'Combining theoretical, historical and political science both international and domestic contexts, this volume breaks new ground in explaining how and why the belief in Britain's continuing 'greatness' has persisted so long and stymied attempts to shape a more realistic appreciation of Britain's foreign policy options. As Britain prepares to forge a new international role outside the European Union, this book will serve as both the best single-volume introduction to recent British foreign policy and a valuable warning of the limitations of a foreign policy based on bluster and wishful thinking.'

– Alex May, University of Oxford, UK.

'*British Foreign Policy since 1945* provides an authoritative and comprehensive evaluation of the critical developments in British foreign policy in the post-war era. Tailored to the needs of lecturers, teachers and students of British politics, the book will facilitate a thorough understanding of the principal themes of British foreign policy – the main factors, events and issues by which foreign policy has been shaped. Garnett, Mabon and Smith provide a fascinating examination of the changes and continuities of British foreign policy.'

– Samantha Wolstencroft, Manchester Metropolitan University, UK.

'*British Foreign Policy since 1945* provides a rich and timely introduction to the past and present of UK foreign policy. It provides a detailed and carefully researched exploration of change and continuity in Britain's approach to world politics from the early part of the twentieth century to the EU referendum of 2016. Accessibly written and with insights into theory and institutional structures, the book provides a very useful guide to understanding Britain's efforts to define its role in the post-War world. Its chronological organisation allows readers to appreciate the connections between different phases of UK foreign policy, Britain's shifting priorities and position in the world, and its path in an increasingly uncertain twenty-first-century global politics. The coverage of Brexit provides a pertinent analysis of what is likely to be a turning point for the UK. *British Foreign Policy since 1945* is an authoritative work and key reading for students of British foreign policy.'

– Jonathan Gilmore, Kingston University, UK.

British Foreign Policy since 1945

British Foreign Policy since 1945 brings a chronological approach to the study of British foreign policy since the Second World War in order to make the principal events and dynamics accessible within a broader historical and cultural context.

The key features included in this book:

- a detailed chronological survey of developments in post-war British politics;
- an integrated discussion of foreign and domestic policy developments indicating connections and interlocking themes;
- analysis of Britain's role in the world, particularly in regard to the UK's 'special relationship' with the US and its decision to leave the EU;
- a range of in-text features, including essay questions and seminar/discussion topics.

This timely book will be essential reading for anyone interested in British politics, foreign policy analysis and British post-war history.

Mark Garnett is Senior Lecturer in Politics and International Relations at Lancaster University, UK. Among many books and articles on UK politics, he is co-author of *Exploring British Politics, 4th edition* (2016) and *British General Elections since 1964* (2014).

Simon Mabon is Lecturer in International Relations and Director of the Richardson Institute at Lancaster University, UK. He is also a Research Associate with the London-based think tank the Foreign Policy Centre, and is the author of *Saudi Arabia and Iran* (2013) and the co-author of *The Origins of Isis* (2017), among other publications.

Robert Smith is a Lecturer in International Relations at Coventry University, UK. He has previously taught at Lancaster University, UK, was a Senior Lecturer in British defence and foreign policy at the Royal Military Academy, Sandhurst and worked for the British Foreign and Commonwealth Office in Iraq advising on the development of human rights policies in the immediate aftermath of the 2003 invasion.

British Foreign Policy since 1945

MARK GARNETT, SIMON MABON AND
ROBERT SMITH

Routledge
Taylor & Francis Group
LONDON AND NEW YORK

First published 2018
by Routledge
2 Park Square, Milton Park, Abingdon, Oxon OX14 4RN

and by Routledge
711 Third Avenue, New York, NY 10017

Routledge is an imprint of the Taylor & Francis Group, an informa business

© 2018 Mark Garnett, Simon Mabon and Robert Smith

The right of Mark Garnett, Simon Mabon and Robert Smith to be identified as authors of this work has been asserted by them in accordance with sections 77 and 78 of the Copyright, Designs and Patents Act 1988.

All rights reserved. No part of this book may be reprinted or reproduced or utilised in any form or by any electronic, mechanical, or other means, now known or hereafter invented, including photocopying and recording, or in any information storage or retrieval system, without permission in writing from the publishers.

Trademark notice: Product or corporate names may be trademarks or registered trademarks, and are used only for identification and explanation without intent to infringe.

British Library Cataloguing-in-Publication Data
A catalogue record for this book is available from the British Library

Library of Congress Cataloging-in-Publication Data
Names: Garnett, Mark, 1963-author. | Mabon, Simon, author. | Smith, Robert (International relations professor), author.
Title: British foreign policy since 1945 / Mark Garnett, Simon Mabon and Robert Smith.
Description: New York: Routledge, 2018. | Includes bibliographical references and index.
Identifiers: LCCN 2017006829 | ISBN 9781138821279 (hardback) | ISBN 9781138821293 (pbk.) | ISBN 9781315743394 (ebook)
Subjects: LCSH: Great Britain–Foreign relations–1945-
Classification: LCC DA589.8 .G36 2018 | DDC 327.41–dc23
LC record available at https://lccn.loc.gov/2017006829

ISBN: 978-1-138-82127-9 (hbk)
ISBN: 978-1-138-82129-3 (pbk)
ISBN: 978-1-315-74339-4 (ebk)

Typeset in Avenir and Dante
by Sunrise Setting Ltd., Brixham, UK
Printed and bound by CPI Group (UK) Ltd, Croydon, CR0 4YY

Contents

List of tables ix
List of boxes x
List of case studies xi
Controversies xii
Acknowledgements xiii

Introduction 1

1 Foreign policy and International Relations theory 7

2 The shaping and making of British foreign policy 28

3 The road to 1945 59

4 The limping lion, 1945–55 97

5 Suez and 'Supermac', 1955–63 132

6 Symbols and substance, 1963–70 157

7 Awkward partnerships and special relationships, 1970–83 176

8 From Falklands fanfare to Maastricht misery, 1983–92 205

9 Ethics and interventions, 1992–2001 240

10 'Not in my name', 2001–7 269

11	Heirs to Blair and 'Brexiteers', 2007–17	**297**
12	Summary, guide to further reading and topics for discussion	**326**
	Bibliography	*342*
	Index	*350*

Tables

2.1 The FCO in numbers, 2015–16　　　　　　　　　　　　　　　30
2.2 Foreign Secretaries since 1945　　　　　　　　　　　　　　31
2.3 FCO ministers, 2017　　　　　　　　　　　　　　　　　　32

Boxes

1.1 Key figures in the Realist tradition	10
1.2 Woodrow Wilson's Fourteen Points	13
1.3 Karl Marx (1818–83)	16
1.4 Alexander Wendt (b. 1958)	19
7.1 The expulsion of Ugandan Asians	184
10.1 Tracking public opinion	276

Case studies

2.1	Valedictory despatches	40
2.2	Christmas broadcasts and soft power	55
4.1	Projecting Britain	101
4.2	Britain and the UN	117
4.3	Graham Greene, *The Quiet American*	129
6.1	Cyprus	163
7.1	Britain and the Yom Kippur War	186
7.2	From Rhodesia to Zimbabwe	197
8.1	Sport, politics and foreign policy	215
8.2	Libya and the 'special relationship'	231

Controversies

2.1	The Falklands War	36
3.1	Palestine and the Balfour Declaration (1917)	76
3.2	Neville Chamberlain – for and against	94
7.1	Cruise missiles	198
9.1	Realism and British policy towards Bosnia	248
10.1	The 'sexed up' September dossier	278
10.2	The Hutton Inquiry	283
11.1	Bahrain, human rights and the return to 'east of Suez'	310

Acknowledgements

The authors are indebted to staff and students associated with the Richardson Institute, Lancaster University, for providing intellectual sustenance and a model of constructive collaboration. Mark Garnett would like to record his special thanks to the students who studied his third-year module Britain in the World at Lancaster in 2016 for having acted as 'guinea pigs' by reading draft chapters of the book. He is also grateful to Alexander Evans, who kindly read a draft of Chapter 2. Simon Mabon would like to thank Swarna, family and friends for their love and support throughout this project. Any errors of fact or interpretation are entirely our own responsibility.

Our greatest debt is to Andrew Taylor and Sophie Iddamalgoda at Taylor and Francis for their remarkable patience and never failing encouragement.

Introduction

There is a good case for regarding the June 2016 referendum on Britain's membership of the European Union (EU) as the most dramatic development in the country's foreign policy since the Second World War. The campaign could also be seen as an unparalleled advertisement on behalf of those who regard a sound knowledge of British foreign policy as indispensable for the exercise of responsible citizenship. Whether they were 'Leavers', 'Remainers' or genuinely undecided, well-informed observers could only lament the general standard of debate. Neither side engaged seriously with the key question of Britain's role in the world. Instead, the 'Remainers' tried to petrify voters with pessimistic forecasts of a future outside the EU, while 'Leavers' insisted that, far from benefiting from membership, Britain was being held back. Voters, the latter argued, should have the courage to throw off their shackles, making 23 June 2016 Britain's 'Independence Day'. Apart from information provided by the BBC website, there was little attempt by the media to inform voters about the nature of the EU itself. On the day *after* the referendum, notoriously, a very popular enquiry to the Google search engine was 'what is the EU?'.

A key purpose of this book is to supply the reader with the background information which was left out of the 2016 debate – and, perhaps, to explain why the protagonists chose not to look too closely into the question of Britain's role. Excellent books on British foreign policy have been published in recent years by authors who take a thematic approach to the subject (Self, 2010; Gaskarth, 2013). While acknowledging the utility of this approach, we prefer a chronological survey of developments since 1945. This seems to give the reader a better opportunity to develop his or her own interpretation of the character of post-war British foreign policy.

This is not to say, however, that the book is an unvarnished (or 'objective') narrative of events. To adapt Churchill's remark about puddings, a book without a 'theme' would be less than satisfactory. This one contains more than one leading strand, ultimately deriving from the inescapable and overriding fact about this period in British foreign policy – the country's relative decline from what can (for shorthand purposes) be described as the status of a 'great power' to that of a state of middle rank but continuing international significance. For some readers, this is too obvious to merit a mention. For others, titles of three books by the careful scholar Frederick Samuel Northedge (1918–85) might be instructive. His study of the 1916–29 period was entitled *The Troubled Giant*; his book about the years between 1945 and 1961 was subtitled *A Process of Readjustment*; and when he updated his account to cover 1961 to 1973 he gave this new study the less equivocal title of *Descent from Power* (Northedge, 1962, 1966, 1974).

While the relative decline became unmistakable to serious observers after 1945, it cannot be explained without a discussion of much earlier developments. Thus the chronological section of the present book (Chapters 3–11) begins in the late Victorian period, providing essential background information for a full appreciation of later years. If Britain's relative decline has been so protracted, why is it that so many Britons seem not to have noticed it? This, for us, is probably the most interesting and important question for any research into modern British foreign policy. The answer includes various elements, such as public inattention, the media's approach to the issue and (by no means least) a reluctance of politicians to address it. As a result, the attitude of many voters to foreign affairs is still shaped by a 'narrative' which developed during the Second World War, drawing on earlier assumptions about Britain's guaranteed place at the 'top table' of international politics.

Among the voluminous literature on Britain's post-war place, a book first published in 1958 provides fascinating testimony to the power of the wartime narrative. The author, Desmond Crowley, was a university lecturer who was also a passionate advocate of adult education; his book *The Background to Current Affairs* was a characteristic attempt to enlighten the 'general reader'. The academic side of Crowley emphatically placed Britain 'foremost among those nations which have become outmoded in scale by the emergence of the two super-powers [the US and the USSR]'. But despite – or maybe because of – Britain's recent humiliation in the Suez Crisis (Chapter 5), the New Zealand-born Crowley was evidently concerned that this might be a little blunt for the 'general reader'. So he followed it up with the reflection that '[i]t is not, as one must add immediately for fear of wounding tender British sensibilities, a question of Britain having declined in strength, so much as of the world situation having altered to her disadvantage' (Crowley, 1963, 4).

What Crowley was really saying was that Britain's decline had been relative rather than absolute; but he refrained from spelling out his message in those terms because he judged that the idea of decline in *any* sense would prove too much for 'tender British sensibilities'. It is understandable that, faced with the need to make practical decisions rather than just writing about them, post-war British politicians have felt intimidated by this dilemma. Their calculations had to incorporate two sharply contrasting 'facts' – the unmistakable evidence that Britain was no longer 'pre-eminent' and the public belief that, if anything, the Second World War had fulfilled the promise of *Land of Hope and Glory* and made their country 'mightier yet'. For politicians in a democracy, facing the prospect of media criticism and electoral defeat, the second of these 'facts' was probably the more tangible.

The need of post-war politicians to engineer some kind of alignment between realities and perceptions explains another theme of the book – the strangely persistent notion of a 'special relationship' with the US. Again, it is too simplistic to attribute this purely to pusillanimous politicians. When Churchill conjured it into existence during the Second World War he rightly felt that it was necessary to give Britain some chance of survival; and it probably played some role in the process which led to the formation of the North Atlantic Treaty Organization (NATO), ensuring US commitment to the security of post-war Europe. After that, though, the rationale grew increasingly tenuous. Since Britain fell so palpably short of equality with the US in terms of power, it was unrealistic to expect 'parity of esteem'. US Presidents quickly learned the rules of the game: venerate the relationship when speaking in Britain but treat the country much like any other ally when taking practical decisions back home.

At times, indeed, British politicians seemed to be confusing 'ends' and 'means' in their foreign policy. It was difficult to see how that ultimate goal of continued (or restored) 'great power' status could be promoted through subservience to another nation. Over time, British foreign policy decisions became more comprehensible if the maintenance of the relationship, rather than recognised global influence, was the real aim. Britain's early responses to European cooperation provide a particularly ironic comment on the 'special relationship'. Initially, the British felt that their global stature, bolstered by the bond with America, made the prospect of a reorientation towards Europe too demeaning to contemplate. This feeling was so strong that, unusually, successive British governments actually resisted US pressure, which was consistently applied in favour of UK membership of the emerging EEC. Shortly after Britain relented and asked for admittance, its existing reliance on the US was augmented by the 1962 Nassau Agreement (Chapter 5), which made it dependent on its transatlantic ally for the viability of its nuclear arsenal which itself, arguably, had been procured primarily for a symbolic purpose.

It would be wrong to describe the 'special relationship' as entirely self-defeating, but there were certainly times when it proved harmful to what (on any realistic view) could be identified as 'British interests'. In particular, it was difficult to reconcile with another recurrent post-war narrative – the idea that even if Britain lagged behind the superpowers in military terms, it deserved to be consulted on all key global issues because of its moral stature. This narrative, which was used (often sincerely) to rationalise Britain's retreat from Empire, was never very convincing: far from being a proactive liberator of subject peoples, Britain almost invariably granted independence only after seeing whether a dose of violent repression could prolong their subjection. But at least the British could argue that there would always be some stones in the road between Empire and Commonwealth, and that once the transition had been effected it could concentrate on the 'ethical dimension' to its foreign policy. This possibility was seriously impaired by the 'special relationship', which entailed British support (even if only verbally) for all of America's initiatives. No longer strong enough to commit sins of its own on a significant scale, Britain enlisted itself as the eager adjutant of a state with a marked propensity to generate lasting resentment (and worse). The resulting ill feeling in regions like the Middle East was the more damaging to Britain, since it was usually mingled with contempt.

This is not to say that Britain is entirely lacking in international goodwill, even after its inglorious part in the Iraq War. It is, for example, ranked very highly in terms of 'soft power'. However, it seems reasonable to claim that its advantages in this crucial area owe a great deal to historical accident. This failure fully to appreciate the value of a 'good name' is another theme of the present study. Too often British policy makers have tended to take for granted their key assets, notably the global popularity of the English language (which would have been cemented through the historic tie with America, even if the term 'special relationship' had never been coined). Instruments of soft power, like the British Council and the BBC World Service, have tended to be viewed as expensive luxuries, whose budgets are among the first to be cut at times of austerity.

This offhand attitude to institutions of continuing importance stands in marked contrast to governmental enthusiasm for one-off 'spectaculars', like the 2012 summer Olympic Games. When London was chosen to host the games – appropriately enough, after a meeting held in its old imperial stronghold of Singapore – Tony Blair hailed a 'momentous day' for Britain. His remark was in stark and telling contrast to the lukewarm reaction of the Attlee government when, in October 1945, the 1948 Olympics were awarded to London. On that occasion the greatest enthusiasm was shown by King George VI (the representative of a monarchy which has always specialised in soft power). On the morning after Blair's 'momentous day' (6 July 2005) 52 people were killed and hundreds injured in a coordinated terrorist attack on London's transport system, launched by British-born Muslims who had convinced themselves that this would be an appropriate form of retribution for Britain's policy towards the Middle East.

While London was under attack on 7 July 2005, few of its residents would have been aware that Britain's involvement in the Middle East had begun long before Blair's fateful decision to offer fulsome support for George W Bush's planned intervention in Iraq. This reflection takes us back to the start of this discussion and the referendum on UK membership of the EU, which offered the imperfectly informed British people an opportunity to exert decisive influence over a key foreign policy decision. Whatever one's reaction to the narrow victory for the 'Leave' campaign, it would be difficult to deny that the result was, in part, a justified reflection on the management of foreign policy by the 'elite' over recent decades. Nearly a century after the introduction of universal suffrage (for adult males, at least), no British government has found a satisfactory way to interpret public opinion and channel it for constructive purposes. In the aftermath of the 'Brexit' vote that elite faces the challenge of exploring new foreign-policy opportunities in a world which seems to lack any of the old certainties. We can only hope that in their ventures they will try to take public opinion with them by working on the assumption that voters can overcome their 'tender sensibilities' so long as they are treated like adults.

If the British foreign policy elite can be deemed to have failed in its duty to serve the national interest, this hardly makes it unique among democratic nations. However, we contend that the British example is uniquely interesting, especially when one considers the unrivalled prestige of the Foreign Office before 1914. The decline of this institution is the subject of Chapter 2. It can also be measured by reading the relevant chapters of the studies of Britain's ruling classes published by the journalist Anthony Sampson between 1962 and 2004. The chapters on Britain's diplomats in the 1962 and 2004 versions are of roughly equal extent; but while the first explains why the British Foreign Secretary had defied all the symptoms of national decline and was still a very significant figure on the international stage, the 2004 chapter is almost entirely taken up by a discussion of the events leading up to the Iraq War, in which the Foreign and Commonwealth Office (FCO) proved as impotent as the million-plus people who demonstrated against the policy of the Prime Minister. Tony Blair was certainly not the first British premier to direct foreign policy against the wishes of the government department which was officially entrusted with that role; indeed, the first of our chronological chapters (Chapter 3) is dominated by discussion of a similar situation, when the policy of 'appeasement' of European dictators was driven by the Prime Minister, Neville Chamberlain. The same was true of the Suez Crisis (Chapter 5), in which Anthony Eden was the main instigator. The essential difference between those periods and the present day is that these Prime Ministers recognised the potential threat from what was then the Foreign Office and were keen to neutralise it by trying to ensure that the Foreign Secretary was a compliant individual. Latterly this precaution has not been necessary, thanks to the diminution of the Foreign Secretary's departmental clout; in 2010 David Cameron felt able to give the job to a former leader of the Conservative Party, William Hague, on the assumption that the key decisions would be taken in Downing Street, while his successor Theresa May caused dismay in the diplomatic community by appointing the controversial 'Brexiteer' Boris Johnson – until it was realised that a modern British Foreign Secretary enjoys a very nice office but no guarantee of significant policy influence.

In addition to its obvious relevance for readers who are interested in British political institutions, this subject also serves as an invaluable case study against which various theories of International Relations theory can be judged. Such theories, which are outlined in Chapter 1, act as interpretive lenses through which the evidence can be viewed. Readers might find any one of these theories so persuasive that they arrive at the enviable position of being able to explain the whole of post-war British policy by reference to a single theoretical perspective. Others might take the view that the whole story is far too messy to lend itself to interpretation within one framework of analysis. On close inspection, indeed, it might be concluded that British governments were taking simultaneous decisions on a variety of subjects, which, taken in isolation, would imply that they were 'Liberals' or 'Realists'. Every one of those decisions, no doubt, could be explained by someone who was convinced by the 'Marxist' approach to international relations; and the 'Constructivist' perspective could also prove helpful, especially in a story which illustrates the complex relationship between 'reality' and 'perception'. The main point is that international theories are essential aids to critical reflection; and the authors hope that, among its other objectives, this book will help readers to extend that critical approach to their own judgements on the fascinating (if often frustrating) story of Britain's international relations.

Foreign policy and International Relations theory

Introduction

Despite the growing popularity of International Relations (IR) as an academic subject, it presents considerable intellectual challenges. Not the least of these is International Relations theory, which confronts students with questions relating to ontology, epistemology and levels of analysis. Those who find such issues somewhat daunting at first glance can at least console themselves with the thought that they can also pose problems for their teachers.

It is, at least, quite easy to understand why theory is so important in the study of IR. The student's task is not merely to accumulate evidence relating to an increasingly complex and fast-changing world. This evidence must be analysed; and even the least sophisticated interpretation will, to some extent, reflect the perspective of the observer. The various IR theories thus represent a range of interpretive 'lenses', which give rise to a variety of judgements. As in all academic disciplines, there is a danger that IR theory can be misused: specific evidence which fits a preconceived theory can be emphasised at the expense of other material which has at least comparable explanatory relevance; foreign policy actors can even be criticised for failing to behave in conformity with an intellectual framework they have never heard of. Nevertheless, IR theory provides crucial equipment for those who seek a deeper, clearer understanding and new insights into this fascinating subject.

The influence of theory is evident in contests over the nature of IR itself. For example, while some suggest that it should focus upon the diplomatic and strategic relationships between states, others argue that it should also encompass transactions across borders. Broadly speaking, the study of IR is the exploration and examination of the interaction of a range of different types of actor within what is commonly referred to as the international system; it deals with the interaction of myriad actors, ranging from states to charities, transnational companies to religious leaders.

The emergence of a discipline of IR can be traced back to the end of the First World War, when a number of scholars sought to explain the path to war in the hope of contributing to the task of avoiding a similar catastrophe. The term 'international relations' can be traced back much earlier, to the time of the British philosopher Jeremy Bentham (1748–1832). A number of thinkers have exercised a profound and continuing influence over the academic study of IR, among them Niccolò Machiavelli, Thomas Hobbes, Immanuel Kant, Karl Marx and, more recently, Michel Foucault. This list highlights two serious problems with IR as a discipline. The first is the dominance of male voices, a problem that haunts philosophy more generally but particularly IR theory. The second is the 'Western' orientation of these authors. One of the most damning criticisms of IR as a discipline is its over-reliance upon Western experiences. Indeed, if one traces the roots of modern diplomacy back to the Peace of Westphalia in 1648, one can appreciate that Western ideals have dominated the discipline since before its existence. In recent years a number of scholars have sought to feed non-Western ideas and values into the study of IR, yet for now it remains dominated by Western voices.

In the formative years of the discipline IR was shaped by what has been termed the first 'great debate', between Realism and Liberalism. Since then other controversies have emerged – for example, between 'traditionalists' and 'behaviourists' (in essence, a debate about epistemology), and between 'rationalists' and 'reflectivists' (a dispute concerned with ontology). We need to clarify what we mean by these unfamiliar terms. 'Epistemology' is concerned with knowledge and how we acquire it; 'ontology' is concerned with what constitutes reality and how we understand existence. These are important differences that shape how we see the world and what processes we use to build our personal interpretations. Different theories have different beliefs and approaches to these questions.

Historically, the discipline of IR was driven by a desire to analyse inter-state relations, yet in recent years the growing prominence of ideas, networks and transactions that transcend the 'black box' of the sovereign nation state has posed a serious challenge to 'state-centric' assumptions. As a consequence, a number of scholars have begun to offer alternative approaches that give more attention to non-state factors and actors.

Many of the theories discussed in this chapter arise from different ontological and epistemological positions and, as such, we should also be aware of the problems associated with them. From this, we can make a crude yet important distinction between positivism (the quest for 'objective' knowledge), post-positivism (also designated as reflectivism), which stresses the subjectivity of events, and Critical Theory, which focuses on social, cultural and economic factors. Positivism is grounded in the 'hard' sciences and asserts that facts relate to concrete realities which are amendable to objective analysis. By contrast, post-positivist and Critical Theorists argue that 'facts' in the sphere of human interactions are subjects of endless contestation as a consequence of the biases and subjectivities which inevitably affect the researcher.

This chapter seeks to introduce the reader to the most prominent IR theories which have shaped the discipline as it approaches its centenary. It begins with a discussion of Realism, before turning to Liberalism, Marxism, Constructivism and Critical Theories. The discussion employs a comparative framework to facilitate a greater understanding of them. Each section begins with a survey of the philosophical traditions underpinning the various theoretical approaches. It then examines the ontological and epistemological presuppositions which inform each perspective, before exploring levels of analysis within each theoretical approach and identifying key questions which arise in relation to each theory. Far from aiming at a comprehensive account, the discussion is intended to give the reader a working understanding of what each theory can do, along with its limitations. Although we regard some perspectives as more applicable than others to an understanding of post-war British foreign policy, we have no conscious intention to act as champions of any one of them. Rather, we believe that all of them have important insights to offer those who want to understand the attempts of various British governments to come to terms with a world which was radically reshaped by the 1939–45 conflict.

The Realist tradition

Although Realism was not the first theoretical 'school' of IR, it has been the most influential of the various perspectives. Claiming to offer a 'fact-based' approach, its attractions seemed obvious following the failure of the League of Nations to facilitate global cooperation, and the process which led to the outbreak of the Second World War in 1939. The notion that Realism engages with the world 'as it is' rather than as one 'wants it to be' still exercises considerable appeal for students and policy makers alike; its focus on the pursuit of the 'national interest' seems especially relevant to the international policy of democratic states, whose governments seek to win the approval of their citizens. As such, it provides an appropriate starting point for our discussion.

An early exponent of what is now referred to as Realism was Edward Hallett Carr, whose seminal work, *The Twenty Years' Crisis* (1939), provided a vivid commentary on the course of events which led to a renewal of global conflict. Shortly after the war, Hans Morgenthau's *Politics among Nations* (1948) added conceptual depth to the basic Realist theory, establishing what became known as Classical Realism. However, the Realist approach is grounded in a broader canon of

> **Box 1.1 Key figures in the Realist tradition**
>
> ### Hans Morgenthau (1904–80)
>
> Along with E.H. Carr, the German legal scholar Hans Morgenthau is regarded as a founding father of what is now understood to be Classical Realism. In *Politics among Nations* (1948) Morgenthau set out a theory of human nature that reflected the influence of Hobbes and Machiavelli. Later in life, Morgenthau served as a consultant to the US administrations of Kennedy and Johnson, although he would later be sacked by Johnson for criticising US policy in Vietnam. Aside from *Politics among Nations*, Morgenthau was also the author of *The Concept of the Political* (1933), *In Defense of the National Interest* (1951), *The Purpose of American Politics* (1960) and many other titles.
>
> ### Kenneth Waltz (1924–2013)
>
> Kenneth Waltz's *Theory of International Politics* invigorated the Realist tradition when it was published in 1979, and it established Structural Realism as one of the essential theories within IR. Waltz served in both the Second World War and the Korean War – experiences which had a profound impact upon his thinking. In addition to his discipline-changing *Theory of International Politics*, he was the author of *Man, the State, and War* (1959), *Foreign Policy and Democratic Politics: The American and British Experience* (1967) and *The Spread of Nuclear Weapons: A Debate Renewed* (1995). Waltz applied a typically Realist style of reasoning in relation to nuclear weapons, arguing that 'more may be better', i.e. if more states possessed such weapons they would deter each other from conventional attacks and thus serve the interests of peace.

philosophical work within the Western tradition, dating back to the fifth century BC. In particular, three authors are worth noting: the Athenian soldier and historian Thucydides, the Florentine politician and author Niccolò Machiavelli (1469–1527) and the English philosopher Thomas Hobbes (1588–1679). It is, however, important to stress that these three were not themselves self-conscious 'Realists'; rather, their work influenced the variants of Realism which emerged during the twentieth century.

Hobbes' work on political organisation, sovereignty and the 'state of nature' which preceded the institution of government provides much of the theoretical groundwork for the Realists. Moreover, the Realist tradition is infused with the Hobbesian understanding of human nature, defined by self-interest and fear.

Hobbes' hypothetical state of nature serves as an admirable illustration of his argument, suggesting that at the heart of action, in the international sphere as well as domestic life, is a quest for survival and security.

A key element of Realist thought is the contention that states are driven by the need for survival and a constant hankering for the power necessary to secure this objective. But how should power be understood? For the Realist, power is often equated to survival, self-interest and influence; yet the Realist canon tends to rest on assumptions in this respect, rather than detailed analysis. Recent scholarly attention has focused on the concept of 'soft power' (see below), yet this work has chiefly been conducted by Liberals.

Concerns about security and power are conceptualised in the 'security dilemma', first identified by John Herz (1908–2005). For Herz (a refugee from Nazi Germany), the security dilemma is a:

> structural notion in which the self-help attempts of states to look after their security needs tend, regardless of intention, to lead to rising insecurity for others as each interprets its own measures as defensive and measures of others as potentially threatening.
>
> (Herz, 1950)

The security dilemma is comprised of two separate stages: the dilemma of interpretation and the dilemma of response. A dilemma is a proposition that contains two potential resolutions, neither of which is unambiguously acceptable. The two components of the security dilemma contain within them uncertainty about the impact of an external 'other' upon state power and national interest.

From this a number of assumptions emerge, which underpin the Realist tradition. First, the international system is 'anarchic', which is to say that there is no overarching power capable of regulating the behaviour of states. Second, states possess a military capacity that will allow them to hurt and potentially destroy adversaries; in the case of the more powerful actors in the post-1945 era, this may be nuclear weapons. Third, uncertainty characterises international relations. Fourth, survival is the main goal of a state and, given the anarchic nature of international relations, self-help is a prominent feature of state calculations.

Within the international system states engage in a 'zero-sum' competition over relative power – that is, every encounter produces clear 'winners' and 'losers'. The unequal distribution of power across the international system requires states to engage in a range of activities to ensure that their needs are met. For stronger states, the quest for 'hegemony', either internationally or regionally, drives foreign policy agendas. In contrast, weaker states fear for their security and habitually devise strategies to balance against the power exerted by other actors.

Over time Realist thought underwent a conceptual development, shifting the focus to 'structural' analysis. Kenneth Waltz proposed Structural Realism (also commonly referred to as Neo-Realism) in 1979, and subsequently the theory was developed by scholars such as John Mearsheimer. For Waltz, the structure of the international system – still anarchic – impacted upon a state's ability to exert and maximise power. Waltz argued that rather than trying to maximise their power, states were primarily concerned with maintaining their security within the system. Mearsheimer, by contrast, contended that states do in fact try to maximise their power. Despite the obvious potential for conflicting conclusions – usually labelled 'offensive' against 'defensive' Realism – and given the general popularity of 'structuralist' analysis in North American universities, it was not surprising that Neo-Realism tended to supersede Classical Realism, whose emphasis on human nature had been a guiding factor in the formative stages of the tradition.

Despite the intellectual appeal of Realism, it has encountered a number of objections which apparently undermine its explanatory value. It is argued, for example, that Realism lacks sufficient depth and nuance to provide an adequate interpretation of international developments. Certainly, the confinements of their positivist epistemology and ontology prevent Realists from appreciating the role of ideas, identities and normative values in motivating international actors. This looks increasingly anomalous in view of the influence of religion and, more broadly, ideology upon the interplay of actors within the contemporary world.

Similarly, since Realists are wedded to the view that states are unitary actors which project coherence onto the world, they pay insufficient attention to developments *within* states. Yet even states which are not formally democratic are clearly influenced by movements of public opinion. Furthermore, the decisions of state actors are increasingly shaped by institutions (such as transnational corporations) whose activities are not constrained by geographical boundaries. Among these transnational forces are groups (including terrorist organisations) which have established a presence in numerous states. Since some of these groups are inspired by ideas, Realist assessments of their importance are doubly disadvantaged, since their analytical framework denies any meaningful role in international politics to either non-state actors or to beliefs.

The Liberal tradition

In the aftermath of the First World War populist sentiment focused on the need to identify and punish the culprits. Intellectuals in various countries sought to understand how the organisation of the international system could allow such savage and self-defeating devastation. The ensuing efforts to conjure tranquil order out of murderous chaos left a lasting imprint on the new academic discipline of IR. Ultimately, the goal of Liberal Internationalism was to develop transparent structures in the international system that would ensure collective security, removing the need for the secretive diplomacy that had helped to precipitate the tragedy of 1914–18.

At the heart of the peace negotiations to end the First World War were fourteen principles of world peace, outlined by US President Woodrow Wilson. On 8 January 1918 Wilson outlined his vision, drawing upon domestic considerations to shape his view of international relations (Box 1.2).

Wilson's vision was favourably received in public, although the British and the French were privately sceptical. George Clemenceau, the French President, exclaimed that 'Le bon Dieu n'en avait que dix!' – 'The good Lord only had 10 points!'. Liberal hopes were dashed by the Treaty of Versailles, in which Wilson's stated principles on self-determination were repeatedly breached; the refusal of the US Congress to commit the US to the League of Nations was another

Box 1.2 Woodrow Wilson's Fourteen Points

- Open covenants of peace, openly arrived at
- Freedom of the seas
- The removal so far as possible of all economic barriers
- The reduction of national armaments to the lowest point consistent with domestic safety
- Impartial adjustment of all colonial claims
- The evacuation of all Russian territory
- The evacuation and restoration of Belgium
- The liberation of France and return to her of Alsace and Lorraine
- Readjustment of the frontiers of Italy to conform to clearly recognisable lines of nationality
- The peoples of Austria–Hungary should be accorded the freest opportunity of autonomous development
- Evacuation of occupation forces from Romania, Serbia and Montenegro; Serbia should be accorded free and secure access to the sea
- Autonomous development for the non-Turkish peoples of the Ottoman Empire; free passage of the Dardanelles to the ships and commerce of all nations
- An independent Poland to be established, with free and secure access to the sea
- A general association of nations to be formed to guarantee to its members political independence and territorial integrity (the genesis of the League of Nations)

serious reversal. As a result, the Liberal approach to IR struggled to establish a firm academic foothold; it was not until the fall of the Berlin Wall and the end of the Cold War that Realist hegemony within the discipline was subjected to serious challenge.

As in the case of Realism, Liberalism reflects a long-established tradition in Western thought. The German philosopher Immanuel Kant (1724–1804) was particularly influential. The Kantian aspiration of a 'perpetual peace' remains central to contemporary Liberal thought, driven by the idea that as states become increasingly invested in internationalism a pacific global order would emerge. The spread of democracy was another vital facet of this tradition, governed by the notion that democracies do not go to war with one another as a consequence of shared interests, regulated by ideas of self-determination, human rights, free markets and the rule of law.

A number of key assumptions can be found within the Liberal tradition. For the Liberal, humans are characterised by their capacity for improvement, particularly in respect of their rational faculties, and this can be facilitated at the international level by the establishment of suitable institutions. This outlook is associated with notions of individual rights and civil liberties, which ought to be enshrined in constitutional law and practice. In sharp contrast to Realism, understanding the domestic construction of the state is important for the Liberal, as the internal organisation of political life will exercise a profound influence upon the external interactions of the state.

As in Realist thought, the Liberal international system is anarchic; yet there is scope for cooperation within these conditions. The Liberal understanding of power is much broader than the Realist approach, encompassing non-military elements. It is also relative, arguing that a state can possess more power than another in one area while being less potent in other respects. Institutions can help to regulate international cooperation, and this consideration played an increasingly important role in the evolution of Liberal IR theory in the 1970s and 1980s. Scholars such as Robert Keohane (b. 1941) suggest that the Liberal view should be formalised within international structures which can serve to mitigate anarchy. For Keohane, institutions can act as both carrot and stick, demonstrating the mutual benefits of cooperation and sharing, while also allowing for the establishment of monitoring mechanisms and, where necessary, sanctions regimes.

Again like Realism, Liberal thought has undergone significant conceptual developments. The Neo-Liberal approach pays greater credence to structural factors than other facets of the Liberal tradition, which have a greater focus upon agency. More contemporary developments of Liberal thought have been predicated upon three aspects: 1) a rejection of power politics, 2) the possible benefits of mutual cooperation and 3) a desire to implement these ideas through institutions. Within the context of contemporary Liberal thought a number of scholars have explored ideas such as Democratic Peace Theory, which suggests that the spread of democracy will prevent conflict, along with a focus upon norms, law and international institutions.

From the Western Liberal perspective, the Cold War was a period of general insecurity in which governments on both sides seemed to act out of hard-nosed 'Hobbesian' calculation rather than following moral norms – an attitude summed up by President Truman's alleged remark about the Nicaraguan dictator Anastasio Somoza: 'He's a bastard, but he's *our* bastard'. The demolition of the Berlin Wall was thus symbolic of a spiritual liberation, heralding the triumph of Liberal ideas in international politics as well as the domestic sphere. This outlook was best expressed in Francis Fukuyama's 'The End of History' (1989; see also 1992), which explained how liberal democracy had triumphed in the Cold War and established the supremacy of Liberal thinking in the theory and practice of IR. In Fukuyama's thesis 'the end of history' did not mean that nothing of interest would ever happen again, but rather that mankind was finally embracing liberal democracy, the final form of government for all states. Fukuyama claimed to be witnessing:

> not just the end of the Cold War, or the passing of a particular period of post-war history, but the end of history as such: that is, the end point of mankind's ideological evolution and the universalization of Western liberal democracy as the final form of human government.
> (Fukuyama, 1989, 4)

'The End of History' was widely acclaimed, but the thesis also attracted considerable criticism. Notoriously, Fukuyama's diagnosis proved premature. By the turn of the century Liberal ideas had largely been discarded by the academy in favour of more emancipatory projects grounded in Critical Theories, the English School or post-positivist approaches. This development reflected a new attention to moral values, at a time when 'humanitarian' concerns were playing a key role in the foreign policy of Western states.

Like the Realist tradition, Liberalism raises serious questions which present a challenge to its explanatory power. Perhaps the most damning of these concern the Liberal 'modernity' thesis, which suggests that all states are on the same trajectory of development and that Western states are leading this process. The assumption that Western values are superior to all others comes naturally to the Liberal but is open to contestation from alternative perspectives. Other serious questions arise from the Liberal view of human nature. This has some points of contact with the typical Realist position, since the concepts of individualism and 'rationality' are common to both. However, the Liberal view that individuals are 'perfectible' and that rational calculation promotes cooperation is rejected by Realists, who regard human nature as flawed and fixed in a manner which generates conflict. Others question the Liberal link between economic and political liberty, on the grounds that the free market produces vast inequalities in wealth which inevitably lead to tension in domestic and international politics. For the Critical Theorist, Liberalism lacks a meaningful emancipatory agenda and, as a consequence, is best understood as a defence of the status quo. Liberal ideas of collective security have also been undermined by the historical failings of the League of Nations, followed by the distinctly mixed record of the post-war United Nations (UN). These developments raise questions about intervention and the role of individual states within the international sphere – issues which have been a major preoccupation for British governments since the 1990s.

Marxism

While Realism places power and survival at the heart of analysis and Liberals stress the role of free trade and cooperation within international relations, Marxists suggest that socio-economic factors outweigh all other concerns. Much like the Realist (and, in some manifestations, the Liberal), the Marxist is thus preoccupied by material considerations. Yet in contrast to those rival perspectives, Marxism within IR reflects a radical agenda of political transformation.

While the Realist argues that the pursuit of power is the driving force of state action within the international system, Marxism suggests that economic interests are the main motivation for political activity. Marxism also challenges Liberalism by rejecting the claim that free trade and capitalism are the most important aspects of international relations. Instead, Marxists focus upon economic inequalities, relating these to domination and exploitation. Like Realism and Liberalism, the Marxist approach has spawned several different approaches. These ideas are perhaps more clearly articulated in Dependency Theory and World Systems Analysis.

Box 1.3 Karl Marx (1818–83)

Karl Marx was born into a middle-class family in Prussia and spent much of his adult life in a variety of major European cities. Ancestrally Jewish, Marx was a scholar, revolutionary activist, journalist and teacher, although he is chiefly known for his writings on political economy. In collaboration with Friedrich Engels, Marx wrote *The Communist Manifesto* (1848), which has exercised a profound effect on the development of Critical Theory. He was also the author of influential books in a range of disciplines, including History and Philosophy.

Marxist scholarship in IR generally accords considerable importance to developments in world history, for the good reason that this approach lends credence to the focus on domination and exploitation. With colonial expansion across the eighteenth, nineteenth and twentieth centuries, Western states accrued plentiful raw materials and new markets. Building upon this, Dependency Theory argues that economic and financial factors are the main determinants in international relations, resulting in a global system of dominance. The theory identifies a flow of resources from the 'peripheral' states to the core, resulting in the enrichment of the latter at the expense of the former. As such, those in the periphery, whose resources and labour are exploited by wealthier states, sustain the quality of life enjoyed by those in the core. The way in which poorer states are integrated into the world system serves to perpetuate this division.

At the heart of Marx's writings is the idea that human societies can be understood by the concepts of 'base' and 'superstructure'. The base deals with the means and relations of production – namely, how capital is generated. The superstructure is everything not directly related with production – for instance, law, politics, ideology, art and education. The relationship between base and superstructure determines the nature of society. Immanuel Wallerstein (b. 1930) builds upon this to suggest that international relations are shaped by positions of power within the international system, in what he termed 'World Systems Analysis'. For Wallerstein, it is the world system, rather than the individual nation state, which should be seen as the primary unit of analysis.

Unlike the traditional, positivist theories, Marxism contains a powerful normative agenda. As Marx himself might have said, scholars of IR have only interpreted the world in different ways: the point, however, is to *change* it. Marxism can thus be seen as a point of divergence from the traditional IR theories, encouraging a more critical approach. Yet the tendency of mainstream Marxist analysis to focus upon material factors arguably leads to an inadequate understanding of less tangible factors, such as ideology, which can sometimes be dismissed as 'false consciousness' created by ruling classes to cement their economic and political hegemony. Also, while identity politics is increasingly important for Marxists, they are predominantly understood through material factors and the socio-economic context within which groups operate.

Social Constructivism

As we have seen, Liberal 'triumphalism' at the close of the Cold War proved short-lived, and those momentous events provided a spur for fresh thinking in IR. A desire to move beyond positivist analytical frameworks inspired scholars such as Alexander Wendt (Box 1.4), John Ruggie and Nicholas Onuf to propose a 'middle ground' between mainstream theories and more critical approaches. As Ruggie noted, the evolution of Realism and Liberalism had generated a sterile 'Neo–Neo' debate, promoting 'a view of the world of international relations in utilitarian terms; an atomistic universe of self-regarding units whose identity is assumed, given and fixed, and who are responsive largely if not solely to material interests that are fixed by assumption' (Ruggie, 1998, 3).

In response, Social Constructivism – henceforth referred to as Constructivism – offered an alternative means of engaging with prominent themes within IR – notably, the nature of anarchy, power and the interaction of identity and interest. It is an approach which engages with the interminable debate about 'structure' and 'agency', looking at the capacity of individual actors to shape and construct their own environments. The Constructivist draws a distinction between 'brute facts' – those whose validity is independent of human perception – and 'social facts', which are amenable to interpretation. The confusion of these positions and misreading of social facts as brute facts can have serious implications for international relations. Indeed, the Constructivist position suggests that the international system is comprised of contestable social facts rather than existing independently of human agency. This argument is particularly problematic for Realists, who pride themselves on their ability to see the world as it 'really is'.

In the years following the end of the Cold War Wendt's article 'Anarchy is What States Make of It' (1992) offered a critical approach to IR while retaining some of the initial Realist assumptions. Constructivism suggests that IR is best understood by means of engagement with a range of interactions, rather than via the materialist lens of the more mainstream theories. At the heart of Constructivism is a concern with identities and culture and their role within the context of social facts. As Ted Hopf (1998) notes, our identities shape our behaviour and the perceptions that others have of us. Moreover, as Martha Finnemore suggests, interests 'are not just "out there" waiting to be discovered; rather, they are constructed through social interaction' (Finnemore, 1996, 2). These insights have consequences for understandings of power and national interests but also for the nature of international relations.

It must be stressed that a range of different Constructivist positions may be held, differentiated, predominantly, by the extent to which a scholar focuses upon the state but also by ontology. Constructivism is located in a curious position, operating as an interpretive 'meta-theory' yet focusing upon discourses, norms and identities, constructed through interactions. As Emanuel Adler suggests, Constructivism holds 'the middle ground between "rationalist" theories – realism, neorealism and neoliberal institutionalism – and "interpretive epistemologies" – post-modernism, Frankfurt School-oriented critical theories and feminism' (Adler, 2005, 89).

> **Box 1.4 Alexander Wendt (b. 1958)**
>
> Alexander Wendt is a German political scientist and philosopher whose work – notably, his 1992 article 'Anarchy is What States Make of It: The social construction of power politics' – has shaped the 'Constructivist turn' of IR. Wendt developed this article into *Social Theory of International Politics* (1999), which made a considerable impression on the discipline. In recent surveys Wendt has been identified as the most influential thinker within IR in the past 20 years.
>
> Wendt's subsequent work has engaged with questions such as levels of analysis, identity formation and international security. This resulted in the publication of *Quantum Mind and Social Science: Unifying Physical and Social Ontology* (2016).

Wendt considers himself to be a 'thin' Constructivist as a consequence of his acknowledgement of certain materialist tenets. For Wendt, Constructivism is comprised of three principles:

> (1) states are the principal units of analysis for international political theory; (2) the key structures in the states system are intersubjective rather than material; and (3) state identities and interests are in important part constructed by these social structures, rather than given exogenously to the system by human nature [as neorealists maintain] or domestic politics [as neoliberals favour].
>
> (Wendt, 1994, 385)

Within conditions of anarchy, the interaction of a range of different actors and discourses, norms and identities can produce sharply contrasting conceptions of the national interest. From this perspective, Wendt argues that 'anarchy is what states make of it'. The views of Thomas Hobbes, John Locke and Immanuel Kant suggest different types of behaviour at the international level – namely, enmity, rivalry and friendship. Wendt suggests that power is constructed – and, perhaps more importantly, can be transformed – through interactions, as ideas and dialogue shape understandings and perceptions. The same thing can also be applied to the national interest, which is constructed through domestic interactions and the broader international climate.

Nicholas Onuf (who in *World of Our Making* (1989) was the first to coin the term 'Constructivism') offers a much more critical analysis than Wendt, who has been accused of endorsing Realist presuppositions by according undue attention to the state. Three distinct forms of Constructivism have since emerged: the systemic, the unit-level and the holistic. The systemic, as posited by Wendt, focuses upon interactions between state actors, downplaying the importance of domestic factors. The unit-level approach, by contrast, focuses upon the domestic realm, considering how norms, identities and interests interact to create 'the national interest'. The holistic variant is an attempt to combine the insights of the other two approaches.

In recent years criticisms have been levelled at the Constructivists for attempting to 'build bridges' with rival theories that reflect very different ontological or epistemological assumptions. Indeed, some criticisms of Constructivism suggest that, far from furnishing a basis for a radical critique of the status quo, it has tended to validate it. For their part, positivists argue that the intangibility of ideas, norms and identities makes it difficult to use them as a basis for reaching anything more than provisional conclusions, which are open to endless contestation.

More critical approaches have stressed that Constructivism fails to appreciate the importance of language within its analysis. Perhaps though, one of the biggest problems with Constructivism comes from those who fail to appreciate the diversity of a position which occupies a space between the rationalism of the more traditional theories, such as Realism, Liberalism and Marxism, and the reflectivism of more critical theories, to which we now turn.

Alternative approaches in IR: Critical Theories, poststructuralism and feminism

The different Constructivist positions articulate the crucial role of identities and ideology within international relations. Critical Theorists take this focus on intangibles a step further, in a project grounded in emancipation from oppressive forms of social relationships such as capitalism, racism, sexuality, nationality and feminism. They insist that IR theory cannot, and should not, be 'value-free'; as Robert Cox has noted, 'theory is always for someone and some purpose' (Cox, 1981, 128). The philosophical roots of Critical Theory can be identified within the work of Marx, although they are supplemented by contemporary continental philosophy – in particular, the Frankfurt School and French scholars such as Michel Foucault (1926–84) and Jacques Derrida (1930–2004).

The legacy of Marx for Critical Theorists is undeniable; indeed, they are often designated as 'Neo-Marxists'. Yet the Frankfurt School suggested that Marx was himself a positivist, with much of his writing reflecting a positivist determinism. Critical Theorists are interested in communitarian interactions, with Jurgen Habermas (b. 1929) suggesting that open dialogue and democracy were essential steps in the move towards human emancipation, while recognising the problems of open dialogue. Such claims reflect the influence of Antonio Gramsci (1891–1937), whose focus upon 'hegemony' – the dominance of a group which seeks to legitimise its position through culture and ideas – has proved central to Critical Theorists. Gramsci's work is especially pertinent when considering the dominance of particular states and institutions within the international system.

While sharing some key premises with the Critical Theorists and, indeed, focusing on broadly similar issues, poststructuralists envisage a much more radical project. For Foucault and other poststructuralists, there are no objective truths about human nature: rather, everything that we think that we 'know' is located within broader discursive contexts, which are reproduced by people or institutions in positions of power. When applied to IR, poststructuralism investigates the operations of power within discourses and practices of international relations, attempting to subvert hierarchies of knowledge, and ultimately power, through a range of approaches.

Although some scholars use the terms 'postmodernist' and 'poststructuralist' interchangeably, a distinction can be drawn. Poststructuralism offers a theory of knowledge and language, whereas postmodernism focuses on society, history and culture. They are united, however, in a mutual desire to deconstruct power relations within international relations – and society more broadly. One consequence of the emergence of these philosophical perspectives has been the development of Critical Security Studies, Critical Terrorism Studies and Critical War Studies. As Chris Brown suggests, the goal of many of these alternative approaches is 'to dislocate our sense of what is "normal", to cause us to re-think assumptions that we did not even know were assumptions' (Brown, 1997, 62).

One important product of a more critical approach to IR has been the increasing prominence of feminist theory. At the beginning of this chapter the lack of female voices within IR was acknowledged and lamented. In recent years its partial correction has opened a new range of issues for analysis. While immediately concerned with the study of gender within international relations – and the power relations embodied in these relations – feminism has also helped to highlight the previous lack of attention to other marginalised groups and more generally challenged many of the in/out binaries that have characterised IR scholarship.

Like the other approaches featured in this chapter, the broad term 'feminism' incorporates a wide variety of perspectives. However, these are typically located on the reflectivist side of the debate. Indeed, feminists typically view gender as a fluid concept and have used this in the process of deconstructing power relations.

It should cause no surprise that Critical Theorists have themselves been criticised. It can be argued, for example, that Critical Theory provides a convenient toolkit for challenging established practices and presuppositions but falls silent when asked to propose concrete solutions. The toolkit, in short, is designed for destruction rather than reconstruction. Critical Theory even seems to run counter to the current trend within academia, which now emphasises the need for scholarship that demonstrates a tangible 'impact' beyond the ivory towers. More seriously, the post-positivist critique is also vulnerable to a challenge which faces all reflectivist positions – namely, the difficulty of engaging with issues and research materials that are not readily observable. A final criticism suggests that Critical Theorists embrace (and indeed celebrate) value-driven research. Even those who reject the standard 'positivist' insistence on scholarly 'neutrality' – and instead take the view that the observer should take pains at least to avoid 'conscious' bias – have some reason to feel unsettled by approaches which direct researchers into arenas of endless contestability.

The 'English School'

A number of alternative approaches have been developed that seek to reconcile the ontological and epistemological differences between these approaches. One such approach falls within what is commonly referred to as the 'English School', so-called because it is chiefly associated with scholars working in English institutions including Oxbridge and the London School of Economics (LSE).

The English School can be seen as occupying a position between Realism and Liberalism, seeking to provide a basis for accommodation between these positions while responding to the changing nature of global politics. A key aim for the English School has been the reconciliation of the Liberal, cooperative approach to IR with the Realist understanding of anarchy in the international system.

Within the English School there are two main ways of interpreting the behaviour of states in the international system. The 'pluralist' framework is a more traditional account of IR, sharing a number of aspects with Realism while also stressing the possibility of cooperation, despite self-interest and anarchy. In contrast, the 'solidarist' account focuses upon the relationship between world society and international society and seeks to incorporate normative aspects in the study of IR. As Barry Buzan suggests:

> This view stresses global patterns of interaction and communication, and, in sympathy with much of the literature on globalization, uses the term society mainly to distance itself from state-centric models of IR . . . [world society] is aimed at capturing the total interplay amongst states, non-state actors and individuals, while carrying the sense that all the actors in the system are conscious of their interconnectedness and share some important values.
>
> (Buzan, 2004, 64)

Compared to the more traditional IR approaches, the English School is still in its formative stages and its full explanatory potential has yet to be realised. Nevertheless, many scholars are attracted by its attempt to draw insights from different approaches – although, of course, Critical Theorists are unimpressed by the School's obvious debt to 'positivism'.

Conceptualising power

The academic study of IR hinges, crucially, on a range of concepts that are understood and framed in different ways, depending upon the theoretical lens being applied. One such contested term is 'power', which Realists conceive as the overriding concern of states seeking to ensure their own survival. In recent years different conceptions of power have become increasingly important within IR. In particular, attention has turned to the concept of 'soft power', first articulated by Joseph Nye (b. 1937), a former official of the US State Department. Nye's argument suggests that there are several ways for a state to meet its objectives: through the use of hard, soft or (more recently) 'smart' power. Hard power, for Nye as for traditional Realists, is the ability to *coerce*. It is the power to get others to do what you want them to do through forceful measures, either militarily or economically. In contrast, the exercise of soft power fosters a sympathetic attitude among other states through the adoption of positive values and the showcasing of other attractive features.

Despite the methodological problems with Nye's approach – particularly in respect of the difficulty of identifying, measuring or indeed utilising soft power – it has received a great deal of attention from policy makers as well as academics. Processes of globalisation have increased awareness of state behaviour and, as a consequence, the need to manage the image of a state is now widely recognised, particularly by liberal democratic states like the UK but also by China and the monarchical rulers in the Persian Gulf. Nye's work can be seen as a much needed supplement to previous scholarly work in IR. Indeed, it can be argued that academic analysis had previously lagged behind the practice of many states, which have always projected soft power by means of state ceremonies and displays of pomp and pageantry.

Theory in practice

Now that the reader has been introduced to a selection of the main theoretical approaches within the discipline of IR, it is useful to apply these theories to a contemporary case study and to consider how each theory can inform a deeper understanding of key developments. To do this, we consider the Iraq War of

2003, in which Britain played a prominent role as a member of the US-led coalition (Chapter 10).

In his 2001 State of the Union address four months after the 9/11 attacks, George W Bush, the US President, announced the commencement of an open-ended 'War on Terror'. Alongside Iran and North Korea, Bush named Iraq as a pariah state – part of an 'axis of evil'. Iraq was clearly America's prime target, on the argument that it possessed weapons of mass destruction (WMD) and had close ties to terrorist organisations such as Al Qa'ida, which was responsible for 9/11. Bush, supported by the British Prime Minister Tony Blair, argued that international regimes designed to prevent the proliferation of WMD had failed and that military action in Iraq was essential for the preservation of international security. Many other states, including some which normally cooperated with the US, were unconvinced, and the UN refused to pass a motion specifically authorising military intervention. Conscious that this was unlikely to deter the American and British governments, millions of people marched in protest against the impending war, including a huge demonstration on the streets of London. Operation Iraqi Freedom was launched by the US, Britain and their allies in March 2003. The theories discussed in this chapter give rise to different questions about the Iraq War, facilitating different types of analysis of events in the run-up to the invasion.

At first glance, despite a range of views within the tradition, Realism appears to offer a persuasive explanation for the Iraq War. For Realists, the conflict was about security and power and, given the inevitable failure of international organisations to restrict Saddam Hussein, the US, as a hegemonic power, was compelled to take decisive action. The Realist could argue that failure of the international community to resolve the Iraq crisis demonstrates the anarchic nature of international politics and that concerns stemming from the 'security dilemma' can explain the military objectives and tactics of the Iraqi regime. Ultimately, however, Iraq did not pose a serious threat even to other states in the Middle East. Realists thus concluded that the war was a mistake, i.e. it was not in the national interest of the states which intervened. It was concluded that 'vigilant containment', based on a regime of sanctions on the Iraqi government, had been working well enough to justify its continuation. For the Realist, British participation in the war is even more perplexing. At best, it could be rationalised on the basis of a calculation that automatic support for the US was *always* in Britain's national interest – a view which runs counter to the Realist insistence that states can never depend on alliances, even if they choose to consider them as 'special'.

Liberalism, like Realism, can explain elements of the Iraq War while struggling to resolve a number of contested points. The Liberal tradition is defined by ideas and norms, which inform the structure of the international system in the hope of promoting stability and cooperation. In the run-up to the invasion Tony Blair devoted considerable energy in the hope of securing explicit UN authorisation of military action. These efforts, according to the Liberal, highlight the importance of the UN within international relations. While the Realist case for war against Iraq rested on the argument that, in the absence of armed intervention, Saddam Hussein would procure WMDs and pose a global threat, Liberals emphasised the need to free Iraqi citizens from a despotic and murderous regime. This kind of 'humanitarian intervention' had been championed by Blair himself, in his Chicago speech of 1999 (Chapter 9). The Liberal would also argue that the establishment of a democratic system in Iraq would improve stability in the Middle East, in accordance with the 'democratic peace' theory. These expectations, arguably, exposed the weaknesses and contradictions affecting both the theory and practice of Liberalism in an imperfect world. In hindsight it was clear that the interests of stability in post-war Iraq depended on the retention of elements of Saddam's regime, i.e. if long-term Liberal goals were to be secured, the US and the UK would have to compromise on their stated ideals and maintain some deeply *illiberal* officials in place.

At the heart of the Constructivist position is the view that norms and ideas are central to international relations. Constructivist attempts to understand the Iraq War focus on the way in which the threat posed by Iraq and Saddam Hussein was constructed, primarily by the advocates of military intervention. Saddam Hussein's WMD programme had long been suspected and was even condoned in the 1980s. The Constructivist would argue that identities and norms influenced a dramatic change in the framing of interests and threats over time, particularly after the 1991 Gulf War. Britain and the US were prepared to do business with Saddam until his invasion of Kuwait; afterwards he was presented as a uniquely evil individual. The new context provided by the events of 9/11 allowed the US and the UK to 'construct' the Iraqi regime as an immediate threat, on the basis of concrete evidence which was no more damning than it had been when Saddam was accepted by both countries as an unpleasant but basically 'rational' actor in international politics.

It will not surprise the reader to learn that Marxists were some of the most critical observers of the Iraq War because of the impact of the conflict upon ordinary Iraqis. Marxists are concerned with the actions of powerful states within the international system, particularly their pursuit of material factors at the expense of those states on the periphery. While few Marxists would suggest that the Iraq War was triggered solely by a quest to secure oil supplies, many protestors (who adopted the slogan 'No blood for oil') were persuaded by that view. Certainly, the US role could be presented as a fulfilment of its self-adopted position as the ultimate guarantor of the capitalist system.

The more critical approaches, such as poststructuralism, would take the concern about power relations a step further by suggesting that the West has an image of the Middle East as its 'other' – the opposite against which it defines itself. The 'Orientalist' discourse depicts a region that lacks democracy, oppressing women and minority groups of various kinds. These representations and definitions have played a central role in the domination – be it economic or political – of the Middle East by the West. Critical approaches to the Iraq War also focus on the use of language, raising questions (for example) about the role of women and how to represent those who fought against coalition forces.

From this brief overview of theoretical understandings of the Iraq War, it should be apparent that different theoretical lenses result in radically different understandings of particular events – even when, in the case of the 2003 conflict, there is an unusual level of agreement that the US-led intervention was misconceived. As a consequence, scholars should think critically about the strengths and weaknesses of the various theoretical frameworks throughout the course of their studies; thanks to the rapid changes affecting international politics, a theory which seems satisfactory today can soon begin to look woefully inadequate.

Conclusions

While necessarily brief, this chapter has provided an introduction to the prominent IR theories that will help readers to engage with British foreign policy since 1945. A number of questions must be asked when applying theory to empirical material, with our choice of theory allowing us to explore particular aspects at the risk of excluding others. In short, when we opt for one theoretical perspective over others we betray our personal order of priorities. By selecting Realism as our lens we overlook the role of identities, of ideologies and of non-state actors. In selecting Liberalism we give credence to cooperation yet fail to engage adequately with agency. Theories that try to incorporate a variety of perspectives might seem appealing at first sight but might be attacked for insufficient clarity or inadequate support from empirical data.

It is important to remember that the role of IR theory is to help to identify patterns and to generalise at an international level, not to understand the factors which affect decision-making processes. Theories help us to do this, but they are not normally theories that diplomats and state officials seek to act out on the international stage. A foreign policy can be understood through the lens of Constructivism; but that would not make it a Constructivist foreign policy, in the sense of a policy maker setting out to enact what she or he may imagine a Constructivist foreign policy to look like. Some influential actors in international politics, such as Henry Kissinger (b. 1923) and Condoleezza Rice (b. 1954), have gravitated towards policy making after studying IR at university and have sought to implement specific theoretical approaches; but such individuals can rarely act alone, and their decisions are affected not only by developments outside their control but also by the input of others who are inspired by different motives.

Theory should be viewed as a toolkit which can enable us to engage with, and attempt to generalise about, international relations. As this chapter has noted, theories reflect different ontological and epistemological positions. As such, theories are not necessarily interchangeable, nor should they be combined without serious consideration of the need for clarity. Above all, we should always remember that, as the philosopher Ludwig Wittgenstein argued, we are unable to stand apart from the world as detached observers. IR deals with controversial decisions and events; that is one of its main attractions as an academic subject. But since the subject matter of IR engages our emotions, we should conduct research with an awareness that our findings will be coloured by our own preconceptions – and, although these can never entirely be suppressed, we should always be aware of them.

2

The shaping and making of British foreign policy

In studies like the present one, where the main text takes a chronological approach, a separate discussion of the policy-making process serves a dual purpose. It allows the student of British foreign policy since 1945 to explore the role which the policy-making process has played in key events during the period under review, while also providing insights into the effect of those events on the policy-making process itself. Indeed, it can be argued that after decades in which the context of international politics was shaped by British decisions, made within an institutional framework which remained broadly unchanged, the post-war period has been marked by changes in the British decision-making process promoted (if not induced) by developments in the international context. In other words, rather than helping to explain Britain's global influence, a chronological survey of the foreign policy making process is suggestive of the extent to which the world has influenced Britain since 1945.

In any account of the foreign policy making process in Britain, the obvious place to start is the Foreign and Commonwealth Office (FCO). The FCO is still regarded (along with the Treasury and the Home Office) as one of the three senior departments within the British government, and appointment to the job of Foreign Secretary normally entails very high rank within the Cabinet. Thus, in the 2010 coalition government the Foreign Secretary, William Hague, was formally ranked above the Chancellor of the Exchequer, George Osborne; Iain Duncan Smith (Secretary of State for Work and Pensions), who had, like Hague, previously served as Conservative Party leader, was placed only ninth. This is not to say that the FCO has ever enjoyed a monopoly over the making of British foreign policy. But in recent years its role has come under increasing scrutiny as other institutions and actors have become more prominent in the policy process. In order to understand the making of British foreign policy, therefore, the FCO can only mark the point of departure; other key sources of influence over foreign policy, both domestic and external, must be examined.

The 2016 referendum which started the process of British withdrawal from the EU has already affected the FCO more than other Whitehall departments, and the ultimate impact of this decision will not be evident for some time. While taking note of 'Brexit' in the relevant places, the following discussion is chiefly coloured by pre-2016 trends; it remains to be seen whether they will be confirmed or challenged by subsequent events.

History of the FCO

The Foreign Office was established in 1782, after a reorganisation of ministerial responsibilities. Previously there had been two Secretaries of State, heading 'Northern' and 'Southern' departments; apart from the conduct of external relations roughly approximating to these geographical terms, these ministers were also responsible for the north and the south of Britain respectively. In 1768 a new post of Secretary of State for the Colonies had been created in response to the rebellion of Britain's subjects in North America (which, confusingly, had previously been administered by the Southern Department). After the loss of the American colonies this governmental position was abolished and responsibility for the remaining British colonies was entrusted to a Secretary of State for the Home Department. Relations with the rest of the world, whether 'north' or 'south', were handled by the newly established Foreign Office.

In strictly institutional terms, the history of British external relations since 1945 could be seen as a process in which the Foreign Office gradually absorbed government departments which had been set up at various times to administer the Empire. The Colonial Office was revived as a separate institution in 1854 to deal with Britain's expanding overseas possessions. In 1925 a new Dominions Office was spun off to handle relations with colonies (such as Canada, Australia and South Africa) which had been granted self-governing status while remaining within the Empire; its remit increased in 1947, when it took on responsibilities for relations with India, which, until the end of British rule, had been allotted to a separate India Office. The political head of the newly augmented department was given the title of Secretary of State for Commonwealth Relations. The Commonwealth Relations Office (CRO) and the Colonial Office maintained a somewhat prickly coexistence until 1966, when their responsibilities were united under a new Commonwealth Office. This arrangement lasted for just two years; in 1968 all of these tortuous institutional pathways converged in the all-encompassing FCO.

In the course of these various governmental gyrations, the magnificent building which now accommodates the FCO was at one time or another home to four separate departments – the Foreign Office, the India Office, the Colonial Office and the Home Office (the latter was not re-homed until 1978). The building, designed by the Gothic-revivalist architect George Gilbert Scott and

Table 2.1 The FCO in numbers, 2015–16

Budget	Staff	Overseas posts
£1.1 billion	Approx. 14,000 worldwide	Approx. 270, in 160 countries

completed in 1868, was threatened with demolition a century later. That such an idea was taken seriously could be taken as a symptom of an indiscriminate rage for 'modernity' in the 1960s; an attempt to downplay Britain's imperial past by erasing its most notable symbol; or, indeed, as an amalgam of both these motivations.

In itself, the institutional history of Britain's external relations sheds interesting light on the landmarks in the country's foreign policy, particularly in the post-war period. It is no coincidence, for example, that the FCO was established in the year after Britain had declared its intention to abandon its role 'east of Suez'; the prospect of a reduced role raised the possibility of institutional simplification. It is also instructive to follow the complicated career of an institution set up by the incoming Labour government in 1964 in an attempt to promote economic development in the world's poorest countries. The Ministry of Overseas Development (ODM) was designed to bring greater clarity and political impetus to a variety of piecemeal initiatives administered by the usual array of Whitehall departments, including the Foreign Office itself. The ODM's champions insisted that it should be independent, but from the outset its status was strongly disputed. The first ministerial chief (the redoubtable Barbara Castle) was included in the Cabinet, but in 1967 the position was deprived of that status. When the Conservatives returned to office in 1970 the ODM was incorporated into the FCO, where it remained (apart from a brief interlude in 1974–5) until 1997, when New Labour launched the Department for International Development (DfID). The new department quickly established a political profile to rival that of the FCO itself. Despite continued public misgivings about the advisability (or affordability) of overseas aid in an era of austerity, the Conservative-dominated coalition of 2010–15 retained DfID as a separate department, and its hard-won independence was affirmed in 2015, when the Conservatives freed themselves from their Liberal Democrat coalition partners. In 2015 DfID expenditure was around £12 billion, dwarfing the FCO's budget (Table 2.1).

FCO structure

As we have seen, the political head of the FCO, the Foreign Secretary, is always regarded as a very senior member of a government, regardless of his or her previous career. Five post-war Foreign Secretaries (Sir Anthony Eden, Harold

Macmillan, Lord Home, James Callaghan and John Major) subsequently served as Prime Minister, compared to four Chancellors of the Exchequer and two Home Secretaries. In addition, in 1970 Sir Alec Douglas-Home (the former Lord Home, who had renounced his peerage) agreed to return to the FCO after his spell as Prime Minister (Table 2.2).

In addition to the prestige of the job, the Foreign Secretary has an opportunity to exercise practical policy influence through his or her access to restricted information and membership of several key Cabinet committees. The Foreign Secretary heads a team of ministers (currently five; there were six before the 2016 referendum on EU membership and just four in the immediate aftermath of the vote (see below)).

Table 2.2 Foreign Secretaries since 1945

Name	Party	Held office
Ernest Bevin	Lab	1945–51
Herbert Morrison	Lab	1951
Sir Anthony Eden	Con	1951–5
Harold Macmillan	Con	1955
Selwyn Lloyd	Con	1955–60
Earl of Home	Con	1960–3
'Rab' Butler	Con	1963–4
Patrick Gordon Walker	Lab	1964–5
Michael Stewart	Lab	1965–6
George Brown	Lab	1966–8
Michael Stewart	Lab	1968–70
Sir Alec Douglas Home	Con	1970–4
James Callaghan	Lab	1974–6
Anthony Crosland	Lab	1976–7
David Owen	Lab	1977–9
Lord Carrington	Con	1979–82
Francis Pym	Con	1982–3
Sir Geoffrey Howe	Con	1983–9
John Major	Con	1989
Douglas Hurd	Con	1989–95
Sir Malcolm Rifkind	Con	1995–7
Robin Cook	Lab	1997–2001
Jack Straw	Lab	2001–6
Margaret Beckett	Lab	2006–7
David Miliband	Lab	2007–10
William Hague	Con	2010–14
Philip Hammond	Con	2014–16
Boris Johnson	Con	2016–

Their responsibilities cover a variety of geographical areas, international organisations and themes, such as human rights and counter-terrorism (Table 2.3).

The political team is supported by a bureaucratic machine whose calibre is invariably compared to that of high-performing motor vehicles. The Diplomatic Service is still a separate branch of the UK's civil service and has sometimes been accused of regarding representatives of the Home Civil Service with ill-concealed disdain. A sense of intellectual superiority was matched by social elitism, at least until the First World War, when independent wealth, as well as powerful patronage, was essential for any ambitious recruit. Women were excluded until the service was reformed by Sir Anthony Eden in the 1940s; until the 1970s they were required to leave if they committed the professional faux pas of matrimony. Women (and members of ethnic minorities) are still under-represented in senior FCO roles; but the department is no less conscious of the case for equal opportunities than its domestic counterparts, and considerable progress has been made recently (Dickie, 2004).

The keys to this 'Rolls Royce' department are entrusted to the FCO's Permanent Under-Secretary (PUS). Free from the Foreign Secretary's party-political distractions, this official has more time to absorb the information flowing into the FCO and thus has a plausible claim to be regarded as the 'Deputy Foreign Secretary'. At the same time, the low public profile of the PUS provides ideal 'cover' for occasional diplomatic ventures into areas where political visits would arouse unhelpful publicity. In the past the PUS would normally accompany the Foreign

Table 2.3 FCO ministers, 2017

Boris Johnson	Secretary of State for Foreign and Commonwealth Affairs	
Sir Alan Duncan	Minister of State	Europe and the Americas, NATO, the Falklands and relations with parliament
Alistair Burt	Minister of State	Middle East and North Africa
Rory Stewart	Minister of State	Africa and international crime
Mark Field	Minister of State	Asia, Australasia and the Pacific, and public diplomacy including the British Council
Lord Ahmed of Wimbledon	Minister of State	Leads for government in House of Lords; human rights, the Commonwealth and UN

Secretary to key meetings abroad. However, in recent decades the FCO has succumbed to the general Whitehall vogue for 'managerialism', ensuring that the diplomatic skills of the PUS are more often deployed in internal personnel issues than in battles of wits with the representatives of other nations.

The work of the FCO is divided into numerous 'departments', dedicated either to geographical areas or policy themes. The FCO's board, which convenes twice weekly, is dominated by officials whose remit is 'thematic' rather than geographical and includes non-executive members. As such, it would be fair to conclude that even before the seismic events of 2016 the hierarchy of the FCO had been reshaped to reflect an era in which international dilemmas are no longer state- (or even region-) specific, and that expertise in 'human resources' or legal questions is at least as highly prized as specialist knowledge of international relations.

Traditionally, the FCO's role in the policy-making process depended on the intelligence-gathering capacity of its formal diplomatic representatives, stationed across the globe in official public buildings. Ambassadors would transmit the knowledge they had gleaned from meetings with significant political actors in their host countries, resulting in a constant stream of telegrams to London. The most significant of these communications would be passed up the departmental channels to the PUS and the Foreign Secretary. This process depended on the judgement of the 'man [and it usually *was* a man] on the spot', which was not always reliable. According to the stereotyped view of the Foreign Office, when its representatives were sent overseas they would seek out people much like themselves as suitable targets for their acumen and charm, resulting in impeccable summaries of the state of 'educated' opinion in a given country, without tapping into the mood among the populace as a whole. Even before the advent of the internet, technological change had facilitated more direct and relevant access to global developments. In 1946 the government's eavesdropping/code-breaking service, which had played a pivotal role in the victory over Nazi Germany, was renamed the Government Communications Headquarters (GCHQ); in 1951 it moved to its current base near Cheltenham, Gloucestershire.

Formally, the Foreign Secretary is responsible for the activities of GCHQ, although it has considerable operational autonomy (thanks to the British government's addiction to secrecy, its existence was not officially admitted until 1983). In comparison to the electronic assistance which this facility provides for those who want to excel in the 'dark arts' of espionage – including the 'hacking' of individual telephone conversations and supposedly private computers – information gleaned from polite conversations at pre-arranged cocktail parties can only seem embarrassingly outdated and even irrelevant. If the intelligence gathered by GCHQ and other clandestine government operatives was confined (at least initially) to the FCO, the department's prestige would be as high today as it has ever been. However, the most sensitive information has always been spread beyond departmental boundaries.

The Prime Minister

For understandable reasons, the most sensitive information is made available to the Prime Minister; and it is equally understandable that, even when she or he is distracted by other issues, the holder of the highest political office can be expected to give close attention to the latest intelligence. Prime Ministerial interest in external policy is certainly not new. Even in the eighteenth century premiers like the Pitts (both 'Elder' and 'Younger') took prominent roles in this field; for his part, Lord North was derided for having 'lost' Britain's colonies in North America. In more recent times the Marquess of Salisbury and Ramsay MacDonald combined the roles of Foreign Secretary and Prime Minister. Despite his lack of relevant experience, Neville Chamberlain seized overall direction of foreign policy from Sir Anthony Eden, who was less than a wholehearted supporter of the Prime Minister's strategy of 'appeasement' (Chapter 3). When Eden himself became Prime Minister in 1955 he found it difficult to work with a strong-minded Foreign Secretary (Harold Macmillan) and quickly replaced him with the more malleable Selwyn Lloyd. The ensuing Suez fiasco cannot be regarded as the Foreign Office's finest hour, but the chief responsibility clearly lay with Eden rather than Lloyd.

Broadly speaking, all these examples of Prime Ministerial dominance of foreign policy can be explained by the fact that the incumbent had a specific interest in the subject; and the office of Prime Minister does not entail any specific departmental responsibilities, allowing the incumbent relative freedom to choose policy priorities. However, Eden's tenure at Number 10 can be seen as marking a watershed in this respect. By the late 1950s air travel had become so convenient that instead of having to make a special effort to attend crucial international meetings, Prime Ministers could anticipate criticism if they *did not* attend – from a media whose representatives had become more mobile thanks to the same technological developments. Thus, while positive publicity had been an unplanned side effect of Chamberlain's attempts to placate Mussolini and Hitler, by Macmillan's time it was possible for Prime Ministers to orchestrate overseas visits (particularly to the Soviet Union) with the specific purpose of impressing the electorate back home.

In short, even by 1960 it was reasonable to regard Britain's head of government as the country's 'chief diplomat' – not just for epoch-making occasions like the peacemaking at Versailles in 1919, when Lloyd George played the dominant role, but also for more mundane meetings like a Commonwealth conference held in an uneventful year. On such occasions the performance of the Foreign Office in preparing the ground in advance – or salving injured feelings during the event itself – could be decisive in terms of success or failure. But since the credit or blame would fall on the Prime Minister, it seemed only sensible that the holder of that office should be able to draw upon additional resources; and if a Prime Minister who already enjoyed unsurpassed access to information could also recruit talented individuals to interpret that material and help with the writing of keynote speeches, the special status of a Foreign Secretary seemed to be endangered.

While modern Prime Ministers have always availed themselves of advice to supplement the suggestions of the Foreign Office, Mrs Thatcher's appointment of a Foreign Policy Adviser in 1983 was another significant step, not least because it was a direct product of her 'disenchantment' with the FCO's performance over the Falklands (Cradock, 1997, 8; Controversy 2.1). The Prime Minister already had a trusted source of advice, since her Private Secretary, Charles Powell, had worked for the FCO both at home and abroad. Rather than seeking to tone down the Prime Minister's forceful views on international affairs, Powell tended to second them, and his presence at the premier's elbow made it unlikely that a Foreign Policy Adviser could ever persuade her into an alternative course of action. As a result, Thatcher saw no reason to follow FCO advice if it conflicted with her own views and those of her favoured 'courtiers'; indeed, at times after 1983 it seemed as if her default position was to ignore or circumvent FCO promptings. This attitude could be explained by her impatience with the diplomatic style of Sir Geoffrey Howe (Foreign Secretary, 1983–9); however, since she had worked alongside Howe quite amicably when he was Chancellor of the Exchequer (1979–83), her apparent desire to humiliate him at every opportunity evidently arose from institutional antipathy towards the FCO as well as personal factors.

After Thatcher's downfall – precipitated by Howe's belated decision to resign from the government – John Major reverted to a more rational and sustainable approach, relying heavily on the counsel of his Foreign Secretary, Douglas Hurd. However, even if Major had not felt a general inclination to revert to a more collegial model of decision-making now that the Thatcherite storm had blown itself out, he would have been inclined to defer to Hurd who had an impeccable FCO pedigree (whereas the new Prime Minister himself had served for just three months as Howe's successor as Foreign Secretary when Mrs Thatcher chose to overlook all of the better-qualified candidates, such as Douglas Hurd).

Thus the restoration of the Foreign Secretary to a key role in foreign-policy making under Major turned out to be the short-lived product of unusual circumstances. After the landslide New Labour victory of 1997 Tony Blair quickly reverted to Thatcherite type. Although Blair had no previous experience in foreign policy, Mrs Thatcher had been in the same position when she became

Controversy 2.1 The Falklands War

The events leading up to the Falklands War of April–June 1982 provide invaluable insights into almost every aspect of post-war British foreign policy (Chapter 7). From the point of view of the policy-making process, several points are worth summarising:

- Although the FCO was castigated for its diplomatic efforts to find a peaceful solution to the Falklands/Malvinas issue, it is difficult to argue that it could have pursued a more fruitful strategy. Public opinion in Argentina was strongly in favour of a transfer of sovereignty over the islands, but the residents were adamantly opposed. A compromise had to be sought; and, since the British government was imposing defence cuts (while simultaneously permitting arms sales to re-equip Argentine forces), the FCO could only hope to secure a deal which left Argentina reasonably satisfied without leaving the islanders with a sense of betrayal. This was a task which would have baffled the greatest of diplomats; the fact that the FCO suggestion of a formal transfer of sovereignty to Argentina, combined with a 99-year 'leaseback' to Britain, was expounded by junior FCO minister Nicholas Ridley – an ideological soulmate of Margaret Thatcher, who had even less taste (or capacity) for tactful discussion than the Prime Minister herself – only abbreviated the passage towards inevitable failure.
- Whatever the reasons for the Argentine invasion, the FCO was rightly blamed for its misreading of the signals from Buenos Aries, which had been registered in security circles (Freedman and Gamba-Stonehouse, 1990, 18). The logic of the FCO's desire for a compromise which, essentially, favoured Argentina over the islanders, implied a recognition that an attempt to seize the Falklands by force was at least theoretically possible; but despite the failure of the 'leaseback' solution to the sovereignty question, the FCO seemed to fall back on the hope that Argentine menaces amounted to no more than sabre-rattling. For this reason, the subsequent resignation of Lord Carrington, along with two junior FCO ministers, can be regarded as a genuine acceptance of responsibility rather than a chivalrous attempt to divert the blame from colleagues (i.e. Thatcher herself and the Defence Secretary, Sir John Nott) who were probably more culpable.
- Despite the impressive House of Commons debate of 3 April 1982, at key moments in the Falklands crisis Parliament unwittingly reinforced the case *against* those who would entrust it with a decisive role in British foreign policy. The MPs of all parties who denounced Nicholas

> Ridley when he reported back to the Commons after his unsuccessful (1980) mission to sell the 'leaseback' idea to the Falkland Islanders might have been justified in giving full vent to their displeasure; but the 'Falklands lobby' was not representative of the Commons as a whole (let alone of the British public, few of whom had heard of the Falklands Islands at the time). After the Argentine invasion Conservative backbenchers treated Lord Carrington so roughly that he felt compelled to resign. If Mrs Thatcher's supporters felt any elation at the ejection of a minister who was unsympathetic to the government's policy on a range of issues, their spirits were quickly doused when Thatcher appointed Francis Pym, a much more outspoken critic, as his replacement. As a result, the friction between Downing Street and the FCO was even greater than it would have been if Tory MPs had treated Carrington more tenderly.
> - Once the Argentine invasion had begun, the FCO lived up to its high reputation. Skilful diplomacy at the UN provided the British government with sufficient grounds for military action to recover the islands (although subsequent UN resolutions calling for a ceasefire had to be vetoed once the military balance had swung Britain's way). Sir Nicholas Henderson, at the Washington embassy, marshalled existing sympathy for Britain within the Reagan administration to maximum effect. 'Europe' was also strongly (and perhaps surprisingly) supportive, although any gratitude Mrs Thatcher might have felt for this symptom of continental solidarity was short-lived.

Prime Minister – and this factor had certainly not deterred her from decisive interventions. In Blair's case, the itch to take a leading role in foreign policy was increased by his previous agreement to allow his Chancellor, Gordon Brown, a dominant position over any domestic issue which involved the significant cooperation of the Treasury. Blair's first Foreign Secretary, Robin Cook, might have been a dangerous rival if he had been given a domestic portfolio; as it was, although Cook made an eye-catching start by signalling a shift to a more 'ethical' foreign policy, within a few months his position was undermined by revelations concerning his personal life, which resulted in a humiliating demand from Downing Street for him to choose between his wife and his mistress. Blair seized the initiative, emerging as a leading advocate of military action in the Balkans and Sierra Leone and rationalising this approach in his 1999 Chicago speech which outlined the case for 'liberal intervention' (Chapter 9).

After the 2001 general election Cook was removed from the FCO, whose officials on the whole were disinclined to lament his departure. His replacement, Jack Straw, was a much less controversial character, having earned the image of an 'elder statesman' through his aptitude for survival during decades of Labour faction-fighting. Any (remote) possibility that the FCO might regain some of its former prestige under his stewardship was extinguished on 11 September 2001, when the terrorist attack on New York's World Trade Center provided Blair with the opportunity to play a starring role. As Straw himself put it, after 9/11 'the pace and focus of our lives changed completely. Tony set that pace' (Straw, 2012, 340). By contrast, a *Guardian* reporter described the Foreign Secretary as 'out of his depth, nervous, over-reliant on officials and completely dominated by the prime minister, who has taken personal command of foreign policy'. In a key interview, the report added, '[Straw's] tie was not straight, his suit was lopsided and his descriptions of Afghanistan sounded like those of a keen geography student who had just been taught about the country from a map' (Watt, 2002b).

Straw was hurt by this critique, particularly (in true New Labour style) by its personal elements (Straw, 2012, 352). His less media-fixated predecessors would have latched on to the brief passage in the offending article which explained why a Foreign Secretary was suddenly vulnerable to such jibes. Blair, the author wrote, had established 'a parallel Foreign Office' in Downing Street, ensuring that the Foreign Secretary would be seen as 'the weakest member of the Cabinet's top four' even if Ernest Bevin himself rose from the grave (presumably in a well-fitting suit and perfectly perpendicular tie) to take the job on the eve of the War on Terror (Watt, 2002b).

In his last snapshot of the FCO the journalist Anthony Sampson, who had been a close and perceptive observer since the early 1960s, contrasted the material grandeur of the FCO's 'Whitehall palazzo' with Straw's menial ministerial function, at Blair's 'beck and call' (Sampson, 2004, 136). In March 2003 Straw had wound up the House of Commons debate on the case for war against Saddam Hussein's Iraq. If Robin Cook had still been Foreign Secretary, the situation would have been much more complicated; while Straw genuinely accepted that Iraq was a threat to Western security, Cook was far more sceptical and resigned from the government on this issue. However, from the FCO's point of view it was probably a good thing that in 2003 it was led by the biddable Straw rather than the combustible Cook. The Prime Minister's indisputable leadership on this foreign policy issue deflected public attention from the FCO's failure to restrain his instinct to support the US, either by questioning evidence relating to Saddam's weapons of mass destruction (WMD) or by presenting more forcefully the argument that 'regime change' might cause more problems than it solved. Perhaps the cruellest comment on the FCO's role in the Iraq War is that it was less damaging than its performance before the Falklands Conflict. In the latter instance it might have averted the invasion of a British Dependent Territory, whereas in 2003 it could only have made things a bit more difficult for individuals who could never have been deflected from their chosen course. An inadvertent, though eloquent, commentary on the relative decline of the FCO can be gleaned from the 'valedictory' despatches of two seasoned ambassadors – Sir Nicholas Henderson, who left Britain's Washington embassy in 1979, and Sir Ivor Roberts, who retired as Ambassador to Italy in 2006. The despatches were equally gloomy; but while Henderson analysed the post-war decline of Britain in political and economic terms (highlighting the failure to engage in European integration at the right time), Roberts riveted his attention on the perceived shortcomings of the department he had served for almost three decades (Case Study 2.1).

The National Security Council

Perhaps the most telling comment on the position of the FCO at the end of the New Labour era was William Hague's stated intention, on becoming Foreign Secretary in the coalition government, 'to place the Foreign Office *back at the centre of government*' (Hague, 2010: italics added). In itself, Hague's appointment did something to restore the FCO's clout within Whitehall; Hague also held the position of First Secretary of State, making him Deputy Prime Minister in all but name. However, the early days of the coalition featured an institutional innovation which raised new questions about the FCO's role in the decision-making apparatus.

In one respect, the newly created National Security Council (NSC) confirmed the importance of the FCO. The first National Security Adviser, who acted as secretary to the body, was the former PUS Sir Peter Ricketts, and his successors (including the current incumbent, Mark Sedwill) have held a variety of key diplomatic positions. However, the NSC was chaired by the Prime Minister, and apart from the Foreign Secretary its membership included no fewer than eight other ministers. The 'Threats, Hazards, Resilience and Contingencies' subcommittee of the NSC was like a meeting of the full Cabinet under a different name. Apart from the Prime Minister and the Foreign Secretary, 15 ministers were listed among the members: even the Secretary of State for Culture, Media and Sport was considered to be a desirable attendee. Although the FCO was reportedly relaxed about the formation of the NSC, the clear implication was that the policy dilemmas arising from Britain's external relations now required the advice of people who were skilled in the provision of 'security', very broadly defined, rather than the diplomacy in which the FCO has always excelled.

The foreign policy role of other departments

Since 9/11 (if not before) matters of national security have obviously been a key concern for the Home Secretary, and the Chancellor of the Exchequer has to be closely involved in the likely event of policy decisions with financial

Case Study 2.1 Valedictory despatches

Sir Nicholas Henderson (1979):

> A representative abroad has a duty to draw the attention of the authorities at home to the realities of how we look . . . Viewed from the continent our standing at the present time is low. But this is not for the first time in our history, and we can recover if the facts are known and faced and if the British people can be fired with a sense of national will such as others have found these past years.

Sir Ivor Roberts (2006):

> The Foreign Office I leave is perforce very different from the one I entered in 1968. And most changes have been for the better, particularly those long-overdue reforms on the status and parity of women . . . But the culture of change has reached Cultural Revolution proportions with no opportunity for new working methods to put down roots . . . Too much of the change management agenda is written in Wall Street management-speak which is already tired and discredited by the time it is introduced. Synergies, [value for money], best practice, benchmarking, silo-working, roll-out, stakeholder, empower, push-back and deliver the agenda, fit for purpose are all prime candidates for a game of bullshit bingo, a substitute for clarity and succinctness . . . our failure to make a successful case for resources adequate to finance the current network while others are literally awash with funds is at the heart of the malaise . . . It is sad that there is not a recognition by government as a whole that allocating greater resources to the FCO saves the spending of far larger resources through the [Ministry of Defence] or DfID.

After the wide dissemination of Sir Ivor's despatch, it was reported that retiring diplomats would no longer be allowed these official opportunities to embarrass their former employers. Given the morale-sapping content of Henderson's effort, it is more surprising that the practice was tolerated for so long.

implications. But the inclusion in the NSC itself of ministers like the Secretaries of State for Business and for Energy and Climate Change served as a vivid illustration of the difficulty in distinguishing 'domestic' and 'external' policy spheres in contemporary Britain. While departments like Business and Energy and

Climate Change obviously had to undertake negotiations with external bodies – non-governmental, as well as the representatives of other states – the FCO has to divert its attention from the making of 'foreign policy', as traditionally understood, to technical matters like economic policy and the environment. The impetus behind these changes is usually designated by the term 'globalisation'; its cumulative effect on the FCO carries a clear risk of turning a department which prided itself on its expertise in one activity (diplomacy) into an institution which is better characterised as a 'jack of all trades', staffed by individuals who can facilitate the work of other departments without being indispensable in any key policy area.

For many academic observers, developments in the foreign policy making process illustrate a more general trend in British government, suggesting that a long-established explanatory framework should be replaced by a more realistic approach. On this view, the traditional understanding of the FCO as a formidable governmental institution reflected 'the Westminster model' of British government, which depicted decision-making as highly centralised and restricted to clearly identified sources of authority. From this perspective, crucial decisions affecting Britain's external relations would invariably (and quite properly) be taken by the Prime Minister after consultations with the Foreign Secretary, who would be briefed by his or her senior officials. For those who continue to understand British government through the lens of the Westminster model, the perception of a decline in the policy-making role of the FCO indicates a faltering (to say the least) in the potency and coherence of British foreign policy. If the FCO no longer exercises control over Britain's external relations, it even becomes pertinent to ask whether Britain still has a foreign policy at all in a meaningful sense.

Other political scientists reach less apocalyptic conclusions on the basis of alternative explanatory models of British government. 'Multi-level governance', for example, takes note of transnational institutions, such as the EU, and (in the British case) the introduction of devolved institutions in Scotland, Wales and Northern Ireland since 1997. These developments have an obvious effect on the relevance of the traditional Westminster model. However, to date they have had a relatively limited effect on the making of foreign policy. Thus foreign and defence policy were among the 'reserved powers' which the British government explicitly retained when it embarked on the process of devolution after 1997. As for the EU, its policy-making competence was limited in scope when the UK joined what was then the European Economic Community (EEC) in 1973. While European legislation was a crucial concern for the Ministry of Agriculture, for example, most other ministers could concentrate on the domestic aspects of their work. Indeed, in the early years UK membership promised to bolster, rather than weaken, the institutional clout of the FCO within Whitehall. It played a very influential role, not least by providing Britain's Permanent

Representatives to the EEC. The foreign ministers of member states have also exercised an important coordinating role in what is now the Council of the European Union (formerly the Council of Ministers) through the General Affairs and External Relations Council, which since the 2009 Lisbon Treaty has been divided into the General Affairs and Foreign Affairs Councils.

However, subsequent developments within what is now the EU have added plausibility to another explanatory framework for decision-making in British government: the 'differentiated polity model'. From this perspective, government in Britain (and elsewhere) can no longer be a matter of 'command and control' from specific institutional locations; rather, decisions can only be made and implemented through a process of negotiation. The old understanding of a nation state is no longer viable: decision-makers have no alternative but to work with a variety of non-state institutions and to collaborate with other actors within their own formal government structures, since decision-making has become subject to overlapping areas of policy responsibility.

Even if the EU has limited authority in foreign and defence policy, it provides numerous venues which encourage a range of government departments ostensibly concerned with 'domestic' policy to develop perspectives formerly associated with diplomatic activity. The Council of the European Union now covers a wide range of subjects, including the Environment; Justice and Home Affairs; Employment, Social Policy, Health and Consumer Affairs; Transport, Telecommunications and Energy; and Education, Youth, Culture and Sport. Through frequent attendance at such meetings the relevant British ministers and officials have inevitably become familiar with the workings of the EU; so although the FCO's expertise in this respect might still surpass that of other UK departments, it can no longer be said to be 'unrivalled'. Ministers and officials from various departments enjoy opportunities to acquire knowledge and personal connections which would once have been monopolised by the FCO. If Britain had joined the European single currency, the ubiquitous Treasury would almost certainly have become the leading departmental player in the EU; as it is, while the Chancellor of the Exchequer attends meetings of the Economic and Financial Affairs Council (Ecofin), he or she is excluded from the core eurozone group of ministers.

The differentiated polity model can certainly be applied to the fortunes of the British FCO since its establishment in its current guise in 1968. Indeed, the blurring of departmental responsibilities was identified as a problem for the FCO by the Duncan Committee's official report into Britain's overseas representation (1969), and William Wallace, who was conducting academic research into the foreign policy making process at that time, observed that 'the role of the Foreign Office has become far less clear than it was fifteen or twenty years ago', and that it was now 'more appropriate to talk about a foreign policy dimension across the whole range of domestic politics, demanding particular attention from particular ministers, civil servants, and commentators' (Wallace, 1975, 272, 270). Wallace's penetrating analysis opened the prospect that the FCO could now only be one of many departments charged with the task of 'doing' foreign policy. It might continue to coordinate the work of other departments at Brussels, but back in Whitehall it seemed more logical to entrust this task to the Cabinet Office. Since this institution was closely linked (in geographical and other respects) to Number 10 Downing Street, the tendency for these developments to augment the foreign policy role of the Prime Minister (whether she or he liked it or not) was readily perceptible.

Since UK membership of the EU was a key driver behind the development of theories which challenged the Westminster model, it is probable that they will require refinement when the dust finally settles on the 'Brexit' phenomenon. For the present purpose, however, the main point arising from all of the theoretical approaches is that the FCO's position within the British policy-making process is no longer as significant as it was when the present department was formed in 1968. On some readings of recent events, the FCO is well placed to reassert its traditional role. Equally, though, it can be argued that the department would have lost even more influence within Whitehall had Britain never been a member of the EU, and that the tendency to lose functions to other ministries (and non-government institutions) can only accelerate after 'Brexit'. Speculation is at the mercy of unpredictable events, and students of the subject are invited to keep a close eye on future Whitehall reconfigurations.

Think tanks and other non-governmental organisations

While the relationship between government and external sources of policy advice has not been as intimate as in the US, Britain has produced several world-renowned institutions which provide policy-relevant information and serve as convenient venues for the exchange of ideas. The Royal Institute of International Affairs (RIIA, also known as Chatham House) was established in 1920 and publishes a highly regarded journal, *International Affairs*. The International Institute for Strategic Studies (IISS) was founded in 1958, in response to growing fears of nuclear conflict. The Royal United Services Institute for Defence and Security Studies (RUSI) has an even longer institutional history, having been established in 1831; however, its research activities were relatively limited until the 1960s.

Generally speaking, the motivation behind the establishment of foreign-policy think tanks has been a feeling that Whitehall lacks a capacity for impartial research geared towards long-term planning; their rationale tends to resist the logic of the differentiated polity model and to reaffirm foreign policy making as a specialised activity, demanding specific expertise. For all prominent think tanks, a persistent challenge is to strike an appropriate balance between policy influence and institutional autonomy, and this dilemma has been particularly acute for organisations working in the defence and foreign policy fields (Garnett and Mabon, 2016). It is all too tempting for governments to cherry-pick the results of serious research to advance their short-term policy goals. For example, an IISS report on Iraq was cited as a source for British government claims concerning the level of threat posed by Saddam Hussein's forces. Ideas advanced by Sir Lawrence Freedman, a prolific academic writer with longstanding connections to Chatham House and the IISS, featured heavily in Tony Blair's 1999 Chicago speech on liberal intervention. On the one hand, such examples suggest that British governments continue to depend upon the advice of foreign policy 'experts' at times of crisis; but they also indicate that in such instances they tend to look outside the FCO for advice. A key issue for think tanks is the source of their funding, which can raise questions about their impartiality. For example, in 2016 it was revealed that the IISS had received considerable donations from Bahrain, a Gulf state with a highly controversial human rights record.

Although the policy influence of think tanks should not be discounted, other non-governmental bodies, notably international charities, are equally (if not more) significant members of the policy networks which characterise the differentiated polity model. Organisations like Oxfam were consulted on a more regular and 'official' basis after New Labour's victory in the 1997 general election; their expertise was helpful to the FCO as well as to the DfID. Senior figures within the key international charities have been recruited as policy advisers; for example, Dianna Melrose was Policy Director for Oxfam between 1993 and 1999 before embarking on a successful career within the FCO (including service as Ambassador to Cuba).

Parliament

In 1815 Lord Grey, the opposition Whig politician and later Prime Minister, told the House of Lords that 'although it was the practice of Parliament during the pendency of all foreign negotiations to leave the management and direction in the hands of the Executive Government', in certain cases 'it became the duty of Parliament to intervene' (quoted in Nicolson, 1946, 187–8). This characterisation of Parliament's foreign policy role still seems plausible, more than two centuries later, despite the fact that the House of Commons, at least, enjoys much greater democratic credibility than it did in 1815 (thanks, at least in part, to the 'Great Reform Act' passed in 1832 by a government led by Lord Grey himself).

The arguments for executive direction of external policy have, if anything, become more pertinent in the intervening years, largely due to technological changes relating to the nature of international conflict:

- In the face of unexpected crises the executive is much better placed to organise a timely response than the legislature, whose members might not even have the chance to assemble before the opportunity for an effective response has passed;
- Even in democratic states, it must be recognised that the unimpeded circulation of information can sometimes have a deleterious effect on diplomatic activity. While full and open debate in the legislative branch of government is a laudable ideal, elected assemblies are unlikely to maintain the kind of balance between disclosure and secrecy which is compatible with the national interest.

In addition, British legislators have tended to resemble their counterparts in other liberal democratic states in their tendency to prioritise domestic-policy issues, which have a direct impact on their constituents on a daily basis, over external affairs which have a more sporadic effect (Richards, 1967). As a result, it has usually been assumed that Parliamentary debates concerning foreign policy will be thinly attended and dominated by a handful of specialists. By the same token, when Parliament has been asked to pronounce on momentous policy issues the turnout of MPs tends to be much more impressive than the result of the ensuing deliberations. Thus, for example, the lengthy debates of 1972 which led to Parliament's agreement to join the EEC were followed by a series of votes which were distorted by the effect of partisan point-scoring (on that occasion, by the Labour Party). In March 2003 the House of Commons authorised British participation in the invasion of Iraq, defeating by 396 votes to 217 an amendment which would have prevented military action without unambiguous endorsement from the UN. Whether or not this outcome was secured by deliberate exaggeration of the threat from Saddam Hussein's regime, it is certainly reasonable to conclude that many MPs who cast their vote in favour of the government's position would not have done so if the available intelligence from Iraq had been presented with some attempt at impartiality.

The Parliamentary vote on Iraq left a lasting legacy, and it was a significant factor in a remarkable Parliamentary defeat inflicted on David Cameron's coalition government. In August 2013 it tabled an ambiguous motion that was (rightly) seen as an attempt to pave the way for British air strikes in support of anti-government forces in Syria. The margin of defeat was narrow – by 285 votes to 272 – but Parliament had been recalled specifically to debate the question, which in itself was intended to stiffen the resolve of coalition supporters who doubted the gravity of the situation. On 26 September 2014 Parliament was recalled again, this time to approve British action against 'Islamic State' (IS) terrorists in Iraq; on that occasion the government won by 524 to 43. The implication of these votes was that the British Parliament was happy for the country's forces to strike against IS in Iraq but not in Syria – a position which was susceptible to rational justification, but which ministers presented as wholly illogical. The government duly asked the Commons to support action in Syria after all, in a vote of 2 December 2015. The motion was approved by 397 votes to 223 – a margin of victory which (even allowing for the subsequent change in Parliamentary support for the major parties) was unsettlingly similar to the one secured by Blair after the Iraq debate in 2003.

Critics of the coalition government's position could argue that although it had been consistent in its desire to extend military action from Iraq to Syria, this apparent consistency masked a dramatic strategic switch – from bombing targets associated with the Assad regime to targeting IS insurgents. However, leaving aside any concrete developments which might have affected Parliamentary opinion between August 2013 and December 2015, a legislature which was capable of such a comprehensive reversal of its initial decision on a key issue would have difficulty sustaining its credentials as a reliable custodian of a nation's foreign policy. Even more damaging was the suspicion that the August 2013 vote had been decided not by a clear-eyed review of the facts but rather by a (somewhat belated) desire in some quarters to purge the Commons of guilty feelings arising from its conduct before the war on Iraq. If so, it would certainly not be the only occasion during the 2010–15 Parliament when the House of Commons allowed emotion to override its capacity for collective rationality. Rather than accepting the 'consensus' view that a referendum on UK membership of the EU should be delayed until significant changes had been proposed in a new treaty, Conservative backbenchers forced David Cameron to promise an 'in–out' referendum on UK membership before the end of 2017, whether or not the 'Brussels bureaucrats' had come up with any new hare-brained schemes.

Recent events have provoked suggestions that British troops should not be committed to action without a previous Parliamentary vote. In typically British style, this has already become something like a constitutional convention – when Parliament has the opportunity to assemble and deliberate in advance of such a decision. The problem, as in the US, is to find a way of ensuring a role for the legislature in cases when instant decisions are demanded. In such cases, whether or not the British Parliament chooses to demand a role, judgements regarding peace or war can only be left in the hands of the executive, with the proviso that the legislature has the right to hold ministers to account if they misuse this power.

Those MPs who take a continuous interest in external relations have a convenient outlet in the Foreign Affairs Select Committee. Like similar bodies in the House of Commons, the Committee (established in 1979) was strengthened by reforms under the coalition government; even before this it had earned a reputation for searching scrutiny of executive decisions. Its prestige is sufficient to ensure the attendance of well-informed witnesses. Thus, for example, a report published in 2011 was based on testimony from the serving Foreign Secretary, William Hague, and five of his predecessors as well as numerous officials and academic observers. The Committee's inquiry, significantly, had been triggered by concerns about the future role of the FCO (House of Commons Foreign Affairs Committee, 2011). Another key report, on the ill-fated British intervention in Libya, attracted considerable attention when it appeared in 2016 (House of Commons Foreign Affairs Committee, 2016). However, although governments usually respond to the Committee's reports, they are under no obligation to adopt its recommendations. Also, like the FCO itself, the Foreign Affairs Select Committee has encountered obstacles because of the growing importance of 'national security', which falls within the remit of the more secretive Intelligence and Security Committee.

Critical comments about the foreign policy performance of the House of Commons are much less applicable to the House of Lords, where debates are relatively free from partisan considerations. Its select committee on the EU, with its various subcommittees, won an enviable reputation for its objective and detailed scrutiny of EU business. However, in more general terms, the Lords cannot hope to rival the potential influence of the Commons over decision-making; it is not unduly cynical to argue that its limited powers are the main reason why debates in the upper chamber are more balanced and better informed than the proceedings in the Commons.

Public opinion

Writing in 1937, the MP and former diplomat Harold Nicolson expressed the view that 'the British people have not yet acquired the habit of judgement in regard to foreign policy', and were subject to 'strange emotional fluctuations'. It was an uncanny echo of the lament of an early Foreign Secretary, William Grenville, who wrote in 1797 that:

> To desire war without reflection, to be unreasonably elated by success, to be still more unreasonably depressed by difficulties, and to call for peace with an impatience which makes suitable terms unattainable, are the established maxims and the regular progress of the popular mind in this country.
> (quoted in Ehrman, 1996, 55)

Nicolson, however, was optimistic that this situation would be rectified as the British public became accustomed to the new role in foreign policy which was implied by the (fairly recent) introduction of universal suffrage.

In the 1930s the problem of public opinion was particularly acute for Nicolson's former Foreign Office colleagues. Whether or not Britain was a democratic country, the state of public opinion would have to be considered seriously, since technological developments meant that a new war would endanger the lives of ordinary citizens as well as the armed forces. Reading between the lines, Nicolson's own view was that British public opinion would have arrived at maturity when an overwhelming majority had realised that in such matters its own judgement would always be inferior to that of the 'experts' in the Foreign Office (Nicolson, 1937, 55).

Unfortunately, even in the 1930s it was clear that the members of the public who were sufficiently motivated to inform themselves on matters of external policy tended (almost by definition) to be passionate supporters of one course or another and thus impervious to the Foreign Office insistence that international affairs should be seen in varying shades of grey. It seemed as if totalitarian states enjoyed a considerable diplomatic advantage, since they had no need to take account of possible public dissent in the decision-making process.

There is good reason to suppose that Nicolson's hopes regarding public opinion have not been realised. Whether or not the general level of knowledge concerning external relations has improved since the 1930s, those who are well-informed are still a minority, and the intensity of their commitment still compensates for their lack of numbers. For the most part, Britain's foreign policy makers have continued to regard public opinion as a force which, within definite limits, can be managed – an attitude which was rudely challenged by the result of the 2016 EU referendum. The best justification for this approach was the fact that governments have been re-elected after apparent foreign policy disasters – the Conservatives won comfortably in 1959 despite the 1956 Suez fiasco, and New Labour repeated the feat in 2005, despite increasing evidence that the 2003 intervention in Iraq had been less than a complete success and had been launched on false pretences. While foreign policy reverses have not necessarily led to electoral defeat, Margaret Thatcher's hopes for re-election in 1983 were undoubtedly helped by a public reaction to the 1982 Falklands War which is best interpreted as a gut reaction against previous humiliations, rather than a sober assessment of the country's international status. But victory in war is no guarantee of electoral success. When the Conservative Party went down to a heavy defeat in the 1945 general election voters might have been influenced by memories of Neville Chamberlain and appeasement; but by 1945 Chamberlain was dead, and the Conservatives were led into the election by Winston Churchill, the man who had resisted appeasement and provided heroic wartime leadership.

From the perspective of liberal democracy, the Iraq War was particularly troubling, since the depth and extent of well-informed opposition had been exhibited in mass demonstrations, which seem to have impressed Britain's American allies more than the country's own government (see the fascinating polling evidence at Ipsos MORI, 2003b). In this instance, although many members of the public were clearly unimpressed by his attempts to make the case for war, Tony Blair could draw on memories of the early 1980s, when demonstrators tried to prevent the siting of American cruise missiles in British territory. The Campaign for Nuclear Disarmament (CND) had enjoyed considerable support, which extended beyond the usual 'troublemakers' who had thought deeply about the subject; in 1982 surveys suggested that the case for unilateral nuclear disarmament was backed by nearly a third of voters. Nevertheless, the Thatcher government and its media allies prevailed, largely by cutting through the complexities of the debate and presenting the issue in terms of patriotism and national security. Blair had special reason to remember this outcome, since he had been affiliated to CND himself for much of the 1980s.

Britain's possession of nuclear weapons, and its membership of NATO, could in certain circumstances have been made the subject of referendums. In practice, governments have not felt it necessary to consult the public on issues which, literally, could make the difference between life or death for their citizens. Instead, in 1975 and 2016 governments agreed to engage the public in direct consultation on the single external policy issue of membership of 'Europe'. However, the initial decision to apply for membership (in 1961) was not even a Conservative manifesto commitment in the preceding election; and (contrary to a popular urban myth) the vote which finally took Britain into the EEC was cast by MPs (in 1972) rather than in the 1975 referendum, which merely confirmed a previous Parliamentary decision. It was thus a remarkable feat for proponents of 'Brexit' to claim in 2016 that citizens who voted against continued EU membership would somehow be *reclaiming* an historic right to play a significant role in shaping their nation's destiny. While the argument for withdrawal could be (and sometimes was) advanced on a rational basis, its supporters in the media tended to rely on the old assumption that the majority of British people knew very little about international realities and were perfectly content to vote on the basis of emotion rather than reason. It could be argued, ironically, that the prevalence of this attitude had prevented British politicians from exerting a constructive influence within 'Europe' from the outset. Thus in 2016 the British public was given an unusual invitation to play a decisive foreign policy role on an issue where its direct input was likely to prove uniquely unhelpful.

External actors

For some observers, domestic influences no longer explain the making of British foreign policy, which instead arises from the country's engagement with a variety of multinational organisations and nation states. As such, the UK's foreign policy (in keeping with its approach on an ever widening range of issues) is testament to multi-level governance. Some go even further, claiming that external influences are so potent that there is no longer any such thing as a distinctively 'British' foreign policy.

No one could seriously deny that Britain's engagement with institutions like the UN, NATO, the EU and the G8 have a significant foreign policy impact. Despite occasional serious disagreements (e.g. over Suez and Iraq), Britain's role within the UN has usually been consistent with its position as a founder member with a permanent seat on the Security Council. Without the UN, Britain's preferred approach to all international disputes – the possibility of peaceful negotiated settlements, the imposition of effective sanctions, the provision of peacekeeping troops and/or humanitarian aid – would be infinitely more remote. Nevertheless, the compromises involved in formulating UN resolutions which will command support without alienating other Security Council members has contributed to the notion that Britain lacks a distinctive foreign policy.

The EU exercises significant influence over its member states, including the UK, in relation to trade policy. Having, arguably, succeeded all too well in one of its original purposes – the maintenance of peace within Europe – to the extent that this is now often taken for granted, the main justification for the EU lies in its ability, as the world's most populous single market, to promote economic prosperity. Apart from its own tariff-free status – finalised, somewhat belatedly, after the Single European Act (1986) – the EU has engaged in numerous negotiations with non-member states. British Eurosceptics have argued that the country could have secured similar free-trade deals if it had not joined the EU. Whatever the truth of that claim – which will be tested in years to come – the EU has certainly been a major influence on UK policy making in relation to trade agreements. It has been a member of the World Trade Organisation in its own right since the latter was founded in 1995.

In terms of traditional foreign policy issues, i.e. those relating to disputes which threaten to lead to armed conflict, the EU has been far less influential than its opponents claim, or than its supporters have hoped. Informal consultation on such matters began in 1970, but the European community's response to the Balkan crisis of the early 1990s was widely criticised and apparently strengthened the case for closer cooperation. However, the creation of a European Union at Maastricht in 1992 generated limited changes in the previous arrangement: foreign and security policy remained 'intergovernmental', requiring unanimous support in the Council of Ministers. The Amsterdam Treaty of 1997 instituted a High Representative for the Common Foreign and Security Policy, whose remit was broadened by the subsequent Treaty of Lisbon (2007); but while these reforms made it easier to identify a single individual who could 'speak for Europe' in the appropriate circumstances, it was still unclear when such circumstances would arise. Certainly, the existence of a High Representative made little difference to the divisions among EU member states in relation to the 2003 Iraq War. Among (many) other things, that conflict checked the momentum towards increased European cooperation on defence and security, which Britain and France had initiated in the St Malo declaration of December 1998. More recently, responses to international crises like Libya (2011) and Ukraine (2013) highlighted different priorities within the EU, with the UK and France taking prominent roles in the former situation and Germany in the latter.

Theoretically, Britain's membership of NATO subjects it to much greater constraints, since Article 5 of the North Atlantic Treaty stipulates the collective defence of any member state which comes under attack. However, this clause has only been activated once (in 2001, after the terrorist attack on the World Trade Center); Article 4, which mandates consultations between member states, has been used five times (all since 2003). The 1949 NATO treaty did not specify that signatory states should have identical friends and enemies, but membership of the alliance can still exert some influence over British policy at times when NATO members and other states are engaged in controversies which fall short of armed conflict. In this respect, the fact that NATO membership has increased from the original 12 states to 28 might be regarded as a mixed blessing.

It can be argued that NATO's influence over British foreign policy is mainly a reflection of the UK's relationship with the alliance's dominant power, the US. It is possible to interpret NATO itself as the product of *British* influence over the US – certainly, it was an immediate post-war priority for Britain to secure an American commitment to the defence of Europe, and NATO provided this. However, it would be a mistake to suppose that the US would have made such a commitment without calculating its own perceived interests. While Britain has influenced US policy in specific instances since 1949 – even in the notorious example of the 2003 Iraq War, the Bush administration is unlikely to have persisted in the attempt to win UN backing if Tony Blair had been less insistent – such instances, even if taken at British evaluation, would hardly satisfy the hopes of observers like Harold Macmillan, who anticipated in 1943 that the transatlantic relationship would emulate that between the Romans and the Greeks, i.e. that virile, headstrong Americans would be prodded onto the path of wisdom thanks to the seasoned (if not world-weary) Brits.

US influence over British foreign policy can be seen throughout the current volume. NATO is not the only forum in which such influence can be exercised; indeed, the UK–US relationship has certainly been 'special' in the extent of informal contact between senior officials. On occasions (notably, but not exclusively, on the Israel–Palestine issue) it has seemed that direct consultation has been unnecessary, and that the guiding 'principle' of British foreign policy has been to wait for the Americans to take a decision and then fall in behind it. If this situation has changed over recent years – particularly with regard to strengthening British ties with China – the overwhelming impulse has been economic necessity. In short, British economic imperatives have promoted relations with China, even at the risk of courting US displeasure, in the hope that the same considerations will keep US–China tensions on more traditional foreign policy issues within manageable limits. If these expectations prove ill-founded, it is likely that British policy will return to its familiar post-war pattern, in which 'rational' considerations of national self-interest are subordinated to the instinctive desire to toe the American line.

The 'Brexit' effect

As noted above, the shock waves triggered by the 2016 referendum on EU membership have affected the making of British foreign policy in several significant respects. Most notably, when Theresa May succeeded David Cameron as Prime Minister in July 2016 she created two new departments of state whose functions intersect with those of the FCO. The Department for Exiting the European Union (DExEU), whose name is self-explanatory, was entrusted with the government's most important policy brief. Its staff were drawn from a range of existing departments, particularly the FCO itself. The other new institution, the Department for International Trade (DIT), was given the task of scouring the world for lucrative market opportunities. While the FCO continued to operate in the field of 'economic diplomacy', its value for this purpose seemed to be threatened by the DIT, which, unlike DExEU, seemed likely to become a permanent Whitehall fixture.

The reduction in the number of FCO junior ministers since 2015 could be taken as a quantitative indication of the department's sagging status. From this perspective, Theresa May's eye-catching appointment of Boris Johnson as the new Foreign Secretary could also be taken as evidence that the new Prime Minister no longer saw the FCO as one of the 'great offices of state'. However, some of the ministerial changes were merely a logical product of 'Brexit'; for example, the position of Minister of State for Europe within the FCO looked anomalous, even if Britain looked set to remain within the EU for at least two years. While Johnson had not previously been noted for his mastery of the enigmatic utterance, he was at least a highly visible public figure, who had an obvious interest in defending the interests of his department.

As such, while there were many ominous signs for the FCO even before the 2016 referendum, the outlook in its aftermath also included potential opportunities. As such, the FCO's situation was much like that of Britain itself.

Conclusions and summary

As this chapter has shown, numerous actors are involved in the making of British foreign policy. It was never the case that the Foreign Secretary enjoyed a monopoly in that field, or anything like it. As de facto head of the executive branch, the Prime Minister has always been consulted: even at the Congress of Vienna, in 1815, Lord Castlereagh took pains to square his decisions with his political chief, Lord Liverpool, back in London. Since 1945 the extent of Prime Ministerial intervention has varied, at least in part due to temperamental differences among the office holders. However, since 1979 there has been a definite tendency for Prime Ministers to play a leading part – and not just at times of crisis – despite the very different characters who have held the position. The itch for intervention, which can make the Foreign Secretary seem like a secondary player, has been augmented by the demands of the media and given institutional backing through the presence of specialist advisers in the Prime Minister's entourage.

If influence over headline-grabbing decisions has been drawn upwards, from the FCO to the Prime Minister's Office, responsibility for more mundane matters has shifted sideways and downwards within the traditional Whitehall hierarchy, lending support to the differentiated polity model of decision-making. An economic dimension to British foreign policy making is nothing new, but the Chancellor of the Exchequer now invariably exercises considerable influence over decisions – as well as enjoying an ever tightening hold over the FCO budget. The presence of a strong security aspect to most of the key foreign policy questions also gives the Home Secretary a leading role. Meanwhile, 'second-rank' ministers, whose predecessors formerly regarded the Foreign Secretary with deference – if not envy – are now regularly consulted on matters which either would not have been regarded as significant elements of 'foreign policy' or would have been handled within the FCO. Ministries responsible for issues like trade or the environment can supply a depth of expertise which the FCO could not hope to rival, and in this respect the emergence of a new Department for International Trade is not helpful to the FCO. The FCO's battle to control overseas aid seems to have ended in defeat, with the DfID now established as a separate institution with a sizeable budget.

The British FCO is not the only institution of its kind to face diminished prestige and an uncertain role. However, the British example is different because the fall from grace has been so dramatic; in the language of political science, the institutional certainties of the Westminster model are a world away from the overlapping (and sometimes conflicting) responsibilities arising from a differentiated polity in an era of multi-level governance. The FCO now seems like as a Rolls-Royce department which has been relegated to a Morris Minor mission. At the beginning of the post-war period the British Foreign Secretary was inevitably a prominent player in any significant international negotiation; now the FCO is chiefly mentioned in news reports as the purveyor of advice to those wishing to travel to hazardous destinations or as a source of solace to the relatives of murdered British nationals.

The importance of the FCO as a coordinator of the overseas activities of other government departments – and as a facilitator for private-sector companies looking for opportunities abroad – should not be underestimated, even if they tend to go unnoticed by the general public. For this reason, however, the FCO has been regarded as 'low-hanging fruit' by successive governments looking for painless spending cuts. Even if the Westminster model is redundant in relation to most UK government departments, it still seems relevant to the outlook and behaviour of the Treasury, which (for various reasons) has rarely been a wholehearted supporter of the FCO. There seems to have been an assumption that Britain could continue to project soft power even if it recalled all of its overseas representatives; from the traditional Treasury perspective, a separate department providing overseas aid would be far more amenable to performance targets based on a cost–benefit analysis. However, a more far-sighted policy would have recognised that the provision of financial assistance to other countries would lose much of its influential force unless it was backed by a strong diplomatic presence on the spot. This realisation might have prompted a resolve to spare the FCO budget from cuts, to give foreign observers the impression that Britain was still confident of playing a constructive role in international affairs even if its 'hard power' was obviously reduced. In the wake of 'Brexit' there was an excellent case for boosting FCO budgets to help foster new relationships outside Europe. Initially, at least, there was little sign that this argument had made much impression in the Treasury or on Downing Street.

Whatever might have befallen the foreign ministries of other Western countries, the British FCO was at least in part the victim of its own virtues. Uncertainty about Britain's role in the post-war world did not arise from failings among the FCO's highly educated senior officials, who understood that things had changed but were prevented from developing a more realistic perspective by party politicians, who, for electoral reasons, continued to claim that Britain was as 'Great' as ever despite persuasive evidence to the contrary. Even after the 1956 Suez disaster British foreign policy was made under a tacit agreement that politicians would persist with their misleading rhetoric, while the professionals at the FCO conducted practical business on the basis of a common-sense appraisal of global realities. Even Britain's tortuous path towards membership of what was then the EEC was conducted without exposing the contradictions in this dual approach. Indeed, during the 1975 referendum campaign mainstream politicians of all parties implied that a leading role within the EEC would provide an admirable springboard for revived British *global* influence.

The Falklands War put an end to this informal *concordat* between the politicians and the foreign policy professionals. It proved impossible to square either of the political narratives –that Britain was still a major power or that it was now on the path to recovery after unavoidable setbacks – with the seizure of

Case Study 2.2 Christmas broadcasts and soft power

During the reign of Elizabeth II successive Prime Ministers have paid tribute to the knowledge she has accumulated since 1952 and to her shrewd judgement. However, the British monarch has no formal role in the making of foreign policy, even though decisions are taken in his or her name. Even the suggestion that the monarch prefers one course of action to another is regarded as constitutionally improper; hence the furore during the 2016 EU referendum campaign when the *Sun* newspaper claimed that the Queen favoured 'Brexit'.

However, it has become something akin to a constitutional requirement that the monarch deliver a Christmas message, broadcast on the radio since 1932 and televised since 1957. Inevitably, these messages have included topical allusions when certain events have been too important to be passed over in silence. Notoriously, during the 1990s Queen Elizabeth referred to developments within her own family; but before then she had mentioned key foreign policy issues in a manner which could be squared with her 'above politics' posture. In 1982, for example, she applauded the courage of British service personnel who had helped to recapture the Falkland Islands, without attributing the conflict either to Argentine aggression or policy failures closer to home. In 1990 she condemned the Iraqi invasion of Kuwait, but this was unavoidable since thousands of British troops were spending that Christmas in expectation of imminent orders for military action to expel Saddam Hussein's forces.

Perhaps the most interesting broadcast in Elizabeth II's long career was the message of 1956. This was crafted at a time when Britain was trying to repair the damage to its international reputation which had been inflicted by the Suez Crisis. Without referring to the cause of dispute, the Queen recognised that the Commonwealth had been sharply divided over Britain's actions:

> deep and acute differences, involving both intellect and emotion, are bound to arise between members of a family and also between friend and friend, and there is neither virtue nor value in pretending that they do not. In all such differences, however, there comes a moment when, for the sake of ultimate harmony, the healing power of tolerance, comradeship and love must be allowed to play its part.

If British politicians had not shown by Christmas 1956 that they were ready to learn at least some of the lessons of Suez, these words of reconciliation might have been unavailing. However, they certainly maximised the chances that the Commonwealth would recover from this serious setback.

From the beginning of her reign the Queen had addressed citizens in Britain's former and existing colonies as if they were part of a 'family'; and while she was the Commonwealth's constitutional 'leader', she always emphasised the equality of its members. More importantly, she took every opportunity to emphasise that individuals, as well as member states, should be regarded as equals. Thus in 1968 – the year that saw the outbreak of civil war in Nigeria, as well as Enoch Powell's 'rivers of blood' speech (Chapter 6) – she went out of her way to express her belief in the 'brotherhood of man', arguing that harmony between nations must begin at the individual level. This tacit assault on racism was underlined by her explicit reference to the great Kenyan athlete, Kip Keino, who had won a gold and a silver medal at the 1968 Olympic Games. With astonishing chutzpah, given the furore over Kenyan Asians which had inspired Powell's engagement with the politics of race, Queen Elizabeth rejoiced in the fact that 'Kenya sent us her great runner Keino. I hope many more sportsmen from Africa will take part in competitions and will establish new contacts between Africa and the rest of the world'. It was the closest that the Queen could prudently come to blowing a raspberry in Powell's direction.

The allusion to Kip Keino's more recent feats was actually a pretext for a generous reference to the 1966 Empire and Commonwealth Games, which had been held in Jamaica – the source of many recent immigrants to the UK and, according to the Queen, an island notable for 'the kindness of the people'. Apart from its usefulness as a weapon against racists at home, the Queen had realised that these sporting contests – the 'Friendly Games', as they came to be called – could help to burnish Britain's external image. The texts of her Christmas broadcasts suggest that for most of her reign she felt that she might be fighting in a losing battle. Even so, she kept plugging away, year after year, with her personal 'narrative' – that whatever its past might have been, Britain's new role was to act as a moral exemplar to the world. Ironically, this was not far removed from the outlook which prompted members of CND to argue that world leaders would sit up and take notice if Britain took the lead in renouncing its 'deterrent'. By another irony, the Queen was such a successful salesperson for Britain's soft power – whether in receiving deputations from other countries or undertaking overseas tours – that she provided indispensable 'cover' for politicians who wanted to claim that the country still mattered and could 'punch above its weight' in terms of global hard power. In other words, thanks to the Queen's Christmas broadcasts, elected politicians could be assured that the 'moral role' narrative was still available for Britain to fall back on, whatever indignities might be involved in the attempt to convince voters that the country was still a great power in traditional hard-power terms.

an Overseas Territory, whose inhabitants clearly wanted to remain under British sovereignty, by a country which was ruled by a right-wing military junta. During the conflict and for years afterwards it was natural for a majority of British voters to accept the argument of the right-wing media and to think that the FCO was full of 'appeasers' who had been unmasked by Margaret Thatcher, the only politician who had the courage to expose their devious designs. On this view, Britain's interests could only be upheld if foreign policy fell under the direction of the Prime Minister; and Mrs Thatcher did not demur from this conclusion.

As Paul Williams has noted, 'the UK simultaneously pursues multiple foreign policies, some of which overlap and some of which may be contradictory' (Williams, 2004, 913). This suggests that the need for the FCO has not been diminished by recent developments; indeed, it could be argued that a department which can coordinate Britain's various international initiatives is more important than ever. It can only be regretted that the transition in the FCO's essential purpose has coincided with a period in which the department has undoubtedly lost prestige – a process which began with the Falklands episode of 1982. In this unhelpful context it has been natural for observers, both within and outside the FCO, to equate a change in role (attendant on a more general switch from the outdated Westminster model to more sophisticated forms of decision-making) with a demotion in status – not least because in 1997 Tony Blair renewed Mrs Thatcher's attempt to win control over foreign policy as if the partial resuscitation under John Major (1992–7) had never happened.

Whatever their constraints in other fields, British Prime Ministers have good reason to assume a licence to try, try and try again in respect of foreign policy until they finally get something right. Unlike the FCO, which has to deal with international 'realities', Prime Ministers have a vested interest in clinging to the delusion that Britain is still (at least potentially) as potent on the global stage as it was in 1945. Previous experience, after all, suggests that palpable policy failures (e.g. Suez and Iraq) are less damaging in electoral terms than even a tacit acceptance that Britain's best days might lie in the past. Since 1945 the best way of reinforcing the preferred construction of Britain's role with some concrete evidence was by turning the country's relationship with the world's pre-eminent power, the US, into an overriding foreign policy priority. Since that relationship is indeed 'special' in significant respects, prudent British policy makers could have used it to the country's perceived advantage, i.e. by regarding it as a useful source of assistance on those occasions when it could help to secure policy objectives identified in the course of objective analysis. Instead, successive British Prime Ministers have forgotten that diplomatic alliances, however intimate, should be regarded as means to specific ends, rather than ends in themselves. Even Prime Ministers who have possessed a basic grasp of modern history – which Thatcher and Blair patently lacked – have felt compelled to persist with the delusional post-war narratives based on an uncritical interpretation of Britain's nineteenth-century status and (with varying degrees of enthusiasm) to accept the consequences. As a result, rather than the FCO or even the Prime Minister's Office, at the time of writing it is arguable that the ultimate source of Britain's foreign policy should be sought in Washington rather than London.

The road to 1945   3

In their satirical survey of English history, *1066 and All That*, Walter Sellar and Robert Yeatman explained that since the US was '100% victorious' in the First World War, it was now 'clearly top nation, and History came to a .' (Sellar and Yeatman, 1930, 113–15). The authors meant that a particular *kind* of history had ended, i.e. the subject as it had been taught in British schools and universities for many decades. 'History', in this sense, had presented the British experience as one in which the hero (the British, but especially the *English* nation) was initially prey to other imperial forces, like the Romans and the Normans, but ended up being so potent that it was able to acquire an Empire of its own without really wanting one.

When *1066 and All That* was published, in 1930, Britons scarcely needed reminding of America's preponderant position in world affairs; it was already clear that they would be among the worst sufferers from the worldwide economic depression triggered by the Wall Street Crash of 1929. To acute observers, indeed, the brutal verdict of Sellar and Yeatman could only be faulted because their fatal full-stop was inserted too late. Britain had ceased to be 'top nation' long before its involvement in the First World War. But for most Britons the message was very slow to sink in. Even in 1945, after another world war in which the US had been '100% victorious', there were plenty of people who clung on to the old story: indeed, the idea that Britain was (or ought to be) 'top nation' could still find supporters in the highest government circles.

Britain's situation in 1914

If, as the historian JR Seeley put it, the British 'seem, as it were, to have conquered and peopled half the world in a fit of absence of mind', the nineteenth century saw their most spectacular displays of amnesia. It is estimated that Britain's Empire expanded by 10 million square miles between 1815 and 1914, and around 400 million people came under British rule of one form or another. Thanks partly to Seeley's writings – notably, *The Expansion of England* (1883) – the British elite gradually became conscious of the potential advantages which could arise from a more coherent approach to their sprawling Empire. Thus in Queen Victoria's Golden Jubilee year of 1887 an Imperial Institute was established to promote research which might benefit the Empire. Ten years later Victoria's Diamond Jubilee was a celebration of Empire, reflecting the fact that in the preceding quarter-century Britain had taken control of Zanzibar, Fiji, Cyprus, Bechuanaland, Somaliland, Kenya, the New Hebrides, Rhodesia and Uganda. In 1902 AC Benson celebrated the nation's status by setting words to Edward Elgar's stirring march *Pomp and Circumstance No 1*. In the year that Britain's war against the Boer Republics of South Africa reached a conclusion, which ultimately led to the creation of a self-governing Union of South Africa within the Empire, Benson seemed on safe ground when he wrote of Britain as a 'Land of Hope and Glory' which God had made 'mighty' and intended to make 'mightier yet', so that its boundaries would be stretched 'wider still and wider'.

Timeline of domestic political developments

1900 General election: Conservative victory with overall majority of 135
1906 General election: Liberal victory with overall majority of 129
1910 General elections (January and December): Liberals command overall majorities thanks to support from Irish Nationalists (Conservatives win the greatest number of votes in both contests)
1915 Formation of wartime coalition government, including Liberal, Conservative and Labour ministers, with the Liberal HH Asquith as Prime Minister
1916 Resignation of Asquith; replaced by fellow Liberal David Lloyd George
1918 Overwhelming electoral victory for coalition, led by Lloyd George but dominated by Conservative MPs
1922 Deposition of Lloyd George as Prime Minister; succeeded by Conservative Andrew Bonar Law until 1923, then Stanley Baldwin
1923 Inconclusive general election: Ramsay Macdonald becomes first Labour Prime Minister, dependent upon Liberal support
1924 General election: Conservative victory with overall majority of 210; Baldwin back as Prime Minister
1929 General election: inconclusive verdict; Labour's Ramsay Macdonald forms a second minority administration

> **1931** Labour government resigns amid global economic crisis; formation of National Government, with Macdonald as Prime Minister but dependent on Conservatives
> **1935** Re-election of National Government, now headed by Stanley Baldwin, with overwhelming majority dominated by Conservatives
> **1937** Baldwin retires; replaced by Neville Chamberlain
> **1940** Resignation of Chamberlain; replaced by Winston Churchill, heading a new coalition government

While Seeley wrote of absent-mindedness, and Benson (as befitted the son of an Archbishop of Canterbury) preferred to perceive the hand of God, it would be more realistic to attribute the creation of Britain's Empire to a mixture of geographical good fortune, the inventiveness of its people and an ability to exploit opportunities which, for various reasons, other nations neglected. As an island nation, Britain had a long history of maritime exploration, and (unlike other sea-faring states) despite being close to the European mainland it was separated from it by sea. In addition to this obstacle to annexation by any European power, it lacked any of the attractions which had made a country like Italy such an alluring target for military adventurers. But while its climate was indifferent at best, it did enjoy significant mineral wealth (especially coal), and, despite occasional outbursts of xenophobia and religious intolerance, its political culture was sufficiently moderate to attract talented individuals who had fled from more repressive states.

With its fortunes founded on international trade rather than the vagaries of overseas acquisitions, Britain was above all a pioneer of financial institutions; the Bank of England was established in 1694. Thanks to its privileged position, Britain was able to subsidise the war efforts of other nations as well as sending its sons to fight on its own behalf. London's Great Exhibition of 1851 had reflected supreme national self-confidence; other nations were welcome to emulate British inventiveness, but by implication they were destined to fail if they tried. While economic statistics – even those of contemporary collation – are always suspect, it has been estimated that in 1880 the UK accounted for nearly 23 per cent of the world's output of manufactured goods; its nearest competitors (the US, with 14.7 per cent, and Germany, with 8.5 per cent) were agreeably distant.

By 1900, however, there had been a dramatic transformation. In terms of manufactured goods, the US had overtaken Britain, producing 23.6 per cent of the world's output compared to 18.5 per cent, while Germany (13.2 per cent) seemed to be gaining fast. Even allowing for a generous margin of error, these figures conveyed an ominous message for the world's 'top nation'. By the outbreak of war in 1914 Britain, having produced far more steel than the US and Germany combined in 1871, was trailing badly behind both countries in this respect. In the 1870s the US had provided a major market for British steel; by the beginning of the twentieth century it was selling steel to Britain. There were obvious explanations for these statistical reversals; once the US had begun to exploit its massive natural resources, and Germany had established political unity (in 1871), these two nations were bound to rival Britain's economic pre-eminence.

In part, the new prosperity of German and US manufacturing arose from the policy of economic protection pursued by both countries, ensuring that their domestic industries could prosper behind tariff barriers. On the face of it, Britain could have taken a similar course. Indeed, it could be argued that its only chance of fending off economic competition from its emerging rivals was to create a protected zone of free trade within its extensive Empire. Those who embraced this vision – notably, Joseph Chamberlain (1836–1914), a dynamic Liberal politician who subsequently defected to the Conservatives and exercised a strong influence over imperial policy as Colonial Secretary (1895–1903) – identified numerous benefits for Britain, since a system of 'imperial preference' promised to forge the Empire into a source of military strength as well as ensuring beneficial terms of trade for the metropolis (Britain would supply the Empire with high-value manufactured goods in return for primary produce).

However, this approach ran counter to the liberal economic doctrine which exerted considerable influence over British economic debates in the second half of the nineteenth century. From this perspective, the Empire was an unnecessary and costly encumbrance – a distraction from the peaceful promotion of prosperity, which was the proper business of humankind. For the Liberal orator John Bright (1811–89), 'there is no permanent greatness to a nation except it be based upon morality'; on this account, the gratitude of satisfied customers was worth far more than the enforced obedience of any number of captive peoples (Porter, 2008, 14). Far from being a reason for regret, the loss of Britain's manufacturing pre-eminence merely reflected the inexorable operation of market forces. The best response was for the country to exploit its position at the hub of world trade, providing various financial services which, although less 'visible' than manufactured goods, were no less profitable. In the years before the First World War there was a noticeable upsurge in the level of British overseas investment, suggesting (in keeping with liberal economic assumptions) that, rather than trying to 'beggar its neighbours', the country should promote productivity in other countries in order to advance the cause of general prosperity and peace.

On paper, the debate between British imperialists and free-trade liberals seemed to be polarised, with no room for compromise. Apart from their disagreement about the best guarantee of economic prosperity, the rival camps were at odds over the true nature of international power. Believing that conflict between nations was inevitable, imperialists tended to regard any kind of overseas expansion as a good thing. Even if new colonies brought neither obvious strategic advantage nor the potential for economic exploitation, they were worth having as expressions of Britain's military prowess. For their part, liberals regarded armed conflict as deeply immoral and looked forward to a time when rational individuals from every land could exchange goods and services without fearing physical violence or having to pay taxes to finance wars which (by their very nature) arose from irrational impulses.

Thankfully, though, a kind of middle way between these positions was available – that the British could accept an imperial role as a kind of divinely ordained obligation while remaining true to the principle of free trade. This compromise proved persuasive for many aspiring British politicians of the late nineteenth century – notably, Winston Churchill (1874–1965) – not least because of its electoral potency. The position allowed the British to regard themselves as reluctant imperialists, who were prepared to relinquish direct control over any part of the Empire which showed itself capable of self-government. Most liberals could be satisfied with this view, on the assumption that the process of liberation for the colonies would not be protracted; once the period of tutelage had ended, the nations would trade freely with each other to mutual advantage. For their part, imperialists could be reconciled in the expectation that, in the majority of cases, decolonisation would be subjected to indefinite delay. The compromise resulted in policy decisions which varied according to the ethnic balance of power within the colonies in question; thus a considerable degree of self-government had been granted to Canada in the 1840s, and similar arrangements were later made in respect of Australia, New Zealand and (after the Boer War) South Africa, making up what came to be known as the White Dominions. This idea – that Britain would conquer people with a view to making them fit for liberation at an unspecified later date – inspired a multitude of adventurers, Christian missionaries, slave-emancipators and people who were a mix of all three. Where their explorations led, annexation of territory to the British Empire was rarely very far behind.

Thanks to the racial stereotyping of the time, the expansion of British territory in Africa was regarded as far less problematic than the country's imperialist activities in India. The latter was probably the most 'absent minded' of all Britain's imperial ventures, starting as a private, profit-seeking venture under the voracious East India Company until the British state took on its responsibilities in 1858. However British imperial expansion was rationalised, its emotional appeal was obvious. India evoked the most overt displays of imperialistic ritual and sentiment after 1876, when Queen Victoria was proclaimed Empress of India. However, the British 'Raj' was always something of a conjuring trick, almost entirely dependent on the ability of a small contingent of British-born administrators and soldiers to retain the goodwill of the Crown's new subjects. Once the British had started playing their trick, they quickly found that it could not be made to look remotely convincing unless they took serious steps to convince the audience that they were in earnest. Thus, for example, in the year before he flattered Victoria with a new imperial title, Benjamin Disraeli had arranged the investment of £4 million in a bloc of shares which gave Britain a significant (though not a controlling) interest in the new Suez Canal. This waterway provided a much more rapid route between Britain and India. Even before the East India Company had ceased trading, British interests in Asia had helped to inspire what must otherwise seem to be one of the nation's most incomprehensible conflicts, the Crimean War (1853–6). As Sellar and Yeatman put it in the hope of raising a laugh among the initiated, one of the primary causes of this war was that 'Russia was too big and was pointing in the direction of India' (Sellar and Yeatman, 1930, 102).

The one factor which united all three possible policies – complete free trade, some form of economic union within the Empire and the Churchilian 'third way' – was the importance of avoiding serious friction (let alone conflict) with any state or combination of states which might disrupt trade or endanger any important part of the Empire. This perspective depended heavily on British diplomacy and entailed that the country throw its weight behind amicable resolutions of global problems without committing itself to any new treaty obligations – an approach enunciated by the Foreign Secretary Lord Derby in 1866 and which came to be known as 'splendid isolation' (although it could also be called 'appeasement' and linked to the fear that the decision to incorporate India within the British Empire meant that the country's overseas commitments had begun to overstretch its resources (Kennedy, 1981)).

The Boer War (1899–1902) confirmed the impression of overstretch. Despite considerable military support from Australia, Canada and New Zealand, the British only repelled an attack from independent South African republics after a prolonged and bitter conflict. In the face of the Boers' effective guerilla tactics, a nation already prone to priding itself on the moral rectitude of its foreign policy had resorted to a system of 'concentration camps', in which more than 25,000 women and children died from malnutrition and disease. Before the end of the war the British government had descended from its isolationist pedestal and accepted the need for allies, negotiating a defensive alliance with Japan. The signatories of the treaty agreed that they would remain neutral if either party became embroiled in a war with another state; either Britain or Japan would come to the other's assistance if it became involved in a conflict with more than one other state. From Britain's point of view, the treaty provided psychological insurance against Russia, which, despite the Crimean War, continued to be 'pointing in the direction of India' and was progressing swiftly with a railway-building programme, which indicated a desire to do more than just 'point'. In the short term, at least, the arrangement worked to the benefit of Japan, which after provocative Russian moves in Manchuria opened hostilities in 1904 and scored decisive victories on land and at sea.

At least Britain still remained free from diplomatic entanglements with other European powers. But the Boer War had shown that the country's isolation in this respect was something less than 'splendid'. Britain and France had been allies against Russia during the Crimean War, but this rare coincidence of interests did not foreshadow a sudden end to their traditional hostility. In 1898, indeed, a small French expedition in Sudan was greeted by more considerable British forces at the village of Fashoda (now Kodak). French *amour propre* had been slighted by Britain's dominance of Egypt since 1882, and the unsuccessful Fashoda intrusion was intended to disrupt the old enemy's conquest of Sudan in a way which might lead to some territorial compensation. The British government's new sense of vulnerability inspired a wider-ranging settlement of colonial disputes with France, known as the Entente Cordiale. In 1907 a similar agreement was negotiated with Russia, mainly in respect of differences over colonial policy in the Middle East.

The unsettling implications of the Boer War meant that by 1907 Britain had 'appeased' three of the world's most powerful states. There was, though, unfinished business concerning relations with Germany and the US. With regard to the latter, Britain's policy of 'appeasement' was particularly appropriate, since the formerly dominant colonial power in North America had accepted long before 1900 that any conflict over Canada would result in a disastrous defeat. Residual territorial disputes with the US were accordingly settled in a manner which was least likely to arouse American resentment. There was no Anglo-American treaty to replicate the 1902 deal with Japan, but this was not felt necessary on the British side and, in any case, the US, set on its own version of 'isolationism', would not have wanted a formal arrangement.

Germany, though, was a different matter. British politicians (especially Joseph Chamberlain) put out feelers for some kind of defensive agreement, but nothing was ever signed. In retrospect it might seem odd that one reason for this was that, unlike in the cases of France and Russia, there were no tangible Anglo-German disputes which demanded resolution (Clark, 2013, 158). Germany was clearly an 'expansionary' state, thanks to its late arrival at the colonial banquet; but France, Russia and (especially) Japan also had expansionist ambitions, and this factor had not deterred Britain from bargaining with them when other considerations seemed to make this necessary. However, German strategists suspected (with good reason) that British policy makers would only seriously seek an alliance with their country if they were feeling particularly jittery about the prospect of war with France and Russia. Understandably, while the German government was willing to reach agreement with Britain, it was only prepared to do so on its own terms, and these were not acceptable to the British.

While this desultory diplomatic flirtation continued, the relationship between Britain and Germany began to be affected by increasingly serious sources of irritation. The German ruler, Kaiser Wilhelm II, showed an 'undiplomatic' degree of sympathy with the Boers during their conflict with the British. In 1906 a Franco-German dispute over the status of Morocco led to the Algeciras conference, at which Britain cemented its new friendship with France by helping to ensure that its case prevailed. This was a clear sign that, by settling their differences with France, British policy makers (whether they liked it or not) were becoming parties to a toxic dispute dating back to the Franco-Prussian War of 1870, which had ended in the German annexation of the provinces of Alsace and Lorraine. In 1908 Germany adopted an ambitious programme of naval expansion, designed to match advances in British shipbuilding. For AJP Taylor, 'In the summer of 1908 estrangement between Great Britain and Germany was clear for all the world to see' (Taylor, 1954, 447–8). In 1911 the Germans responded to an intrusion by French forces into Morocco by despatching a gunboat to the port of Agadir. Although the British government had warned the French against provocative actions in Morocco, it again decided to support its new ally against Germany and sent naval forces of its own to the area. The result was another German climbdown, followed by the establishment of a French 'protectorate' over Morocco and an agreement between Britain and France over a division of naval responsibilities in the event of war.

The Agadir crisis certainly increased the expectation of war among well-informed British (and German) observers. For example, when the journalist Norman Angell wrote *The Great Illusion*, his powerful counter-thrust against the advocates of war within Europe, he focused on recent articles and published correspondence which identified the growing likelihood of a conflict in which Britain and Germany would fight on opposite sides (Angell, 1910, 13–24). Negative emotions towards Germany were also present within the British Foreign Office: Sir Edward Grey, Foreign Secretary since December 1905, was receptive to alarmist analyses, particularly a famous memorandum written by the German-born official Eyre Crowe in January 1907, which warned of the country's atavistic expansionary tendencies (Clark, 2013, 159–67). Yet none of this made war inevitable; although Britain's naval agreement with France followed years of discussions between the respective military staffs, all of these were precautionary in nature and fell short of concrete commitments.

After the First World War the question of moral responsibility was widely canvassed; and, unsurprisingly, the victors blamed the vanquished. For the present purpose, rather than rehearsing the endlessly fascinating and often discussed causes of the war, it is sufficient to examine the more contentious aspects of Britain's role. In recent years 'revisionist' historians have sought to restate the old adage which was so easily forgotten in the immediate aftermath of the Great War – namely, that it takes two (and in this case rather more than two) to make a quarrel. However well intentioned, of their very nature revisionist accounts run the risk of replacing an initial mistake with a different one, so that the attempt to see nothing but premeditated evil in the decisions of German policy makers tends to be superseded by an unduly critical interpretation of the thought processes of their adversaries in the years immediately preceding the outbreak of war. Britain, it can be argued, had ample motive for war with Germany, based on the hope of forestalling a challenge from a potent and seemingly rapacious challenger. However, if the anti-German faction within the British governmental machine had wanted to provoke a 'pre-emptive' war, it would have been much more vigorous in its attempts to turn its ententes with France and Russia into concrete defensive alliances, which would have been interpreted by Germany as deliberate acts of military encirclement. This did not happen, and Britain ended up taking sides with France and Russia without any formal treaty agreements.

The official reason for Britain's declaration of war in August 1914 was Germany's refusal to respect Belgian neutrality, which was guaranteed by the London Treaty of 1839. German military strategy (based on the 'Schlieffen plan') required that its assault on France should be launched *via* Belgian territory. This consideration was certainly an important influence over elements of British opinion, including some members of the Cabinet. However, a fortnight before the British government delivered its ultimatum to Germany, *The Times* newspaper had argued that British intervention in any war resulting from the current crisis in the Balkans would be dictated by 'an elementary duty of self-preservation' (quoted in Kennedy, 1981, 139). From this perspective, the true objective of armed intervention was not the territorial integrity of Belgium but rather (in *The Times*' words) an attempt to ensure that war did not result in 'a Europe dominated by any single power'.

For British policy makers since the time of Elizabeth I, the dominance of the European mainland 'by any single power' had been a dreadful prospect, and the fear had increased in tandem with Britain's rise to 'top nation', since a European hegemon was almost certain to take a hostile stance towards the offshore imperialists. However, from the mid nineteenth century onwards the threat had taken a different and more tangible form – of a Europe without a single dominant power, but whose leading nations were united in antagonism towards Britain. For understandable reasons, British policy makers preferred a scenario which was often characterised as a 'balance of power' in Europe, but which is better described as a condition of disunity and mutual suspicion among the country's neighbours. This was a state of affairs which had been extremely helpful to Britain during the eighteenth and nineteenth centuries – it had, one might say, made possible the world view expressed in the words of *Land of Hope and Glory*. Although AC Benson had suggested that the boundaries of that nation should be pushed 'wider still and wider', in 1914 Britain was essentially a 'satisfied power', anxious to avoid any incidents that might disturb the advantages it had gained. In reality, to observers like Eyre Crowe of the Foreign Office, it seemed to be Germany which wanted to extend its boundaries both within Europe and beyond; it certainly expected that God would make it 'mightier yet'.

In terms of IR theory (Chapter 1), Britain's participation in the First World War looks like an example of 'defensive Realism'. However, this practical example also provides an early warning that Realism – broadly understood as a calculation of the 'national interest' in advance of any response to dilemmas in international politics – can arise from an assessment of a nation's situation which is heavily coloured by emotion rather than cold 'reason'. When *The Times* alluded to 'national self-preservation' its editorial team was thinking not of the literal defence of Britain as an independent country but rather of the *continuation* of its previous role (in Sellar and Yeatman's words, that of 'top nation'). In short, when the British Cabinet decided that peaceful coexistence with Germany was no longer possible and reversed its previous inclination to stay out of the impending conflict, it did so feeling that the country had no alternative if it wanted to conserve the vision of itself enshrined in the words of *Land of Hope and Glory*. At the same time, those who did not delude themselves with the assumption that this war could be concluded in a few victorious months had good reason to suspect that, whatever the outcome, the conflict was likely to confirm and even accelerate the existing process of relative British decline.

The consequences of conflict

The consequences of the 1914–18 war are difficult to exaggerate and defy concise analysis. For the purposes of this book, four major implications for British foreign policy can be identified, on the understanding that this approach cannot hope to present an adequate summary of a conflict which, in Zara Steiner's words, 'was like a terrible volcanic eruption that left immeasurable destruction in its wake' (Steiner, 2005, 1).

Developments in weaponry

A war on this scale, taking place in an era of considerable technological innovation, was always likely to revolutionise the resources at the disposal of armed forces. From the British perspective, the most ominous developments concerned submarine warfare and aerial bombardment. The first of these presented a continuous threat to Britain's trading routes, and when Germany embarked upon a policy of indiscriminate submarine attack in January 1917 the country which boasted of 'ruling the waves' seemed in danger of defeat from a foe lurking beneath them. Ultimately, unrestricted submarine warfare was highly damaging to the Germans, since it helped to bring the US into the war after the sinking of several of its vessels. The British also adopted improved defensive tactics, notably the convoy system, to protect merchant shipping. Nevertheless, the experience opened up the possibility that Britain, which had prided itself on an ability to starve its enemies of vital supplies through a naval blockade, could now be treated to a taste of its own medicine.

In terms of aerial bombardment, technological innovations during the war were particularly dramatic, starting with small bombs thrown out of light aircraft and ending with purpose-built craft whose crews could deliver explosives more precisely, thanks to visual aids. Although bombing raids had a limited effect on the overall fortunes of war, their psychological impact was understandably considerable; and although defensive techniques were developed to meet the threat, it was natural to suppose that, as Stanley Baldwin put it in 1932, 'the bomber will always get through' to devastate its selected target, since 'aerial warfare is still in its infancy, and its potentialities are incalculable and inconceivable'. On this view, another war among the major combatants of 1914–18 could spell the end of European civilisation (*Hansard, House of Commons Debates*, 10 November 1932, Vol. 270, cols 630–40).

Developments in domestic politics

The new weaponry helped to ensure a heavy death toll among civilians – possibly more than 2 million as a direct result of conflict, leaving aside the additional losses inflicted by associated famines and diseases. In Britain itself the tally among civilians and members of the merchant navy (many of whom were killed by submarine action) was probably less than 17,000. Nevertheless, this meant that between 1914 and 1918 British non-combatants had been at greater risk of death or injury than at any time since the seventeenth-century civil war. Yet this was only one indication that Europe had entered an era of 'total war'. Conscription for military service was introduced in 1916, initially for single men aged 18–41 but later extended to married male civilians. This remedy for the drastic shortage of voluntary military recruits had an obvious knock-on effect among the domestic workforce, not least in key areas like the manufacturing of munitions. To fill the gap women were recruited; almost a million were working in government-controlled munitions factories by the end of the war. Rationing of certain foodstuffs was also introduced from the beginning of 1918 in response to shortages resulting from unrestricted submarine warfare.

With so much of the population either actively involved in the British war effort, or facing death or bereavement as a result of the struggle, it was increasingly difficult to defend an electoral system which, despite successive reforms in the nineteenth century, still excluded a majority of adults on the basis of economic status or gender. The 1918 Representation of the People Act was an attempt to redress this obvious democratic deficit (while refusing to accept gender equality, thus giving the vote only to women aged over 30, compared to the

21-year qualification for men). Even so, in numerical terms the effects of the act were spectacular: a British electorate of 7.7 million had expanded to 21.4 million.

While this measure was bound to have repercussions of some kind throughout British politics, the field of foreign policy presented unique challenges. Traditionally, this area had been regarded as one in which duly qualified specialists were authorised to act in what they considered to be the national interest without having to wait for the verdict of imperfectly informed public opinion (Chapter 2). In the nineteenth century, indeed, British governments had tended to take advantage of the imperfection of public opinion by whipping up patriotic emotions (or, in William Gladstone's case, moral indignation) in favour of their preferred causes. After the 1918 franchise reform even Foreign Secretaries had to admit that the balance of domestic power had changed, and that they, along with other government ministers, had to regard themselves at least to some extent as 'servants of the people'. In the first century after the First World War foreign policy was rarely a decisive or even a serious factor in determining the outcome of general elections; but decision-makers could never afford to be complacent, so some attempt had to be made to gauge 'the public mood' before significant steps were taken.

How, though, should public opinion be interpreted in the days before regular surveys were conducted on a 'scientific' basis? The most convenient litmus test was to consult the coverage of foreign affairs in widely circulating newspapers. In this respect, the years leading up to the First World War had also seen significant developments with the emergence of a 'popular press' catering for the tastes of people who were now literate (thanks to educational reforms since 1870) but not necessarily equipped for sophisticated analysis of contemporary affairs, whether domestic or foreign. Of one of these new papers, the *Daily Mail* (founded in 1896), Lord Salisbury disdainfully remarked that it was 'written by office boys for office boys'. Salisbury held the post of Foreign Secretary during more than 13 of the years between 1878 and 1900, combining the job with that of Prime Minister for most of his stint; and if there was any doubt concerning the longevity of his influence over policy making, his equally elitist nephew Arthur Balfour succeeded Salisbury as Prime Minister (1902–5) before taking over from Grey at the Foreign Office (1916–19). For people like Salisbury and Balfour, the best understanding of 'public opinion' could be derived from a reading of the editorials (and the correspondence pages) of *The Times* newspaper; but even that august publication could not be immune from the voice of the 'office boys' as expressed by their favourite newspapers.

The first concrete test of public opinion after the extension of the franchise was the 1918 general election, resulting in a victory for the wartime coalition which won 449 of the 707 seats. These figures, however, concealed a major change in the British party system. The Liberal Party, previously the main competitor against the Conservatives, divided during the war into rival factions led by Herbert Asquith (Prime Minister from 1908 to 1916) and his supplanter in the top job, David Lloyd George. In the election Asquith's group won almost the same number of votes (1.39 million) as Lloyd George's Liberal supporters, but only 36 compared to 127 seats, thanks to an agreement between Lloyd George and the Conservatives not to run candidates against each other. As a result, Lloyd George continued as Prime Minister but was effectively the prisoner of 332 Conservative MPs. Meanwhile, the Labour Party won more than 2 million votes and 57 seats. Since Labour had also suffered serious divisions, between pro- and anti-war factions, the outcome strongly suggested that when peacetime conditions were re-established the main contestants for office under Britain's disproportional first-past-the-post voting system would be Labour and the best organised of the two formerly dominant parties; and since the Liberals were unable to resolve their differences until Asquith's death in 1928, they effectively handed that role to the Conservatives.

The Versailles settlement

At the Congress of Vienna (1814–15), which attempted to settle European affairs after Napoleon Bonaparte's meteoric career, British policy makers were generally able to exercise a dominant influence, thanks to their diplomatic dexterity as well as the country's pivotal role in Napoleon's defeat. The discussions which led to the 1919 Treaty of Versailles were very different. Although the Americans only declared war on Germany in April 1917, the main effect of which was not felt until the following year, their position in the peace talks which led to the Treaty of Versailles was similar to that of the British back in 1815. The chief difference was that the American contribution to the First World War represented only a foretaste of what that nation could achieve if it entered any future conflict without reservation. To that extent, Sellar and Yeatman were right to identify the end of the First World War as the point at which US supremacy became evident to anyone capable of discarding the *Land of Hope and Glory* narrative; and British negotiators were acutely conscious of a change in the global batting order, which had been foreshadowed 20 years earlier in Rudyard Kipling's controversial poem *The White Man's Burden*.

During the negotiations at Versailles US President Woodrow Wilson ostensibly stood by the Fourteen Points – statements of principle (see Box 1.2, Chapter 1), both general and specific, which he had unveiled in a speech of January 1918. As well as asserting the need for 'open' diplomacy and a reduction of armaments, Wilson advocated the removal of all barriers to free trade and 'absolute freedom of navigation upon the seas'. Although German policy since 1870 did not escape criticism in some of Wilson's specific points, Britain seemed to be the main target of his generalities. Complete free trade would destroy the dreams of British imperialists who wanted to develop the Empire as an economic asset; complete freedom of navigation would mean that Britannia no longer ruled the waves, which raised doubts about the preservation of the Empire in any form and threatened to undermine the essential basis of Britain's influence within Europe, let alone its status as a significant global power. Wilson followed up his Fourteen Points with a speech asserting the right of peoples to determine their own future. If Wilson's overall vision was to be taken literally in an overall settlement after the war, the resulting treaty would potentially be at least as detrimental to Britain and its Empire as any conceivable terms that might have been dictated by a victorious Germany. Indeed, a literal interpretation raised doubts about the future of the UK itself, in view of the growing agitation for Irish independence.

Assailed on one flank by Wilsonian idealism, Lloyd George also had to contend with the attitude of the French, who sought the redress of historic grievances against Germany, full compensation for the damage wrought by the war and additional measures which would enhance the country's future security. The first of these objectives was accepted even by Wilson, and Alsace and Lorraine were duly restored to France. The second and third requirements, however, proved to be contradictory. In combination, the French demand for direct financial 'reparations' and the attempt to strip Germany of key strategic and economic assets helped to create the context for an eventual renewal of hostilities. Although Britain had suffered far less direct war damage than France, Lloyd George was sensitive to the vengeful mood among many British voters and initially seconded the French demand for reparations, on the grounds that Germany should contribute to the support of war widows and pensioners. Later he recognised that the imposition of a crippling financial burden on Germany would do little to help Europe's economic recovery, but by that time the principle of reparations had been accepted. The remaining question was the level of German payments; this was not finalised until 1921, when a sum of 132 billion marks was named. By that time Germany had already fallen behind the schedule of interim payments stipulated at Versailles, and its currency had depreciated to an extent which undermined any calculation of the 'true' war debt. The resulting inflation also undermined Germany's new democratic 'Weimar' constitution.

France had also demanded the annexation of the coal-rich Saar Valley region, on its north-east border, but the Americans and the British preferred a compromise under which the area would be governed by an international commission for 15 years, after which the local people could determine their own national allegiance through a plebiscite. In the meantime the French took control of the Saar's coal mines. Also, the industrial Rhineland area of Germany was to be occupied by allied forces for up to 15 years; no German fortifications could be established within 50 kilometres of the Rhine's eastern bank. Again, this settlement was a suboptimal compromise with the French, who had wanted to separate the Rhineland from Germany (and to control its government).

In short, the position that France adopted at the peace conference, hosted on its own territory, implied a continuing antagonism between itself and Germany, and that it could only feel safe if its hostile neighbour was made even weaker than itself. But France had only been able to emerge on the winning side of the First World War because of its allies; and since those allies had a different vision of Germany's future, the final settlement at Versailles fell a long way short of France's hopes. Even so, despite the likelihood that the loss of the Saar and the occupation of the Rhineland would only be temporary, these clauses were humiliating enough for most Germans, whose representatives were excluded from the negotiations. The punishment did not end there. The German provinces of West Prussia and Posen were awarded to a resuscitated Polish nation state. Lloyd George managed to insist that the mainly German coastal city of Danzig should come under the authority of a newly created League of Nations (see below), rather than being awarded to Poland, but this still meant that the German territory of East Prussia was physically separated from the remainder of the country. After a 1921 plebiscite, Upper Silesia was divided between Germany and Poland. Another new state, Czechoslovakia, emerged from the ruins of the Austro-Hungarian Empire; it, rather than Germany, absorbed the predominantly German Sudetenland. Meanwhile, the new boundaries of Austria were drawn to coincide with the main German-speaking region of the old Habsburg Empire; in the most remarkable of their many contraventions of the principle of self-determination, instead of allotting this area to Germany the peacemakers of Versailles explicitly prohibited a union (or *Anschluss*) between the two countries, whatever their inhabitants might want.

In hindsight it is easy enough to say that since the French were not in a position to destroy Germany entirely, their best option was to extinguish the perceived threat through acts of generosity. However, given the unprecedented level of slaughter and destruction, it is unsurprising that magnanimity was in short supply in 1918–19, and that Lloyd George, on behalf of Britain, was disinclined to emphasise his own misgivings during the negotiations. The war had also robbed France of a key ally, since Russia had made a separate peace with Germany after the Bolshevik Revolution of 1917. Of course, the prospect of having to fight a war on two fronts had not inhibited Germany in 1914; but it was natural for the French to expect that even a weakened Germany would feel less reluctance about embarking on war in the west if it felt secure on its eastern borders. For this buffer zone to have any deterrent effect, Poland and Czechoslovakia would have to be viable (and, of course, friendly towards France). Even then, the buffer zone would only be useful to France in the event that it became embroiled in a direct conflict with a resurgent Germany. As it was, Hitler's Germany turned east rather than west, and instead of providing useful assistance Czechoslovakia and Poland merely underlined the extent of French weakness.

The League of Nations

While hindsight suggests that French attempts to insure itself against future German aggression were self-defeating, even at the time it was possible to regard them as unnecessary. Among his Fourteen Points, President Wilson had suggested the establishment of an international organisation for the peaceful resolution of disputes. A 'League of Nations' – the term was originally coined by the British political scientist Goldsworthy Lowes Dickinson (1862–1932) – would provide arbitration on any disputes between member states and apply sanctions against states which defied its rulings. The League would also oblige its members to reduce their armaments 'to the lowest point consistent with national safety and the enforcement by common action of international obligations'. Initially, the main difficulty with the League reflected a difference of interpretation between Britain and France; the former wanted it to be a forum in which disputes could be resolved before the eruption of hostilities, whereas the latter hoped that it would bring the united force of the international community (including military action) to bear against any power (i.e. Germany) which had already embarked on aggressive action.

Although the idea of such an organisation violated the traditional British reliance on the balance of power as a preserver (or, more accurately, a long-term restorative) of international peace, one can appreciate why it seemed attractive in 1919. With the defeat of Germany, and the apparent neutralisation of Russia as a potential disrupter of the status quo, it was difficult for the British to anticipate any future source of disturbance to peace and prosperity. Despite (or perhaps because of) the slaughter of land-based armies between 1914 and 1918, the British were entitled to look positively on the prospect of a permanent peace which was policed by navies; and since the German fleet of warships and mercantile vessels had either passed into friendly hands or been scuttled by their crews at the end of the war, Britannia and its friends (France, Japan and the US) 'ruled the waves' to an extent which James Thomson and Thomas Arne could not have anticipated when their combined efforts created that patriotic song back in 1740. If the arbitration procedure of the League proved unavailing and conflicts broke out, Britain would obviously be called upon to help restore order, but the task would be shared with other states of comparable potency. More likely, while Britain was agreeing to be one of 'the world's policemen', the deterrent effect of this powerful posse would mean that it would never have to wield a truncheon in anger. Lobby groups in Britain – indeed, within Parliament – had been pressing for the formation of such an international body. More importantly, the idea of the League chimed with a more general demand among the newly expanded electorate that this should be 'a war to end all wars'.

This beatific vision might have come to pass if the new 'top nation', the US, had ratified the Treaty of Versailles and thus committed itself to membership of the League. However, Woodrow Wilson's efforts to muster Congressional support only succeeded in undermining his health, and the treaty was rejected by the Senate. This decision had an understandably dampening effect on initial enthusiasm for the League. The Senate debates on ratification of the treaty also exposed continuing American antipathy towards the British Empire; one of the arguments against the League was that member states like Australia, South Africa and Canada would constitute a formidable voting bloc which could ensure that Britain's interests were always preferred to those of the US (Doerr, 1998, 50). In declining to ratify Versailles, the US Senate also nullified a proposed agreement which committed Britain and America to defend France's frontiers against future German aggression. The prospect of such a guarantee had persuaded Clemenceau, the French Prime Minister, to drop his insistence that the German Rhineland should be made into a separate state. Britain had accepted this arrangement on condition that it was also ratified by the US, so the Senate's rejection of Versailles aborted the whole enterprise.

Thus within a few months of the Versailles conference the supposedly victorious allies were at least partially estranged from each other. Italy, which had joined the war against Germany in 1915, was also aggrieved because its territorial aspirations had not been fulfilled in the 1919 settlement. On this ground, at least, British imperialists had few reasons for dissatisfaction. Germany's defeat meant the loss of its colonies, and while Britain acquired several territories in Africa – parts of Cameroon, Togo and Tanganyika – Australia, South Africa and New Zealand became imperialists in their own right, mopping up German New Guinea, South West Africa (now Namibia) and Western Samoa respectively. The 1920 Treaty of Sevres, which marked the final dissolution of the Ottoman Empire, gave Britain authority over Transjordan, Palestine (Controversy 3.1) and Mesopotamia (Iraq); by 1926 Britain had succeeded in its aim of extending the territory of the latter to include the oil-rich Mosul area. Overall, the treaties subsequent to the First World War brought almost 2 million square miles of additional territory – and 13 million more people – under British control. Rather than outright annexations, these new acquisitions were characterised as 'mandates' authorised by the League of Nations, to underline the expectation (of Wilson and others) that the British would interpret their role in terms of 'trusteeship' rather than exploitation. In reality, the determination to take control of Iraqi oilfields was symptomatic of a new British emphasis on the economic (and strategic) potential of its overseas territories; Persia (Iran) was another target of Britain's oil-extracting interest. It seemed that the country's imperialist impetus had been stripped of its theoretical benevolence – let alone its imputed absent-mindedness – and that its policy makers were unwittingly validating the criticisms of anti-imperialist authors such as Lenin and JA Hobson. Certainly, they were belatedly recognising

Controversy 3.1 Palestine and the Balfour Declaration (1917)

On 2 November 1917 the British Foreign Secretary and former Prime Minister Arthur Balfour sent a letter to Lord Rothschild, which was subsequently published. With the War Cabinet's authority, Balfour wrote that 'His Majesty's Government views with favour the establishment in Palestine of a natural home for the Jewish people, and will use its best endeavours to facilitate the achievement of this object'.

There were three motives behind Balfour's notorious 'Declaration'. First, although Balfour himself took a detached and sceptical view in theological matters, he had been impressed, while Leader of the Opposition in 1906, by a private conversation with the Zionist leader Chaim Weizmann, who refused to be fobbed off by the suggestion of a Jewish homeland in Uganda. Second, Balfour calculated that a pro-Zionist statement of intent might have a galvanising effect on opinion in Russia, where anti-war sentiment had precipitated the deposition of Tsar Nicholas II in March 1917. Third, while British policy makers saw limited economic potential in Palestine, the Middle East as a whole was sure to assume more geopolitical importance after the war, and it would do no harm to long-term national interests if a part of that area was populated by people who felt a strong sense of obligation to Britain.

In relation to one of its objectives, Balfour's declaration was made to look futile even before it was published; the letter to Rothschild was sent just a few days before the Bolsheviks took control of Russia, leading inevitably to that country's withdrawal from the conflict. In other respects, however, the document can only be seen as a self-inflicted disaster, produced by highly intelligent ministers who were being 'too clever by half'. Balfour and his colleagues evidently thought that Zionists would be so heartened by the commitment to a 'natural home' in such an emotive place as Palestine that they would continue to feel gladdened even when they had digested the small print. After all, there was no commitment to a Jewish *state* – merely to a 'home' within Palestine. Furthermore, the final version of the text (though not the original draft) contained the proviso 'that nothing shall be done which may prejudice the civil and religious rights of existing non-Jewish communities in Palestine'. As soon as Balfour's letter was published it became evident that the idea of a Jewish homeland in Palestine was unacceptable to Arab opinion; and, far from being hypothetical prospective allies, the Arabs (thanks to protracted negotiations) were already providing invaluable assistance to the British war effort in the Middle East.

> Subsequent attempts to rationalise the Balfour Declaration – not least those of Balfour himself – have been wholly unconvincing. It was an avoidable mistake with terrible and lasting consequences for the Middle East and for Britain itself.

the need for Britain to maximise its resources, since 'the war to end wars' had evidently ushered in a period of uncertainty and insecurity.

Between the wars

In fact, the phrase 'war to end wars' was coined by HG Wells in 1914, rather than being inspired by the efforts of the Versailles peacemakers. Their deliberations took place while a murderous civil war was raging in Russia, with thousands of British troops joining a multinational effort to assist anti-Bolshevik forces. Before the end of this unsuccessful intervention, in 1920, the British were engaged in a brutal campaign of repression in Ireland and had killed hundreds of non-violent protestors in the Jallianwala Bagh garden at Amritsar in north-west India. These episodes set the tone for Britain's overseas activities between the wars, which featured precious few shafts of light to contrast with the general gloom which also prevailed in domestic politics.

Economic background

Despite initial hopes of national resurgence on the back of a hard-fought military victory – encapsulated by Lloyd George's promise of making 'a country fit for heroes to live in' – Britain experienced a brief economic boom before entering a period of stagnation, followed by a slump at the end of the 1920s. Once the victory celebrations were over, it was clear that the negative trends which had affected Britain before 1914 had only been accentuated by the conflict. Previous trading partnerships had been disrupted, and the US (in particular) had been ideally placed to establish new links which the British were unable to sustain. Elsewhere, countries which had previously absorbed exports of British goods developed manufacturing capacity of their own (e.g. India's textile industry).

Even before 1914 Britain's relative decline as a manufacturing nation had increased the importance of the financial sector, based in the City of London. Once formed, the notion that the benefit of the doubt in any policy decision should be awarded to those who made money out of other people's money, rather than those who actually made *things*, proved very difficult to contest.

In the inter-war period this outlook gave rise to a determination that the value of sterling in relation to gold should be forced back (up) to its pre-1914 level, so that international financiers could have renewed confidence in Britain's financial reliability, regardless of the cost to individuals engaged in the manufacturing process. This goal was achieved in 1925, when the Chancellor of the Exchequer, Winston Churchill, announced in his budget speech that Britain would return to the gold standard. The measure was applauded in the House of Commons and by much of the press, though the newspaper proprietor Lord Beaverbrook privately commented that he knew his friend Churchill 'would give in to the bankers' (Gilbert, 1990, 117–18).

By 1929 the outlook had improved to some extent. Although the traditional labour-intensive heavy industries were still depressed, the City had recovered and industries exploiting new technologies were emerging. But in October 1929 a stock-market slump in New York triggered a sharp decline in world commodity prices; two years later the withdrawal of overseas investments from London forced the Bank of England to request American loans. In September 1931 Britain abandoned the gold standard, and this time there would be no return. With many nations – notably, the supposedly free-trading US – raising tariffs to protect domestic producers, world trade declined by two thirds between 1929 and 1934. A World Economic Conference held in London in the summer of 1933 failed to resolve the situation. In such circumstances the system of war reparations and debt repayments collapsed; Britain remitted a last token sum to its US creditors in December 1933, with $265 million still outstanding.

As early as August 1919 Britain's weak economic situation had affected its defence expenditure, with obvious foreign policy repercussions. At that time Lloyd George's Cabinet adopted the guiding principle that estimated defence spending should be based 'on the assumption that Great Britain will not be involved in any great war during the next ten years'. Whether or not this reflected a calculation of the length of time which Germany would need to rebuild its military strength in order to renew hostilities in Europe, in 1928 Chancellor Churchill persuaded his colleagues that the 'Ten Years' Rule' should continue to govern defence estimates unless it was explicitly revoked. The revocation occurred in March 1932, four months before Hitler's Nazis became the largest party in the German Reichstag. By that time the British defence budget had fallen from £766 million in 1919–20 to just over £100 million.

The British government's abandonment of the Ten Years' Rule coincided with the opening of a World Disarmament Conference, under League of Nations auspices, after several years of preparation. It was, of course, possible to support disarmament from two contrasting positions. On the first (moral) position, the chain of reasoning was 'armaments lead to war: war is wrong: therefore Britain must disarm to set a moral example'. The second argument was 'armaments lead to war: war is expensive: therefore Britain will have to disarm and hope that potential enemies will see things the same way'. In either case, the British government (whose circumstances inclined it towards the second view) was probably sincere in its hope that the conference would be successful. However, from the outset the event was dogged by disagreements between France and Germany (which had been admitted as a member of the League of Nations in 1926). In October 1933, after Hitler's appointment as Chancellor, Germany withdrew from the Conference and also gave up its membership of the League (following the example of Japan earlier in the year).

This development provoked the British government into a serious re-examination of its defensive deficiencies, and a slow process of rearmament commenced in the following year. In sharp contrast to the situation before the First World War, when vote-hungry politicians found it difficult to resist public demands for naval expansion, the British were now seriously concerned by the economic implications of an 'arms race'. As early as the Washington Conference of 1922 Britain had abandoned any thought of outbuilding its main nautical rivals and accepted parity with the US in relation to battlecruisers and destroyers; it retained an advantage over Japan, but only in the ratio 10:7.

The Empire

Superficially, it might seem that the First World War, which had consumed so many empires, had reaffirmed the strength and solidarity of the British variant. The British declaration of war had also committed the Empire to the conflict, without consultation. The response was invaluable to Britain's war effort; eventually more than 600,000 Canadians enlisted, along with 400,000 Australians, and nearly 150,000 South Africans. Including nurses, more than 100,000 New Zealanders (out of a total population of 1 million) were involved. The death toll among Canadians and Australians was roughly equal at around 60,000; more than 17,000 New Zealanders died, along with nearly 7,000 South Africans. Soldiers from these self-governing Dominions were involved in some of the most infamous slaughters of the war, on the Western Front and in the ill-starred Gallipoli campaign against the Ottoman Empire.

Sacrifice on this scale could only result in a revision of the relationship between Britain and its Dominions which had already been changing from one of central direction to one in which the metropolitan power was more 'first among equals'. Given their contribution, it seemed appropriate that the Dominions should be represented at the Paris peace talks. General Jan Smuts, so recently a Boer War opponent, became a member of the British War Cabinet in 1917. In the same year, Smuts used the term 'Commonwealth of Nations' to characterise the future relationship between Britain and its Dominions. In 1922, when Britain's support for Greece against Turkey in the Chanak crisis took the country to the brink of war, the refusal of Dominion governments to offer automatic support was crucial to the subsequent British climbdown. Four years later another (and more statesmanlike) 'Balfour Declaration', at the 1926 Imperial Conference, affirmed that this was now a free association of autonomous states, 'though united by common allegiance to the Crown'. The 1931 Statute of Westminster gave formal legislative recognition to the revised relationships.

Although imperial idealists continued to cherish the vision of an Empire-wide free-trade area in which business would be conducted to Britain's advantage, the Statute of Westminster merely confirmed that this was no longer a realistic vision. The Dominions were free to develop their own trading networks and to construct their own tariff arrangements. As a result, when in 1932 the Chancellor Neville Chamberlain announced a system of tariffs which included more lenient terms for imports from the Empire/Commonwealth, the subject only caused serious agitation among the most dogmatic free traders; even Churchill was unruffled. At the ensuring Imperial Conference at Ottawa Chamberlain was taken aback by the extent to which the Dominions were now prepared to act on economic interests of their own. Far from realising the visions of his father, Joseph, the Ottawa conference had merely halted a process in which the countries of the old Empire were 'drifting apart pretty rapidly' (quoted in Self, 2006, 174).

From the narrow perspective of British foreign and defence policy, these developments were not entirely unwelcome; if the Dominions were ready to utilise their economic autonomy in full, the British moral responsibility to provide for their protection could be reduced to a similar degree. By the same token, however, it was not realistic for Britain to expect the Dominions to respond to any new international crisis by backing Britain with the enthusiasm they had shown in 1914. Since Neville Chamberlain was the minister who received a direct foretaste of the likely Dominion response to a future war in Europe, the morale-shredding Ottawa Conference must be regarded as a significant contributory factor in his later attempt to appease Adolf Hitler's Germany.

At least Britain's relations with the Dominions were altered without confrontation and bloodshed. In other territories, where Britain had either seen no need for amicable arrangements or failed to negotiate satisfactory settlements, the ominous outlook should have been apparent even for those enthusiasts (like King George V) who celebrated the expansion of British rule after Versailles. The most spectacular development was uncomfortably close to home – in Ireland, which after centuries of antagonistic relations had been coaxed (or coerced) into a political union with Britain in 1800. From the British perspective, the main reason for this unsentimental union was strategic – the fear that an invading force could use Ireland as a springboard. The union was widely resented from the outset, leading to frequent outbreaks of violence in Ireland. In 1886 and 1893 William Gladstone's Liberal government introduced bills to give Ireland Home Rule within the Empire, but these attempts at a compromise solution foundered in the House of Lords. Even the liberal ideologue John Bright, so sceptical of imperial adventures far from home, recoiled from the notion that Ireland should be allowed to govern itself.

In 1914 another Home Rule bill received the Royal assent, since the House of Lords had been stripped of its power of veto. However, this legislation was fiercely opposed by the Protestant majority in the six counties of the north of Ireland, whose cultural identity (underpinned by religious allegiance) was vehemently 'British' rather than 'Irish'. The Parliamentary process was completed after the outbreak of war; and since it would have been difficult to implement even in peacetime, the legislation was suspended for the duration. In 1916 an armed rising of around 1,200 Irish nationalists resulted in the seizure of strategic buildings in Dublin and the proclamation of an Irish Republic. As AJP Taylor noted, 'This was the only national rebellion in any European country during the First World War – an ironical comment on the British claim to be fighting for freedom' (Taylor, 1963, 56). Vastly superior British forces quickly quashed the insurrection, but the execution of the leaders predictably inflamed feeling among Irish nationalists who had not initially supported the 'Easter Rising'. In January 1919 a further declaration of Irish independence led to more than two years of conflict between Britain and Irish Republicans, which ended with an agreement that Ireland should be granted Home Rule at last, but that the island should be partitioned; the northern counties would remain within the UK, while the South (the Irish Free State) became a self-governing Dominion within the British Empire.

Ireland was far from being the only venue for armed resistance to British rule between 1918 and 1939. In 1920 there was an uprising in that unstable and artificial British creation Iraq, in which up to 10,000 Iraqis lost their lives along with almost 500 British troops. Iraq became independent in 1932, but not before a British-based company had negotiated a long-term monopoly over oil extraction. In Palestine British attempts to square the circular logic of the first Balfour Declaration led to alienation on all sides, and although armed Arab resistance was delayed until 1936, the British government was forced to allocate 20,000 troops to this mandated territory just a few months before the outbreak of the Second World War.

The wind of change had even reached India, Britain's 'Jewel in the Crown'. In 1919 the British government granted limited powers of self-government to a country which had provided around 1.5 million people for the war effort in varying capacities and almost £150 million in financial contributions. Far from appeasing the demand for self-government, the measures of 1919 merely exposed the patronising assumptions behind Britain's continuing role in India. A further Government of India Act, creating a federation and ensuring the representation of minority groups, followed in 1935, after bitter resistance by Conservative backbenchers led by Winston Churchill. There were some violent disturbances, notably in Peshawar during a general strike in 1930, and in the same year Mahatma Gandhi led his supporters on a 240-mile march in protest against a salt tax first imposed in the 1880s. Gandhi, whose Congress Party had issued a declaration of independence in January 1930, was famously committed to non-violent methods, but his repeated arrests by the British authorities ran the risk of precipitating a violent reaction. As it was, a 200,000-strong police force and an army of almost equal size somehow ensured that British rule survived the strains of the 1930s (James, 1994, 422).

Even without the benefit of hindsight it was obvious that the British 'Raj' had a limited shelf life. The colonial power was now in the situation of an individual who has managed to reach the centre of a maze by luck rather than judgement and now faces the task of finding a way out. The task was complicated by imperialist diehards, like Churchill, who were desperate to avoid the necessity of leaving, but also by growing evidence of schisms within the society of India itself – the sort which had previously been exploited to British advantage. While British prestige could just about sustain a negotiated withdrawal, a forcible ejection of any kind was deeply unpalatable. The defence of India from external threats therefore remained a priority, though after the Bolshevik Revolution the Russian threat seemed to have subsided.

India, of course, was not the only source of British concern in Asia. As noted above, Britain had concluded a defensive alliance with Japan in 1902, and this was renewed in 1905 and 1911. In 1910 an Anglo-Japanese exhibition had been held in London to augment cultural and economic ties between the two countries. Despite such tokens of mutual goodwill, and Japan's pivotal role in protecting British assets during the First World War, Japan took the opportunity to expand its own Empire between 1914 and 1918. Its growing power raised the possibility of future conflict with the US, in which Britain would have to be neutral at best. While other Commonwealth countries advocated a continuation of the Japanese alliance, Canada was understandably alarmed by any possibility of conflict between America and the British Empire. Such considerations ensured that the Anglo-Japanese alliance was not renewed; in December 1921 it was superseded by a 'Four-Power Treaty' between Britain, France, Japan and the US, which guaranteed the existing overseas possessions of all the contracting parties and provided for consultation if any disputes should arise in future.

The ending of the Anglo-Japanese alliance was as momentous as its commencement had been. The original treaty had been a tacit acceptance that Britain could not defend its imperial interests in south-east Asia unaided. It needed a partner, and initially Japan fitted the bill admirably. However, the Anglo-Japanese alliance could only camouflage British weakness: it did nothing to remove the underlying problem – namely, that Britain was no longer able to defend the most distant territories within its Empire. The events of the First World War suggested that America, rather than Japan, was the right horse to back; if tensions between Japan and the US erupted into conflict there could only be one winner. However, while Japan was dynamic and acquisitive, the US was a somewhat hesitant horse – reluctant to exert its potential power when the going seemed good, and disinclined to enter the race at all unless it was forced to do so or could be certain of a relatively cost-free victory. British misgivings about the preference for the US over Japan is suggested by the fact that in 1923 – the year in which the treaty with Japan was formally terminated – the British announced their intention to construct a massive naval base in Singapore. Development of the base was painfully slow, and it was only completed in 1939; three years later it was captured by Japanese forces, just a few weeks after the attack on Pearl Harbor had brought America into the war on the British side.

Europe

From the British perspective, the priority in the aftermath of the Treaty of Versailles was to ensure a lasting peace by rehabilitating Germany without making France feel insecure. Unfortunately for the British, the French took the view that a rehabilitated Germany would automatically pose a threat to their security. The concept of a League of Nations briefly offered a solution to this dilemma; under its auspices, France would (or *should*) gradually feel more relaxed about a more prosperous Germany, with its territory restored within more realistic borders, so long as any future misconduct would incur the collective wrath of the fledgling international community. When this prospect – along with a specific Anglo-American guarantee against future German attack – was swept away by the US Senate it was not surprising that French policy should revert to the idea of exploiting Germany's supine condition in a way which might prevent its antagonist from posing a threat in the future. Deprived of its Russian alliance, France also began to put out feelers of friendship towards states on Germany's eastern borders – notably, Versailles creations, like Poland and Czechoslovakia. These initiatives meant that France was committing itself to the Versailles settlement as a whole and not just those aspects of the treaty which affected its border with Germany. In 1922 attempts to negotiate a defensive alliance against Germany succumbed largely because Britain refused to expand its terms into an Anglo-French guarantee of Versailles, backed by discussions between senior military planners. Friction between the erstwhile allies increased in 1923, when French and Belgian troops occupied the German mining district of the Ruhr to enforce the delivery of coal and other industrial materials. Britain also protested against fruitless French attempts to stir up separatist sentiment in the occupied Rhineland.

In 1925 a potential escape route from this diplomatic impasse was offered by the German Foreign Minister, Gustav Stresemann. His initiative resulted in the Locarno Treaties, the most important of which was an agreement between Germany, France and Belgium not to attack each other. Britain and Italy also joined this pact, guaranteeing to defend any of the other signatories which might come under attack in a 'flagrant violation' of the Versailles settlement (including the terms relating to the Rhineland). Although a 'flagrant violation' was not defined in the treaties, the effect of Locarno was to reaffirm the 1919 settlement in Western Europe. However, there was no such system of mutual guarantees for Germany's eastern neighbours, although the Weimar Republic agreed to submit any disputes to international arbitration.

Having accepted at Locarno the kind of peaceful procedures characteristic of the League of Nations, the logical step was for Germany to join that organisation, which it did in 1926. In the same year the foreign ministers of Germany and France (Stresemann and Briand) were awarded the Nobel Peace Prize. However, their British counterpart Austen Chamberlain (not to be confused with his more abrasive half-brother, Neville) had pre-empted them, scooping the 1925 award; and of the trio he had the surest grounds to be satisfied with Locarno. Despite his emotional preference for France over Germany, Chamberlain had established equally cordial personal relations with Stresemann and Briand. While France and Germany had accepted that Locarno was the best deal that they could achieve in the circumstances, for Britain it was almost the perfect solution to the problems bequeathed by Versailles – almost good enough, one might say, to make the adoption of the Ten Years' Rule on defence spending seem rational. Chamberlain proclaimed Locarno as 'the real dividing-line between the years of the war and years of peace' (quoted in Carr, 1937, 97). In reality, the signature of the treaties almost marked the halfway point between the beginning of the First World War and the resumption of hostilities in 1939.

Stresemann died, still in office, in 1929; Briand followed in 1932. By the latter date the Locarno Treaties still existed on paper, but their spirit had been undermined by the Great Depression. Austen Chamberlain, by contrast, lived just long enough to see the final destruction of his prize-winning exploits. In March 1936 Hitler, whose rise to power in Germany owed much to the Great Depression, ordered the reoccupation of the Rhineland and openly repudiated Locarno on the same day. The pretext was the recent revival of the fateful Franco-Russian alliance. His actions, however, would have satisfied any reasonable person's understanding of the term 'flagrant violation'. Chamberlain, certainly, felt that way; now a backbencher increasingly disillusioned with the Baldwin government, in which his half-brother Neville was serving as Chancellor of the Exchequer, he favoured the establishment of a unified Ministry of Defence headed by Winston Churchill, the most outspoken critic of the administration's foreign policy

(Dutton, 1985, 319). Austen Chamberlain died suddenly in March 1937; his half-brother became Prime Minister ten weeks later.

Whatever Austen Chamberlain might have thought, the German remilitarisation of the Rhineland met a muted official response in London and Paris. The French, having almost completed a fortified barrier against a German invasion (the Maginot line), were less concerned about the Rhineland by 1936. Any aggressive reaction to Hitler's dramatic move would have to be coordinated with Britain; and (probably to the French government's relief) the British government offered words of sympathy but no material support. In fact, while AJP Taylor was exaggerating when he described Hitler's reabsorption of the Rhineland as 'a success for British policy', it was not entirely unwelcome to the Baldwin government (Taylor, 1964, 132). After all, in the previous year that government had signed a naval treaty with Germany, which gave a comfortable margin of superiority to British vessels but nevertheless allowed German naval rearmament to levels which clearly breached the terms of the Treaty of Versailles. In answer to the argument that 1936 marked the last chance for Britain and France to stop the process which led to the Second World War, Taylor points out that even if French troops had succeeded in throwing their armed enemies out of the Rhineland, Germany would have continued to exist, harbouring redoubled resentments and merely awaiting a better opportunity to strike back. However, Taylor himself presents Hitler as a gambler whose dominant position in German politics depended on the success of his calculations; and if this throw of the dice had proved unsuccessful, it might have been his last, since at this stage there were still plenty of highly placed German officers who wanted to revert to Stresemann's measured approach to the revision of Versailles and Locarno. By sharp contrast, the political leaders of Britain and France felt that they enjoyed public trust precisely because of their refusal to take risks with the lives of their fellow citizens; as a result of their inaction, Hitler's successive gambles could be made to look like the strategic masterstrokes of an inspired leader.

The role of public opinion

As we have seen, although British politicians had to acknowledge the importance of public support for their policy in the era of total war and universal suffrage, this factor was difficult to evaluate, and it was understandable that they tended to draw concrete conclusions from questionable evidence. Historians of the inter-war period – even eminent ones – also have to resort to generalisations. For example, EH Carr wrote that after an initial thirst for vengeance against Germany at the end of the First World War, 'passions on the British side abated rapidly'. Indeed, Carr felt confident enough to explain the changing mood: 'Time-honoured British conceptions of fair play and chivalry' caused a reaction in Germany's favour. All that was missing from Carr's analysis was an allusion to the equally traditional British preference for the 'underdog'. This might have been true, but it also could just be a rationalisation of the changing attitude of the British government and leading newspapers (Carr, 1937, 50).

A fascinating (and famous) example of perceptions of public opinion influencing foreign and defence policy was Stanley Baldwin's attempt to defend his coalition (more usually known by the misnomer 'National') government's record on rearmament in a Parliamentary debate of November 1936. Baldwin's case was that he and his colleagues had become alarmed by developments in Europe three years earlier; in fact, he would have been justified in dating the end of complacency to March 1932, when the Ten Year's Rule was dropped. However, a by-election at East Fulham in October 1933 had resulted in a surprising defeat for the Conservative candidate, who was criticised strongly for supporting British rearmament. Baldwin could also have alluded to the notorious decision of the Oxford Union in February 1933, by 275 votes to 153, to oppose the idea of fighting for 'King and Country'; or the rather more substantial snapshot of public opinion provided by the National Declaration, or 'Peace Ballot', organised by the League of Nations Union and held between November 1934 and June 1935. Eleven million people – nearly two fifths of Britain's adult population – cast a vote, but only 60 per cent endorsed the use of military action to resolve international disputes if all else failed. On this evidence, Baldwin argued, he could not have asked the voters to back a full-scale programme of rearmament in a general election; his government had won an overwhelming majority in 1935, and he chose to interpret this as a 'mandate' for a more tentative rearmament (*Hansard, House of Commons Debates*, 12 November 1936, Vol. 317, col. 1144).

To some critics, what Baldwin called his 'appalling frankness' on that occasion was, frankly, appalling. Churchill was not alone in thinking that the Prime Minister had confessed openly to putting the electoral interests of his party before the security of his country. Baldwin could also be accused of having deliberately misled the public during the 1935 election campaign about the gravity of European threats. Whatever the merits of these arguments, Baldwin certainly gave the impression that while he and his colleagues had been aware of growing dangers in 1933, the public was too bovine to understand – and (for whatever reason) the government had not even bothered trying to enlighten them. In case the implications of his remarks offended some voters, Baldwin made sure that his 1936 speech included some flattery of a public who 'may come a little late, but my word, they come with a certainty when they do come'. Yet his avowal that 'I shall always trust the instincts of our democratic people' came hard on the heels of eloquent testimony which suggested that, in 1933 at least, those 'instincts' had been entirely untrustworthy. On his own account, Baldwin had often rehearsed a theory 'that a democracy is always two years behind the dictator'. If true, this suggested that the leaders of a democracy had a duty to be at least two years *ahead* of their own voters, leading public opinion rather than pandering to it. Ironically, while 'East Fulham frightened the government out of what senses they had', AJP Taylor thought that this reaction merely exemplified the common tendency of politicians to exaggerate the electoral importance of foreign affairs. Domestic issues certainly played a major role in a by-election result which in any case coincided with a more general Labour recovery from a disastrous showing in the 1931 general election (Taylor, 1965, 367).

Neville Chamberlain had wanted to take a more robust line on rearmament in the 1935 general election campaign, albeit for narrowly partisan reasons (Self, 2006, 253). But when he took over the premiership from Baldwin in May 1937, Chamberlain was far more proactive than his predecessor in pursuing appeasement of Britain's potential enemies (Controversy 3.2). Chamberlain wanted to *mould* public opinion rather than to trail behind it, which would have been a laudable intention had he not wanted to lead opinion in the wrong direction. He took considerable pains to influence the press, with the help of shadowy assistants well versed in the dark arts of manipulation. When challenged about this practice in the House of Commons the Prime Minister blithely denied that it was happening (Price, 2010, 104–5). In this respect, at least, Chamberlain was doing his best to make up some ground on the dictators.

Final steps to war

The main problem with Chamberlain was not his novice status in the field of foreign policy but rather an excessive confidence in his own capacity. He disliked Anthony Eden, the Foreign Secretary he had inherited when he succeeded Baldwin as Prime Minister in 1937; and although his subsequent defenders have pointed out that the policy differences between the two men were relatively trivial, these were bound to be magnified in Eden's mind by the Prime Minister's tendency to embark on important initiatives without consulting him. Like many interventionist premiers, Chamberlain also disliked the Foreign Office, and it was certainly true that the department housed several powerful officials (notably the Permanent Under-Secretary, Sir Robert Vansittart) who loathed Germany. Some Prime Ministers might have seen this as a reason to pause and reflect whether their policy was really in the national interest, but Chamberlain was not made from such flexible materials.

After the remilitarisation of the Rhineland the course of events allowed little opportunity for anyone to pause for reflection. In July 1936 – just before the opening of the Olympic Games, which had been awarded to Germany in the pre-Hitler days of 1931 – civil war broke out in Spain. German troops and aircraft were involved from an early stage, although Italy played a more prominent role in the conflict, which ended in 1939 with the toppling of the democratically elected Popular Front government. In March 1938 Hitler skilfully exploited disorder in Austria to establish an unopposed union of that country with Germany – the *Anschluss* which the Treaty of Versailles had explicitly prohibited. This latest of many breaches in the peace terms was particularly ominous, since it raised the possibility that Woodrow Wilson's principle of 'self-determination' could now be utilised against the victorious peacemakers. The significant German-speaking minority living in Bohemia, Moravia and Silesia – now incorporated within Czechoslovakia – were 'stirred to ungovernable excitement' by the *Anschluss* (Taylor, 1964, 191). Czechoslovakia was an ally of Soviet Russia (since 1935) as well as France, but the Soviet commitment to go to war over Czechoslovakia would not take effect unless France acted first, and France did not want to act. In effect, Chamberlain rescued France from its moral dilemma by taking charge of this stage of appeasement, leading to the Munich conference of September 1938 at which – in the absence of the Czechs and the Russians – Britain, France and Italy agreed to the German annexation of the Sudetenland region of Czechoslovakia.

If history had really come to a '.' at this point, the British policy of appeasing Germany might have been judged at least a partial success. What seemed in hindsight like abject national humiliations – Chamberlain taking repeated flights across Europe to hear Hitler's latest demands and then bullying other states into compliance – might have seemed excusable, since it could be squared with the logic of Locarno and the procedure (if not the active participation) of the League of Nations. Germany had made no move to revise its western borders; and its expansion in Central and Eastern Europe had been negotiated (after a fashion) rather than imposed after armed conflict. Chamberlain's idea that Hitler should sign a document committing his country to peaceable methods in future, and hinting that relations between Germany and Britain should be cooperative, might look sensible; waving the document around in triumph on his arrival back in Britain could be excused; and even his appearance at the window of 10 Downing Street to claim that he had brought back 'peace with honour' would not seriously have been held against him. Significantly, the deal had been struck without any help from the US, whose Congress had passed a Neutrality Act in 1935 and whose President, Roosevelt, had been rebuffed by Chamberlain in January 1938 when he floated the idea of an international conference. If, for better or worse, Britain was asserting a leadership role in global affairs, Chamberlain's personal responsibility for the policy had been cemented in February 1938 when Anthony Eden resigned from the Foreign Office.

Unfortunately for Chamberlain and those who continued to hope for a peaceful end to the nightmare that the advent of Hitler had triggered, historical events continued to happen. On 9 November 1938 the murder of a German official of the embassy in Paris gave Hitler a pretext to turn petty persecution into more draconian action. *Kristallnacht* unleashed a wave of retribution against German Jews, whose homes, shops and synagogues were attacked and looted, and thousands were rounded up and sent to concentration camps. At least *Kristallnacht* proved that Hitler could be regarded as a man of his word, when he issued threats rather than promises and felt sufficiently strong to fulfil them. Those who had studied Hitler's profession of faith, *Mein Kampf* (1925), might have been surprised that he had postponed a concerted campaign of violence against German Jews for so long after his seizure of dictatorial powers in 1933.

In March 1939 – just a few days before the Spanish Civil War ended in another defeat for democracy – Hitler took advantage of unrest in the remaining parts of Czechoslovakia and sent his troops into the capital, Prague. According to AJP Taylor, in Britain '[t]here followed an underground explosion of public opinion such as the historian cannot trace in precise terms' (Taylor, 1964, 251). Certainly, Chamberlain was shaken by an increased level of criticism among Conservative backbenchers, and newspaper editors, who had previously seemed reliable purveyors of the government's message. The Prime Minister finally realised that something would have to be done – not to tell Hitler that he had gone too far but to signal that there might be trouble ahead if he went any further. Assuming that Poland would be the next Nazi objective, at the end of March Britain and France agreed to guarantee its independence. By that time the predominantly German city of Memel, absorbed by Lithuania after the First World War, had been annexed by Hitler's Reich. On 7 April Italian troops invaded Albania. This prompted another British guarantee, this time to Greece and Romania. In practice – despite London's lingering hopes – this also marked the parting of the ways between Chamberlain and the Italian dictator, Mussolini, who had been regarded as a potential restraining influence on Hitler, even after his conquest of Abyssinia (1935–6), which destroyed any of the credibility the League of Nations retained following Japan's invasion of Manchuria. Using Mussolini as a potential brake on German expansion was like asking a fox cub to impose limits on its parents' hunting activities; only now, however, did Chamberlain confide privately that Mussolini was no better than 'a sneak and a cad' (Self, 2006, 359). In May 1939 Hitler and Mussolini signed a 'Pact of Steel' – an economic and military alliance to which Japan might also have adhered if it had not so obviously been directed against Britain and France rather than the Soviet Union.

As a practical proposition, the Polish guarantee was obviously futile – if Germany did choose to attack, there was no way that an effective Anglo-French force could be assembled in time, even if those countries had been determined (and sufficiently equipped) to fulfil their pledge. Since Britain and France had failed to act even against Hitler's infringement of the Munich agreement to respect what remained of Czechoslovakia, the German dictator had every reason to regard the Polish guarantee as yet another bluff which he could call without undue risk. After all, the British and the French had tacitly accepted the German case in relation to the Sudetenland, and the moral argument about the status of Danzig seemed very similar. One might conclude that having done his best to appease the Germans and the Italians, Chamberlain had suddenly realised the necessity of some domestic appeasement to placate the 'resurgent determination to resist Hitler that had swept over the public, the opposition, the government backbenches and even members of his own cabinet' (Doerr, 1998, 245). Privately he continued to dangle inducements in the hope of satisfying Hitler's lust for *lebensraum*, and he dropped hints that the guarantee of Polish *independence* did not rule out revisions of its territorial boundaries.

There was one context in which the Polish guarantee *might* have made some sense – if the Soviet Union was also a party to the agreement. However, this presupposed that the Poles and the Soviets were on good terms, whereas recent evidence demonstrated that, of the predatory dictators on their eastern and western doorsteps, the Polish government preferred Hitler to Stalin. There is also ample evidence that Chamberlain shared this preference; in common with many Conservatives, he regarded 'Bolshevism' as something akin to a plague which could sweep across the whole of Europe, whereas even in 1939 he could still regard Nazi ideology as a malady which only afflicted people (mainly German) whose reasoning powers had been disturbed by the injustices of Versailles. Grudging respect for the Red Army might have persuaded Chamberlain to soften his view of the Soviet Union, but, in view of Stalin's recent murderous purges of senior officers, it was widely believed to be far weaker than its Tsarist counterpart had been back in 1914 – and even then it had not been able to sustain its initial attack on Germany's eastern flank. Even in April 1939 Chamberlain clung to the hope that war could be avoided, which meant that he could regard an alliance with the 'contagious' Soviets as a very last resort. When, in that month, the Soviet Union proposed a treaty of mutual assistance with Britain and France, complete with guarantees of the states on the Soviet border, Chamberlain procrastinated before suggesting a revised agreement under which the Soviets would offer help to the Western powers without receiving any guarantee in return. Naturally this one-sided deal was rejected by Stalin.

In May 1939 the British government authorised more serious talks with the Soviet Union, and eventually a deputation was despatched to discuss military cooperation. However, Stalin had already opened clandestine conversations with the Germans. On 17 August 1939 the Soviet talks with Britain and France broke down because of the reiterated Polish refusal to allow the Red Army to infiltrate their territory in order to fight the Germans. Less than a week later the Nazi and Soviet regimes signed a non-aggression pact. Despite repeated warnings that something like this might happen, the deal came as a disagreeable surprise to Chamberlain, who could now add Stalin (and, at last, Hitler) to his 'sneak and cad' list alongside Mussolini. His official response was that the pact made no difference to the Polish guarantee, but the Soviets saw things the other way round.

By guaranteeing Poland (however ineffectually) the British had tacitly interposed themselves between Hitler and Russia. At worst, when Hitler finally decided to tear up the pact with Stalin and invade the Soviet Union through Poland, he would now be faced with a war on two flanks; and since the deal with Hitler allowed the Soviets to annex slightly more than half of Polish territory, their own country would be furnished with an extensive buffer zone to buy some time for defensive preparations.

Whatever the motives behind Britain's lame attempt to include the Soviet Union within an anti-German alliance, its failure, and the subsequent Molotov–Ribbentrop pact, can only have made Adolf Hitler feel that the gamble he had already decided upon – a full-scale invasion of Poland – was more likely to be a winning one. Whether or not its armed forces prevailed in the ensuing struggle, in crucial respects Britain was bound to be a loser.

Conclusions: Liberalism, Realism or a mixture of both?

The foregoing discussion of British foreign policy in the decades before 1945 is necessary and useful, not just as 'background' to the post-1945 period, but also because it allows us to engage critically with the theoretical framework of IR (Chapter 1).

Marxist observers would emphasise the economic aspects of European disputes; and, as we have seen, these factors were of enormous underlying importance. However, in respect to relations between Britain and Germany this explanatory framework seems inadequate. From 1919 onwards British policy makers were anxious to restore Germany's status as a prosperous trading partner, and as a new war approached they were even willing to contemplate German colonial expansion. The most effective Marxist card in this game is the British reluctance to forge an alliance with the Soviet Union as war approached in 1939. However, although Chamberlain and his political allies might have preferred Hitler's brand of tyranny to the Stalinist regime, there were plenty of British anti-communists (like Churchill) who favoured a deal with the Soviets; and although in hindsight Hitler's Reich posed the more potent threat to the capitalist order, even from the Marxist perspective it must be difficult to decide whether Stalin or Hitler was a greater friend to the interests of the European proletariat.

Of the mainstream theories which can be brought to bear on British foreign policy, this leaves Liberalism and Realism. It would be wrong to underestimate the extent to which British imperialists of the nineteenth century had been actuated by a self-adopted mission to elevate the human condition, however much their efforts might be execrated today; equally, those who believed that global free trade would eventually lift all boats way above their existing level were often (if not always) sincere. One scholar has argued that a key reason for Britain's failure to prevent the Second World War was its 'pursuit of conciliation and tolerance to the point of failure to recognize [Nazi] evil, and in evil danger' (Reynolds, 1954, 167). On this view, British policy makers seem to stand accused of being too saintly for their own good, putting moral values above the kind of cynical calculation which, if backed by timely actions, might have kept their country out of war. As we have seen, public opinion was a significant factor in British foreign policy between the wars, even if it could not be measured with precision and often acted as a pretext for decisions which would have been taken anyway. The League of Nations Union, which at its peak attracted around 400,000 members, constituted a force which no government could entirely have ignored; and it seems clear that Stanley Baldwin, at least, was strongly affected by a general revulsion against a possible recurrence of total war fought with even more destructive weapons.

However, British policy between the wars is susceptible to a different construction. 'Conciliation and tolerance' sounds like a motto for the League of Nations, and senior British politicians certainly endorsed the idea of collective security in theory. Yet when the League's system of economic sanctions against recalcitrant states came into conflict with perceived national interests – as it did over Italy's aggression against Abyssinia in 1935 – Britain (and France) made only token efforts to implement the measures before abandoning them entirely in the summer of 1936 (after Neville Chamberlain had described the policy as 'the very midsummer of madness' and attacked the concept of sanctions because they could easily lead to war (Northedge, 1966, 424–5)). On the face of it, Britain had taken a constructively conciliatory role in the negotiations which led to the Treaties of Locarno; but even this prize-winning effort featured an element of 'cynical calculation', because it left open the possibility that if Germany revived it could expand its borders eastwards rather than directly threatening Britain's key interests.

Insofar as Britain was forced to take a 'conciliatory' role in Europe, this ultimately arose from the infringements of the principle of national self-determination included in the Treaty of Versailles – in the shaping of which Britain had played a leading role. In other elements of the post-1918 settlement Britain had taken control of territories without consultation of their inhabitants – indeed, in 1917 its politicians had even promised a homeland for the Jewish people without paying the slightest heed to Arab opinion. After the war these champions of 'tolerance and conciliation' tried to repress independence movements in longer-established imperial 'possessions', like Ireland and India. In this context one need only consider Neville Chamberlain's bleat of incredulity in September 1938 at the thought that Britons were preparing for war 'because of a quarrel in a faraway country between people of whom we know nothing'. At the same time that Germany was preparing to attack Czechoslovakia individuals who had never heard the name Balfour were being killed in Palestine because 20 years earlier the British Cabinet had authorised a declaration which concerned another area 'of which it knew nothing'.

This is not, of course, to endorse a swing to the opposite extreme and claim that British policy between the world wars was uniquely wicked. Rather, the irresistible conclusion on the basis of concrete evidence – as opposed to the subsequent rationalisations of historians who liked to think that Britain had declined gracefully from its former status of 'top nation' – is that the statesmen and officials who took decisions on the country's behalf were actuated throughout the period by an overriding concern for its own perceived interests. If this priority prompted actions which were satisfactory from the moral point of view, so much the better – especially since decisions of that kind were easier to sell to the voters of a newly democratised country. But if the nation's perceived interests lay in a different direction – say, in the 'toleration' of German and Italian involvement in the uprising against the elected Spanish government – that direction was invariably taken.

Britain's foreign policy in these years is thus best understood under the category of Realism. However, Realism never reflects an *objective* 'reality', for the good reason that no such standpoint exists. When British policy makers sought to pursue the national interest they had a particular vision of the 'nation' in mind. Moral values – particularly those which assumed the guidance of farsighted, incorruptible governments – had been integrated into that vision from the beginning of Britain's overseas expansion. As an Anglophile German writer put it in 1922, 'England is the single country in the world that, in looking after its own interest with meticulous care, has at the same time something to give to others' (Dibelius, 1930, 108). However, when the British acted in accordance with this approach, they tended to rely on the idea that their rule would bring incorruptible government in the long run – and in the long run, as John Maynard Keynes might have remarked, a lot of the country's colonial subjects met violent deaths. Some moral purpose could be salvaged after 1918 from the argument that Britain's role was to guide its colonies towards self-government; but the behaviour of the Dominions after 1918 showed that self-government led to the development of interests that differed from those of the 'mother country', let alone those of other Dominions. Although idealistic British intellectuals were inspired by the emergence of the Commonwealth to speculate about the eventual creation of a world government which would eradicate war, the legacy of Empire was just too complex for policy makers to resolve into a coherent policy approach in the relatively brief period between 1918 and 1939. As a result, patriotic politicians like Churchill felt instinctively that another world war was worth fighting in order to preserve Britain's global destiny, without having any clear idea of what Britain's position might look like after another full-scale conflict. All that was certain was that if Britain was to defeat Germany and its allies for a second time, the US would have to lend effective support – and however much people like Churchill might hope to persuade themselves and others that the US shared the British vision, a clear-sighted 'Realist' of 1939 would have been fairly certain that such was not the case.

Controversy 3.2 Neville Chamberlain – for and against

After decades of vilification as the 'man of Munich', who pulled out all the stops to appease Hitler – and who spoke publicly about the collapse of his policy as if it had been a tragedy for himself rather than for the British people as a whole (let alone the victims of Hitler's attempted extermination of the Jews) – Neville Chamberlain has found some doughty defenders since the 1980s. In 1989 John Charmley's forensic examination of Chamberlain's policy of 'appeasement' managed to imply that his opponents – Churchill and particularly Anthony Eden – were the real villains. Robert Self's magnificent biography of Chamberlain (2006) guides the reader to a sympathetic understanding of the terrible dilemmas he faced, while criticising the Prime Minister for obvious errors of judgement.

Chamberlain is an ideal candidate for posthumous rehabilitation, since he wrote frequently to his sisters in a way which allows biographers and revisionist historians a unique insight into the development of his policy towards the dictators. The main 'revisionist' points are:

- While 'appeasement' has become a dirty word in diplomacy since the Munich conference of 1938, there is nothing shameful about the attempt to avoid war, and Britain had been pursuing a policy of that kind even before the First World War.
- Chamberlain's version of appeasement bought Britain valuable time in which to prepare for war.
- Chamberlain inherited the indefensible Versailles settlement and took over from Baldwin as Prime Minister when it was clear that the League of Nations could not resolve the problems that were arising in central Europe.

It is reasonable to suggest that this defence of Chamberlain is the product of hindsight; since Hitler's Germany was eventually defeated, no one can ever know the full extent of the brutality that Nazi forces could have visited on conquered European peoples, whereas the revisionist historians can cite concrete evidence of the sufferings which were inflicted by Stalin's Soviet Union on the inhabitants of the territories which it occupied before and after 1945. Indeed, by the late 1980s, when Chamberlain's champions decided that it was safe to ride out in his defence, the Soviet Union itself was in terminal decline; it could appear that Churchill had been equally guilty of pointless 'appeasement' of a merciless dictator when he strained every sinew to get on good terms with Stalin.

However, none of this should have any bearing on an objective assessment of Chamberlain's record as a practitioner of foreign policy in the years during which he exercised a decisive influence. Against the positive points mentioned above one could argue that:

- Chamberlain *made* appeasement into a dirty word by continuing to conciliate Hitler (and Mussolini) after those dictators had shown themselves to be unreliable (at best). He met both Hitler and Mussolini and persisted in placing the most positive construction on their pronouncements to the end, whereas his lack of personal acquaintance with Stalin and Roosevelt did not prevent him from regarding the Soviet Union with profound suspicion and the US with contempt.
- The 'buying time for Britain' argument was used by Chamberlain himself before his death as a rationalisation of his conduct. Yet Chamberlain's diplomacy arose from desperation to preserve peace at all costs, rather than a desire to defer the outbreak to a more convenient time. His attitude was exposed all too obviously in his willingness to fly to Germany to talk with Hitler and his anxiety to bring back from Munich some evidence that Germany would rather not go to war with Britain. It is true that the resulting 'piece of paper' made Chamberlain seem like the chosen apostle of peace at home and in many other countries; but the leader of the country that really mattered could only draw the conclusion that Britain was so afraid of war that it would allow him a completely free hand outside Western Europe. From that perspective, far from buying time for Britain, Chamberlain's interventions merely ensured that the money it had started to spend on rearmament was not entirely wasted.
- While revisionists have a tendency to overreact against Chamberlain's dismal reputation by implying that he was in fact an infallible oracle of wisdom in the field of foreign policy, they would have done better to focus on his inheritance. When he became Prime Minister in 1937 Chamberlain had to find a way to resolve differences arising from the Treaty of Versailles in a political context which had been reshaped to his further disadvantage by the repercussions of the Great Depression. As one scholar of the period has put it, since Chamberlain had been 'dealt a near-impossible hand' by Versailles, the economic crisis which followed so soon after the promising Locarno Treaties gave rise to consequences which were 'well beyond the control of any diplomat' (Doerr, 1998, 272). The circumstances after 1937, in short, required a miracle worker. Unfortunately for revisionists, who want their readers to sympathise

with Chamberlain's personality as well as his policy, there is ample evidence that their hero deluded himself into thinking that he was indeed capable of diplomatic miracles – and his self-evaluation, rather than his decisions in themselves, leave him open to adverse historical judgements.

If nothing else, the controversy over Chamberlain's conduct and decisions in the last months of the 'fragile peace' suggests that the role of individuals should not be overlooked in studies of foreign policy. It is important not to draw general conclusions from a period of intense and continuous crisis like 1937–9. The British Foreign Office was still a very powerful institution at home and abroad, and the Secretary of State at any time was regarded as one of the most powerful members of the Cabinet, ranking alongside (if not slightly above) the Home Secretary and the Chancellor of the Exchequer (Chapter 2). Nevertheless, the extent to which Chamberlain succeeded in imposing his personal policy on the Foreign Office was an ominous precedent for the politics of a country which, having failed to prevent a Second World War, seemed certain to face plenty of serious problems in future, whatever the outcome of the new conflict.

The limping lion, 1945–55

Introduction: a tale of two narratives

Britain's involvement in the Second World War, which its political leaders had tried so hard to avert, gave rise to two sharply contrasting narratives. The first presented the successful struggle against evil dictators as a new and uniquely glorious instalment of a continuous story, depicting Britain as a great power which was also essentially a peace-loving nation whose considerable weight had always been cast on the side of justice, regardless of the odds and the material cost. The second – whether or not it included an exalted view of Britain's previous foreign policy role – argued that on this occasion the material cost had been unsustainable for a nation with realistic prospects of being regarded as a great power in future. Underlying these sharply contrasting perspectives were two different analyses of a nation's strength. On the first view, this is chiefly a reflection of spiritual attributes which can only be appreciated when sorely tested; for specially favoured nations, adversity cannot quench this spirit but rather confirms and even augments it. On the second interpretation, a nation's reputation for choosing the right course rather than the expedient one, and the qualities of its citizens, are certainly relevant considerations; but they can never compensate for a paucity of more tangible resources. From this vantage point, while Britain might have gained considerable moral credit from its isolated defiance of Nazi Germany and its allies, the inescapable fact was that the conflict had accelerated an economic decline which had been apparent to acute observers since the late nineteenth century, cruelly exposing its pretensions to great-power status.

Winston Churchill was the laureate of the first narrative. His evocation of British spirit came naturally to a politician whose personality exemplified (and even exceeded) this ideal. In a more cynical age it is possible to question whether his magnificent oratory made much difference to those who were actually fighting. Publicly, at least, Churchill downplayed his contribution, saying as he approached retirement in November 1954 that:

> I have never accepted what many people have kindly said, namely that I inspired the nation. It was the nation and the race dwelling around the globe that had the lion heart. I had the luck to be called upon to give the roar.
> (quoted in Gilbert, 1988, 1075)

It is, though, instructive that Churchill's best-remembered leonine effusions took place in the first half of the war, encompassing the near-calamity of Dunkirk, the Battle of Britain and the fall of France. After Britain's first significant victory, in the battle of El Alamein (October–November 1942), Churchill hailed an event which was not the end, or even the beginning of the end, but perhaps the end of the beginning of the war. In this speech, delivered in front of an adoring audience at London's Mansion House, he went on to proclaim that:

> We have not entered this war for profit or expansion. Let, me, however, make this clear: we mean to hold our own. I have not become the King's First Minister in order to preside over the liquidation of the British Empire.

Churchill was right in stressing that El Alamein was not even the beginning of the end of the war; but it was certainly the beginning of the end of his great wartime oratory. Churchill's 'roars' in the period between November 1942 and the unconditional German surrender of May 1945 are far less celebrated today; whether or not they were necessary for national survival when things were going badly, his phrases, however vivid, found a less ecstatic reception after the tide of war had turned. Churchill, in short, was a great leader in adversity; his attractions were less obvious when people began to think about a return to 'normality'. Once the war was over, Churchill's 'luck' ran out; he turned the 'lion's roar' against the Labour Party in the 1945 general election campaign, but his attempt to associate his former coalition colleagues with the Nazi Gestapo in the public mind was a predictable failure.

Labour in office

In theory, Labour's landslide victory of 1945 brought to office a party whose vision of Britain's destiny could hardly have been more different from Churchill's. In practice, though, despite all the changes which were enforced by the circumstances of the immediate post-war period, there was a remarkable degree of continuity. This elite foreign policy 'consensus' can best be described as an attempt to reconcile the competing narratives outlined above: Britain had indeed suffered serious damage during its heroic fight against the dictators, but it would soon recover thanks to the dauntless spirit of its citizens. In a debate of May 1947 Labour's Foreign Secretary Ernest Bevin gave perfect expression to this new consensus approach shared by front-bench politicians on both sides of the House, when he declared that:

> His Majesty's Government do not accept the view . . . that we have ceased to be a Great Power, or the contention that we have ceased to play that role. We regard ourselves as one of the Powers most vital to the peace of the world and we still have our historic part to play. The very fact that we have fought so hard for liberty, and paid such a price, warrants our retaining such a position; and indeed it places a duty upon us to continue to retain it. I am not aware of any suggestion, seriously advanced, that by a sudden stroke of fate, as it were, we have overnight ceased to be a Great Power.
>
> (*Hansard, House of Commons Debates*, 16 May 1947, Vol. 437, col. 1965)

Timeline of domestic political developments

1945 Landslide Labour victory in general election; Clement Attlee becomes Prime Minister
1949 Enforced devaluation of sterling from $4.03 to $2.80 (30 per cent)
1950 General election: Labour holds on, with overall majority of just five
1951 General election: Conservatives under Churchill win an overall majority of 16 (though Labour won more votes)

For those who doubted Bevin's optimistic 'spin' on Britain's post-war situation, the giveaway phrase here would have been 'sudden stroke of fate'. The 'alternative' narrative suggested that, far from ceasing to be a great power 'overnight', in 1945, the country had been slipping against its international rivals for decades, since before the First World War. In presenting the upbeat narrative so starkly, Bevin was inviting those who questioned it to advance their own argument in full or to keep quiet. In the circumstances of 1947, so soon after a struggle which had cost their country so much, it is understandable that the overwhelming majority of potential critics chose to remain silent. After all, such an analysis ran the risk of looking unpatriotic and even defeatist, and it was unwise to discount the possibility that a genuine 'sudden stroke of fate' might turn up to make Bevin's optimistic view seem well founded.

The economic cost

Despite the political rhetoric, however, the reality was that while the First World War marked a serious setback to a country which was already beginning to lag behind its major competitors, the second global conflict brought Britain to the verge of bankruptcy. In order to maintain the struggle it had liquidated more than half of its overseas assets. Despite this sacrifice, it was left with debts of around £3 billion; its creditors included not just countries like Canada and South Africa, which had been self-governing for many years, but imperial possessions such as India. In August 1945, abruptly and without consultation, the US ended the 'lend-lease' agreement which had been crucial in maintaining Britain's military contribution to the war in Europe.

In the following year a loan agreement was negotiated between Britain, the US and Canada. The interest on repayments (2 per cent) was reasonably generous – though not excessively altruistic, since Britain's understandable focus on war production since 1939 had left its established overseas markets exposed to North American penetration, so that to an extent it was bailed out by the profits which it had been forced to forego. More controversially, the terms of the loan also stipulated that sterling should be freely convertible into dollars within a year. When convertibility duly occurred, in July 1947, international holders of sterling were quick to take advantage; the ensuing dash to convert pounds into dollars forced the British government to suspend convertibility within a few weeks. In 1949, after considerable resistance, the government bowed to the inevitable and the pound was devalued against the dollar, from $4.03 to $2.80. While politicians who accepted the Churchillian narrative saw this decision as a massive blow to national prestige, the drastic devaluation began to take the pressure off an economy which had been switched from war production to an 'export or die' basis in order to preserve the value of sterling. The wartime system which subjected domestic consumption to rationing was actually tightened for some items after the war and only came to an end in 1954.

To some critics – notably, Correlli Barnett – Britain's post-war plight was accentuated by a failure to equip the country for future economic challenges. This verdict is ironic, given that the 1945 election manifesto of the victorious Labour Party was entitled *Let Us Face the Future*. The manifesto did foreshadow a much more dynamic and interventionist economic role for the state; and, of course, Labour fulfilled its promise to take 'the commanding heights' of the economy into public ownership. However, as if to signal the limits of its interventionist ambitions – or, more likely, to underline the scarcity of resources – in office after 1945 the Labour Party seemed to assume that the remaining private sector of the economy would revive of its own accord, rather than stepping in with the kind of support and direction which proved so successful in other Western European countries, like France and West Germany. Before the war even the government of free-market America had devoted significant sums to research and development; Britain's corresponding effort had been puny in comparison, and this remained the case after the war (Barnett, 1986, 266–7).

Case Study 4.1 Projecting Britain

In 1851 the Great Exhibition held in London had been (among other things) a lavish demonstration of Britain's industrial prowess. To mark the centenary, a Festival of Britain was held, showcasing British achievements, particularly in architecture, design and the arts. Although the main site was on the South Bank of the River Thames, events were held in numerous British cities. The Festival was thus an attempt to reaffirm the wartime feeling of national unity as well as to show the world that Britain was a forward-looking nation which was still capable of creativity.

Winston Churchill rather sourly criticised the event as a festival of 'socialism', although (like so many developments under the 1945–51 Labour governments) the idea had originated when Churchill's own wartime coalition was in office. Churchill had fewer reservations about another opportunity to project a favourable image of Britain – the coronation of Elizabeth II, on 2 June 1953. Typically, Churchill was against broadcasting the event live on television, but his Head of State overruled him (and the Archbishop of Canterbury, who disliked the idea that the ceremony would be watched in pubs). If the objectors had prevailed, an estimated 277 million people across the world would have been deprived of a spectacle which easily eclipsed the Festival of Britain as a means of conveying a positive image. In particular, although the Queen was unable to emulate Victoria as Empress of India, she seemed more than happy with her role as Head of the Commonwealth. Britain's aptitude for ceremonial pomp, which had once been just one facet of its great-power status, was beginning to be regarded as a tolerable substitute for it. Richard Dimbleby, for example, who provided the solemn television commentary, opined that overseas visitors 'were envious of everything they saw, and none more so than the Americans – a race of such vitality but so lacking in tradition'. From this condescending perspective, it was convenient that the coronation was held as Britain's costly contribution to the Korean War – undertaken to appease the 'envious' Americans – was coming to an end (Hennessy, 2006, 242–3, 271, 245).

Churchill's concentric circles

At the 1948 Conservative Party conference Churchill (then Leader of the Opposition) laid out his vision of Britain's future role as a power which enjoyed a unique place 'at the very point of junction' between three 'co-existent' circles – the Commonwealth and Empire, the English-speaking world and 'United Europe'. According to Churchill, if the three circles were linked together 'there is no force or combination which could overthrow them or even challenge them'. Britain was ideally placed to facilitate the crucial coupling:

> If we rise to the occasion in the years that are to come it may be found that once again we hold the key to opening a safe and happy future to humanity, and will gain for ourselves gratitude and fame.
> (Churchill, 1950, 417–18)

Churchill's circles have rightly attracted much comment in discussions of Britain's post-war foreign policy, and, for the purposes of this chapter, they provide a convenient basis for analysis. However, at the outset it is worth considering Churchill's implicit evaluation of Britain's situation in 1948. For someone who had been accounted a Realist in his approach to international politics before the Second World War, it was striking that Churchill should allude (even in a speech to a partisan audience) to the prospect of 'a safe and happy future' for the human race. As we have seen (Chapter 1), it is far more characteristic of Realists to invoke a nation's independent strength as the best guarantor of 'safety'. While membership of the three circles could indeed make Britain a powerful international actor, on Churchill's presentation this would derive from various combinations, rather than Britain's independent strength. Indeed, if Britain's global influence were to rest on its ability to act as a facilitator or catalyst rather than as a state capable of independent initiative – what would later be called soft power – in theory it could gain 'gratitude and fame' even if it decided to dispense with its own armed forces. In any event, although 'gratitude and fame' were very meaningful to Churchill himself, he could not be sure that they would be regarded by his fellow Britons as sufficiently tangible rewards in future.

The Empire: a saga of selective retreat

In the brief period between 1945 – Churchill's year of international triumph and domestic disaster – and his 1948 speech there already had been several crucial developments which affected Britain's position in the first two circles. In those years Britain also faced challenges which related to wider commitments. While Britain had been awarded League of Nations 'mandates' after the First World

War, Churchill accepted a more informal allocation of 'spheres of influence' in a meeting with Stalin in October 1944. As a result, the British took on the primary responsibility for Greece, whose occupation by Germany and its allies between 1941 and 1944 had ended in a power vacuum which communist insurgents were eager to fill. The Soviet Union, however, held aloof from the struggle, and the revolt was suppressed. In a 1946 election boycotted by the communists, right-wing parties won a comfortable overall majority, and a subsequent referendum approved the return of the exiled pro-British King. However, the British could no longer afford their military presence in Greece or the assistance they were giving to Turkey. The burden in both cases was swiftly assumed by the US.

Humiliating as it was for a nation which had recently acted as one of the 'Big Three' powers, helping to oversee the settlement of a second global conflict, the withdrawal from Greece was soon overshadowed by a setback with even more disturbing implications. In Palestine, Britain reaped the indigestible crops which Balfour had cultivated through his ill-advised promise of a Middle Eastern homeland for the Jewish people. As we have seen, Balfour's Declaration (1917) was promulgated despite the near certainty of conflict between incoming Jewish settlers and Arabs who were living in Palestine. By 1945 it looked as if Palestine might become the source of serious contention between Britain and another of the 'Big Three', the US. Britain had sponsored the formation in 1945 of the Arab League, whose members were naturally hostile to the idea of a Jewish homeland. The US, by contrast, had no official role in Palestine, and (despite its obvious material interests in the Middle East) it lacked Britain's reasons for sensitivity to Arab opinion. As a result, US politicians were far more susceptible to the arguments of Zionist lobbyists who sought greatly accelerated Jewish migration to the area. In Palestine itself Jewish militants began a campaign of terror in the hope of driving out the British. In February 1947, as non-essential British personnel were being evacuated from Palestine, the Labour government decided to refer the issue to the newly formed UN. At the UN both the Americans and the Soviet Union supported a plan to partition Palestine, despite British warnings that it would not ask its troops to impose this. Subsequently, Britain announced that its mandate would be terminated in May 1948. The withdrawal was followed, predictably, by a sanguinary conflict between the Jews and a coalition of Arab nations. For the British, the only surprising thing was the outcome – a resounding defeat for the Arab forces, leading to the establishment of the state of Israel and the displacement of hundreds of thousands of Palestinian Arabs. During the conflict several British planes on reconnaissance missions were shot down by the Zionists.

These unmistakable signs that Britain was intent on cutting its global responsibilities to suit its reduced resources were matched by developments within the Empire. In February 1947 – when the government passed the problem of Palestine to the UN – a new Viceroy of India was appointed. The plan was that Lord Louis Mountbatten would preside over an orderly handover of power, scheduled for June 1948. However, during the war the Indian desire for self-government had been augmented to a point where the British position could not be sustained without savage repression. In addition, Mountbatten quickly decided that the preferred solution, of an independent India which retained its unity in a federal structure, was unworkable. Partition along religious lines, he deemed, was inevitable; furthermore, amid growing inter-communal violence, the timetable for British withdrawal would have to be accelerated, to August 1947.

Up to a million people died and more than 14 million were displaced in the genocidal butchery which attended the birth of independent India and Pakistan. Yet from the response of the British press (and, by all accounts, of most members of the public), this abrupt excision of 'The Jewel in the Crown' was something which their country had always been hoping to arrange at an early opportunity. Had India been prised from Britain's grasp by any hostile power, the very same politicians would have lined up to swear unyielding resistance to India's removal from British rule. As it was, the veneer of voluntarism allowed them to indulge in an orgy of self-congratulation when the Indian Independence Bill was debated in the summer of 1947. The loss of a single portion of the British Empire was transformed into a gain of two new members of the British Commonwealth. Thanks to Britain's wise guidance, India and Pakistan knew all about the benefits of freedom, democracy and justice; and if they did not take advantage of these lessons, it would be their own fault. This view had been sketched out by Stanley Baldwin as he approached retirement in 1937, when (in defiance of the facts) he claimed that the British Empire could provide 'spiritual leadership' in a benighted world because it was animated by democratic ideals and held together by a belief in 'the free development of the individual' (Baldwin, 1937, 120, 160, 164). It was given eloquent expression in the House of Lords by Lord Templewood, who as Secretary of State for India from 1931 to 1935 had overseen the introduction of limited self-government to India:

> The two new Governments [of India and Pakistan are] pioneers of a great experiment in Asia. They are pioneers also of a great experiment in the British Commonwealth of free peoples. We, to-day, an ancient and historic people, hand to them well-tried political principles – freedom of speech, toleration of minorities, government by discussion. And, greater even than those political principles and institutions, the two invaluable gifts of peace and justice. Let them take those two treasures which we have ensured over more than a century. Let them maintain them in their own country, and let them help to spread them over the whole world. It is peace and justice that the world chiefly needs to-day. Let the two new Governments of India take their share in spreading the fruits of these gifts from one end of the world to the other.
>
> (*Hansard, House of Lords Debates*,
> 16 July 1947, Vol. 150, col. 825)

Independence for Ceylon (later Sri Lanka) came in February 1948, just a few weeks after the same status was awarded to Burma (which declined membership of the Commonwealth). In Malaya, by contrast, the British chose to resist nationalist forces, partly because these were ostensibly communist in inspiration but also because the islands were of considerable strategic value and produced vital dollar-earning exports (notably, rubber). The High Commissioner, Gerald Templar, spoke of the need to base a successful campaign on winning 'hearts and minds'. In practice, though, the British strategy was more about lives and limbs, with forced resettlement programmes and the visitation of 'collective punishment' on villages which were suspected of collaborating with insurgents (Curtis, 2003, 340–2). Singapore, which was not included within the Malayan Federation, was another important source of raw materials; in addition, the fall of Singapore to the Japanese in February 1942 (a month after Malaya had suffered the same fate) had been a crushing blow to British prestige, so the preferred option in this case was a period of restored rule leading gradually to self-government and Commonwealth membership (1958).

Britain's old imperialist logic would have suggested that a retreat from the Far East rendered its presence in the Middle East redundant, allowing it to cut its losses in the area once it had abandoned its mandate in Palestine. However, vast oil reserves had made the Middle East crucially important in itself. In particular, while the Suez Canal had once been prized because it furnished a relatively speedy 'Passage to India', by 1950 Britain's partial ownership of the canal had become arguably the country's most valuable overseas asset. Certainly, British politicians could not contemplate the prospect of the canal falling under the control of a hostile power, which would have the potential to choke off its oil supplies. Unfortunately, there was every chance that Egypt itself would become a hostile power of considerable significance, not least because of resentment against British troops stationed in the canal zone in accordance with a treaty which had been signed (in very different circumstances) back in 1936, but also because Egypt had ambitions to take on a leadership role in the Middle East. In October 1954 Britain (with Churchill restored as Prime Minister) struck a deal under which it agreed to withdraw from the canal base within 20 months; in return, among other things, Egypt promised to uphold the principle of free navigation through the canal itself. Dissident Conservatives alarmed by the implications of Britain's weak negotiating position had already formed a small but determined 'Suez Group' to resist future concessions to Arab nationalism.

In North Africa Britain had taken over the administration of former Italian possessions – notably, Libya. However, this was never intended to be more than a temporary measure, and although Britain encouraged the formation of a separate emirate in the eastern coastal region of Cyrenaica, this was absorbed back into Libya when the latter became an independent kingdom in 1951. Britain's Empire in other parts of Africa remained substantially intact in the decade after the war, but there were abundant signs of impending change. The general rule was for the countries with the fewest European settlers to progress fastest on the road to self-government. The Gold Coast, which became independent Ghana in 1957, had a black prime minister (in all but name) as early as 1951. In 1954 neighbouring Nigeria was given a new, decentralised constitution, which the British presented as a kind of trial run for full self-governing status (Brendon, 2008, 535).

By contrast, the adoption of democratic procedures seemed implausible (even outrageous) in countries where self-government would take power out of the hands of a substantial British-born minority. Even if one accepts the 'official' British view that it had been preparing Asians to 'take up the white man's burden' for many years prior to independence, in its Empire in Africa it is indisputable that the 'preparation' had been of brief duration or non-existent. For many future leaders of independence movements, the British had only offered 'training' for future responsible roles in the form of frequent prison sentences, like those bestowed on Gandhi and Nehru in India. Discrimination on racial grounds was particularly flagrant in Kenya, where the situation bore more than a passing resemblance to that of South Africa after 1948, when that country adopted a system of apartheid, which translated the European assumption of racial superiority into law. It was unlikely that apartheid offended the sensibility of the average Briton in the late 1940s – or, indeed, for many decades afterwards – but if the moral arguments on behalf of a continuing connection between Britain and its former colonies were to withstand even cursory scrutiny, it was difficult to see how the Commonwealth could accommodate any country which practised apartheid. In Kenya the emergence of a ferocious 'liberation' movement known as Mau Mau was met by an equally brutal response from the British, so that 'by the mid-1950s it was an open secret that Kenya had become a police state that dispensed racist terror' (Brendon, 2008, 560). In the post-war climate repression of this kind could not continue indefinitely; and although the Mau Mau uprising was eventually quelled, even by 1955 it was only a matter of time before Kenya was given its independence.

While South Africa remained a Commonwealth member (which it did until 1961), the poisonous effects of its apartheid system continued to hamper British attempts to salvage something lasting and positive from its imperialist project on 'the Dark Continent'. Thus in 1953 the British established a Central African Federation, which yoked Nyasaland (now Malawi) with Northern and Southern Rhodesia (now Zambia and Zimbabwe respectively). Optimists saw this as a potential test bed for racial cooperation, in an area with considerable potential for economic development. Yet Southern Rhodesia, which was always likely to be the dominant partner within the Federation, was dominated by a minuscule European minority, including some who were attracted rather than repulsed by the South African system. The Federation might have had a future of sorts had it been instituted between the wars; but in the new atmosphere after 1945 the only surprise was that it took a few years to die.

While the Central African Federation was probably the best example of an imperial development which might have worked if British imperialists had been sufficiently enlightened at the most propitious time, in hindsight other initiatives between 1945 and 1955 create the irresistible impression of desperate attempts to derive economic benefits from Africa before the British agreed to an inevitable and enforced departure. In 1946, for example, the Labour government decided to back a scheme to cultivate groundnuts, as a source of vegetable oil, in Tanganyika – part of what had formerly been German East Africa and was later to become independent Tanzania. Despite heavy expenditure, the scheme suffered numerous foreseeable setbacks and was abandoned in 1951, having no positive results to set against the considerable environmental damage it had caused.

Although Britain's disengagement from its Empire gathered pace after 1955, the impetus was already present by that year, so this is an appropriate place to evaluate its effect on domestic opinion. As in any disorientating development, there was a natural desire among Britain's leaders to furnish a rationale which bolstered their own self-image, as well as promising to mollify the misgivings of voters who might wonder why their country had divested itself of overseas possessions so rapidly after what Churchill had acclaimed as 'its finest hour'. Since the Second World War had demanded so much sacrifice from so many, voters proved receptive to the idea of *national* self-denial – that if Britain was taking measures which flatly contradicted what had previously been proclaimed as its manifest destiny, this was attributable to a punctilious sense of duty, in keeping with the tenor of Bevin's speech quoted above.

The success of this moral rationalisation of Britain's imperial retreat effectively neutered the arguments of those (like the Conservative 'Suez Group') who protested either that it was all happening too quickly, or that it should not have happened at all. In its 1955 manifesto the Conservative Party promised that '[w]e shall work to raise living standards and to guide Colonial peoples along the road to self-government within the framework of the Commonwealth and Empire'. Labour's document devoted just two paragraphs to the subject, inviting voters to applaud the role played by the 1945–51 governments in working 'to transform the British Empire into a Commonwealth of free and equal peoples'. Former Prime Minister Clement Attlee was lauded as 'the man who freed India', as if he had liberated that country, without significant bloodshed, from the grasp of some merciless (and unnamed) tyranny. Labour was clearly hoping for some electoral benefit from its proud record, and its stress on racial equality and the need for further Commonwealth development suggested that it did indeed recognise a continuing obligation which the Conservatives were less keen to advertise. Nevertheless, the overall impression is that the two main parties regarded this as an issue on which consensus had been established to a degree which removed it from electoral contention. They were not far apart in their attitudes towards the Cold War, but they obviously regarded that subject as a much more promising source of electoral dividends.

Britain and the Cold War

At Westminster College in Fulton, Missouri, on 5 March 1946 former Prime Minister Winston Churchill delivered a speech which is often cited as the opening salvo of a conflict which was to last more than 40 years – the Cold War. He was introduced to his audience by Harry Truman, the US President, who had been happy to accompany him on the journey to Missouri. Truman and his officials had approved the text of the speech, including a phrase which Churchill had tried out before – 'From Stettin in the Baltic to Trieste in the Adriatic, an iron curtain has descended across the continent'.

Connoisseurs of political rhetoric who concentrate on the immortal 'iron curtain' phrase to the exclusion of the rest of the speech will overlook a riotous display of verbal dexterity. For one thing, Churchill was hoping to beguile his US audience into a much more positive view of British imperialism. Thus he referred to 'the liberties enjoyed by individual citizens throughout the British Empire', as if all citizens under British rule enjoyed equal rights. Of course, in terms of racial equality, 'The Land of the Free' had very little to boast about either, as Churchill knew very well, so he could feel safe from criticism on that score. He also included a tribute to the Soviet contribution to victory in the Second World War, accepting (in true Realist style) that Stalin had good reason to seek a buffer zone against Germany on the western frontiers of the USSR. Yet he also referred to the 'expansive and proselytising tendencies' of the USSR and claimed that although the Soviets did not seek a renewal of conflict, they wanted 'the fruits of war and the indefinite expansion of their power and doctrines'. There could be a peaceful settlement of emerging differences, but Britain and its allies must avoid appeasement at all costs and could only hope for a satisfactory deal if they negotiated from a position of strength.

It was no surprise that Stalin reacted strongly against the speech. For his part, Truman instantly regretted his apparent endorsement of Churchill's uncompromising rhetoric, which was denounced by senior Democrat Senators as well as respected press commentators in the US. In Britain, however, Attlee and Bevin refused to second the criticisms of left-wing Labour backbenchers, and their muted response betrayed their substantial agreement with Churchill's sentiments.

As an outspoken opponent of 'Bolshevism' since its first manifestations, Churchill could be accused of trying to turn a dispute between states into an ideological crusade. However, he had dealt with Stalin quite amicably during the war – not least in 1944, when he and the Soviet leader rapidly reached agreement over spheres of influence. In fact, while Churchill's position was partly derived from his distaste for Communism, it chiefly reflected the Realist fear of Russia which had been prevalent among British policy makers long before his birth. The best explanation of his view can be found in his 1947 account of what he claimed had been a dream. The somnolent Churchill was visited by his late father, Lord Randolph, who posed a series of pertinent questions. When asked if Russia was still dangerous, Churchill replied that 'we are all very worried about her'. Lord Randolph followed up by inquiring whether there was still a tsar, and Churchill said that there was, 'but he is not a Romanoff. It's another family. He is much more powerful, and much more despotic' (Gilbert, 1988, 371).

Attlee and Bevin had good reason to welcome Churchill's 'iron curtain' intervention, since their main objective was to coax the US into a lasting commitment to Western European security without openly contradicting their claim in the 1945 general election campaign that a left-wing British government would be better placed than the Conservatives to reach an accommodation with the Soviet Union. In fact, as believers in the non-violent, Parliamentary road to what they called 'socialism', in 1946 Attlee and Bevin were actually more concerned than Churchill about Soviet proselytisation, which might inspire revolutionary thoughts among the British working classes. By mentioning, without overstressing, his own ideological opposition to the Stalinist brand of communism, Churchill had injected into the American consciousness the feeling that freedom was under threat, while allowing Attlee and Bevin to distance themselves from any negative domestic fallout from the Fulton speech.

Apart from the danger of Soviet-inspired ideological infiltration of their own party, the Labour government also had good evidence by 1946 that Stalin had embraced the strategic ambitions of his tsarist predecessors. As Churchill noted in the Fulton speech, both Turkey and Iran were targets for Soviet intervention; the old Russian ambition to make waves in the Mediterranean seemed to have been reactivated; India might fall under direct Soviet influence; and, according to some Foreign Office alarmists, the collapse of Britain's position in the Middle East might open the road for Stalinist expansion in Africa. As Sellar and Yeatman might have put it, Soviet Russia was pointing in more than one 'wrong direction': it still threatened to expand its influence eastwards but was now a potential threat to Western Europe. While the fate of Britain's African empire might previously have seemed a matter of indifference to US policy makers, by an exquisite coincidence Churchill's Fulton speech – which could easily be read as a warning to American anti-imperialists that the British Empire could be replaced by something even less benign – was delivered less than a fortnight after the despatch of a telegram written by the American diplomat George Kennan. This document argued that the Soviets would be eager to exploit the 'vacuum' left when European states abandoned colonial possessions which were populated by 'backward or dependent peoples' (Kennan, 1946).

If in March 1946 US opinion was still divided over the best attitude to take towards the Soviet Union, in the next few months the situation began to change. Not unexpectedly, Germany was the focus of contention. After that country's capitulation it had been divided into three zones of occupation, for the US, USSR and Britain (which later created a fourth area for France from within its own zone). The Soviets, seeking reparations for the economic devastation wrought by the Third Reich, requested payments drawn from the British and American zones, which included Germany's most productive industrial areas. In May 1946 the US halted reparations payments from its zone, and in January 1947 the British and American zones were merged. The transatlantic allies agreed on the need to establish a reunified, Western-oriented Germany; the Soviets, for understandable reasons, balked at this prospect and wanted to ensure that the restored Germany would be a friendly power. These incompatible visions of Germany's future made for sterile discussions at the Council of Foreign Ministers, which had been established to coordinate the occupation of Germany. When the Council's meeting in late 1947 ended without agreement, the Western powers effectively accepted the partition of Germany and set about making their respective zones into a federal state, though it was not until 1949 that the separate states of West and East Germany officially came into existence.

In the meantime other key features of the Cold War landscape were becoming discernible. In March 1947, prompted mainly by Britain's inability to sustain the struggle against communism in Greece, President Truman felt able to supersede his ambiguous response to Churchill's Fulton speech and pledged his support for 'free peoples who are resisting attempted subjugation by armed minorities and by outside pressures'. It was impossible to mistake the implied source of these 'outside pressures'. Taken literally, the Truman Doctrine meant that the old, isolationist American outlook had been exchanged for an interventionist approach framed around ideological conflict with the Soviet Union. However, the doctrine was clearly based on a presumption that, in countries which were not yet under Communist control, the majority of the population consisted of freedom lovers who would welcome 'outside pressure' – so long as it emanated from America. Since Western Europe (including Britain itself) was struggling to recover economically from the devastation of war, and communist parties were attracting considerable support in countries like Italy and France, something tangible was needed to reinforce the ideological case for freedom.

Thus, on 5 June 1947, the US Secretary of State George Marshall announced that if European countries could collaborate on a plan for economic reconstruction, the American government would provide the necessary financial support. Marshall's speech was a rare and brilliant manifestation of enlightened self-interest. Whether or not it was explicitly designed to put Stalin on the spot and dare him to draw a dividing line between 'free peoples' and countries which were fated to remain, for the indefinite future, behind an Iron Curtain of totalitarianism, it certainly had that effect. In July 1947 a meeting was held in Paris to which all major European states (with the exception of Franco's Spain) were invited to send representatives. As expected, the Soviet Union was unable to accept the terms on which the financial aid had been offered and refused to attend; its East European 'satellite states', like Poland, Czechoslovakia and Hungary, followed suit.

With the economic division of Europe now firmly established, it only remained to provide a military dimension. In March 1947 Britain had signed the Treaty of Dunkirk with France, guaranteeing the latter against attack from a resurgent Germany. Whatever the French might have thought – and, for understandable reasons, they continued to oppose a reunified Germany, whether allied to the West or the East – from the British point of view the agreement was also valuable as a potential stepping stone towards the organised defence of Western Europe against the Soviet Union. The next step was the agreement of the Brussels Defence Pact of March 1948, which brought Belgium, the Netherlands and Luxembourg into the existing arrangement between Britain and France. In addition, Britain agreed to station troops in Germany for 50 years. This is not to say that British policy makers really feared that the Red Army was an unstoppable instrument which could be wielded against Western Europe at short notice; rather, it was an admission that Britain was now too weak to act alone if the delicate post-war arrangement with the USSR should break down and lead to hostilities. Just a few days earlier a Soviet-inspired coup in Czechoslovakia helped to persuade the Americans of the need for a transatlantic military alliance.

Thanks to the infamous Munich agreement of 1938, aggression against Czechoslovakia was bound to be regarded as a key test of Western resolve. Although the country had been liberated from the Nazis by the Red Army and was thus clearly going to be under Soviet influence, the 1948 coup provided adequate proof to any doubters that Stalin was only prepared to tolerate democratic procedures when they resulted in victories for his favoured parties. However, probably an equally significant factor in Washington's calculations was a deterioration in relations with the Soviet Union in respect of Germany. In the battle for future control of the country, Stalin's trump card was the fact that Berlin (which like Germany as a whole had been divided into four sectors) was located about 100 miles inside the Soviet zone. In January 1948 the Soviets started to hamper the access of its erstwhile allies to Berlin, starting with unnecessary and intrusive 'security checks', followed in April 1948 by more blatant provocations which threatened to cut off the Western zones of Berlin from the rest of non-Communist Germany. In response the Americans and the British began to supply West Berlin by air. In June they decided to proceed with the issue of a new currency, the Deutschmark, in all the areas of Germany which were free from Soviet control. The Soviets replied by introducing a rival Ostmark in their own areas and by extending the existing restrictions on access to West Berlin, so that the new situation was rightly characterised as a blockade.

It was the first occasion on which the Cold War very nearly resulted in open conflict between the Western powers and the Soviet Union. The airlift was a considerable gamble, given the vast superiority of Soviet forces in the Berlin area. The avoidance of open hostilities proved that neither side was ready to risk the outbreak of all-out war, which might easily have involved the use of nuclear weapons, of which the US enjoyed a monopoly. By the time that the Soviets conducted a successful test of their own atomic capacity (August 1949) they had accepted that, as things stood, they would never be able to control a united Germany, and that half of that country was much preferable to none. The Soviet blockade was lifted in May 1949. By that time more than a million and a half tons of supplies had been delivered, in 200,000 flights (Northedge, 1974, 89). Despite the serious economic problems which afflicted Britain in the immediate post-war years, it made a significant contribution to the airlift in terms of the tonnage of delivered supplies; 39 British airmen lost their lives during the operation, compared to 31 Americans.

The Berlin blockade undoubtedly helped to clear the remaining obstacles to a transatlantic military pact. In June 1948 the almost unanimous passage of the Vandenberg Resolution showed that Congressional fear of Soviet intentions had finally surpassed US aversion to European entanglements. On 6 July formal negotiations for a defensive treaty against the USSR got underway in Washington, involving the US and Canada as well as the Brussels partners. In the same month long-range US bombers, capable of carrying nuclear weapons as far as Moscow, were stationed in East Anglia. After his unexpected re-election in November 1948 President Truman announced that he would soon be offering a transatlantic treaty for Congressional approval. However, detailed diplomatic negotiations over the final text were still necessary. It was not until 4 April 1949 that the North Atlantic Treaty was signed in Washington, by twelve countries (Denmark, Iceland, Italy, Norway and Portugal were added to the European signatories).

The 14 articles of the North Atlantic Treaty represented a revolution in foreign and defence policy, for Britain as well as the US. The final wording stopped short of an automatic *military* response if any signatory was attacked, but still contained an obligation to offer assistance of some kind in such circumstances. The sense of obligation was sure to be strengthened by the Council established by the treaty; although there was no stipulation that this body should assemble on a regular basis, it should 'be so organised as to be able to meet promptly at any time', implying frequent gatherings. The Council was also empowered to establish 'subsidiary bodies', which could be expected to convene for regular discussions. As such, the North Atlantic Treaty was different from the strictly intergovernmental deals which Britain had previously preferred to strike (when it felt constrained to reach agreements of any kind). Entailing lasting commitments of some kind, and creating decision-making institutions of indefinite duration, it sat on the indistinct boundary – between the intergovernmental and the supranational – which many politicians and other interested observers tend to regard as crucial in terms of the preservation of 'national sovereignty'. From the British perspective, it seems fair to conclude that the traditional definition of 'sovereignty', implying complete freedom of action in foreign relations, was perceived as less important in 1948–9 than the apparent requirements of national *survival*. The overriding priority at the time was the negotiation of a deal which would commit the US to the defence of Western Europe – and in this respect the North Atlantic Treaty certainly fulfilled the hopes of the British government. In the short term the establishment of NATO was probably a factor in the Soviet decision to end its blockade of Berlin, ending the aerial relief operation which had been a considerable drain on Britain's financial resources.

The 'special relationship'

The signature of the North Atlantic Treaty is often presented as a triumph for British diplomacy, casting Labour's Foreign Secretary Ernest Bevin as the hero of the hour. One historian has written that:

> The period between Marshall's Harvard Speech on 5 June 1947 and the coming into being of NATO in April 1949 is a period of sustained creativity such as few, if any, British Foreign Secretaries have produced since the time of the Elder Pitt.
>
> (Morgan, 1984, 275)

This verdict overlooks the inadvertent contribution of Josef Stalin to the creation of NATO. Nevertheless, Bevin certainly possessed abundant negotiating skills and an opportunist instinct, which allowed him to take advantage of the circumstances that Stalin's policy created.

Above all, as we have seen, unlike his most illustrious predecessors as Foreign Secretary, Bevin was anxious to maintain Britain's reputation as a great power, while taking decisions which were not readily reconciled with that status. While others quickly understood that Britain might continue to claim to be a great power because of its close friendship with the US, Bevin persisted in a fruitless search for alternative global roles, on the optimistic view that Britain's relative decline was temporary, rather than a lasting phenomenon which had been apparent for half a century and still had some way to go. Thus, for him, NATO was essentially a transatlantic marriage of convenience, whereas someone like the half-American Churchill was bound to regard it as a permanent union of a quasi-spiritual kind. Both of these attitudes, however, were based on a neglect of inconvenient evidence. Churchill was unrealistic because although American priorities might coincide with those of Britain in some respects, there could never be a true unity of purpose between such different countries; Bevin's error was to suppose that a marriage of convenience with America might turn out to be more advantageous for the junior rather than the senior partner.

Certainly, by 1949 it was possible to perceive that the occasional interludes of generosity in the American treatment of Britain were at least partly inspired by self-interested considerations. The abrupt cancellation of lend-lease had been followed by the unsentimental conditions attached by the US and Canada to Britain's post-war loan. The McMahon Act of 1946 established procedures for the management of nuclear technology, ending US cooperation with Britain and Canada which had led to the development of America's atomic weapons. This could be seen as a prudent measure, since a Soviet defector had recently warned about the extent of nuclear espionage, and the British physicist Alan Nunn May was revealed as a Soviet informant. However, the act breached the terms of an agreement struck by Roosevelt and Churchill in 1944. As Peter Hennessy has plausibly argued, rather than the Soviet threat it was the McMahon Act – and Bevin's feeling that Foreign Secretaries would never be taken seriously by their American counterparts unless the country could pack a nuclear punch – which provided the main impetus for the development of a British bomb. Lack of US cooperation inevitably added to the financial outlay – £100 million – but in the Cabinet subcommittee Bevin insisted that 'we've got to have this thing over here, whatever it costs' (Hennessy, 1992, 268–9).

It would be misleading to claim that antipathy towards Britain was the primary motivation for these US decisions, but it was certainly a key contextual factor. While Churchill and others tried to persuade themselves and their fellow Britons that the 'special relationship' was a reality, it is tempting to argue that the only unusual thing about the relationship even at this early stage was the underlying existence of so much friction between politicians who spoke the same language and shared a large number of global objectives. While British ambivalence towards America emanated almost entirely from jealousy and cultural condescension, for their transatlantic 'cousins' the sticking point was obviously the Empire. The most poignant comment on Churchill's inexhaustible courtship of President Roosevelt is the note of a conversation with the latter's Secretary of State, Edward Stettinius, in February 1945. Having heard Roosevelt attacking the British for their imperialistic tendencies, Stettinius concluded that '[i]t is very apparent that he distrusts the British and dislikes them immensely' (quoted in Beloff, 1986, 252).

Significantly, Roosevelt's comments echoed recent criticism of Britain in the American press and were made in the aftermath of the Yalta conference, during which the British position within the 'Big Three' global powers had begun to seem anomalous (Orde, 1996, 156). During one of the Yalta sessions Churchill had evidently (and probably rightly) sensed that Roosevelt and Stalin were using their mutual dislike of the British Empire as a means to establish warmer personal relations: as in the familiar playground scenario, the two big bullies who felt the need to come to terms were cementing their friendship by picking on someone palpably weaker than themselves. Instinctively grasping what was going on, Churchill launched into a passionate denial of anyone's right to put Britain 'into the dock' because of its conduct of imperial matters and ask us 'to justify our right to live in a world we have tried to save' (quoted in Louis, 1977, 458–9). One can easily imagine the knowing glances that Roosevelt and Stalin must have exchanged during this tirade; it must have been difficult for Stalin to conceal his glee while witnessing such vivid symptoms of division between his two supposed allies. Unsurprisingly, it was at Yalta that Roosevelt accepted Soviet promises about the future of Poland, which very quickly proved to be false; but it fell to Churchill to defend this regrettable American-inspired deal in a subsequent House of Commons vote of confidence.

The vehemence of American anti-imperialism, which could be detected even in initiatives which seemed to promise full-hearted cooperation with Britain, helps to explain why elements within the Labour Party continued, even after the Berlin blockade and the advent of NATO, to hanker after the role of a 'third force' in global politics, allied neither to Washington nor Moscow. In January 1950 these dissidents were cheered by the British decision to recognise the Maoist People's Republic of China, rather than the nationalist regime led by Chiang Kai-Shek, as that country's official government. This implied that, notwithstanding NATO, Britain could still take decisions based on its perceived national interest, rather than trailing in America's wake; while Britain prioritised the survival of its Hong Kong colony over any ideological considerations, the US felt that it had to back Chiang, even though his anti-Communist forces had been compelled to take refuge on the island of Taiwan. Britain's pragmatic outlook led it so far as to dissent from the American view that Chiang's representative, rather than Mao's, should attend the UN. The message seemed clear – whatever British policy makers thought about communism as an ideology, they would only stir themselves to oppose its advance when it infiltrated territories for which they bore responsibility, or when it seemed to be giving new impetus to the Russian ambitions which had haunted the Foreign Office since before the Crimean War.

Korea

Superficially, Britain's posture towards China presents a jarring contrast to its unstinting support for the US response to the invasion of South Korea by the Communist North in June 1950. No essential British interests were at stake: the fate of Korea was certainly less relevant to British interests than Mao's victory in China had been. Perhaps, then, Britain had belatedly accepted the Truman

Doctrine and was now ready to oppose Communism wherever it threatened 'free peoples'? In reality, the same pragmatic impulses were at work, associated with, but not driven by, an aversion to communist ideology.

At the outset the Foreign Office view was that the Korean crisis offered a marvellous opportunity to demonstrate 'the United Kingdom's capacity to act as a world power with the support of the Commonwealth'. Sir Oliver Franks, Britain's Ambassador to the US, urged that Britain should send ground forces to Korea as well as the naval assets which had already been despatched. Franks told Attlee that this would provide a vivid demonstration of Britain's loyalty to the US; it would also serve British interests by boosting the prestige of the UN, which had passed resolutions in favour of armed action against North Korea thanks to a timely Soviet boycott of the UN (in protest against the failure to give a Security Council seat to Communist China) (Morgan, 1984, 422).

If British participation in the Korean War of 1950–3 showed that it was prepared to join the US in a systematic attempt to extirpate Communism, from the Whitehall perspective it was a pretty cynical crusade. This is not to say, however, that a fundamentally pragmatic outlook was proof against the kind of mistake which might have arisen from ideological fervour. For example, the British Chiefs of Staff initially advised against sending ground troops to Korea, but they changed their minds once they realised that their political masters wanted to make this gesture (or, in Tony Blair's later parlance, to 'pay the blood price'). More seriously, amid the narrow political calculations which inspired the Labour government to pledge complete allegiance to the US over Korea, the likely economic cost was underestimated, despite warnings from the Chancellor Sir Stafford Cripps (Bennett, 2013, 24–31). Under Cripps' successor, Hugh Gaitskell, planned defence expenditure of £3.4 billion for the four years between 1950 and 1954 had to be upgraded to £4.7 billion for 1951–4. As Kenneth Morgan has written, in Cabinet on 25 January 1951 Gaitskell 'spelt out the economic problems that the new rearmament programme would cause in such remorseless detail that he might almost have been an opponent of it' (Morgan, 1984, 433–4).

This was a pivotal episode in the post-war history of the Labour Party, since Gaitskell's determination to drive the increased defence expenditure through Cabinet resulted in the imposition of charges on certain items which had previously been provided freely by the National Health Service (NHS), leading to the resignations from the Cabinet of Aneurin Bevan, the architect of the NHS, and the future Prime Minister Harold Wilson. However, this controversy (and the Korean War as a whole) deserves closer attention than it has received from scholars of post-war British foreign policy in general. The first thing to strike any well-informed observer is that while Cabinet crises usually arise when a Chancellor tries to trim ministerial budgets, on this occasion Gaitskell enraged his critics because of a request for *additional* expenditure in a specific area. Second, Bevan's most substantial charge against Gaitskell – that the surge in

Case Study 4.2 Britain and the UN

Britain was, along with the US, the main architect of the UN, whose first meetings took place in London (January 1946) before transferring to New York. The initial impetus for the UN can be traced to a meeting between US President Roosevelt and Winston Churchill, resulting in a statement of principles known as the Atlantic Charter (August 1941). This document bore some kinship to Woodrow Wilson's Fourteen Points, not least because it pledged the signatories to 'respect the rights of all peoples to choose the form of government under which they live' – but Churchill was ready to accept abstract commitments like this so long as Roosevelt reciprocated with a more concrete commitment to the war effort.

For the British, the UN which took shape after negotiations between the US, the Soviet Union, Britain and China at Dumbarton Oaks, Washington, DC in Autumn 1944 was far preferable to the earlier League of Nations, because American participation was much more likely this time. Britain would also be a permanent member of the UN Security Council, along with the US, the Soviet Union, China and France. As such, it could veto resolutions passed by the UN Assembly, consisting of the representatives of other member states (initially, the overall membership was 51 states). This was helpful, because from the outset it was possible that such resolutions would be hostile to British interests, particularly in relation to its remaining imperial possessions. Britain's support for the UN also reflected the fact that its main mission of peacekeeping was based on a respect for state sovereignty – its operations were supposed to prevent conflict *between* states, rather than intervening *within* a state to uphold (or impose) its interpretation of human rights. Yet Britain had learned the obvious lesson of the inter-war era and ultimately trusted its security to regional pacts like NATO, rather than to a global organisation which owed so much to idealism.

defence expenditure would result in serious problems for Britain's balance of trade and would take much needed resources away from other priority areas (notably, housebuilding) – proved to be substantially correct. Third, while these considerations might not be felt by individual voters for some time – and, with luck, might not result in a serious loss of electoral support for the government – other consequences were bound to be damaging. For example, the term of compulsory National Service was increased from 18 months to two years, which was hardly likely to endear the Labour government to young citizens who had been brought up to expect that the defeat of Hitler would be followed by the creation of a 'New Jerusalem' in 'socialist' Britain.

Gaitskell is still remembered fondly by British social democrats, despite his chequered record as Labour Party leader (see below). But his conduct over Korea is difficult to defend from any point of view. He might have been trying to precipitate a Cabinet crisis which would force his rival, Bevan, into resignation. If so, he was successful in the short term, and public opinion polls suggested that a significant majority of voters supported the increased spending on defence (Snyder, 1964, 56). Yet even before Bevan's resignation it was apparent that Korea, and the associated defence expenditure, had opened fissures within the Labour Party which contributed to its defeat in the 1951 general election.

The emerging British foreign policy consensus between 1945 and 1950 had implied that good relations with the US were important enough to become in themselves a major factor in considerations of the national interest, i.e. if British policy makers were faced with finely balanced decisions, they should normally take the option which happened to be preferred by the US. Gaitskell, by contrast, seems to have thought that the maintenance of the 'special relationship' was so vital that, in itself, it outweighed more traditional calculations of the national interest – that standing shoulder to shoulder with the Americans constituted *the* national interest, whatever the implications of a particular course of action for Britain, even in terms of its economic prospects or the fortunes of Gaitskell's own party. The conclusive symptom of this arresting perspective was a tendency to brand one's opponents as 'anti-American', even when the basis of their objection was self-evidently a contrasting perception of British interests rather than ideological subservience to the Soviet Union. Gaitskell was quite willing to castigate his opponents in this way, and at a party meeting at the beginning of February 1951 even Attlee had referred to 'a lot of anti-American feeling', adding, with a mixture of pragmatism and condescension, that 'they [the Americans] do talk too much – but they are essential for European defence' (Dell, 1996, 145; Benn, 1994, 135). Overall, it is likely that this furore contributed to Labour's defeat in the 1951 general election, but whatever damage was done to the party, Gaitskell's personal ambition was unhindered – he went on to succeed Attlee as party leader in 1955.

Participation in the Korean War, inevitably, had momentous consequences for Britain aside from its significance as the first occasion when backing for the US was equated with the national interest. Britain ranked second behind the US in the number of troops it sent to Korea, and the exploits of units like the 'glorious' Gloucestershire Regiment were deservedly celebrated. Even so, the American contribution to the UN operation dwarfed that of Britain and other Commonwealth countries; the overall tally of British combatants (about 90,000) was easily exceeded by the number of US personnel who were killed or wounded. It was thus inevitable that the key decisions were taken by US commanders – notably, the controversial General Douglas MacArthur. After UN forces had repelled the North Korean attack and driven up towards the Chinese border, China (with Soviet encouragement) launched a vigorous and successful counter-attack. With MacArthur's troops now in retreat, Truman hinted at a press conference in November 1950 that the US might resort to a nuclear strike on Chinese territory. By this time Britain had agreed (without any public announcement, let alone a formal treaty) that American atomic weapons could be stored on its soil. In view of Truman's comments, and the cavalier attitude that the US had shown towards previous pledges in respect of nuclear weapons, the British Cabinet was understandably alarmed at the possibility that such weapons might be used without any consultation. Clement Attlee flew to Washington to seek clarification. Truman provided what Attlee considered to be adequate reassurance, but, thanks to the intervention of his Secretary of State Dean Acheson, the US President stopped short of a binding written promise.

As Kenneth Morgan has written, on his return 'Attlee was hailed in parliament and in the press as the bringer of peace, who had calmed down impulsive and ideological Americans, and pulled the world back from the brink of a wider war in the Far East' (Morgan, 1984, 429). Although Morgan argues that the praise was justified to some extent, other evidence suggests that Attlee's flight was hardly more fruitful than Neville Chamberlain's airborne excursion to Munich in 1938. Indeed, the parallels with Munich extend as far as the production of a hastily written document expressing pious hopes rather than concrete pledges (Hennessy, 1992, 408). In return for Truman's verbal pledges, Attlee felt compelled to offer substantive concessions to his American hosts, particularly in terms of Britain's future defence spending (precipitating the Cabinet resignations described above). Thus an incident which British historians usually cite as an example of UK influence over American policy is susceptible to a more nuanced interpretation. Tellingly, while Truman himself discussed Attlee's visit in lavish detail in his memoir, a voluminous 1992 biography of the President dismisses the supposedly decisive intervention in less than one page (Truman, 1965, 451–69; McCullough, 1992, 825–6).

The question, then, is how a mission which was induced by serious British suspicions about American intentions managed to be translated into a triumphant affirmation of the 'special relationship'? The most plausible answer is that Attlee had inadvertently added a new element to the 'meta-myth' which was beginning to dominate the British world view. It now appeared that although Britain could not hope (or even want) to compete with the US in terms of 'brawn', it brought an essential element of 'brain' to the alliance. This offered the British public the best chance to accept a fact which had become abundantly clear since 1945 – that what they had presumed to be a relationship of (roughly) equal powers was unmistakably asymmetrical. Indeed, the new version of the British post-war narrative could convince even some well-informed observers that the 'special relationship' was rendered *more* special by its very inequality. On this view, without the injection of common sense from the less powerful partner, the superpower would be fated to blunder from one disaster to the next. Britain's new mission was thus no less than the salvation of the world from atomic oblivion – and, thanks to the stature of its statesmen and its unimpeachable moral conduct, it was the only power which possessed sufficient soft power to attempt, let alone perform, this role. Attlee's mission was thus the direct antecedent of Harold Macmillan's view that Britain's world role was to act as wise Greeks to the virile Romans of the US (Chapter 6).

Whatever the real efficacy of Attlee's intervention, the Romans showed a remarkable lack of deference towards the Greeks when, in September 1951, they signed a defensive pact (ANZUS) with Australia and New Zealand from which the British were excluded. Since the fall of Singapore in 1942 it had been obvious that these former colonies would depend on America rather than Britain for their defence; but it was not surprising that the British were 'deeply wounded' by the snub, given their historic links with the area (Frankel, 1975, 216). Indeed, the ANZUS pact – which was agreed while Attlee was Prime Minister, but came into effect after Churchill had resumed his old office in 1951 – could hardly have been better calculated to expose the wishful thinking which lay behind the latter's concentric-circles idea and to make him switch his focus to the circle which he had obviously regarded as the least important.

Europe

On 8 July 1950 the junior Foreign Office Minister Kenneth Younger recorded in his diary that '[t]he Korean situation has . . . knocked Schuman right into the background of public consciousness' (quoted in Hennessy, 1992, 407). Younger was alluding to the announcement on 9 May 1950 by the French Foreign Minister Robert Schuman of a plan to create a European Coal and Steel Community (ECSC), in the hope of building on previous initiatives to foster European cooperation. If Younger had not been a passionate advocate of the Schuman Plan, he would have been less surprised at its failure to retain the attention of the British public.

In 1950 the leadership of Europe was Britain's for the asking: indeed, it was available even if the British did not ask for it. Whatever damage the 1939–45 war had done to Britain, it was the only Western European country whose prestige had not been seriously tarnished. Six months after his 1946 'iron curtain' speech, and still Leader of the Opposition, Winston Churchill seemingly endorsed the cause of European unity in another memorable oration, this time delivered in Zurich. However, while Churchill was obviously sincere in his hopes for European integration as a general principle, on this occasion his resonant phrases were amenable to different interpretations. The Zurich speech could mean that Churchill wanted Britain to be a key player at the heart of the new Europe – or that it would offer encouragement from the outside. The latter interpretation of

Churchill's attitude was supported by previous speeches. For example, in 1930 he had argued that although unity for the rest of Europe was a very good idea, 'we have our own dream and our own task. We are with Europe, but not of it. We are linked but not compromised. We are interested and associated but not absorbed' (Churchill, 1930).

By 1945 even Churchill must have accepted that Britain's pre-war 'dream' had faded at least to some extent, and the 'task' – presumably, on Churchill's usual form, an imperial one – lacked the clarity of 1930 – so enthusiasts in the cause of a united Europe had plausible reasons for taking Churchill at his apparent word and embracing him as one of their own. Yet this interpretation overlooked the post-war narrative which Churchill himself had done so much to foster among the British public, i.e. that the Second World War had just been a temporary setback for Britain, which still had every reason to 'dream' of a 'task' which was global rather than parochial. Oddly enough, from this perspective Churchill's warm words about European integration can be read as a radical variant of the usual British Euroscepticism. He seemed to be taking for granted that European cooperation would take the form of a quasi-federal 'United States' of Europe, which was perfectly acceptable for the peoples of mainland Europe but unthinkable for Britons who had inherited broader horizons and a right to govern themselves without having to cooperate with others.

Developments between the Zurich speech and the promulgation of the Schuman Plan made close European cooperation more urgent but also suggested that Britain would have to take a more active role in continental affairs. The terms on which the US Congress had endorsed the Marshall Plan implied much closer integration between democratic European states, and in response the Organisation for European Economic Co-operation and Development (OEECD) was established in April 1948. Britain was a prominent member of this organisation and of the European Payments Union (EPU), which followed in 1950. A Congress of Europe, held at The Hague in May 1948 with an impressive cast of political heavyweights, including Churchill, led to the creation of a Council of Europe. Significantly, this body would have its headquarters at Strasbourg, in the Alsace-Lorraine region, whose annexation by Germany in 1871 had triggered so much subsequent conflict; but the agreement to establish the Council was signed in London, on 5 May 1949.

For Attlee's Labour government, the Council of Europe and the OEECD were adequate responses to the American desire for post-war European amity. The OEECD answered the immediate practical need for some kind of economic organisation to administer Marshall Aid; for its part, the Council of Europe provided a venue for the discussion of political issues. The British government ensured that neither body could be seen as a direct infringement of national sovereignty; and if this meant that the Council of Europe (in particular) was regarded as a toothless 'talking shop', that was a price worth paying so long as it gave the Americans the impression that European politicians had learned the lessons of two world wars and were now prepared at least to engage in regular dialogue.

However, the idea of Britain as a 'benevolent bystander' in Europe was no longer realistic. The country had committed itself to European cooperation in some form, and the remaining question was whether other European states were satisfied with the strictly intergovernmental institutions in which Britain was prepared to participate. Ironically, Britain itself helped to make this question more complicated by taking a leading role in the process of drafting a European Convention on Human Rights, which began in the summer of 1949. The initial intention was to reinforce the lessons learned since 1914 and to advertise the impression that Europe as a whole would no longer tolerate the barbarities committed in the name of various governments during those years. But in practice the establishment of a European Court of Human Rights to rule on alleged breaches of the Convention introduced an element of supranationality. If the court's decisions were genuinely binding on all member states, then the Council of Europe was capable of infringing traditional understandings of 'national sovereignty'; if not, it would seem that despite all their fine-sounding phrases, the states of the new Europe regarded human rights with the same insouciance shown by their pre-war predecessors.

The discussions which led to the establishment of the Council of Europe should have alerted the British government to the strength of support for some supranational element to European institutions. France and the Benelux countries had argued that the Council should be elected (albeit indirectly) to give it greater credibility, while the British, keen to keep credibility within limits, insisted on an appointed membership. For the British, Schuman's initiative of May 1950 was deeply unwelcome, not least because Schuman had chosen not to consult Bevin in advance (whereas the US Secretary of State, Dean Acheson, seemed well informed). This manoeuvre was probably intended to avoid a repetition of previous discussions, in which Britain had used its considerable influence to water down radical proposals; this time, hopefully, Britain would see that its European neighbours were in earnest and either accept the principle of supranational institutions or reject it decisively, leaving the architects of 'United Europe' to get on with their self-appointed task without obstruction. If the promoters of unity really hoped for a positive British response, the precise nature of Schuman's scheme – to place the coal, iron and steel industries under supranational supervision – was ill chosen. Having just brought all of these industries into state ownership as key elements in the creation of a 'democratic socialist' Britain, the Attlee government was most unlikely to relinquish control to institutions with incompatible ideological visions.

If the Conservatives had been in office in May 1950, the British response might have been different – Churchill and many of his colleagues asserted as much in the House of Commons debate subsequent to Labour's rejection of the Schuman Plan. Almost certainly, the Conservatives would not have been deterred by a sentimental attachment to the Commonwealth, which weighed heavily with the Labour Party, thanks to its promotion of a retreat from Empire. However, Churchill would have committed Britain to Schuman's project with the intention of changing its nature – basically, repeating Bevin's approach to the Council of Europe and weakening the supranational elements of the original proposal.

In essence, the Conservatives agreed with Labour in deploring the impact of supranational institutions on Britain's 'national sovereignty', and in 1950 both major parties accepted the definition of this term, which had become common currency in Britain's Victorian heyday, i.e. that a nation is 'sovereign' insofar as no outside body can overrule the outcome of its domestic decision-making process. Arguably, though, by its enthusiastic sponsorship of what became the NATO alliance, the Labour government had already signalled that sovereignty, in that sense, was not absolute. NATO, after all, very seriously circumscribed Britain's freedom of action in a crucial area – so long as the alliance persisted, the country was obligated to lend assistance if one of its partners was attacked; and if a constitutional purist insisted that this obligation would cease if Parliament chose to terminate the alliance, exactly the same thing would be true of Britain's membership of any supranational European arrangement. Unwittingly, Labour's claim that the Schuman Plan would act as a distraction from the Atlantic alliance lends support to this argument – it implied that commitments like NATO and the Marshall Plan had already become immovable landmarks within the British constitution, and that the British were not prepared to accord the same importance to European agreements. According to taste, one could either retort that an acceptance of European unity was wholly compatible with the Atlantic alliance – indeed, the Americans were warm supporters of the enterprise and of British involvement – or that NATO membership embodied a permanent revision of the traditional British definition of 'sovereignty', making an acceptance of Schuman's proposals much less difficult than it would have been had NATO never existed.

Britain's refusal to commit itself to a primarily European role was less fraught with consequences in respect to plans for military cooperation. In October 1950 the Schuman Plan was supplemented by the proposal of another senior French politician, René Pleven, for a European Army with a single European Defence Budget and a European Minister of Defence responsible to a European Assembly. While Schuman's proposal was designed to ensure French influence over German production of the sinews of war – coal, iron and steel – the Pleven Plan was designed to subject a revived German army to supranational supervision, as well as offering a basis for a coordinated European response should the Soviet military threat ever materialise.

Although in opposition Churchill himself had spoken out in favour of a European Army and a European Minister of Defence, in November 1951 Anthony Eden, restored to his old berth as Foreign Secretary in a new Conservative government, signalled that, as in the case of the Schuman Plan, Britain favoured European cooperation in this area but would not itself join the proposed European Defence Community (EDC). Although the treaty was signed in May 1952, the French were unwilling to ratify it without British participation. Significantly, French Gaullists who had been prepared to accept the ECSC were much more troubled by the possible implications for their own national sovereignty of a supranational organisation in the areas of defence and foreign policy – unlike the British, who had flung themselves into NATO without contemplating the full range of possible implications.

In September 1954 the French Assembly decisively declined to ratify the EDC. This presented a serious dilemma even to politicians who harboured misgivings about the abortive Community, since it left unanswered the problem of finding a basis on which West German rearmament could proceed. It was Anthony Eden who came up with the idea of strengthening the existing Brussels Treaty (itself based on the Anglo-French Dunkirk Treaty of 1947), incorporating West Germany, which would be admitted to NATO at the same time. Unusually for a post-war British initiative, Eden's suggestion was well timed; apart from the warm response of the relevant European governments, the scheme promised to satisfy the Americans, who continued to favour West German rearmament. Nevertheless, Eden's skilful personal diplomacy was needed to secure an agreement. At a London meeting of EDC signatories (with the US and Canada as observers) Eden announced the commitment to European defence of four British army divisions, with tactical air support, unless and until other EDC members decided that they were no longer wanted or if 'an acute overseas emergency' meant that the UK forces were required for service elsewhere. Thus, even when taking a leading role in the resolution of a key European question, Britain's leaders contrived to slip in a quiet reminder of its extra-European interests. However, this was accompanied by an admission of Britain's reduced economic status; the situation would be reviewed '[i]f the maintenance of UK forces on the mainland throws too heavy a strain on the external finances of the UK' (quoted in Northedge, 1974, 169).

These mixed messages were consistent with the nature of the settlement itself, which was agreed in London on 3 October 1954. It established a Western European Union (WEU), with its headquarters in Brussels. The fearful supranational features of the Pleven Plan – the European Minister of Defence, etc. – were gone. Instead, the key decision-making institution would be an intergovernmental Council of Ministers; the associated assembly would be purely consultative. At the same time, the terms of WEU genuflected towards the principle of European cooperation in economic and cultural matters as well as defence. Finally, while

WEU foreshadowed a much more amicable relationship with West Germany, it also embodied some old suspicions: the troops on German soil were no longer strictly speaking an 'army of occupation', but their presence was at least in part a guarantee to France and Poland against a revival of aggressive intentions.

The importance of individuals: Anthony Eden as Foreign Secretary

Since Sir Anthony Eden exercised considerable appeal over Conservative supporters thanks to his aristocratic demeanour and pleasing appearance as well as his record of opposition to Neville Chamberlain's policy of appeasement, he seemed the ideal person to build on Ernest Bevin's achievements. According to Robert Rhodes James, Eden 'realised – few better – how circumscribed British power was, but at heart he did not accept the implication of Britain as an inferior nation, devoid of influence' (Rhodes James, 1986, 353). In short, like Bevin he was an exemplar of the view that the 1939–45 conflict had been a temporary setback for Britain rather than a pulverising blow. In particular, Eden took an unsentimental view of the Anglo-American relationship, recognising that the interests of the two countries coincided in many respects but could also diverge over specific issues. Significantly, while Eden echoed Churchill's notion of three concentric circles, he differed from his chief in mentioning the Commonwealth *before* the Atlantic alliance (Shlaim *et al.*, 1997, 91). This order of allegiances was underpinned by Eden's assessment of the Soviet challenge as a manifestation of 'traditional' great-power politics, rather than the ideological threat perceived by his American opposite number, John Foster Dulles.

The contrasting perspectives were illustrated vividly by respective attitudes to Iran. In 1951 Mohammed Mossadegh had been appointed Iranian Prime Minister on a progressive platform of social reforms, which would be financed by oil revenues. To this end Mossadegh approved the nationalisation of the Anglo-Iranian Oil Company (the forerunner of British Petroleum (BP)), which had exploited Iranian reserves on very favourable terms: its revenues were greater than those enjoyed by the Iranian government itself (Curtis, 2003, 304). The British were not prepared to accept this expensive rebuff meekly and began to work out ways in which Mossadegh could be removed from office.

Since Mossadegh seemed strongly opposed to Communism, the Truman administration had taken a favourable view of his rise to power. Restored to the Foreign Office by the Conservative victory in the 1951 general election, Anthony Eden had sought to cajole the Americans into a more hostile stance. Truman's successor, the Republican Dwight D Eisenhower, proved more receptive to these arguments. Mossadegh, it was now alleged, was a secret Soviet stooge.

Eden's initial public reaction to the nationalisation had been cautious, mixing a tacit acceptance of Mossadegh's move with demands for compensation which could be made as unreasonable as the occasion required. Others were inclined to resent the incipient blow to the British economy less than the affront to the country's prestige. Before the Conservatives returned to office the former Permanent Under-Secretary to the Foreign Office (and vociferous anti-German) Lord Vanssitart used a House of Lords debate to 'point out that a good many of us are getting not only uneasy but angry at the disrespect with which we and our interests are now so often treated' (*Hansard, House of Lords Debates,* 21 March 1951, Vol. 170, col. 248).

Vanssitart could rest assured that his message was heeded in the relevant quarters. As soon as the American enthusiasm for the Mossadegh regime began to cool the Soviets adopted a warmer attitude towards Iran. The threat of Soviet influence provided the trigger for intervention by the American Central Intelligence Agency (CIA), who (in collaboration with the British secret services) financed a political coup in Iran. Mossadegh was seized in August 1953 and placed under house arrest; the more reliably pro-Western hereditary monarch, the Shah, who had fled into exile, was restored to his throne.

Although the most footling adherent of the *'cui bono?'* school of detection would have identified the culprits behind the 1953 Iran coup in an instant, it took six decades for the US government to own up to their responsibility, whereupon the former British Foreign Secretary Jack Straw admitted the Churchill government's guilt. By that time the events of 1953 had been forgotten (in Britain, at least) by all except a handful of activists and scholars. Back in 1954 the re-division of oil spoils benefited the US partially at British expense, but, overall, Eden could be satisfied with the result of this neo-colonial transaction. Indeed, it set a dangerous precedent – an incident in which Eden seemed to have been proved right in his negative assessment of an ambitious Middle Eastern politician, while the Americans could be accused of dangerous naïvety until brute reality had demonstrated the need to defer to British experience and to take action on the spot regardless of the democratic will of the people.

Eden's hostility to Mossadegh, prompted by sensitivity over the security of British oil supplies, contrasted sharply with his initial attitude to nationalist politicians in Egypt. In 1952 the Egyptian monarchy was overthrown in a military coup. Britain's base in the Suez Canal was a key focus for unrest, and even before the coup the Egyptian government had denounced the 1936 Anglo-Egyptian treaty, which had permitted the British to retain their base until 1956. After concerted British efforts to reach a rapprochement with the new regime in Egypt (now led by Colonel Gamal Abdul Nasser), in October 1954 the two countries agreed a phased British withdrawal from the canal zone.

However, Eden's plan for a graceful disengagement from Suez was endangered within a few months by his decision to commit Britain to the Baghdad

Pact – an agreement which also provided a further illustration of the less than 'special' UK–US relationship. In February 1955 Turkey and Iraq agreed a military pact and were joined by Pakistan, Iran (newly liberated from democratic government) and Britain. The idea of a pact between these countries, creating a defensive line against possible Soviet expansion to the south-west, held obvious attractions for Britain and the US. The latter, however, chose to be a benevolent non-participant in the Baghdad Pact, partly because its adherence would not have been welcome to Israel, but also because it preferred not to taint itself by association with 'imperialist' Britain in this area. Unlike the US, Britain had a practical reason for joining; the terms of the pact could be interpreted as a tacit renewal of a 1930 treaty which had allowed the RAF to use Iraqi facilities (Northedge, 1974, 124–5). However, Iraq's newly installed Prime Minister, Nuri As-Said, was already regarded as a rival to Egypt's Colonel Nasser for political leadership in the Middle East. Britain's apparent championship of Nuri was bound to incur Nasser's displeasure, undoing at a stroke the careful diplomatic work of the previous two years. A personal meeting between Eden and Nasser before the signing of the treaty seems to have resulted merely in the confirmation of existing suspicions (Rhodes James, 1986, 397–8).

While Britain's diplomatic activity in the Middle East was clearly – perhaps *too* clearly – inspired by a consideration of its perceived national interest, Eden also played a considerable part in attempts to settle the growing problems of Indochina. As Douglas Hurd has written, although Britain 'had no direct involvement' in this area, 'Eden, like Churchill, believed that as Britain was a first-class power, she [sic] had a role in defining the world's direction' (Hurd, 2010, 354). After Japan's defeat in 1945 France had resumed its colonial role in Vietnam, Laos and Cambodia; but its restored position was on the point of collapse in the face of a Chinese-backed Communist insurgency. In February 1954 a conference was convened in Geneva, comprising representatives of the US, the Soviet Union, Britain and France; it would discuss the end of the conflict in Korea before moving on to address the situation in Indochina along with representatives of the Chinese government, whose involvement in the negotiations had been supported by the British. Since the US continued to withhold official recognition from Mao's government, Dulles refused to talk to the Chinese.

This left Eden as, effectively, the major spokesperson of the Western democracies at Geneva. With no British vested interests at stake – and no ideological axe to grind – Eden was in his element. The result was a partition of Vietnam, but one which was intended to be temporary, to be followed two years later by a nationwide democratic election. Ultimately, the Geneva Accords did nothing to prevent the developing tragedy in Indochina; the US government, which did not sign the accords, stepped into the vacuum left by the withdrawing French forces and began to build an anti-Communist South Vietnam, with well-known consequences. However, Hurd is surely right to praise Eden for his attempt to create a context for a more rational settlement, if other, more interested parties had been wise enough to pursue one. The US initiative in Vietnam was followed by the signature in September 1954 of the Southeast Asia Collective Defence Treaty, leading to the creation of the Southeast Asia Treaty Organisation (SEATO). Britain was a founder member but doubted the efficacy of a body which was clearly intended to provide cover for aggressive US action in Indochina.

Eden's anxiety about US policy towards Indochina was greatly increased by developments in nuclear weaponry. By 1954 both of the superpowers had tested hydrogen bombs with far greater destructive capacity than the devices dropped on Hiroshima and Nagasaki in 1945. Hampered by the restrictions on cooperation with the US, Britain was lagging behind. The decision to develop a British hydrogen bomb was, true to form, taken without a full discussion in Cabinet, let alone a public debate. However, the new prospect of imminent destruction for the human race had a profound effect on Winston Churchill, whose preference for 'jaw-jaw' over 'war-war' was now given additional piquancy.

In his eightieth year, Churchill was convinced that his personal style of diplomacy could engineer some kind of *modus vivendi* between the US and the Soviet Union. This notion was not entirely implausible; since the death of Stalin in 1952 the Soviets had seemed more amenable to constructive discussions, and President Eisenhower offered Churchill encouragement. In fact, by 1954 the main opposition to Churchill came from within his own Cabinet, which was sceptical of the value of any meeting between the Prime Minister and the current Soviet leader, Malenkov. It would be easy to dismiss Churchill's talk of a high-level summit which reunited the wartime 'Big Three' in the shadow of the hydrogen bomb as merely a ruse to delay his retirement from office; Eden, his anointed successor, certainly seems to have formed that view and was obviously irritated that the Prime Minister had begun to communicate with world leaders without prior consultation, as Chamberlain had done in the late 1930s. But the stakes were so high, and the supportive hints from Washington so tangible, that a more positive interpretation is possible. After all, Churchill knew Eden well enough to have good reasons for doubting that he could play an equally effective role at such a meeting. Only when Eisenhower, in March 1955, decided against holding a summit in the near future did Churchill reluctantly agree to relinquish the reins, resigning on 5 April.

The substitution of Eden for Churchill meant that a great, flawed statesman, who finally had to accept that he was too old and ill to occupy Downing Street, was replaced by a younger man who did not appreciate the extent of his own infirmities. In the interests of Britain's international reputation, this did not turn out to be a change for the better.

Case Study 4.3 Graham Greene, *The Quiet American*

For an insight into the differences between Anglo-American attitudes in the early post-war period, particularly in relation to Indochina, Graham Greene's novel *The Quiet American* (1955) is a thought-provoking source. Greene knew the area well, having worked there as a journalist. His experiences, along with his appreciation of the wider political context, enabled him to create a human drama which also stands as an allegorical critique of the 'special relationship' in the mid 1950s.

Greene's main protagonists are Thomas Fowler, a British journalist, and Alden Pyle, who is covertly working for the CIA in the Vietnamese capital, Saigon. Although he is a complex character, Fowler is a cynic who knows the real world only too well; Pyle, by contrast, is an idealist whose views are derived from books. Fowler is living in Saigon with a young dancer, Phuong, but her family disapproves of the relationship, because he is already married. Pyle falls in love with Phuong and assumes that she will leave Fowler for him.

At first it looks as if Phuong will choose Fowler, and he writes to ask his wife for a divorce; predictably, Mrs Fowler refuses to comply, but her deceitful husband tells Phuong that she has agreed. Pyle then saves Fowler's life during a firefight in the war zone; when they return to Saigon Pyle tells Phuong that Fowler has lied to her about the divorce, and she seems set to transfer her affections to 'The Quiet American'. However, Fowler discovers that Pyle's undercover activities include active collaboration with terrorists, inspired by the theoretical hope that the ensuing atrocities will help promote the establishment of a pro-American government in Vietnam. For all his cynicism, Fowler is disgusted by this evidence that an apparent idealist can participate in the slaughter of innocent civilians in pursuit of abstract aims; on a more mundane level, he is jealous of Pyle's relationship with Phuong. In combination, these considerations overcome Fowler's gratitude to the man who saved his life, and he agrees to cooperate with a plan to assassinate Pyle. Once this has been accomplished, Phuong returns to Fowler and his long-suffering wife agrees to a divorce. On the personal level, this might approximate to a happy ending, but in 1955 Greene's readers would be well aware that there was unlikely to be such a satisfactory resolution for Indochina as a whole.

Greene's novel was well received in the UK, but in the US it was attacked as 'anti-American'. This response is highly instructive. Fowler, after all, is an ageing and impecunious drug addict, while his transatlantic rival is young

> and resourceful. If Fowler represents post-war Britain, it is not a very endearing portrait. Nevertheless, the novel seems to argue that in moral terms Britain is (just) preferable to America: Fowler (Britain) might commit serious offences for bad reasons, but Pyle (America) is capable of indiscriminate killing in the name of superficially attractive abstract values.

Conclusions

Foreign policy issues were unusually prominent in the 1955 general election campaign but offered limited scope for party conflict, since Labour and the Conservatives agreed on the key questions of the time. Both parties favoured multilateral nuclear disarmament – a cause given fresh urgency by the recent advent of the hydrogen bomb. They both wanted, as the Conservative manifesto put it, 'to guide Colonial peoples along the road to self-government', backed by British economic assistance.

This foreign policy consensus between the dominant factions within the two main parties was not surprising, since they had been coalition partners for most of the Second World War. However, it also reflected the constraints of the international arena, which left British politicians with little choice but to indulge in wishful thinking about the future intentions of the superpowers. These constraints fostered the development of a decision-making mentality which prevailed under governments of both parties for most of the period reviewed by this book. Indeed, even in 2017 many key elements of policy were still being made along lines first laid down by the 1945–51 Attlee governments.

In particular, these comments are pertinent in relation to the 'special relationship' and to 'Europe'. In the immediate aftermath of the Second World War policy makers hoped that America would continue to help Britain through its difficulties on favourable terms. Failing that, circumstances demanded a willingness to accept US assistance on *any* terms, since Britain desperately needed help, and the US was the only country which could give it. Senior figures like Bevin hoped that the period of enforced obsequiousness would be of short duration; but although the British economy recovered to some extent from the devastating consequences of the Second World War, by 1955 the habit of deferring to the Americans in the field of foreign policy had taken root. As Chapter 5 will show, Anthony Eden's attempt to think and act independently merely resulted in a reaffirmation of the previous arrangement.

If the UK had been *entirely* subservient to America during these years, the history of its involvement with 'Europe' would have been very different. The US strongly recommended British participation in any serious plan for cooperation, partly because this would implant an anti-federalist cuckoo in the European nest but also because it would confirm Britain's abandonment of its pre-war colonial visions. In the early 1950s, however, the British were not prepared to contemplate such a drastic step, even at the risk of displeasing their American paymasters. At this stage, at least, decision-makers tended to echo Bevin by assuming that their country's decline would shortly be arrested and at least partly reversed, allowing it to maintain a global role. Subsequent events showed that Britain's relations with the fledgling EEC would have been impaired even if it had behaved in a way which hedged its bets in respect of European cooperation; instead, it evinced a mixture of contempt and unease which ensured that if and when it finally 'joined Europe', it would have trapped itself in the role of 'awkward partner'.

In short – provided that mankind did not annihilate itself, which seemed more possible in 1955 than ever before – Britain's foreign policy decisions over the decade after the end of the Second World War gave shrewd observers a very good chance of predicting the country's long-term future. The only surprising thing was the zeal with which senior British policy makers applied themselves to the verification of those predictions, almost as soon as the 1955 general election results were announced.

Suez and 'Supermac', 1955–63

5

Introduction

A collection of essays on Britain between 1951 and 1964 was given the title of *The Age of Affluence*, which seemed highly appropriate when the book was published in 1970. This was indeed a period of transformation in the lives of most British people, thanks chiefly to the easy availability of consumer goods (and of loans to pay for them). Harold Macmillan's remark of July 1957 that 'most of our people have never had it so good' is a ubiquitous quotation in studies of the period; and, although Macmillan was actually warning that the British public might not 'have it so good' for much longer if inflation could not be controlled, he was right to refer to 'a state of prosperity such that we have never had in my lifetime'. Far-sighted politicians were beginning to brood over a new problem – how to cajole citizens into the constructive use of the hours of leisure which they could now expect, as changes in the production process meant that even manual labourers could combine comfortable lifestyles with a much shorter working week. For some pessimistic observers, it seemed all too clear that 'the problem of leisure' had already been solved – by the television set. By 1964 these dubious devices adorned 17 million households in the UK.

By 1970, though, the first half of this period seems to have been characterised not so much by affluence as by complacency. With hindsight, future trouble was easily discerned by those who were willing to peer below the surface of events. For example, in the year before Macmillan told the British to count their blessings, the playwright John Osborne produced *Look Back in Anger*, which attracted mixed reviews at first but found enough favour among members of the cultural elite to win a reputation for having tapped into the zeitgeist, which the purveyors of far more popular fare apparently failed to do. Among Osborne's cast of characters is a retired army officer, Colonel Redfern, who served in India between

> **Timeline of domestic political developments**
>
> **January 1957** Anthony Eden resigns as Prime Minister; replaced by Harold Macmillan
> **October 1959** General election: Conservatives increase majority to 100
> **August 1961** Britain applies for membership of the EEC
> **18 January 1963** Sudden death of Labour leader, Hugh Gaitskell
> **29 January 1963** French President Charles de Gaulle vetoes British application for EEC membership
> **October 1963** Macmillan resigns as Prime Minister; replaced by Sir Alec Douglas-Home

the outbreak of the First World War and the granting of Indian independence in 1947. Redfern is presented as a warm-hearted individual who is perplexed by the Britain to which he has returned.

No doubt Redfern would have been reassured to some extent by the Conservative Party manifesto for the 1959 general election, which betrayed few twinges of self-doubt and featured a foreign policy programme designed to '[maintain] British influence in the world unimpaired'. Redfern would have been well advised, though, to ignore Labour's 1959 offering, which accused the Conservative government of engaging in 'an act of folly, hopelessly misconceived, bungled in execution and covered with a tissue of lies told by the leading Ministers concerned'. Labour was referring to an episode which occurred during the months between Osborne's outburst of anger and Macmillan's praise of prosperity – Suez.

The Suez Crisis

In the Middle East the rising popularity of Arab nationalism presented a serious challenge to Britain's position in the region. For many, the events in Iran in 1951–3 (Chapter 4) were a dress rehearsal for a burgeoning crisis in Egypt, where the stakes were even higher. In 1955 Anthony Eden finally succeeded Winston Churchill as Prime Minister. Back in 1929 Eden had argued that

> If the Suez Canal is our back door to the East, it is the front door to Europe of Australia, New Zealand and India. If you like to mix your metaphors it is, in fact, the swing-door of the British Empire, which has got to keep continually revolving if our communications are to be what they should.
>
> (quoted in Kyle, 2003, 7)

With the discovery and large-scale reserves of crude oil after the Second World War, the Middle East was no longer a region to pass through on the way elsewhere: it was now a destination in its own right, and the Suez Canal was vital for both purposes.

One of the leading figures within the Arab nationalist movement was the Egyptian Gamal Abdel Nasser. For Nasser, the Suez Canal had not served Egyptian interests since it opened in 1859; rather, Egypt had been made to serve the needs of the canal and its major shareholders.

Conscious of the canal's importance, Britain had declared Egypt a 'Protectorate' during the First World War. Under the terms of a treaty signed in 1936, Egypt would regain its autonomy, but British troops were allowed to be stationed within the Canal Zone, at least until 1956. Formally, Egypt remained neutral during the Second World War, but this meant little in practical terms, given the strategic importance of the country and the commitment of substantial British forces, who repelled attempted invasions by the Italians and the Germans. After the war the creation of the state of Israel added considerably to Anglo-Egyptian tensions.

Attacks on British troops in the Suez Canal Zone increased after 1950, prompting the government to authorise a crackdown through Operation Eagle on 'Black Saturday', 25 January 1952. The excessive force used by British troops, resulting in at least 50 Egyptian deaths, further galvanised an already vocal opposition to colonial rule. British commercial interests were targeted, and several Britons were murdered. Anti-British sentiment across Egypt was spearheaded by the Free Officer Corps within the Egyptian army, led after 1950 by Colonel Gamel Abdel Nasser. In July 1952 the Egyptian King, Farouk, was overthrown and replaced by a military government. Two years later Nasser became effective ruler of Egypt and gained considerable popular support by positioning himself against the British, opposing Israel and starting the construction of a dam to irrigate the Nile valley.

It became quickly apparent that Nasser posed a serious threat to British interests in Egypt. Nasser was able to capitalise on populist sentiment both in Egypt and across the Middle East, with the canal serving as an easy – and highly evocative – focus for resentment. Realising the severity of the threat, in October 1952 the British agreed to withdraw their troops from the canal zone by June 1956, while reserving the right to reoccupy their old bases if Egypt was threatened by a third party (by which the British meant the Soviet Union).

British ministers were also concerned by the possibility that, far from invading Egypt, the Soviets would woo Nasser by supplying him with arms. The Middle East – and its vast natural resources – had become a key arena of Cold War competition. While Britain had sought to consolidate its position with the establishment of the Baghdad Pact (later the Central Treaty Organisation; see Chapter 4), relations between the signatory states were uneasy, and Egypt was openly hostile. The US had declined to sign up to the Baghdad Pact, but its own attempts to cajole Nasser into the anti-Soviet camp made little progress. Furthermore, Eden's decision not to sell British arms to Nasser only served to push Egypt closer to the Soviet orbit. As Nasser argued, the Soviets had never occupied Egypt and posed far less of a threat to Cairo's interests than the British, who had been in Egypt for 70 years. Ultimately, Nasser sought to play the Cold War contestants against each other in the name of Arab nationalism.

When Eden succeeded Churchill as Prime Minister in 1955 he called a general election which increased the Conservatives' Parliamentary majority to 60, with almost 50 per cent of the popular vote. Eden had not changed his mind about the importance of the Suez Canal since 1929, and his more recent dealings with Mossadegh in Iran had done nothing to diminish his confidence that Britain could exercise considerable influence in the region. Since the general election seemed to have provided him with the resounding democratic 'mandate' which Churchill had never enjoyed, Eden felt emboldened to act on his impulses in the Middle East. In December 1955 he decided to reassert his authority over the Foreign Office, where his initial choice of Foreign Secretary, Harold Macmillan, had proved too independent-minded for his liking. Selwyn Lloyd, Macmillan's replacement, was a far more compliant character.

In the same month Britain joined the US in pledging financial support for Nasser's dam. However, Nasser had already agreed to buy arms from Czechoslovakia, which the British interpreted as a sign that he was prepared to stop merely flirting with the Soviet bloc and place the relationship on a permanent footing. Any development which cemented Nasser's power within Egypt was likely to augment his influence within the wider region; and it was no longer so likely that Nasser would turn his back on the Soviet Union in gratitude for the financial assistance offered by the US and Britain to the Aswan Dam project. Nasser certainly showed no sign of modifying his anti-colonial rhetoric, which threatened to undermine British interests in other parts of the Middle East – notably, Iraq and the Kingdom of Jordan (known as Transjordan until 1949). In the latter country Nasser's influence was detected behind the sacking of the British officer General Glubb, who had led Jordan's armed forces from 1939 until his sudden dismissal in March 1956 (and had provided some of the sternest Arab resistance to Israeli aggression in 1948 and afterwards).

Despite these concerns, the last British soldiers were withdrawn from the canal zone in July 1956, in accordance with the 1954 deal and just ten days before Nasser promoted himself from Prime Minister to President of Egypt. Belatedly, the US took alarm at Nasser's ascendancy and withdrew its offer of funding for the dam. If this was an attempt to blackmail the Egyptian government, it was markedly ill advised, since the Soviet Union had already offered financial support. Instead of the typical Cold War card game in which the major powers played to win control over a state with no promising cards of its own, Nasser's Egypt had an independent strategy and now seemed to have a winning hand. On 26 July

1956 Nasser played his trump, ordering his army to seize control of the Suez Canal Company, whose status had not been affected by the deal with Britain. His justification was that the British and the Americans had forced him into this step, since their withdrawal of funds endangered the Aswan Dam project, and the revenues from those who wished to navigate the canal would supply the deficiency. In reality, Nasser could feel relatively confident that financial backing would materialise, from one state or another. In the meantime he had little reason to fear retaliation against a move which advanced his claims to Arab leadership, since inherent British weakness was compounded by the withdrawal of troops from the area; and although American power might be immensely strong on paper, the country's lack of engagement with the Middle East in general had been betrayed by its dramatic oscillations between a policy of coercion and conciliation over the funding of the dam.

When the news of the nationalisation broke, Eden favoured a firm response. However, since British troops were engaged in conflicts across the Empire, a unilateral reaction could not be swift. In a Cabinet meeting of 27 July the Foreign Secretary, Selwyn Lloyd, sketched a plan of action:

> First need = common [position]. with U.S. & France . . . Suggest immediate talks, at high level – where convenient, but [London]. might be best.
>
> Our line : we are ready to act – mil[itarily], pol[itically]. & economic[ally]
> (www.nationalarchives.gov.uk/releases/2008/
> october/suez-27-07-1956.htm)

Given the British military overstretch, the need to ensure US approval was paramount in strategic calculations in the summer of 1956. Although the US had acted unilaterally in the withdrawal of funding for the Aswan Dam, it was reluctant to become embroiled in any resulting conflict.

Cabinet notes from this time show that ministers were concerned to proceed in a way that would ensure support from both the UN and US. All involved realised the importance of ensuring domestic support. As Selwyn Lloyd argued on 14 August, some gesture towards the UN was necessary in order to keep public opinion onside. In the same meeting Eden underlined the gravity of the situation, declaring that 'if we lose the [Middle East] we are finished' (www.nationalarchives.gov.uk/releases/2008/october/suez-14-08-1956.htm).

In a Commons debate of September 1956 the Prime Minister argued that the fate of the canal affected the interests of many countries besides those of the UK:

> Our economy is increasingly dependent upon oil, much of which has now to be brought through the Canal. In this country alone our oil consumption has doubled since 1949. It has increased by 8 per cent in the last

six months. More than half of Western Europe's oil passes through the Canal. That concerns not only the consumer countries; it is vital to producers as well. . . . A large part, for instance, of Persian oil production, which is now steadily rising, and upon which Persia's prosperity largely depends, is shipped through the Canal; and for other eastern lands the Canal matters almost as much, for purposes of ordinary trade.

(Hansard, House of Commons Debates,
12 September 1956, Vol. 558, col. 2)

In particular, France and Israel had good reason to monitor Nasser's decisions with concern. France was engaged in a bitter conflict in Algeria, where rebels against colonial rule had been assisted by Nasser. For understandable reasons, tensions between Israel and Egypt had persisted since 1948, and ships showing the Israeli flag had been subjected to intrusive searches as they passed through the canal. Nasser had also supported various groups which launched small-scale attacks on Israel through Gaza. This meant that if Britain decided on military action against the Nasser regime it would not necessarily have to act alone. Furthermore, Eden's real intentions could be concealed through the creation of a cover story, which depicted Britain not as an aggressor but rather as a calming influence seeking to bring order out of the chaos which, Eden presumed, would ensue once Egypt took responsibility for managing the canal. A secret agreement was duly reached at Sevres, near Paris, between Israel, Britain and France. The three states had different orders of priority, but they shared enough objectives to make the operation seem worthwhile. Whether as a primary or a secondary concern, they all welcomed the possibility that their actions would lead to 'regime change' in Cairo.

As the military preparations progressed, British policy makers seemed increasingly uncertain about their primary purpose. Selwyn Lloyd, for example, thought that negotiations might result in an agreement to 'internationalise' control of the canal, but he seemed to find this solution unsatisfactory, since it would rob Britain of the chance of 'cutting N[asser] down to size'. Furthermore, the negotiations necessary for a peaceful solution were likely to outrun the preferred timetable for military action, particularly since Nasser proved inconveniently amicable to negotiations (www.nationalarchives.gov.uk/releases/2008/october/suez-23-10-1956.htm). For those familiar with the course of events leading up to the Iraq War of 2003, these considerations will have a familiar ring – only the cast of characters was different, with Britain playing the role assumed by the US almost half a century later. As in 2003, the political and military momentum for war prevailed over any suggestions of last-ditch diplomacy. On 27 October 1956 Israeli tanks crossed into the Sinai and within the space of a week had occupied the entire Sinai Peninsula. Two days later British and French troops invaded the canal zone, under the pretext of separating Israeli and Egyptian forces and to ensure safe passage through the canal, but in reality to promote their own interests. Their joint mission – Operation Musketeer – was successful, defeating Egyptian forces around Port Said. However, instead of marching on to Cairo, the 'musketeers' had been withdrawn by the end of December 1956. The US – which had not been properly consulted – had orchestrated resistance to the operation through the UN and its own financial muscle, making it impossible for the invasion to continue. On 2 November the UN General Assembly passed Resolution 997, calling for an immediate ceasefire and the withdrawal of all forces. Only New Zealand and Australia joined Britain, France and Israel in opposing the resolution: 64 states voted in favour. On 7 November Britain and France accepted a UN-supervised ceasefire.

In the autumn of 1956 the US President Dwight D Eisenhower had grown concerned about the possibility of British action against Egypt. However, he expected this to be delayed until after the Presidential elections in November. Eisenhower was campaigning as an apostle of peace; it would be worse than unwelcome if war erupted in the Middle East, thanks mainly to the aggressive intentions of a country which might now be a friend but which had once sent its armies to retain colonial control over the US itself. Eisenhower's own reputation as an international statesman was at stake; if he had influence anywhere, surely he must be able to restrain Britain, to which he had intimate wartime ties.

President Eisenhower's immediate reaction to the invasion was that 'I've just never seen great powers make such a complete mess and botch of things':

> I think that Britain and France have made a terrible mistake. Because they had such a poor case, they have isolated themselves from the good opinion of the world and it will take them many years to recover. . . . this is something of a sad blow because, quite naturally, Britain not only has been, but must be our best friend in the world.
>
> (quoted in Dundabin, 1994, 293)

By the time of the 2003 Iraq War British politicians had learned to treat the American electoral calendar with as much (if not more) respect than their own; doing anything to upset the occupant of the White House in the crucial weeks before a Presidential or Congressional mid-term election was unthinkable unless the nation's survival was at stake. Anthony Eden lived in different days; and even if he had been acutely conscious of Eisenhower's electoral needs, he believed that Britain's survival *was* wrapped up in the fate of the Suez Canal. From this perspective, it was easy for Eden to convince himself that Eisenhower had given tacit approval for British action whenever the time seemed suitable.

To compound his chronological miscalculation, Eden also misjudged the reaction of the Soviet Union, whose ruler, Nikita Krushchev, had signalled a less confrontational approach towards the West since emerging as Stalin's successor.

Krushchev, though, was not so convinced by the case for peaceful coexistence with the capitalist enemy as to look a diplomatic gift horse in the mouth. On the one hand, the international furore aroused by the Suez intervention distracted attention from the Soviet repression of its satellite state Hungary, where a revolt against its heavy-handed rule had broken out a few days before Operation Musketeer swung into action. On the other, the Soviet relationship with Nasser's Egypt had become close enough for Krushchev to behave as if it was already a confirmed ally, allowing him to threaten a fearsome retaliation, even including the use of nuclear weapons. For Eisenhower, this was a nightmarish prospect just before a Presidential election – the terms of the NATO alliance might force him to engage in a life and death struggle with the Soviet Union, because of an act of aggression taken by fading allies who had not consulted him fully before taking the fateful plunge. The Eisenhower administration accordingly used its economic leverage to reinforce its diplomatic efforts at the UN. With the British pound sterling under international pressure, the country needed an emergency IMF loan; but the US vetoed any support. This left Britain with no choice but instant and ignominious capitulation.

'No end of a lesson'

As in the case of the 2003 Iraq War, impressions of public opinion at the time of Suez have been distorted by hindsight, making it seem that the nation's armed forces were committed against the overwhelming and clearly expressed view of ordinary people; but despite large demonstrations against the intervention, Eden's policy enjoyed widespread support. Newspapers were largely divided along partisan lines, with the traditionally left-wing press, such as the *Manchester Guardian* and the *Daily Mirror*, openly critical of the conflict, while the right-wing press – notably, *The Times* and the *Daily Telegraph* – endorsed Eden's actions.

The public response to the sudden withdrawal of British forces was one of general consternation. The extent of Eden's failure in Suez is perhaps best summed up by his biographer DR Thorpe, who outlined the four goals of the policy: first, to secure the canal; second, to ensure that the canal remained open and that oil supplies would continue; third, to remove Nasser from power; fourth, to prevent the Soviets from gaining influence. As Thorpe argues, the 'immediate consequence of the crisis was that the Suez Canal was blocked, oil supplies were interrupted, Nasser's position as the leader of Arab nationalism was strengthened, and the way was left open for Russian intrusion into the Middle East' (Thorpe, 2010, 357–8). By any standards, this was a pretty comprehensive failure, which stood in need of explanation.

The most convenient narrative depicted Suez as the product of irrational decisions by a single, sick individual. Anthony Eden was, indeed, seriously unwell, as he had been almost continuously since unsuccessful abdominal surgery in 1953. This feverish condition can help to explain why Eden became fixated with Nasser, who he saw as a reincarnation of the European dictators of the 1930s. The personal parallels were enhanced in Eden's mind by the fact that he felt double-crossed by Nasser, just as Chamberlain had been fooled by Hitler. He came to regard Nasser as

> our Enemy No. 1 in the Middle East and he would not rest until he destroyed all our friends and eliminated the last vestiges of our influence. . . . Nasser must therefore be . . . destroyed.
>
> (quoted in Mason and Asher, 1979, 638)

Anthony Nutting, a Junior Foreign Office Minister, who had been an admirer of Eden's, subsequently revealed that Eden had wanted Nasser to be murdered (Tunzelmann, 2016), 1–2.

However, the 'madman in Downing Street' thesis is unsatisfactory, not least because it portrays Eden, rather than Nasser, as the real 'dictator' in the story, able to orchestrate major foreign policy initiatives without any restraining influences. Eden was certainly flagrant in his disregard for constitutional conventions; he misled Parliament (by denying any collusion with other countries), ignored the advice of the government's own law officers, failed to consult any British diplomats in relevant locations (especially Egypt) and ordered the destruction of incriminating minutes from key meetings (Hyam, 2006, 231–8).

A more nuanced account suggests that Eden's mind was indeed affected by illness, but that, in any case, he and some senior colleagues had been sent into a panic by a mixture of reality and perception generated by Nasser's nationalisation of the Suez Canal Company. The 'reality' was that oil-dependent Britain was indeed extremely vulnerable to any threatened disruption of its fuel supplies. The 'perception' was that, unless Britain did something to stop Nasser, it would look impotent in the eyes of observers both abroad and at home. From this perspective, inactivity would be costly to Britain in economic and reputational terms. There was a risk that a military operation would meet a serious setback of some kind; equally, though, it might be conducted efficiently, lifting the economic clouds and reminding the world that Britain still mattered on the global stage.

The spectacular failure of Suez produced its own set of new realities. In particular, it dissipated the dreams behind Churchill's idea of a 'special relationship'. During the Second World War a fading colonial power (Britain) had momentarily shared a common purpose with a rising nation (the US). Churchill had tried his best to argue that this alliance should not merely be temporary; and his case could be backed by linguistic and cultural evidence. Nevertheless, the points of mutual interest between a rising and a fading global power were likely to prove fleeting, even if the diplomatic exchanges between them could proceed without interpreters. Indeed, the ease of communication between American and British diplomats could actually facilitate *disagreement*, since it could hardly be claimed that their exchanges were subject to the kind of technical verbal misunderstandings which can arise from inadequate translations. 'Misunderstandings', in short, were most likely to be due to *deliberate* evasions and misleading assurances. Whether or not Eden genuinely thought that he had US permission to embark on his Suez adventure, he certainly did not convince Canada that his cause was just. As with the US, Commonwealth states felt (with considerable justice) that Britain had developed its response to Nasser's nationalisation without adequate consultation. Since France was the only European state to support British policy in the UN, Eden had managed to alienate Britain from all three of Churchill's concentric circles at a single stroke. These relationships would have to be reconstructed by Eden's successors, but clearly the time was right for a reassessment of Churchill's order of priorities, which had placed the 'special relationship' at the top.

Anthony Nutting thus chose a very apt title for his 1967 book on Suez – *No End of a Lesson*. The remaining question was whether the appropriate lessons would be grasped and digested. Many British politicians and civil servants were well aware of the implications and now regarded their main task as the civilised management of inevitable decline. But would they pass on this message to the British public, which had been divided by Suez but was now united in bewilderment? The charitable answer is that Britain's politicians decided to shield the public from the trauma which would follow full disclosure. Put another way, they decided to act as if nothing of great moment had happened; and, in so doing, some even managed to convince themselves that this was the truth. Eden's successor set the tone. In his first broadcast as Prime Minister Harold Macmillan said that:

> Every now and again since the war I have heard people say: 'Isn't Britain only a second- or third-class power now? Isn't she on the way out?' What nonsense! This is a great country, and let us not be ashamed to say so.
> (quoted in Wallace, 1975, 207)

As such, it can be argued that among its other effects, Suez was a key moment in the development of British public opinion on foreign policy matters. There had always been a 'knowledge gap' between those who took an active interest in politics and those whose engagement was more sporadic. It was also common for people to draw different conclusions from the knowledge they gathered. However, after Suez the knowledge gap was accompanied (and in many cases reinforced) by a gulf in popular perceptions. Those who attended to the lesson of Suez had to acknowledge that Britain's place as one of the 'Big Three' in the immediate post-war era had been misleading at the time and had now been exposed as a potentially dangerous illusion. Others – with the encouragement of senior politicians – saw no reason to dispel their memories of Churchill sitting alongside Roosevelt and Stalin at Yalta in February 1945. If the lessons of Suez had been taught properly by Britain's elected representatives, it would have brought to an end the incompatible narratives which had emerged from the war, i.e. that Britain deserved its place at the 'top table' because it stood for moral rectitude in global affairs and that, as a key global player, it could be excused if, when hard-pressed, it took policy decisions which relegated moral rules to secondary considerations (at best). The harshest indictment of British politicians during the years when their country 'never had it so good' is that in defiance of all rational evidence they allowed these narratives to continue, side by side and sometimes in awkward conjunction, and bequeathed them to their successors.

Europe

It is reported that on the day that Eden decided to end the Suez misadventure the West German Chancellor, Adenauer, told the disconsolate French Prime Minister, Guy Mollet, that:

> France and England will never be powers comparable to the United States and the Soviet Union. Not Germany either. There remains to them only one way of playing a decisive role in the world: that is to unite Europe. England is not ripe for it but the affair of Suez will help prepare her spirits for it. We have no time to waste; Europe will be your revenge.
> (Kyle, 2003, 466–7)

Adenauer's alleged words implied that, for Britain, 'revenge' for Suez would be a dish served very cold indeed, if ever.

Britain's frigid reception of the 1950 Schuman Plan for cooperation among European states set the tone for the ensuing decade. Those who wanted British participation were heartened by a change of government in 1951, restoring to office Winston Churchill and Anthony Eden, both of whom had made positive noises about European unity. However, it soon seemed apparent that Churchill had only ever wanted to be a benevolent spectator, and in January 1952 Eden told an American audience that joining a European federation was something 'we know in our bones we cannot do' (Young, 1998, 74). Coming after the establishment of the European Coal and Steel Community (ECSC), which involved unmistakable federal elements, Eden's comment conveyed a clear and demoralising message for Britain's continental well-wishers. When a politician claims that an initiative is against a nation's gut instincts – or in this case its 'bones' – he or she is usually signalling that it will never join, even if it seems likely to promote the nation's interests.

In June 1955 representatives of the six founding ECSC member states conferred at Messina in Sicily. The meeting led to the appointment of a committee to investigate options for the formation of a customs union. The resulting report was discussed at an intergovernmental conference, which opened in Brussels in June 1956 and extended over several months (neatly overlapping the Suez Crisis at both ends). After some hesitation, the British decided to send an observer to the conference; and instead of a senior minister, they despatched a civil servant from the Board of Trade, Russell Bretherton. According to his own testimony, from his attendance at the Brussels meetings Bretherton not only formed the impression that a customs union was feasible, but that if Britain had thrown its weight behind the idea at this early stage, it would have been able to exercise a decisive influence over future European cooperation. Whatever his personal convictions, though, Bretherton was constrained by instructions from Whitehall; and since 1951 the Conservative government's view had changed from one of 'benevolent neutrality' to thinly veiled hostility. According to witnesses, at a meeting on 7 November 1956 – the very day that Britain and France accepted the US-dictated Suez ceasefire – Bretherton laid his country's cards on the table:

> Gentlemen, you are trying to negotiate something you will never be able to negotiate. But if negotiated, it will not be ratified. And if ratified, it will not work.
>
> (Young, 1998, 93)

All in all, as the authors of *1066 and All That* might have put it, 7 November 1956 was at least as 'memorable' as 5 November 1605, when a plot to blow up the Houses of Parliament was thwarted. It is all the more telling that the more recent date has been forgotten, not least by people who regret the failure of the Gunpowder Plot.

From the British point of view, Bretherton's predictions turned out to be wildly optimistic. The Treaty of Rome, inaugurating the EEC, was signed by the consenting six states on 25 March 1957 and came into force in the following year. In January 1960 Britain signed the Stockholm Convention to establish a European Free Trade Association (EFTA), along with Austria, Denmark, Norway, Portugal, Sweden and Switzerland. This alliance was much more to British taste; creating a free-trade area without an external tariff to discriminate against the exported goods of non-members, it allowed states to negotiate trade agreements with third parties and had minimal implications for those who took a traditional view of national sovereignty. Yet the rate of British economic growth was sluggish in comparison to that of EEC member states, especially West Germany. This, it was felt in some quarters, was because the EEC fostered competition between firms located within the different member states, so that only the efficient ones would survive. British industry, with its lamentable workplace relations and a poor record of investment in modern machinery, seemed destined to stagnate if the country refused to expose itself to the bracing environment which could only be offered by the EEC.

Anthony Eden's successor as Prime Minister, Harold Macmillan, had emulated his two Conservative predecessors by seeming to endorse European cooperation before sounding more sceptical when his chance came to take concrete decisions. However, Macmillan's growing unease about the apparent success of the EEC prompted second thoughts. These, indeed, began in the immediate aftermath of Suez, when ministers wondered if a more positive attitude to the EEC would help to rebuild the 'special relationship', since the US was keen for Britain to join (Hyam, 2006, 238). Macmillan had no illusions about either the magnitude or the necessity of the task which faced him as he prepared to commit his government to an application to join the EEC. As he put it in his memoirs,

> It was ... asking a great deal of the Conservative Party, so long and so intimately linked with the ideal of Empire, to accept the changed situation, which might require a new concept by which Britain might serve Commonwealth and world interests more efficiently if she were linked with Europe than if she remained isolated, doomed to a diminishing power in a world in which her relative wealth and strength were bound to shrink.
>
> (Macmillan, 1973, 5)

Macmillan was right to be concerned about the likely reaction from the British public, in view of the gulf in popular perceptions which had been exposed and further expanded by Suez. He could be confident, however, of persuading the Cabinet to agree on an application for EEC membership, and this was achieved formally on 27 June 1961. However, gaining the approval of the House of Commons was a far greater challenge. Apart from MPs on Macmillan's own side who were unrepentant about Suez, the Parliamentary Labour Party included many members who either retained an idealistic attachment to the Commonwealth, which allegedly would be betrayed if Britain adopted a European role, or who opposed EEC membership because the Community was a 'capitalist club' which would obstruct the development of socialism. As a result of these considerations, when explaining the change of policy to the Commons on 31 July 1961, Macmillan was careful to avoid enthusiastic expressions. In particular, his account of the implications for national sovereignty would have done little to enlighten or reassure any listener who had failed to digest the lessons of Suez:

> I am bound to say that I do not see any signs of the members of the Community losing their national identity because they have delegated a measure of their sovereignty. This problem of sovereignty, to which we must, of course, attach the highest importance is, in the end, perhaps a matter of degree.
>
> (Macmillan, 1973, 22–3)

In these words – which Macmillan obviously did not regret, since he quoted them unapologetically in his memoirs – the British Prime Minister acknowledged the gulf in perception among British voters by attaching 'the highest importance' to the question of 'sovereignty' before dismissing the object of their fears as a mere 'matter of degree'. Macmillan was astute enough to point out that the pooling of decision-making authority between states did not necessarily involve any diminution of a sense of national *identity*; but he did so in a defensive manner, which in itself was an unavailing concession to his opponents, who (despite the implications of the NATO alliance) took the view that Britain's sense of self would collapse after the slightest dilution of Westminster's decision-making role.

Against this inauspicious background, negotiations for UK membership began immediately after Macmillan's statement of intent, fronted by the consistently pro-European Edward Heath.

Africa

As we have seen, after 1945 the British attitude to overseas possessions became deeply inconsistent – if not schizophrenic. In some instances, where the cost of clinging on would be exorbitant, independence was readily granted, in keeping with the developing picture of the Commonwealth as a voluntary family of nations bonded by moral norms rather than force. Elsewhere, though, the Empire struck back hard at its opponents. Usually, this very different attitude was prompted by economic concerns – as in Malaya – but elsewhere there were other considerations at work. In Kenya, for example, where a state of emergency had been declared in 1952 (Chapter 4), the government felt a sense of obligation to white settlers who had been encouraged to make their homes there. This was seconded by the impression that the Mau Mau insurgents were unusually brutal – in contrast, of course, to the humane methods employed by British troops. At the end of the rebellion around 80,000 Kenyans were held in prison camps.

In March 1959 11 detainees were beaten to death in Hola Camp in south-east Kenya. Despite an attempted cover-up, the facts emerged and the matter was debated in the Commons. In a speech which was remembered long after his name was associated with other causes, the Conservative MP Enoch Powell argued that:

> We cannot say, 'We will have African standards in Africa, Asian standards in Asia and perhaps British standards here at home'. We have not that choice to make. We must be consistent with ourselves everywhere.
> (*Hansard, House of Commons Debates*,
> 27 July 1959, Vol. 610, col. 237)

Powell was speaking as an official inquiry into events in another African trouble spot – Nyasaland, now Malawi – was about to deliver its report. The three-man inquiry, headed by a respected (and highly conservative) judge, Patrick Devlin, depicted a scenario which closely resembled the British response to unrest in Kenya – the declaration of a state of emergency, followed by repression and what Devlin described as the institution of a 'police state'. Yet Nyasaland was a key part of a British constitutional experiment in Africa, having been joined to Northern Rhodesia (now Zambia) and white-dominated Southern Rhodesia (now Zimbabwe) in a federation which was supposed to promote racial harmony. The British government's embarrassment can be measured by the pressure it applied to Devlin to persuade him to revise his draft report, and by Macmillan's diary comment that the judge was 'Irish – no doubt with Fenian blood which makes Irishmen anti-Government on principle' – in addition to being a 'hunchback' (Catterall, 2011, 235). Subsequent governments would be more careful in the appointment of judges to preside over such sensitive inquiries.

By coincidence, Iain Macleod, Enoch Powell's oldest friend in politics, was given responsibility for these matters in October 1959 when he became Colonial Secretary. Macleod's tenancy of the Colonial Office lasted just two years, and it was known that he would be leaving the job when he told the 1961 Conservative Party conference that 'I believe quite simply in the brotherhood of man' (quoted in Garnett, 2015, 67). It was a defiant parting shot to his numerous Conservative critics, as well as implying that he, at least, took seriously the narrative which depicted Britain as a positive moral influence in world affairs.

Thanks largely to Macleod's predisposition in favour of African independence movements, Harold Macmillan was able to provide this moral narrative with its most memorable sound bite. In January 1960 he had embarked on a tour of Africa, which included Nyasaland and was rounded off with a visit to South Africa. On 3 February 1960 he addressed the Parliament in Cape Town and told his all-white audience that 'the wind of change is blowing through this continent'. Typically, Macmillan did not divulge whether or not he approved of the direction in which the wind was blowing, although he made a few positive remarks about the principle of equal opportunities. The main thrust of his argument was that the real battle was between Communism and the 'free world', rather than between races; and if racist South Africa continued along its chosen path, it would encourage all of Africa's 'liberation' movements to regard the Soviet Union as their greatest potential benefactor.

Macmillan's argument left his audience unmoved, but he could still feel that his speech had served its intended purposes, even before South African police unwittingly reinforced its message by killing 69 demonstrators at Sharpeville six weeks later. Little more than three years after Suez – and less than a year after the murders at Hola Camp – Macmillan had read a moral lesson to a regime whose principles were at least as repugnant as the ones which Britain had acted upon in those notorious incidents. By subjecting himself to a bath in some of the world's most foetid waters, Macmillan could remove Britain's moral stains in the eyes of his domestic audience. But he had contrived to do so without departing from the staple text of his American allies – 'if you think we're bad, just wait until you see what happens if the Soviets take over'. Even those who disliked 'the wind of change', in short, should bow to it if they wanted to win the Cold War.

Restoring relations with the superpowers

Whether or not its government was contemplating a radical rethink of foreign policy in the wake of Suez, Britain was unlikely to flourish if it remained on bad terms with both global superpowers. Macmillan was optimistic that he could restore amicable relations with the US, not least because he had been on friendly terms with President Eisenhower since the war. Macmillan had no such personal advantage in his dealings with the Soviet Union, but he could at least hope to bring back the wary tolerance of pre-Suez days.

Whatever Eisenhower's personal estimation of Macmillan, he was not prepared to forget Suez in a hurry. When Selwyn Lloyd – still Foreign Secretary, despite his support for Eden's calamitous policy – visited Washington in December 1956 he was unable to secure a meeting with the President (Wallace, 1975, 207). The Middle East continued to cloud the 'special relationship'. In the summer of 1957 an insurrection broke out in Oman, backed by Saudi Arabia. The Sultan of Muscat and Oman appealed to the British, who had supported the regime in an earlier conflict. Swayed by British interests in the oil industry, rather than a cool assessment of the Sultan's regime, the government responded positively. The RAF launched air strikes against rebel positions, and the Special Air Service (SAS) played a key role in the suppression of the rebels in 1959. Much to Macmillan's annoyance, the US government was strongly opposed to British involvement, although it decided not to support an Arab League protest in the UN (Lamb, 1995, 30).

Gradually, the US administration began to perceive that Macmillan, unlike Eden, was not activated by personal rancour against Nasser or by imperialist nostalgia. On this basis Britain could be useful in the overriding struggle to resist Soviet influence in the Middle East. Within a few weeks of the disagreement over Oman, Britain and the US were cooperating to forestall a Soviet attempt to take control of Syria. In the following year the Iraqi Hashemite monarchy was overthrown in a military coup which seemed to have taken inspiration (if not material support) from Nasser. The Soviet Union quickly recognised the new regime, arousing in Washington a suspicion that Eden might have been right all along in identifying Nasser as a potent threat to Western influence in the region as a whole. Lebanon and Jordan were also destabilised; this time, in contrast to the Omani incident, requests for military assistance were sent to the US as well as Britain. Macmillan seems to have been seriously tempted by the idea of avenging Suez, this time co-opting the US into a grand design which would reassert Anglo-American influence over Syria and Iraq, thus thwarting Nasser as well as the Soviets. Although Eisenhower resisted Macmillan's proposal, the leaders were in regular communication throughout the crisis and reached a tacit agreement that US troops should defend Lebanon while the British concentrated on Jordan. Iraq withdrew from the Baghdad Pact, but the new regime was unwilling to side openly either with Nasser or the Soviet Union. This allowed the British and the Americans to turn a blind eye to the brutal suppression of the regime's opponents – an attitude which persisted until the 1990 Iraqi invasion of Kuwait. However, expansionary tendencies were a different matter. In 1961, when the Iraqi dictator Abd Al-Karim Qasim threatened Kuwait, the British despatched troops with US consent, whereupon Qasim abandoned his planned aggression. The US saw no reason either to restrain the British or to send forces of its own.

It seemed as though the US, after a period in which its government regarded colonialism and communism with roughly equal hostility, had decided that it had taught Britain too much of a lesson over Suez and was now prepared to accept that colonial countries had a valid role in the struggle against the ideological enemy – even if countries such as Britain and France had not entirely repented of their imperialist misdemeanours. This new willingness to compromise with colonial countries was prompted by a deepened concern about the threat to US security posed by the Soviet Union. On 4 October 1957 the Soviets demonstrated their technological prowess by launching the world's first artificial satellite, Sputnik. This came just a few weeks after successful Soviet tests of an intercontinental ballistic missile (ICBM). Inevitably, this new sense of US vulnerability affected relations with the country's allies; and since Britain had successfully tested a hydrogen bomb in May 1957, it had to be taken seriously in this context. The news of Sputnik reinforced a new spirit of nuclear cooperation in Washington, following the installation of US-made Thor intermediate-range missiles at 20 RAF bases. In 1958 the restrictions which had been imposed by the 1946 McMahon Act were swept aside by Congress, to be replaced by agreements which really did denote a 'special' degree of cooperation between the two nations.

Macmillan was quick to appreciate that 'events' – the things which, famously, he once said that he feared the most – had operated in his favour. If Sputnik had been launched *before* Britain had mastered the technological requirements for an H-bomb, his government would not have been so well placed to take advantage of American vulnerability. As it was, for a brief moment in October 1957 Britain and the US looked rather like equals in terms of military hardware, despite the ever widening gap in their economic resources. Both of them possessed the power to wreak hideous devastation on the territory of any enemy state, but neither seemed able to match their mutual enemy, the Soviet Union, in their ability to deliver their weapons of mass destruction.

It is not improbable to regard the Sputnik launch as the moment when the 'special relationship' took on a semblance of reality, after the Suez blow which could otherwise have proved fatal. However, as Macmillan well knew, it was likely to prove little more than a 'moment'; for the US, the embarrassment of being outpaced by the Soviet Union in the 'space race' could only result in a massive increase in funding for similar American projects, and one way or another the technology gap with the Soviets would be closed as quickly as possible. For Britain, the real message of Sputnik was that it was possible to match the superpowers in terms of developing weapons with unlimited killing potential but much more difficult to rival their ability to deliver these infernal devices to their intended targets.

In 1955 the British had realised that their existing delivery systems, based on the V-2 bomber, would become obsolete within a decade at best. A new air-launched missile, Blue Streak, was duly commissioned. However, Soviet technological advances and British financial constraints led to the cancellation of the project in 1960.

If the UK could not produce an effective delivery system for its nuclear devices, Macmillan's only recourse was the US; and his only hope of persuading the Eisenhower administration to cooperate was the latter's post-Suez mood, in which Britain was seen as a potentially useful ally rather than a clapped-out country with outmoded imperial aspirations. The Americans were developing a missile, Skybolt, which could be used by existing British bombers; this made it marginally preferable on grounds of cost to the Polaris system of submarine-launched missiles, although Polaris would have the advantage of being more difficult to detect and intercept. Before leaving office at the beginning of 1961 President Eisenhower had agreed a deal whereby Britain would secure Skybolt in return for allowing the US to use Holy Loch in Argyll and Bute for nuclear submarines. However, the US preference was for nuclear weapons under NATO, i.e. American, control, rather than individual countries possessing arsenals of their own.

Against this unhelpful background, Macmillan pulled off a remarkable coup of his own. Recently dubbed 'Supermac' by the (hostile) cartoonist 'Vicky', in February 1959 he embarked on a ten-day tour of the Soviet Union, during which he talked with Krushchev about the prospects for peace. Little was to be expected from such conversations, but they were bound to impress the British electorate. Just before the 1959 general election Labour's leader, Hugh Gaitskell, made the same trek to Moscow; but this had little potential to sway undecided voters, since he was accompanied by his Shadow Foreign Secretary, Nye Bevan, who had always been a very divisive figure, and President Eisenhower had decided to visit Macmillan in London at almost exactly the same time.

Yet even as Macmillan celebrated a personal triumph when the Conservatives were re-elected just three years after the Suez humiliation, he was too astute to regard the result of the 1959 general election as more than a superficial snapshot of a deeply divided and rapidly changing country. That division can be regarded as a symptom of the gulf in popular perceptions mentioned earlier. For those who continued to think of Britain as a great power, the possession of nuclear weapons was a matter of course, and it was only right that the country should try to keep up with the technological developments of other states, whether hostile or friendly. However, those who had seen Suez as final confirmation that Britain owed its position at the 'top table' to an historical hangover were all the more likely to protest against its possession of weapons of mass destruction, if these were now to be paraded in justification for a role which Britain could (and should) no longer play. Very often, these were individuals who endorsed the parallel post-war narrative – that Britain *deserved* to be treated as a major global force, because of its moral rectitude – and now argued that the country should renounce its nuclear weapons in a gesture which other states would be sure to follow. Others thought that, given the destructive power of such weapons, Britain should get rid of them whether or not this would entail a loss of global influence.

Views of this kind were strongly represented within an organisation which, from relatively modest origins in November 1957, by 1960 was attracting around 150,000 people to its annual marches from the Aldermaston Atomic Weapons Research Establishment to London. The Campaign for Nuclear Disarmament (CND) attracted supporters from all parties, but its call for the unilateral renunciation of nuclear weapons was particularly attractive to radicals within the Labour Party. At the party's conference in 1957 Nye Bevan, who had been an outspoken critic of Eden's Suez policy, helped to defeat a unilateralist motion by arguing that such a position would prevent Britain from persuading other nuclear states to lay down their arms – it would send a future Foreign Secretary 'naked into the conference chamber'. Bevan, though, died in 1960; and, without his ability to appeal to the party's left wing, the Labour conference of that year endorsed unilateralism. It was not surprising that the pro-American Labour leader, Hugh Gaitskell, characterised the decision as a devastating blow for his party, pledging to 'fight, and fight, and fight again, to bring back sanity and honesty and dignity, so that our party – with its great past – may retain its glory and its greatness'. After all, the US had helped the Conservatives win the 1959 general election, and it was unlikely to transfer its preference to a Labour Party which was pledged to make Britain into a nuclear-free zone.

Thanks to Gaitskell's panic-stricken efforts, the 1961 Labour conference abandoned the position which the party had adopted in the previous year. Possibly hoping to shore up his credibility with the left, Gaitskell dismayed his usual allies at the same conference by claiming that membership of a 'federalist' EEC would mean 'the end of Britain as an independent nation state . . . the end of a thousand years of history'. It would certainly destroy the Commonwealth. Clearly, Gaitskell (despite his opposition to Suez) connected 'glory and greatness' with Britain as a whole and not just the Labour Party. His logic, though, was a little odd. By 1961 it was clear that the retention of nuclear weapons would increase Britain's dependence on the US; but Gaitskell evidently thought that this, unlike cooperation with other European states, would not put an 'end to Britain as an independent nation'. Others – including many Labour MPs – believed that membership of the EEC presented a possible way in which Britain could disentangle itself from the supposed 'special relationship' – or that nuclear dependence on America, as well as a commitment to 'Europe', were both fully compatible with the maintenance of Britain's sense of self in an increasingly interdependent world.

Labour's gyrations over nuclear weapons and the EEC were not helpful to Macmillan, since the Americans could only expect that Labour was likely to return to office at some point in the near future, raising the possibility that Britain would be governed by a party which was both unilateralist and anti-EEC. In January 1961 the Democrat John F Kennedy succeeded Eisenhower as US President. By a remarkable coincidence, the two leaders had been related by marriage – Kennedy's late sister Kathleen had been the wife of the Marquess of Hartington, whose aunt Dorothy was Macmillan's (unfaithful) spouse. The oddity of this connection was increased by the fact that both Harold Macmillan and 'JFK' were the privileged products of families which, in the recent past, had been anything but affluent and far removed from either London or Washington. 'Supermac''s grandfather had been a small farmer on the Scottish island of Arran, while Kennedy's grandfather's rise to riches had begun with a manual job in Boston's docks.

The fact that these humble lineages had both intermingled with members of one of England's longest-established aristocratic families, whose leading figure was the Duke of Devonshire, seems not to have affected Kennedy's relationship with Macmillan. Certainly, it did not make the latter any more sympathetic to Kennedy – or to Americans in general. After their key meeting in Nassau, Bermuda, in December 1962 Macmillan recorded of Kennedy and his team that '[i]t is *very* hard to judge whether they speak the truth or not' (Catterall, 2011, 527). This was harsh, especially since the same comment could have been applied to Macmillan himself; and the terms of the Nassau Agreement could hardly have been more congenial for the British Prime Minister. The Americans were very doubtful about the advantages arising from a deal which would allow Britain to claim (however improbably) that it still had an 'independent' nuclear capacity. Influential members of Kennedy's administration, particularly his Secretary of State, Robert McNamara (1916–2009), preferred that British nuclear forces be placed under multinational control, through NATO. Macmillan – perhaps thinking that such a detail really would put an end to 'a thousand years of history' – would not accept this. Britain, after all, had played a leading role in the development of nuclear weapons and had shared its knowledge freely with its US allies. Since this argument suggested that America was under an historic obligation, Kennedy would have been naïve to accept it in full. Nevertheless, he did put his name to a very vague deal, in which Britain's Polaris fleet would nominally be under NATO control unless a 'supreme national interest' arose, in which case it could act independently. In essence, since Britain was bound so closely to the NATO alliance, this meant that Polaris would not be under Britain's control unless some incident arose in which Britain was uniquely concerned. By the time of the Nassau summit the Americans could feel satisfied that Britain was committed to the liquidation of its Empire and had settled on a European role. Thus, in agreeing that the UK should be able to use its deterrent independently at a time of national emergency, the Kennedy administration was assuming that this time would never arise, and that the only 'emergencies' which could affect Britain in future would be considered a threat to Western civilisation as a whole.

Kennedy's conciliatory attitude at Nassau was not universally welcomed by members of his administration. However, since Eisenhower's departure from office the US had suffered more than one serious scare which reminded it of its need for allies, at least insofar as these provided psychological reassurance. A new crisis over the status of Berlin, which had been brewing since 1958, came to a head at the Vienna Summit of 1961, when Kennedy was forced to concede what looked like the permanent division of the city. In August 1961 construction began on a wall which provided a physical manifestation of this division.

The Western powers, including Britain as well as the US, seemed ready to accept this as a logical corollary of the Cold War; indeed, since the wall was designed to stop East Germans defecting to the West, rather than vice versa, it could be seen as an impressive advertisement of Communism's totalitarian methods and spiritual bankruptcy. Nevertheless, whatever the Soviet Union's deficiencies in soft power, it still be ahead of the West in terms of hard technology – and on 12 April 1961 the cosmonaut Yuri Gagarin confirmed a Soviet advantage in both respects. By becoming the first human being to orbit the earth he was launched as a celebrity as well as proving that his country was winning the space race.

The subsequent Cuban Missile Crisis, of October 1962, gave the US a chance to strike back in the war of nerves, since Krushchev agreed to dismantle the weapons which his regime had despatched to Cuba. Western propaganda presented this as a triumph for JFK, who had held his nerve despite the presence of weapons of mass destruction within easy reach of American cities. However, this 'official' narrative omits relevant facts – notably, the deployment of US weapons to Italy and Turkey, within easy reach of the USSR, and the various American attempts to unseat the Cuban President, Fidel Castro, culminating in the 1961 Bay of Pigs Invasion, which made Suez look like a well-planned incursion into friendly territory. If Anthony Eden had exaggerated the threat from Nasser, it could be argued that America had forced Castro into becoming a potential threat to its security by its unrelenting hostility towards any Cuban regime which was not slavishly supportive of its interests. Initially a nationalist rather than a communist, Castro had been pushed into the arms of the USSR by its Cold War rival.

Thus before the Nassau meeting of December 1962 Kennedy had strong reasons to adopt a conciliatory approach in the hope that, if Macmillan could emerge with a satisfactory deal, the US could rely on Britain in the unlikely event that its military assistance would be helpful. But if Nassau was a victory for Macmillan, it was typically tactical rather than strategic. If Britain really did have an 'independent deterrent' – a phrase comprising two endlessly debatable words – what, exactly, did that amount to? Nye Bevan had suggested one answer – that it would ensure Britain's place in any future negotiations to rid the world of nuclear weapons. However, this was an unlikely prospect, since the weapons could not be 'uninvented' – it was even doubtful whether members of the 'nuclear club' could bar the way to future applicants, despite Macmillan's energetic pursuit of a ban on nuclear testing, which, at most, would make things a bit more difficult for a state which wanted to join. During the Cold War the terrible (and unanswerable) argument against Britain's possession of nuclear weapons was that if they were located in British bases – and Britain remained a secondary player in the Cold War – they could make it more, rather than less, likely that the country would be targeted by a Soviet 'first strike'. In this sense – rather like Tony Blair's subsequent decision to attack Iraq, when, according to his own claims about Saddam Hussein's military strength, such a move would trigger a fearsome retaliation – British policy makers saw the possession of nuclear weapons as a one-way bet: the logic for their retention hinged on an assumption that the attack they were supposed to guard against would never happen. In both of these cases, the real motive was a desire to maintain Britain's international prestige at something like the pre-1939 level; and in neither instance did anyone within policy-making circles seriously ask whether it was really worth continuing this losing game. It was left to a Realist American academic observer, Kenneth Waltz, to reflect with elegant cruelty on the true significance of Nassau: 'A nuclear establishment maintained because of the desire to "put the 'great' back into Great Britain" turned England [sic] into a nuclear satellite of the United States' (Waltz, 1967, 152).

Outside observers, though, were content to raise the questions which most Britons were happy to ignore – either because they thought their country was weakened by the Second World War but had proved its moral mettle, or because they assumed that in terms of military (if not economic) prowess it was still a great power. A few days before the Nassau summit Dean Acheson (1893–1971), who had been US Secretary of State under Harry Truman between 1949 and 1953, told graduates from the United States Military Academy at West Point that:

> Great Britain has lost an Empire and has not yet found a role . . . The attempt to play a separate power role – that is, a role apart from Europe, a role based on a 'special relationship' with the United States, a role based on being head of a 'commonwealth' which has no political structure, or unity, or strength – this role is about played out.
>
> (Beisner, 2006, 631)

Like the title of John Osborne's play *Look Back in Anger*, the first part of this quotation almost invariably features in studies of the Macmillan years. The difference is that while Osborne was articulating the outlook of a truculent minority which probably would not have felt happy with the state of Britain at any time, Acheson was a well-known Anglophile whose remark identified an immediate existential crisis. When he negotiated the Nassau Agreement Harold Macmillan still thought that it was possible for Britain to cut a deal which would leave its security in American hands, while reassuring the member states of the EEC that the country was wholly committed to cooperation with them. However, on 14 January 1963 France's President de Gaulle called a press conference which put an abrupt end to Macmillan's transatlantic juggling act. Although de Gaulle (rightly) saw Britain's preference for the US over 'Europe' – so recently attested by the Nassau Agreement – as a reason for casting his veto, he also referred to the Commonwealth as an obstacle. Thus the first two of Churchill's concentric circles had been cited as reasons why Britain should not become a full participant in the third one. It was almost as if Acheson had been colluding with de Gaulle to make the latter's veto as hurtful as possible to British pride.

Conclusions

At the time of de Gaulle's veto Winston Churchill was still a member of the House of Commons, despite his failing physical and mental condition. In April 1963, after votes in both Houses of Congress, President Kennedy made Churchill an honorary citizen of the US. Although Kennedy thought that the French soldier and politician the Marquis de Lafayette (1757–1834) had received the honour, Churchill was in fact the first person to be singled out in this way.

Unlike some of his successors, Churchill understood that his departure from Downing Street had brought down an 'iron curtain' on his lengthy career as an important influence on public life. According to his Private Secretary, while once he would have been 'thrilled' to be made an honorary US citizen and 'would have used the occasion for at least a resounding pronouncement on Anglo-American relations', his response was 'muted'. Only after some prompting did he agree that his response should include a reference to Dean Acheson's recent remarks: 'I reject the view that Britain should now be relegated to a tame and minor role in the World'. The content of Churchill's speech was well received – even, apparently, by Acheson – but he was too ill to deliver it in person (Montague Browne, 1995, 319). If the occasion had been less solemn, Acheson could easily have retorted that Churchill had missed the point – he had not said that Britain had become a 'tame and minor' player in world affairs, but rather that it had not found a suitable post-imperial role which reflected its reduced (though still significant) status. The Prime Minister, Macmillan, played the man rather than the ball, recording in his diary that Acheson 'was always a conceited ass' (Catterall, 2011, 523). This approach was followed by the *Daily Express* and the *Daily Telegraph*. It was left to the Conservative-leaning *Spectator* magazine to articulate the true reasons for British resentment:

> in this transitional period we have a right to ask that our friends should not make matters worse. It is the nature of nations diminished in power to feel humiliated when that fact is called to their attention.
> (quoted in Wheatcroft, 2013)

When Churchill had handed over to Eden in 1955 it was already clear to close observers that Britain was in a period when it would have to 'adjust' to Cold War realities. Yet technological advances, and increased international opposition to colonialism, meant that mere 'adjustment' was not enough: there would have to be a full-blooded 'transition' from one role to another. If the lessons of Suez were not clear enough, within a few weeks of Acheson's speech the Nassau Agreement and de Gaulle's veto reinforced them. Taken together, they implied that British policy makers had decided to run the risk of being regarded internationally as subservient clients to the US, in the hope that domestically this would lend credence to the idea that Britain was still capable of exercising some degree of global influence. The fact that this residual power would, in most cases, be deployed on behalf of the US was apparently a matter of no consequence to Macmillan, who had expected that his government would fall as a result of the Suez Crisis and had developed an ability to talk strategically, while acting tactically, ever since.

Churchill had remained in office until 1955, even though his faculties were obviously impaired. The judgements of his successor, Eden, had been affected at least to some degree by ill health. By January 1963 it could confidently be predicted that this situation would never recur: an obviously ailing Prime Minister would be persuaded to step down in good time, before he or she took decisions which damaged the national interest. But in January 1963 it was far from certain that even a Prime Minister in robust mental and physical health could face the challenges presented by Acheson and de Gaulle. Harold Macmillan, who was about to enter his seventieth year at the time of de Gaulle's veto, still felt fit enough to guide his country to a new role which would be meaningful enough to satisfy the increasingly demanding (and decreasingly deferential) British electorate.

Symbols and substance, 1963–70

Introduction

If the task of finding a suitable role for Britain was not onerous enough, in the 1960s the country's decision-makers faced a new domestic challenge. In the early post-war period electoral politics in Britain was dominated by socio-economic factors – as one academic famously put it, 'class is the basis of British party politics; all else is embellishment and detail' (Pulzer, 1967, 98). Combined with the first-past-the-post voting system, this ensured the dominance of Labour (which commanded the allegiance of most members of the working class) and the Conservatives (who enjoyed the support of around three quarters of middle-class voters in these years). However, in the 1960s the rigid boundaries of Britain's class system began to blur. The electorate became more volatile and unpredictable, particularly between general elections, when voters suddenly registered the availability of the Liberal Party as a vehicle for 'protest votes'. Politicians of all parties were now expected to make themselves available for television interviews, which developed a more critical edge; and satirists began to make fun of leading establishment figures (Denver and Garnett, 2014, 2–3).

It is tempting to attribute at least part of Britain's diminishing deference to foreign policy issues – to a feeling that other world leaders were embracing the spirit of the nation's television audiences and treating British politicians as impotent figures of fun. However, surveys of public opinion suggested that foreign developments played a limited role in voting decisions, which were overwhelmingly swayed by domestic factors. The Conservative recovery between Suez and the 1959 general election had not, then, been a fluke, although Harold Macmillan could still take pride in his outwardly unflappable conduct of the diplomatic retrieval mission.

However, de Gaulle's veto of Britain's belated application for EEC membership was potentially even more damaging to the Conservatives than Suez. Macmillan was not exaggerating (much) when he wrote in his diary that '[a]ll our policies at home and abroad are in ruins' (Catterall, 2011, 539). When he had taken over from Anthony Eden Macmillan knew that, so long as he could keep his Parliamentary following broadly united, he would not need to call a general election for more than three years. A major factor in the ensuing Conservative recovery had been the replacement of a failed leader; and for obvious reasons Macmillan was anxious to prevent the same thing happening in 1963. This time, indeed, it was Labour which would have a fresh face at the top, since Hugh Gaitskell had contracted a devastating viral infection and died on 18 January 1963, days after de Gaulle decided not to bring an end to 'a thousand years of history'. Since the next election could not be delayed beyond autumn 1964, Macmillan was left with less than two years to rescue his party from a policy disaster which (unlike Suez) had happened on his own watch. If he failed, there was every reason to expect that Gaitskell's successor would be Prime Minister for most of what looked likely to be a difficult decade.

Timeline of domestic political developments

October 1964 General election: Labour wins overall majority of just four; Harold Wilson becomes Prime Minister
July 1965 Edward Heath replaces Douglas-Home as Conservative leader
March 1966 General election: Labour wins overall majority of 96
November 1967 Devaluation of pound sterling, from $2.80 to $2.40
January 1968 Announcement of decision to withdraw from bases 'east of Suez' by 1971
April 1968 Enoch Powell's 'rivers of blood' speech
June 1970 General election: Conservatives win overall majority of 31; Edward Heath becomes Prime Minister

---

Caligula's horse

When he succeeded Anthony Eden Macmillan had retained the services of the Foreign Secretary, Selwyn Lloyd, partly to give the appearance of 'business as usual', partly because Lloyd was likely to give loyal service and partly because if senior ministers were to lose their jobs as a result of misjudgements during the Suez crisis, Macmillan would have been forced to sack himself as well as Eden's Foreign Secretary.

In 1960, however, Macmillan moved Lloyd to the Treasury. In his place he appointed Lord Home, who had been Secretary of State for Commonwealth Relations since 1955. Home's appointment was controversial, not least because a Foreign Secretary who was not a member of the elected House of Commons represented a reversion to pre-war practice, rather than being in keeping with the new spirit of 'meritocracy'. Hugh Gaitskell alluded to the constitutional impropriety; the *Daily Mirror* called it the worst appointment since the Emperor Caligula had made his horse a member of the Roman Senate. More seriously, Home had been an enthusiastic supporter of Neville Chamberlain's policy of 'appeasing' Hitler and Mussolini.

Back in 1939 Macmillan and Home had been poles apart in their attitudes to key foreign policy issues, but by 1960 they could easily share a hymn sheet. Their common refrain was that the future – not just for Britain but for all nations – lay with 'interdependence'. Britain was already stronger, thanks to its alliances with the US and the Commonwealth, and its position would be enhanced further by developing ties with other European states (whether or not the country joined the EEC). Unfortunately, this benign rationalisation looked far less plausible by 1963, after de Gaulle had slammed the brakes on cooperation with the EEC in the wake of the Nassau deal, which suggested that the relationship between Britain and the US was characterised by one-sided 'dependence'. Meanwhile, the idea of an 'interdependent' Commonwealth was becoming increasingly difficult to sustain, with many British observers feeling that this relationship involved considerable responsibilities (and incessant criticism) with no compensatory benefits.

With his eye on an impending election, Macmillan had few reasons for satisfaction in the months after de Gaulle's veto, but some developments did seem to provide an element of personal vindication. Among his various charges against recent British governments, Dean Acheson had claimed that 'Great Britain, attempting to be a broker between the United States and Russia, has seemed to conduct policy as weak as its military power' (Wheatcroft, 2013). In other words, Macmillan might have reaped electoral advantage from his dealings with the superpowers, but the idea that Britain could find a viable role as a catalyst for deals between Washington and Moscow was fanciful. Nevertheless, in August 1963 it seemed that Britain had indeed acted as an effective go-between. Along with the US and the Soviet Union it signed a Partial Test Ban Treaty, confining the detonation of prototype nuclear weapons to underground sites. The main purposes of the treaty were to prevent further environmental damage arising from atmospheric tests and to make it more difficult for future aspirants to join the 'nuclear club'. As such, it was hardly a major sacrifice for existing members to sign up, and enforcement was always going to be problematic. Nevertheless, the negotiations had been sufficiently protracted to suggest that the issue was being taken seriously on both sides of the Iron Curtain, and the British certainly played a notable part in the final stages.

Macmillan experienced a similar frisson in relation to the imperial outpost of British Guiana, on the northern coast of South America. In 1953 elections had been held in the colony, under the first-past-the-post voting system. The result had been a comfortable victory for the People's Progressive Party (PPP), which surprised and discomfited the British, who felt that the party was susceptible to communist influence. A state of emergency was declared, and the colony returned to direct rule from London. When various attempts were made to reintroduce democratic procedures the people showed an inconvenient propensity to retain their preference for the PPP. In 1961 British Guiana was given self-governing status, but full independence was withheld pending evidence that would satisfy London of the country's future stability. Eventually, the British decided that first-past-the-post was inappropriate in this context and that the interests of democracy would best be served by a system of proportional representation. When this was applied in 1964 the PPP fell short of an overall majority, forcing it to govern in coalition.

This kind of heavy-handed interference in a country within America's long-established sphere of influence would have aroused considerable resentment at almost any other time in the preceding century. However, in the aftermath of the Cuban Missile Crisis the US was petrified by the possibility of a repetition, and the geographical situation of British Guiana made it a possible destination for Soviet weapons which could pose a direct threat to American cities. In such circumstances the Kennedy administration decided that Britain could be as heavy-handed as it liked in its attempts to thwart the PPP. After talks on this subject in July 1963 Macmillan recorded that it was 'rather fun making the Americans repeat over and over again their passionate plea to us to stick to "Colonialism" and "Imperialism" at all costs' (Catterall, 2011, 578).

The irony of this situation might have been delicious for Macmillan, but it was unlikely to win him any votes. In this respect, 1963 had opened badly for him, and things took a turn for the worse in March, when the Secretary of State for War, John Profumo, was forced to deny rumours that there had been any 'impropriety' in his relationship with a young model, Christine Keeler. In early June Profumo admitted that he had lied to the House of Commons and resigned. It emerged that Ms Keeler had taken the spirit of 'interdependence' a little too far by also befriending an official who was working for the Soviet embassy. This provided the Labour Opposition with an ideal opportunity to present Profumo's personal indiscretion as a threat to national security.

Macmillan's response to the scandal was generally regarded as being weak, making him seem out of touch with a fast-changing country. The former minister Nigel Birch provided these criticisms with a literary punchline, quoting Robert Browning's attack on William Wordsworth: while Macmillan remained as Prime Minister it could never be 'glad confident morning again'. Despite adverse findings in public opinion polls, Macmillan decided to stay in office, and on 7 October he was preparing to inform the Cabinet to this effect. However, during that night he was suddenly afflicted by a prostate condition which enforced his resignation. Macmillan's recovery from the ensuing surgery was speedy enough to allow him to take an active (if not decisive) part in the choice of his successor, which in those days was still determined by informal 'soundings' rather than a vote. Reflecting on the options, Macmillan noted that 'the party in the Country wants [Quintin] Hogg; the Parliamentary Party wants [Reginald] Maudling or [RAB] Butler; the Cabinet wants Butler' (Catterall, 2011, 607). Armed with this information, the outgoing Prime Minister reached the improbable conclusion that the party as a whole would be best suited by a candidate who was not the first choice of any of its component parts – Lord Home. Caligula's horse would have been envious – not only had Home been chosen as a key political decision-maker, but he had also been designated as the Emperor's successor.

Macmillan's support for Home can be explained in terms of personalities – he genuinely liked Home, whereas his feelings towards the other possible successors ranged from mild sympathy to (in the case of Butler) unquenchable aversion. However, while Butler, Hogg and Maudling might easily have proved unsuccessful Prime Ministers, at least their failure could not be predicted in advance, whereas only some improbable turn of events could have made Home seem electable, for reasons which were evident to any impartial observer. Before acceding to his hereditary peerage in 1951 Home had been an MP for 20 years; but between 1951 and 1963 the House of Commons had changed considerably, and Home, who had just turned 60 when he became Prime Minister, was ill equipped for rapid adaptation. As it was, having returned to the Commons (thanks to a convenient by-election) as plain old Sir Alec Douglas-Home, the new Prime Minister was pitched against Harold Wilson, one of the quickest-witted Leaders of the Opposition in British history. Douglas-Home's lack of debating skill was also evident in his inability to master the newly dominant medium of television, which Wilson seemed to relish.

Even Douglas-Home's greatest strength proved to be a serious weakness in the context of 1963–4. Whatever his defects as a politician, he had been involved in diplomacy for a long time, and it was reasonable to suppose that he possessed considerable knowledge of foreign affairs. Some of his judgements, however, were strikingly superficial. For example, in his memoirs he mused that '[t]he individual Russian is, I think, a naturally friendly and gay person, but the Communist system is like a wet blanket and stifles fun' (Home, 1976, 245).

Whatever Douglas-Home's real qualities as a servant of British interests abroad, we have seen that even in exceptional circumstances British voters tended to take their decisions on the basis of *domestic* factors. Douglas-Home's best ploy would have been to organise photo-opportunities with world leaders, giving an impression of statesmanship which would provide a positive background for an election campaign dominated as usual by the economy, public services, etc. However, he had no intention of reordering his personal priorities, and the 1964 Conservative campaign was organised to accommodate him. The first section of the party's manifesto was devoted to global developments, followed by a lengthy disquisition on the Commonwealth. Labour's strategists, by contrast, saved their indictment of the government's foreign policy record until the last pages of their own manifesto.

Just conceivably, during Douglas-Home's tenure of Downing Street – which lasted almost exactly a year – some dramatic development might have transpired, allowing him to showcase his long-practised diplomatic acumen. Just a few weeks after Douglas-Home took office the assassination of President Kennedy seemed to provide such an opportunity. However, the Prime Minister's contribution to a BBC memorial programme was considered 'stilted and formal' in comparison to those of Wilson and the Liberal leader, Jo Grimond, and Tory MPs could only wonder how Macmillan, who had some real fondness for Kennedy, would have exploited the occasion for electoral advantage (Howard and West, 1965, 106–7).

Douglas-Home's premiership featured other relevant events. For example, the long-running ethnic conflict in Cyprus (Case Study 6.1) resurfaced, leading to the despatch of a UN peacekeeping force which illustrated the benefits of 'interdependent' action. However, the deep-rooted problems of Cyprus – and the fact that Britain had left these unresolved when the island became a Republic in 1960 – could scarcely be regarded as a vindication of Douglas-Home's belief that the Commonwealth would be an electoral trump card for the Conservatives. In December 1963 a grenade attack on British officials in the South Arabian colony of Aden led to the announcement of a state of emergency and a vicious crackdown on dissident groups, who took their inspiration from the notorious Nasser. However, this made little impact on the British public (and was not deemed to be worthy of mention in Douglas-Home's published memoir, *The Way the Wind Blows* (1976)). It was left to the next government to extricate Britain from this late-imperial imbroglio.

In its contest with a governing party which seemed to have outstayed its welcome and had just saddled itself with an unsuitable leader, Labour was well placed to secure a comfortable overall majority in the general election of October 1964. Its failure to surpass all other parties by more than four seats was, and remains, difficult to fathom. Labour was well aware that it could no longer rely on its working-class base for electoral victory, and Wilson (as a brilliant Oxford graduate) had considerable cross-class appeal as the figurehead of a campaign which was targeted on 'aspirational' voters, whatever their social origins. While Wilson could present himself as the champion of a 'meritocratic' society, Douglas-Home was at best a passable representative of the British aristocracy, whose best days were clearly over.

Case Study 6.1 Cyprus

The Mediterranean island of Cyprus was always likely to prove an awkward candidate for decolonisation. In part, this was because the island was divided on ethnic lines – between the majority Greek Cypriot population and those of Turkish ancestry, mostly living in the North – but also because of its strategic importance. This seemed to grow after 1954, when Britain agreed to withdraw from its military installation in the Suez Canal zone. At the time, a British minister gave the impression that the country would never grant full independence to Cyprus.

The chief source of resistance to British rule came from Greek Cypriots seeking 'enosis' – a union between Cyprus and Greece. This prospect was unpalatable to the British, despite the fact that Greece (as well as Turkey) had become a NATO ally in 1952. British ministers were particularly exercised by suspected links between the Orthodox Archbishop of Cyprus, Makarios, and pro-enosis insurgents. In March 1956 Makarios was forced into exile. By this time there were around 12,000 British troops on Cyprus as unrest escalated; in 1956 there were more than 200 violent deaths (Brendon, 2008, 620–1). The Greek government began an action against Britain in the European Court of Human Rights, to the consternation of British ministers who had assumed that the European Convention would never be applied to them.

Cyprus was used as a key base for British operations during the 1956 Suez crisis, and this was held to have exposed its strategic limitations. As a result, when Harold Macmillan succeeded Anthony Eden in 1957 one of his first key decisions was to release Makarios in the hope that this would help to quell the insurgency. Just three years after the ministerial hint that Britain would never cede sovereignty Macmillan noted that 'I am as anxious as anyone to get clear of Cyprus . . . I am not persuaded that we need more than an airfield . . . Then the Turks and Greeks c[oul]d divide the rest of the island between them' (Catterall, 2011, 18). Even though Makarios was not allowed to return to Cyprus, the Marquess of Salisbury, the Leader of the House of Lords, resigned in protest. Determined to avoid a settlement that smacked of appeasement, the British poured more troops into Cyprus to conduct a campaign which included the familiar features of mass arrests and torture.

In 1959, however, the Greek government decided that enosis was not practicable and sought a deal with Britain which would facilitate Cypriot independence. Makarios was persuaded to accept this and to allow that two areas of the island would remain as British Overseas Territories for

> military purposes. Independence was duly delivered in August 1960. However, inter-communal violence erupted in 1963 after Makarios proposed constitutional changes which were rejected by the Turkish government, and the British troops stationed on the island were unable to restore order. As a result, UN peacekeepers were called in and an uneasy truce persisted for the next decade.

Douglas-Home's contribution to British politics did not end with his 1964 defeat or his deposition as Conservative leader in the following year. He agreed to serve as Shadow Foreign Secretary under his successor, Edward Heath, and when his party won the 1970 general election he became Foreign Secretary once again – this time as an MP, rather than a member of the House of Lords. When he came to write his memoirs Home identified a common error 'about Britain's conduct of foreign policy' – a 'failure to recognise that our role in the world had changed as our relative power had diminished, and that the change was permanent' (Home, 1976, 173). Even this mild protest against the obtuse nature of British public opinion, which could not rid itself of the post-war great-power narrative, becomes less persuasive in comparison with the tone of the manifesto issued by the Conservative Party under Douglas-Home's leadership in 1964. In his foreword the Prime Minister invited voters 'to conclude that we should retain British power and influence', re-electing his party in order to 'gain the vitality to keep our country great'. Thus despite – or maybe because of – his personal shortcomings, Douglas-Home provides the most telling evidence of the post-war tendency among British politicians to acknowledge relative decline in private but to deny it in public.

Labour's 'New Britain'

In a speech of November 1964 Harold Wilson claimed that he would ask the British people for just one sacrifice – the sacrifice of illusion. The policy area most encumbered by illusion was foreign affairs, as Douglas-Home had correctly diagnosed. However, it soon transpired that Harold Wilson was keen to give these illusions a semblance of reality, rather than dispelling them. Ironically, this ill-conceived objective arose from Wilson's expertise in a key area of *domestic* policy. By far the best-qualified academic economist ever to have served as Prime Minister, Wilson saw Britain's relative global decline in economic terms: put the economy right and the country would be recognised once again as the global power that it had always been. Furthermore, this goal was readily achievable. The Conservatives, Wilson imagined, had failed to embrace technological change and had overlooked the positive role which government could play in promoting economic growth. In fact, Macmillan had encouraged a form of economic 'planning' through discussions between government, employers and trade unions. Rather than starting on an entirely new economic project, Wilson merely wanted to take it further in the hope that this would generate something akin to the West German 'economic miracle', without the unpleasant necessity of having to join the EEC.

In fact, while posing as the personification of a new and enticing future for Britain, Wilson's view of the world was anchored in the past. In his first major Commons speech on foreign affairs, Wilson referred to Britain's world role, 'which no one in this House or indeed in the country, will wish us to give up or call in question' (*Hansard, House of Commons Debates*, 16 December 1964, Vol. 704, col. 420). This was a more significant remark than Wilson's earlier statement that '[w]e are a world power and a world influence or we are nothing' (Guildhall speech, 16 November 1964); the Prime Minister was implying that even those who dared to *question* this proposition were beyond the political pale.

Wilson, in short, rejected the idea that British governments had no alternative to the civilised management of inexorable decline. However, his optimistic visions were banished as soon as he took office. It turned out that his accusations of Tory economic mismanagement had been all too accurate. Although British exports were increasing, they were not keeping pace with the demand for imported goods. As a result, the Treasury was forecasting a balance-of-payments deficit of around £800 million for 1964. In an attempt to relieve the inevitable pressure on the value of sterling, Wilson's government embarked on a deflationary course which overshadowed the remainder of its term of office.

Wilson now had to confront the consequences of the inconclusive 1964 general election. If he had secured a comfortable majority, he could have announced that the mess bequeathed by his opponents could only be cleared up by drastic measures. He could weather the political storm created by a devaluation of sterling, in the expectation that the economy would have established a more healthy equilibrium by the time of the next election. As it was, he could not hope to survive for long with a wafer-thin majority and a Parliamentary Labour Party which was split on ideological lines. A new election would have to be called in the near future – indeed, if sterling was devalued, the ensuing political crisis could easily trigger an immediate contest. Having formed part of the government which was forced to accept devaluation in 1949, Wilson was in an excellent position to estimate the potential damage arising from a second dose of the same medicine.

Thus in 1964 political imperatives trumped economic considerations – another recurrent theme of Wilson's first administration. But there would also be a heavy price to pay in terms of foreign policy. In the long term Wilson's idea of restored global influence backed by economic resurgence was gravely endangered, if not negated, by the policy of deflation. In the short term the need to curtail government spending raised the prospect of sharp cuts in the defence budget. Indeed, Britain's global presence was in itself a source of difficulties for the balance of payments and for sterling. A retrenchment on overseas commitments seemed to be indicated. Yet, according to Wilson himself, this would mean that from being a prominent world power Britain had dwindled away to 'nothing'.

In acting to preserve the value of sterling (and his own position) rather than consulting Britain's long-term economic interests, Wilson had effectively decided to cling to *symbols* of prestige at the risk of undermining the *substance* of power. Whatever their other uses, nuclear weapons could be regarded as another potent symbol of Britain's continuing global relevance. In Labour's 1964 manifesto, Polaris had been treated as a luxury which the country could easily deny itself; the so-called 'British independent deterrent' 'will not be independent and it will not be British and it will not deter. Its possession will impress neither friend nor potential foe'. Rather than engaging in the self-defeating nuclear game, Britain would entrust its existing arsenal to a multinational force. However, the fate of Polaris was left uncertain; Britain would merely renegotiate Macmillan's Nassau deal. Despite this ambiguity, Whitehall officials expected the Polaris project to be cancelled, and Wilson had given the same impression during a pre-election visit to Washington (where, of course, Nassau had been regarded with mixed feelings).

Within days of taking office the Labour government had committed itself to Polaris – after a discussion between Wilson, his formidable Defence Secretary Denis Healey and the Foreign Secretary Patrick Gordon-Walker (Ponting, 1989, 87–8). The proposed Multi-Lateral Force (MLF) was also dropped. Even if Britain's place at the 'top table' was justified by nothing more tangible than its membership of the 'nuclear club', the deterrent would have to be retained; indeed, if nuclear weapons were the last remaining fig leaf, they became all the more necessary as a means of concealing the country's nudity. Although Labour's unilateralist MPs were numerous enough to bring down the government on this issue, they held their fire, even finding the fortitude to overlook Rab Butler's provocative observation that 'in general terms the Government are following the main lines of the foreign policy which we laid down' (*Hansard, House of Commons Debates*, 16 December 1964, Vol. 704, col. 402).

Aden, Vietnam and Rhodesia

One area of apparent continuity between the Conservative and Labour governments was Aden. According to Mark Curtis, under Labour 'Britain sought to counter a national liberation movement in favour of continued rule by friendly despots' (Curtis, 2003, 280). In reality, this verdict credits the new government's policy with a coherence which it lacked. The Colonial Secretary, Anthony Greenwood, had in fact been 'determined to reverse Conservative policy by ditching the feudal rulers who had become allies' (Hyam, 2006, 355). However, it was difficult to contemplate withdrawal with rival rebel groups fighting each other as well as targeting British troops. In addition, American politicians, who in 1945 had regarded 'colonialism', rather than 'communism', as the worst of the two C words, had now turned full circle and were urging the British to cling on to military bases 'east of Suez'. Clinging on, in Aden, entailed the adoption of increasingly squalid tactics, including the regular use of torture. It provided an ironic commentary on Labour's 1964 manifesto, which had boasted of the party's record of decolonisation, claiming that there was '[n]o nobler transformation in the story of the human race' than the transition from Empire to Commonwealth.

The 'noble transformation', of course, had largely been prompted by US economic pressure. By 1964 the same weapon was being used to push the British in the opposite direction. As well as encouraging the Wilson government to maintain the value of sterling (to prevent a more general destabilisation of international currencies), the Lyndon Johnson administration hoped that Britain would make at least a token contribution to its escalating struggle in Vietnam. This, after all, was the quid pro quo which had operated during the Korean War. This time, however, Wilson could plead that his hands were tied, not just because of Britain's relative poverty but because his vulnerable Parliamentary position would be endangered if he agreed to despatch British troops. In 1965 the two governments agreed that British assistance would be chiefly diplomatic, but also logistical – US troops were offered training in counter-insurgency tactics, and (despite Parliamentary denials) weapons were sold for use against the Vietcong (Ponting, 1989, 219–21).

Wilson's attempts to resolve the Vietnam conflict were genuine enough – not least because successful mediation would win him plaudits at home. However, his efforts were often maladroit and lent further support to Acheson's view that Britain could not find a viable role as a conduit between the superpowers. In February 1965 Wilson suggested a visit to Washington in order to give Lyndon Johnson the benefit of his advice. The US President replied with a volley of invective, suggesting that Wilson's advice might be more welcome if the British had actually contributed to the war effort (Pimlott, 1992, 387). In February 1967 Wilson thought he was making progress in talks with the Soviet Prime Minister, Kosygin, only to be thwarted by a hardening of the American position. Wilson protested vehemently, but Johnson was unmoved. The only cause for surprise was that, on this occasion, the Soviet leadership seemed to take Britain seriously as an intermediary, despite its great and growing dependence on the US. The country was simply too broke to be a broker.

Since it is difficult to see how even an efficient contribution to a successful intervention in Vietnam could have brought concrete advantages for Britain, this can be regarded as an instance where Wilson was forced by circumstances to put his country's immediate needs above his desire to propitiate the US. The Labour left was well aware of Wilson's true motives and knew that he scarcely deserved credit for keeping Britain out of the conflict, but at least they could be happy with the outcome. They were less content with Britain's relative inactivity in relation to Rhodesia; on this occasion the main celebrants were right-wing Conservatives.

Like the balance-of-payments crisis, Rhodesia was a toxic problem inherited from the Conservatives. The Central African Federation, which they had established as recently as 1953, only survived for a decade. Northern Rhodesia (Zambia) and Nyasaland (Malawi) were given independence. In those states the privileged position of tiny white minorities was clearly unsustainable, and Britain accepted the inevitability of majority rule. Southern Rhodesia, however, was different. With a more sizeable white population (around 8 per cent), and a geographical proximity to South Africa which was too close for comfort, it seemed well placed to brave Macmillan's 'Wind of Change' and move from a system which was already highly discriminatory to full-blooded apartheid. Without constitutional changes which allowed for majority rule, Britain could not grant independence without incurring international odium. The growing likelihood of a collision with the imperial power increased political polarisation within Southern Rhodesia, leading to the election of a more rigid government led, after 1963, by Ian Smith. A tough negotiator, Smith also had a record of distinguished service as a Second World War fighter pilot. If he had been blessed with a touch of charisma, he would have been the opponent of Wilson's worst nightmares; and even a humourless Smith proved to be a redoubtable antagonist.

If giving Southern Rhodesia independence without meaningful reform would make Britain look immoral, the obvious alternative – that the colony would declare itself independent without British permission – would expose its impotence. Smith was well aware that Britain lacked either the resources or the political will for military intervention. After fruitless negotiations Southern Rhodesia made a Unilateral Declaration of Independence (UDI) in November 1965.

The British government was resigned to this step and had been exploring the possibility of imposing sanctions on the rebel colony. The main problem, even with American backing, was making such measures effective without causing considerable hardship in neighbouring African states. At the Commonwealth conference of January 1966 Wilson saw a way past this dilemma, predicting that sanctions 'might well bring the rebellion to an end within a matter of weeks rather than months' (Pimlott, 1992, 377). It was an uncharacteristic verbal indiscretion from a politician who normally weighed his words carefully – why precede such an ambitious claim with a qualifying clause ('might well')? It turned out that Wilson should have said 'decades rather than years'; it was left to the first Thatcher government to settle the Rhodesian issue (Chapter 7).

After the 1966 general election Wilson continued his own dispiriting search for a settlement. In December of that year he met Smith on board a British warship sailing off Gibraltar – a venue for talks which conveyed ambiguous messages about Britain's past and present status. Wilson offered concessions which might not have proved acceptable to his Parliamentary party – or to Britain's Commonwealth partners – but was spared that indignity by Smith's rejection of the terms. In October 1968 the pair held another Gibraltarian rendezvous, this time aboard the inaptly named *HMS Fearless*. By now Wilson was prepared to contemplate a deal which would have allowed independence without majority rule. Smith, emboldened by clear evidence that the sanctions regime was not working (thanks to endemic evasions), returned the same negative answer. Wilson tried to convince himself that the talks had been worthwhile because Smith's rigidity would cost him support among the British public – a typical misreading of non-progressive opinion by moderate post-war politicians of all parties. A more important source of consolation was the fact that Conservative MPs were as sharply divided on the issue as their Labour counterparts. Just before the 1970 general election the rebel colony declared itself the Republic of Rhodesia.

Wilson's second term

At the end of February 1966 Wilson felt confident enough of victory to call a new general election. After the poll, on 31 March, Labour was left with an overall majority of 96.

As in 1964, foreign and defence policy was covered at the end of Labour's manifesto. The tone, however, was very different in the 1966 document. In 1964 the party had accused the Conservatives of losing 'any sense of vision of Britain's role in the second half of the twentieth century'. In 1966 Labour's own 'vision' seemed to have faded. The voters were admonished that '[a]lthough we are a world power with world responsibilities, this is not the nineteenth century when Britain ruled one-quarter of mankind. We have to see ourselves realistically in the right proportions'. Instead of applauding itself for its part in decolonisation, the party now seemed inclined to be apologetic and nostalgic.

A greatly enhanced Parliamentary majority only remedied one portion of Wilson's political problems. In June 1967 the Six Day War between Israeli and Arab forces resulted in another conclusive defeat for the latter. Any satisfaction which might have been felt at this devastating setback for Egypt's President Nasser was nullified by the closure of the Suez Canal, exposing once again Britain's dependence on oil imports and causing further damage to its balance of payments. On 15 November 1967 Wilson finally bowed to a combination of pressures, and accepted that sterling would have to be devalued, from $2.80 to $2.40. After the announcement the Prime Minister delivered a broadcast to the nation. In his anxiety to minimise the change – which he had done so much to resist – he committed another serious gaffe, implying that the value of 'the pound in the pocket' would be unaffected. On 27 November General de Gaulle rejected Britain's renewed application for EEC membership, which Wilson had launched in May. Compared to the General's first veto of 1963, his unsurprising decision was felt as little more than a pinprick within Whitehall, which was still reeling from the decision to devalue.

To make devaluation effective the government had to embark on a new round of spending cuts; and once again the defence budget was identified as low-hanging fruit. In 1966 a wide-ranging review had pared expenditure, recommending among other things the end of Britain's unwelcome presence in Aden. However, the net result envisaged a continuation of the global role, with fewer resources. Once the election was safely won, the government showed more of its real intentions with a further White Paper (of July 1967), which proposed a withdrawal from major facilities east of Suez by the mid 1970s. In the wake of devaluation, this timetable was accelerated. The withdrawal would now be completed before the end of 1971. Among other consequences, this decision meant that Britain would no longer require American-built F-111 fighter-bombers, which were intended for a role east of Suez. The order was duly cancelled.

From one perspective, the series of events and enforced decisions since Eden embarked on the Suez enterprise in 1956 was regrettable only because it had unfolded slowly and inexorably, rather than culminating in a single calamitous episode which might have triggered a national debate. The ultimate result, after all, had been implicit at the outset; long before 1956 it had been obvious that Britain could not sustain a global role unaided. After devaluation and military disengagement the country could face the future free from any hangovers from an irrelevant past. While realigning itself as a middle-ranking power whose interests lay mainly in Europe, it could retrieve something from the wreckage of the post-Suez period and wholeheartedly embrace the moral narrative which had been invoked sporadically since 1945. On this view, even if it was not a global *power*, Britain could draw on residual reserves of international goodwill (its soft power) to remain as a potential source of constructive *influence*. The experiences of Macmillan and Wilson suggested that Britain certainly could not *command* this role; however, the country continued to pursue global interests and it should be ready to play a mediating role in future if invited to do so.

However, there were two serious obstructions to this scenario. The first was the nuclear question. Even in 1968 there was no possibility that Britain would give up its deterrent. In some quarters this position may have reflected a sincere feeling that the country would be vulnerable to Soviet aggression if it relinquished nuclear weapons. However, this logic depended upon the attribution to the Soviet Union of expansionist tendencies, which seemed more than a little fanciful; indeed, it could plausibly be countered that the possession of nuclear weapons actually made it *more* likely that the Soviets would identify Britain as a prime military target, even if their purpose was self-defence rather than an irrational desire for territorial acquisition. A more tenable argument was that, as a nuclear power, Britain could be sure of playing some part in negotiations which might lead to multilateral disarmament. However, whether or not Britain's nuclear weapons were truly independent, the country's arsenal was dwarfed by that of America and the Soviet Union (not to mention China, which tested a hydrogen bomb in 1967). In disarmament talks Britain would have a voice, but it would be distinctly muffled. And in order to enjoy even this marginal influence the country would be dependent on the US for technical assistance and thus less likely to be called upon as an ethical arbiter in any of the world's serious disputes.

The extent of that dependence was illustrated, crudely and covertly, in a deal struck between Britain and Mauritius before that Indian Ocean colony was granted independence in 1965. The British proposed to detach Mauritius from a group of small neighbouring islands, the largest of which, Diego Garcia, had been identified by the US as a potential military base. In compensation the British paid Mauritius £3 million. They proceeded to force out the local population of around 2,000 people by various unscrupulous methods before handing Diego Garcia to the Americans for £5 million, on a minimum lease of 50 years. The transaction was completed without any Parliamentary discussion, and it was hoped that the British public would never know about it. Assuming that they were liberated at last from the leash of domestic and international scrutiny, Foreign Office personnel seemed to relish the opportunity to articulate their private feelings about colonial subjects. One official jeered that the inhabitants of Diego Garcia 'have little aptitude for anything other than growing coconuts'. In 1982 the British government offered a total of £4 million as compensation to the displaced people – a sum which, allowing for subsequent inflation and the fall in the value of sterling since the mid 1960s, was far less than Britain had been paid for Diego Garcia by the Americans (Curtis, 2003, 414–31). It can safely be said that had the treatment meted out to the inhabitants of Diego Garcia been replicated by any unfriendly power after 1945, Britain would have seized on the evidence as proof of its own moral superiority.

The episode presented an interesting contrast to Britain's treatment of the Falkland Islands in the South Atlantic, which was home to a similar number of people. Under pressure from Argentina, which claimed sovereignty over the islands, by 1968 Wilson's government was prepared to reach a compromise. However, it was felt that these particular islanders deserved to be consulted about their fate, not least because they enjoyed support from a vocal group of Parliamentarians – thus they should gently be guided towards the right decision, i.e. to accept the technical sovereignty of Argentina, while remaining under British administration through a 'leaseback' arrangement, rather than being forced to abandon their bleak isolation. Unfortunately for the British, ministerial soundings suggested that the islanders were oblivious to the promptings of rational-choice theory and overwhelmingly preferred the constitutional status quo. For the time being, at least, it was clear that Labour would not be able to add the Falkland Islands to its lustrous record of voluntary decolonisation.

If Britain's claim to moral influence was difficult to reconcile with its dependence on a superpower whose decisions were characterised by amoral calculations, domestic developments endangered its remaining ethical stature within months of the decision to withdraw from east of Suez. A repressive policy adopted by the Kenyan government towards its Asian residents, culminating in legislation of 1967 limiting their right to pursue business interests, prompted a precipitous rise in migration from that country to Britain. In 1948 the Attlee government had created the status of 'Citizen of the United Kingdom and Colonies', giving the right of migration to the UK to people throughout the Empire and Commonwealth. This situation was modified by the Macmillan government in 1962, as part of the general policy of imperial retreat. However, in 1968 many Kenyan Asians retained the right of settlement in the UK in recognition of the fact that they (or their ancestors) had been uprooted from their original homes in pursuit of Britain's imperial goals.

The Act of 1962, which restricted the right of migration to Britain of people from what became known as the 'New' Commonwealth, had been prompted at least in part by a feeling that unrestricted immigration was exercising an undue influence on the balance of the country's population. In short, while Macmillan was exhorting white settlers in Africa to accept the 'Wind of Change', politicians in Britain had decided that it was time to shield the mother country from this climatic development. The desire to appease racist sentiment increased after the 1964 general election, when Patrick Gordon-Walker, Wilson's preferred candidate to serve as Foreign Secretary, lost his Midlands Parliamentary seat to a Conservative who had campaigned on the slogan 'if you want a nigger for a neighbour, vote Labour'. In a hurried response to the Kenyan crisis further restrictions on immigration were introduced, which were indisputably discriminatory to Black and Asian people. In its defence the Wilson government could argue that this measure had been preceded by legislation to outlaw the ugliest manifestations of racial discrimination in Britain. However, on 20 April 1968 the Conservative front-bench spokesman Enoch Powell delivered a speech which quoted Virgil's *Aeneid*, warning of 'rivers of blood' which would flow unless the migrant question was addressed with more urgency.

It was possible to square Powell's position with his oration on the Hola Camp atrocities (Chapter 5) but only with some imaginative licence. Whether or not Powell himself was a racist, in the 'rivers of blood' speech he quoted the views of prejudiced individuals without critical comment. Powell was ejected from the Conservative front bench as a result of his speech. However, it raised him from his previous obscurity to superstar status compared to other British politicians; rightly or wrongly, many Britons thought that he had spoken out on their behalf while other senior figures had turned a blind eye to the evidence of rising racial tension, especially in Britain's inner cities. In fact, Powell had known that he was pushing at an open door – or, rather, helping to slam a door that was already being closed. Most British politicians now accepted that the 1948 British Nationalities Act had been a mistake, which had itself been inspired by imperialist emotions, akin to those which had induced the Romans to extend equal citizenship to every individual within the boundaries of its Empire. The difference was that these 'orthodox' politicians were reluctant to criticise the practical impact of this legislation for fear of sounding too much like Ian Smith or (as in the case of the EEC application) of saying things which tended to subvert the post-war narrative, which continued to serve as an electoral comfort blanket for the main parties. Powell had no such inhibitions; indeed, a selection from his speeches on foreign affairs constitutes a cull of his country's sacred cows, attacking among (many) other things the fetish for nuclear weapons, the 'special relationship' and the reality of a military threat from the Soviet bloc. In exchange for the possibility of holding high office in a future Conservative government he was rewarded by a degree of adulation which he could not otherwise have expected from people who probably disagreed with the overwhelming majority of his views. On the surface the emergence of 'Powellism' was a problem for the Conservative Party, rather than the Labour government; but in a world where racial differences were being acknowledged as a rival to ideology as a source of division the popularity of Powell's message could only impair the country's claim to moral superiority.

At least the Labour government could claim to be a resolute opponent of the racist South African regime, having included in its 1964 manifesto a pledge to stop supplying it with arms. In reality, the government did allow the export of equipment (including helicopters) with military capacity; and in other respects trade with South Africa continued to flourish. In June 1967 the South African government proposed a major arms sale, worth around £100 million, including frigates and planes. The issue caused a bitter and protracted Cabinet dispute, with ministers almost equally divided at a time when the pressure on sterling made a deal seem expedient. Wilson himself seemed unwilling to commit himself, before coming down firmly against the sale. For the Prime Minister, a change of policy towards South Africa would evidently have been a volte-face too far (Ponting, 1989, 297–8).

Wilson and his colleagues were less inclined to agonise over arms sales when they felt unconstrained by racial considerations. In July 1967 civil war had erupted in Nigeria after the Biafran region in the east of the country announced its secession. The British Cabinet had no hesitation in supporting the federal government, ostensibly because Nigeria's territorial integrity should be upheld. More importantly, the interests of the oil industry were at stake. A further issue was the provision of arms to the federal side by the Soviet Union; mindful of the dreadful Suez precedent, British ministers felt that they could not afford to be less generous. However, the Biafran rebels proved adept at publicising the sufferings of their people, who were subjected to a blockade by the government and thus endured famine as well as direct war damage. In 1968 and 1969 Labour conferences voted for an arms embargo, but the government stuck to its policy in the knowledge that it was supported by most Conservative MPs. Once again, ministers were economical with the truth, falsely claiming that the level of arms sales to Nigeria had not increased during the conflict (Ponting, 1989, 230–1). Before leaving office Wilson had the satisfaction of seeing the capitulation of Biafra (in January 1970).

Conclusions

For a man whose concern for global poverty had supposedly helped to inspire the creation of the charity War on Want back in 1951, the widely publicised plight of Biafran children must have been deeply unedifying. At least Harold Wilson could claim that British aid organisations were in a better position to respond to humanitarian disasters like Biafra thanks to the separate Ministry for Overseas Development established in 1964 (Chapter 2). However, this initiative had not escaped the effects of economic crisis; although the first Minister for Overseas Development (the dynamic Barbara Castle) had been a full Cabinet member, in 1967 the role was downgraded. There could hardly have been a more potent symbol of Labour's failure to make good on its initial idealism.

This is not to say that the 1963–70 period was entirely devoid of success. In 1967, for example, British diplomats played a prominent part in the passage of UNSCR 242, which established key principles for a resolution of the Arab–Israeli conflict. However, a positive outcome depended on the constructive intentions of more powerful states than Britain. Wilson also deserves credit for a decision which was widely derided – the award in 1965 of MBEs to The Beatles. Rather than being an example of Wilson's 'gimmickry', as critics complained, this is best seen as a recognition that, since all else seemed to be failing, Britain's interests could be advanced by marshalling its cultural advantages – its soft power. The Duncan Report of 1969 gave more official recognition to this trend, arguing that the British Council and the BBC's external services would become increasingly important as 'Britain turns from politico-military relations towards other ways of making her presence known to other countries' (quoted in Donaldson, 1984, 241). Unfortunately for Britain's cultural ambassadors, the realisation that they performed considerable services to the nation at minimal cost to the state was regarded as a reason for keeping the costs minimal, rather than an incentive to increase expenditure in the hope of securing even greater advantages. In any case, there was a danger that prominent celebrities might exhibit a propensity for independent thought: the recognition of the Beatles looked less inspired in 1969, when John Lennon sent a message to the Queen disclaiming his MBE as a protest against 'Britain's involvement in the Nigeria-Biafra thing' as well as the Vietnam War.

It is, of course, possible to argue that Wilson was unlucky in crucial foreign-policy areas. Equally, though, he had an unusual ability to make his own bad luck. For example, in advance of the 1968 US Presidential election Wilson had arranged that the former MP John Freeman should become the next British Ambassador to Washington. Freeman had close contacts with the Democratic Party, which Wilson confidently expected to win the election. However, Freeman's friend Hubert Humphrey was defeated by the Republican Richard Nixon, whom Freeman had attacked in a *New Statesman* article as self-seeking and unprincipled. Nixon chose not to show any resentment, but the incident added a dose of personal embarrassment to a result which in itself exposed the element of wishful thinking behind the concept of a 'special relationship' (Watt, 1984, 150).

It is testimony to the low political salience of foreign affairs that, despite dramatic events in Vietnam and elsewhere, they barely featured in the 1970 general election campaign. Even discussion of the EEC was muted, since public opinion had turned sharply against membership and the two main parties had little incentive to dwell on their inglorious applications (Butler and Pinto-Duschinsky, 1971, 440–3). If the country's role in the world had been high on the political agenda, it is unlikely that Labour would have entitled its manifesto *Now Britain's Strong – Let's make it great to live in*. This could be taken as an invitation for voters to make their own appraisals of Britain's apparent strength and to wonder why four years of majority Labour government had failed to make it 'great to live in' already. If they did, it might explain why, against Wilson's expectations and the guesswork of most other pundits, Labour lost.

Awkward partnerships and special relationships, 1970–83

7

Introduction

The popular retelling of the history of post-war Britain, whether in fiction or documentary, evokes deceptively vivid images of each decade. The 1960s revolve around social revolution, fashion, music, Mini Cooper cars and miniskirted models in a period of brash optimism. Fast forward to the 1980s, and Britain is imagined as a nation transformed, suddenly swarming with sharp-suited entrepreneurs pressing mobile telephones to their ears and eschewing both sleep and meals in the pursuit of profit. Sandwiched in between these two dynamic decades sits the 1970s, the decade when 'the worst of times' were visited on the nation (Beckett, 2010). In the years that followed the 1970s became most closely associated with economic decline and dysfunction, when the prolonged period of economic growth that had followed the end of the Second World War subsided into industrial unrest and stagflation. While some historians have suggested that this represents a caricature, offering a selective account of the history of the decade, it remains the pervasive narrative and was supported by well-placed contemporary observers (Garnett, 2007, 1–2). Certainly, the perception of decline framed the debate about Britain's domestic and international policy options; while the remarkable flowering of Britain's cultural soft power in the 1960s had to some extent camouflaged the retreat from Empire and economic malaise, the 1970s offered fewer agreeable distractions (even the England football team went from world-beaters to whipping boys). It was thus no surprise that the 1970s saw various attempts to establish new narratives which would explain Britain's post-war experience to audiences at home and abroad.

Applicants

The state of the British economy was the key issue in the general election campaign of 1970. The 'technological revolution' hailed by Harold Wilson in 1963 had seemingly bypassed Britain, and trade with the Commonwealth nations was in steady decline. Through the 1960s both parties had reached out to the EEC as a corrective for Britain's economic malaise. There had been two failed applications for membership, in 1963 by the Conservatives and in 1967 by Labour, both of which couched the case for membership in economic terms. Wilson, who led Labour to a narrow election victory in 1964 and a decisive one two years later, was an instinctive 'Little Englander' rather than a 'Eurofanatic', which makes his belated conversion to the case for membership all the more noteworthy. By contrast, Edward Heath, an early advocate of European cooperation who had become Conservative leader in 1965, felt a strong emotional attachment to the European mainland as well as seeing the EEC as a palliative for Britain's post-war economic decline as well as the prospect of 'modernising' the country's global outlook.

Timeline of domestic political developments

October 1971 'Great debate' on principle of EEC membership: government wins Parliamentary vote by 356 to 244

January 1973 UK joins the EEC

February 1974 Inconclusive general election: Labour forms a minority government under Harold Wilson, although the Conservatives win more votes

October 1974 General election: Labour wins an overall majority of just three

February 1975 Margaret Thatcher replaces Edward Heath as Conservative leader

June 1975 Referendum on continued EEC membership: 'Yes' secured 67 per cent of the vote

May 1979 General election: Conservatives win an overall majority of 44 and Margaret Thatcher becomes Prime Minister

July 1981 Rioting in many English cities

January 1982 Official unemployment figures top 3 million

Heath argued 'that Britain would inevitably be drawn towards a Community with a market of 200 million people'. But his arguments did not stop there. For the Conservative Party and for Britain as a whole, membership of the EEC represented a 'new beginning', turning away from the historical attachment to Empire and 'establishing new policies of competition and efficiency' (Turner, 2000, 54). Far from being deterred by the failure of the 1963 membership application – which he had overseen – Heath's faith remained unshaken, and the vast majority of his party followed his lead at that time, despite lingering nostalgia for the imperial past. Having given the initial impetus to the process of decolonisation, the Labour Party ostensibly carried less historical baggage into the encounter with 'Europe'; but many of its members acknowledged genuine obligations towards the Commonwealth, while others saw the EEC as 'a capitalist club, undemocratic in its decision making, membership of which would . . . undermine Britain's ability to pursue socialist policies at home' (Young, 2004, 140). Increasingly, though, senior Labour politicians were swayed by the economic case for membership. Both main parties thus adopted pro-EEC policies, with the Conservative Party offering Parliamentary support for Wilson's application for membership in 1967. When the second application was rejected, however, a degree of scepticism towards the European project began to enter British politics; this would be most keenly felt within the Labour Party, but it was also registered in the party manifestos for the 1970 general election.

In that contest, as in 1966, Heath presented himself to the British electorate as the man who would halt the nation's economic decline. Central to his strategy was the notion of reinvigorating the economy by increasing competition. Heath offered at least a partial break from the consensus of the post-war era, challenging the power of the trade unions and seeking to reshape the welfare state. In his promised 'Quiet Revolution', the state would be reformed to foster the spirit of competition. Central to this would be membership of the EEC. Heath believed that by joining the EEC Britain would have greater influence in the world and that this would be beneficial both to the nation and ultimately to its Commonwealth partners. But he also believed that membership of the EEC, with the provisions of the Treaty of Rome that enshrined economic competition, would embed the institutional change required to achieve the goals of his economic strategy: for Heath, 'Europe was to provide the linking theme between domestic and foreign policy' (Turner, 2000, 59).

In addition to this Heath argued that the EEC was central to the future security of the continent. He regarded the development of European unity as the natural progression of a world order that was shaped by the needs of states. The Soviet invasion of Czechoslovakia in 1968 was, for Heath, a cautionary example that the US's strategic priorities may not always coincide with those of Britain or 'Europe'; it was noticeable that the reaction to this event was not as strong across the Atlantic. The bitter experience of Vietnam was also likely to make Americans more reluctant to risk their own security through involvement in a future European conflict. European states should therefore collaborate more closely in their own defence, reducing the financial burden on the US and thus creating a more equal (and no less friendly) relationship.

Despite Heath's personal enthusiasm for 'Europe', the 1970 Conservative Party manifesto couched Britain's prospective engagement with the EEC in sober language. While British membership would make a 'major contribution to both the prosperity and security' of Britain, there would be obstacles to entry, and the Conservative Party was keen to reassure the electorate that there was 'a price we would not be prepared to pay'. The manifesto failed to quantify this price but asserted that a new government would enter office with a 'commitment to negotiate; no more, no less'. The caution of the Conservative manifesto reflected the fact that the rejection of British applications for membership in 1963 and 1967 had left scars. Measured in Parliamentary votes, there was a significant majority in favour of membership; but this did not necessarily translate into real enthusiasm for the project. Heath's resolve to pull his party away from its historical connections to Empire was not widely appreciated. At the final party conference before the 1970 general election, of 35 motions submitted on the EEC only seven supported membership (Turner, 2000, 64).

Unease concerning the European project reflected the tendency of many Britons to nurse 'stubborn hopes of remaining a global rather than merely European power' (Beckett, 2010, 80). At this stage, at least, this feeling could not overcome the widespread belief that membership would be beneficial for British business. Even the then leading Conservative critic of membership of the EEC, Enoch Powell, accepted the logic, remarking that 'I took it for granted that if we were excluded from the Common Market our trade with Europe was bound to fall off and shrivel to nothing' (quoted in Turner, 2000, 56).

When Heath unexpectedly won the election of 1970 the way was cleared for another membership bid. British hopes had been lifted by the resignation of the obstructive French President, Charles de Gaulle, in the preceding year. Even so, success was far from a formality. President de Gaulle's replacement, Georges Pompidou, indicated his support for British membership, but progress through 1970 was slow. One of the problems that negotiations had to overcome was Britain's economic ties with the Commonwealth. Although Britain was entering the EEC partly to counter the decline in trade with its former Empire, the trade in agricultural produce from New Zealand and the Caribbean was not insignificant. Negotiations between the British and the established members of the EEC stumbled over the issue of 'New Zealand butter, Commonwealth sugar and Britain's budget contribution' (Reynolds, 2000, 227). These negotiations had been made more complicated by the fact that, in the year before their renewal, the EEC had agreed a new deal for its Common Agricultural Policy (CAP). The CAP represented the bulk of EEC expenditure, financed by taking 1 per cent of VAT raised by member states and all of the tariffs levied on food imported into the EEC. This was a double blow for the British. First, its agricultural sector was small in comparison to its European neighbours, and the economy as a whole would gain little from the subsidies that CAP brought in. Second, with its dependence on food imports from Commonwealth nations, Britain would now be making a disproportionate contribution to the EEC budget. In 1970 it was calculated that the 'net cost' of British entry into the EEC would be between £550 million and £750 million (Young, 1996, 266–7).

The difficult terms of Britain's entry into the EEC were mostly glossed over by the White Paper presented to Parliament following the successful conclusion of negotiations over membership. But Britain was joining the European project at a difficult point in its post-war history. The long period of economic growth that had followed the Second World War was reaching its end. Although Heath sought to present the deal on membership as a continuation of the bipartisan approach of 1967, the Labour Party was in no mood to reciprocate. The failure of the 1967 application had undermined support for the European project among Labour MPs and party members. In addition, offering unambiguous support for the Heath government would not produce any political advantage for the Labour Party. Therefore, official party policy was to oppose the terms that Heath had negotiated on entry, while leaving open the possibility that a future Labour government would reapply in the hope of securing a better deal. Tony Benn reported on these divisions in his diaries, as former Cabinet members clashed at a meeting of the Parliamentary party. Barbara Castle, a committed anti-marketeer, argued that Labour had been cornered by 'the Tories on the terms [of membership]'; in turn, the Tories themselves had been 'caught out' by the French by their manoeuvres on the CAP (Benn, 1988, 357). Others – even high-ranking members of both main parties – sensed even at this stage that the political 'establishment' was trying to cajole the British public into an institutional arrangement which contradicted the familiar narratives of the country's post-war history – and that once the European option had been selected from among the rich alternatives offered by Churchill, there would be no escape.

Nevertheless, in 1972 the legislation to allow Britain to become a member of the EEC made its way through Parliament, with the support of pro-Europeans on all sides of the Commons. While the Parliamentary Labour Party officially opposed the government through the detailed legislative process, pro-Europeans within the opposition organised themselves to ensure that the government had a majority in all the key votes. The process was duly concluded after a year of Parliamentary business, and Britain became a member of the EEC in January 1973. Polling of public opinion at the time suggested an equally divided nation, with the majority against membership (39 to 38 per cent) falling within the margin of error. Subsequent polling, however, suggested that around 80 per cent believed that membership was inevitable (Turner, 2000, 66). The public, of course, was not to be consulted before the decision was taken; a proposal that a referendum should be held was defeated in the House of Commons in April 1972 by 301 votes to 272, despite the opportunistic support of the Labour Party.

Members

Heath had little time to savour the realisation of his chief political goal, being ejected from office only 14 months after Britain officially joined the EEC. But even in this short period of time problems began to emerge in the deal that had been struck to achieve British membership, laying the foundations for the Eurosceptic canard that, contrary to his pose of pragmatic patriotism, Heath was either an unworthy defeatist or a traitor who had spent his adult life plotting the extirpation of the British nation state. As had been predicted, Britain's contribution to the CAP created a serious imbalance; its terms ensured that Britain was a major net contributor to EEC resources. The planned corrective measure – the European Regional Development Fund, which was supposed to funnel EEC money into the poorer communities of Britain – was yet to make significant contributions to the British economy. The situation had not been helped by the actions of the Heath government. Its Budget of 1972 had attempted to prepare British companies for the challenges of EEC competition. This was done through a series of measures to increase demand for British manufactured goods, which in turn would result in increased profits for companies and rising investment prior to EEC membership. The theory seemed entirely plausible, but reality disproved it. The injection of additional domestic economic demand only introduced inflationary pressures into the British economy, which were reinforced by the increase in the cost of foodstuffs, attributed to the CAP. Heath's strategy was given the *coup de grâce* by the quadrupling of the price of oil in October 1973 (thanks to developments which were entirely unrelated to the EEC). Britain's economic woes were domestic and global, but in the public debate they were associated with membership of the EEC. This was particularly damaging, since the argument for joining had been carefully expressed in terms of the economic advantages. By the time Heath left office, in March 1974, '[b]laming Brussels was on its way to becoming one of the most entrenched British political habits' (Beckett, 2010, 86).

The two general elections of 1974 (February and October) took place against a backdrop of further economic gloom and industrial strife. The inflationary shock of the rise in oil prices in late 1973 was now feeding through to industry, where workers were seeking pay rises to keep up with the giddy upward spiral in the cost of living. Most significantly, a strike by the National Union of Mineworkers (NUM) exploited the oil crisis in a way which threatened government pay policy and domestic energy supplies. Seeking a fresh mandate to deal with the unions – without being entirely clear about the way in which such dealings would be conducted – Heath called a general election for late February 1974.

The Conservative Party manifesto set out its prospectus for a country that faced 'great dangers' at home and a 'difficult period' in the immediate future. Amongst the gloom, one bright spot was the achievement of EEC membership, 'a major national objective which had eluded successive British Governments'. The manifesto continued that while it was too soon to make a full assessment of the 'implications for Britain', the country 'was better able to secure [its] national interests both economic and political within the Community than would have been possible had we remained outside'. In the absence of concrete supporting evidence, this optimistic assessment was not widely shared.

While the Wilson government had renewed Britain's application, the Labour Party's divisions on the subject were as profound as ever, and the opponents of membership seized the initiative after the 1970 election. The Labour manifesto of February 1974 presented a bleak assessment, warning that membership threatened Britain 'with still higher food prices and with a further loss of . . . control of its own affairs'. The only resolution was for a Labour government to renegotiate the terms of Britain's membership and then allow the British people to decide through a referendum. Harold Wilson saw the idea of a referendum – the first poll of its kind in the UK as a whole – as an opportunity to keep the party together.

The two general elections of 1974 did not result in a decisive majority for either party, but the Labour Party emerged after the second election in October with a slender majority of four seats and felt able to claim a mandate to continue the renegotiation of Britain's deal with the EEC. Discussions were drawn out through the year, but by the end of 1974 agreement was reached that would see Britain receive a refund for its budget contribution. This was followed in February 1975 by 'some vague promises on reform of the CAP' (Young, 2004, 144). In January the date of the referendum was set for 5 June 1975, and in March the Cabinet backed a 'Yes' vote. For reasons of party management Wilson suspended the convention of collective Cabinet responsibility, allowing ministers to speak on either side of the debate in the expectation that the advocacy of controversial figures like Tony Benn would help to persuade undecided voters to support the status quo. Public support for the EEC had actually been increasing since 1974. The pro-EEC Britain in Europe group was well funded and slick in comparison to the anti-EEC National Referendum Campaign. The referendum resulted in a clear endorsement of Britain's membership of the EEC, with a positive 'Yes' from every region of the UK. Whether the public ended the campaign with enhanced knowledge of the EEC's institutions was more questionable than the verdict.

New faces

The elections of 1974 and the EEC referendum marked a point of transition in British politics and foreign policy. The two dominant figures of the previous decade, Edward Heath and Harold Wilson, had both left their respective front benches by the summer of 1976, while Roy Jenkins took leave from British politics to become President of the European Commission. Heath clung on to the Conservative leadership despite having lost three general elections out of four. But by early 1975 he could survive no longer and was replaced by the political outsider Margaret Thatcher. Heath's removal did not mark a Conservative turn away from the EEC: the party offered strong support for a 'Yes' vote in the referendum. It was more a personal rejection of Heath as an individual and a leader. However, in her campaign against Heath Margaret Thatcher had outlined a narrative of British decline since 1945. In this story, it was difficult to see how Britain's membership of the EEC could be regarded positively; at best, it could only feature as a symptom of a depressing trend which Thatcher was determined to reverse.

Wilson's resignation, in April 1976, caused considerable surprise and indeed gave rise to various conspiracy theories and allegations, including the claim that he had been a Soviet spy. The more mundane truth – that he had lost his appetite for politics – was partly due to failing health, but must also have reflected the unpromising prospects for his country and his party, in which doctrinaire socialists were becoming increasingly influential. The EEC-referendum vote was almost the only positive development of his last spell in Downing Street; it was, one biographer noted, 'perhaps the greatest triumph of his career' (Pimlott, 1992, 654). Yet it was a *negative* achievement – helping to prevent an outcome which, on balance, he considered to be more damaging – and, in any case, much of the success of this process of renegotiation was credited to his successor as Prime Minister, James Callaghan.

Callaghan had been made Foreign Secretary by Wilson after the first election of 1974. He was a wily operator who had proved his mettle as a trade unionist before rising through Labour's ranks. As such, he was a Foreign Secretary in the mould of Ernest Bevin (though with a much keener interest in self-advancement). Callaghan had been introduced to the new realities of British power through the negotiations with the EEC which dominated his first months in office. There was an even ruder reminder of Britain's diminished status in 1975, when Callaghan flew to Uganda to bring home the British writer and teacher Denis Hills. Hills had published a book which included an attack on the eccentric Sandhurst-educated Ugandan dictator, Idi Amin, and had been sentenced to death for his literary endeavours. Amin – already a bogeyman in Britain thanks to his decision to expel Asians from his country in 1972 (Box 7.1) – clearly relished this opportunity to humiliate the former colonial power, and Callaghan paid a very public price. This was all the more ironic since the Foreign Secretary had acquired a reputation for 'progressive' views in the field of Commonwealth relations; however, there was no possibility that Britain would use its sole weapon against the distinctly illiberal Amin by suspending Uganda's Commonwealth membership. While

> **Box 7.1 The expulsion of Ugandan Asians**
>
> Edward Heath set himself the task of liberating Britain from the idea that (as Harold Wilson had put it) 'we are a world power and a world influence or we are nothing'. The immediate and predictable problem for Heath was to persuade Britons that their future lay in 'Europe'. This would have been difficult enough even if voters had decided to put aside memories of the Second World War. As it turned out, the task was complicated further by jarring reminders of the country's Imperial past.
>
> In August 1972 the Ugandan dictator, Idi Amin, abruptly announced that the country's Asian residents were to be expelled within 90 days. For Britain, this was a double dose of imperial 'blowback'. Uganda itself had been granted independence in 1962, and the government of the country was clearly not in hands which reflected well on the ex-colonial power. Furthermore, the treatment of Ugandan-based Asians was a matter of pressing moral concern to the British, who had brought them to Africa to perform various (often menial) tasks. Many Asians had retained British passports (under the 1948 Nationality Act).
>
> By 1972 the remaining Asian population of Uganda was the subject of repression and discrimination, not least because its members had proved so industrious and successful. As such, the British government and public might have regarded Amin's dramatic gesture as an opportunity to inject some new entrepreneurial vitality into the country's economic activity. However, after a similar move by the Kenyan government in 1967, public opinion had been agitated by the prospect of a flood of refugees who would 'swamp' the indigenous population. Since then various attempts had been made to deprive citizens of the old Empire of the right to settle in Britain. It was thus to the government's credit (though decidedly not to its electoral advantage) that, after trying to persuade Amin to change his mind, it accepted around 27,000 of the displaced people. Sizeable contingents were resettled in Commonwealth countries such as Australia and New Zealand, almost certainly reflecting the enlightened self-interest of their governments rather than a desire to help Heath out of an awkward dilemma created by his predecessors.

the significance of this episode (which Callaghan tactfully omitted to mention in his memoirs) was chiefly symbolic, there was a more serious reminder of Britain's fading influence in what used to be considered its own backyard when, in July 1974, Turkey invaded Cyprus in response to a coup engineered by the military rulers of Greece with a view to annexing the Commonwealth island. Despite considerable diplomatic activity, Callaghan was unable to prevent the partition of Cyprus, with a Turkish republic in the north.

Callaghan was on more congenial ground when he dealt with the Atlantic alliance, and during his time as Foreign Secretary and then Prime Minister he prioritised the restoration of a relationship which had languished over the previous decade. Doubts concerning the 'special relationship' between the two nations had arisen in part because of Heath's public pronouncements during his time in office, consistent with the need to reassure De Gaulle's successor, President Pompidou, that Britain would not be an American 'Trojan horse' if accepted into the EEC. While Heath's emollient words may have received support in France, his actions were greeted more critically in the US. The US Secretary of State, Henry Kissinger, characterised Heath as the British leader who was 'the most indifferent to the American connection and perhaps even to Americans individually'. The two countries continued to cooperate at a diplomatic and military level, but in 1973 Kissinger raised his concerns with the British Cabinet Secretary, stating that for 'the sake of an abstract doctrine of European unity . . . something that has been nurtured for a generation was being given up' (Dumbrell, 2001, 73–4). The British response to the 1973 Yom Kippur War, when Syrian and Egyptian forces launched an unsuccessful surprise attack on Israel, was a concrete example of Heath's refusal to toe the American line (Case Study 7.1).

In private conversation Callaghan showed a commendable ability to subvert the great-power post-war narrative, observing bluntly in 1976 that '[t]he mistake we made was to think we won the war' (Morgan, 1997, 622). However, his decisions and public utterances were fully compatible with the familiar conception of Britain's post-war status. On arriving at the FCO, Callaghan sought to rebuild relations with Washington, to reassure both the US and the EEC. In particular, he established an extremely close working relationship with Henry Kissinger, who regarded him as a friend (Morgan, 1997, 439–41). For the US, Callaghan made it clear that he would deviate from Heath's approach, and he condemned the notion that the EEC would only develop as a power if it set itself in opposition to America. Wilson and Callaghan were both keen to reassert cooperation on Britain's nuclear-weapons programme with the US, moving on from Heath's ambitions for an Anglo-French nuclear alliance. Despite the worsening economic circumstances of the mid 1970s, the government continued to fund the modernisation of its Polaris submarine fleet and to maintain military expenditure in line with NATO requirements. Both policies faced considerable opposition inside and outside government. The Chevaline upgrade to Polaris was made with the usual secrecy, to avoid political disputes. Wilson and Callaghan believed that by maintaining Britain's nuclear deterrent they were upholding the nation's great-power status and retaining influence over America's nuclear strategy. The European powers were growing increasingly concerned by the impression that they were being bypassed by the US, as the Cold War moved into the period of

Case Study 7.1 Britain and the Yom Kippur War

The Yom Kippur War of 1973 is a vivid illustration of Britain's reduced global status. As we have seen (Chapter 4), the creation of the state of Israel had been foreshadowed by the 1917 Balfour Declaration but was finally achieved more than three decades later after Zionist terrorism made it impossible for the British to maintain their 'mandate' in Palestine. It would have been natural for the British to regard the new Zionist state with mixed feelings; in any case, there was good reason to suppose that it would be short-lived, due to the hostility of neighbouring Arab countries.

Regardless of British expectations the new state survived, and in 1967 it launched a pre-emptive strike on its enemies, making considerable territorial gains. Six years later Egypt and Syria attempted a similar *coup de main*, hoping (at least) to reduce Israel to its 1967 borders. The result was a devastating defeat for the Arab forces.

In Britain these events were viewed with sharply contrasting emotions. Within the government there was considerable support for the Arab side, animated not so much by anti-Israeli sentiment as by a more pragmatic feeling that a successful recapture of the areas occupied by Israel in 1967 would restore a semblance of stability to the Middle East. Some ministers, however (notably Margaret Thatcher, whose North London constituency included a significant Jewish population), hoped for a different outcome, feeling that the existence of Israel itself was at stake. This view commanded considerable public support, suggesting that by 1973 the memory of terrorist outrages committed by Zionists against British service personnel had been replaced by a sense that Israel was a plucky underdog, surrounded by brutal enemies. In other words (leaving aside the reputed power of well-funded Zionist 'lobbyists'), many Britons had voluntarily transferred the narrative of Britain standing alone against Nazi Germany to the Israeli situation, which in itself was a poignant reminder of the Second World War.

Against this background, the Heath government maintained its general record of pursuing the most 'rational' course and reaping the minimum benefit. It imposed an embargo on arms shipments to both sides in common with its EEC partners. Initially, the US was minded to follow the same course, but in the face of massive arms shipments from the Soviet Union to the Arab side it began to supply Israeli forces. Heath refused permission for these supplies to be flown from British bases, which was also consistent with the policy of most EEC countries. This move was viewed with considerable displeasure in Washington and did Heath no good, since the ensuing

> conflict (which he had predicted long before Yom Kippur) had a serious impact on the British economy as well as helping to end the long economic boom in Western Europe which had made membership of the EEC seem so alluring.

détente and the US favoured direct negotiations with the Soviet Union 'over the heads of the Europeans' (Dumbrell, 2001, 78).

The improved relations between the US and the Soviet Union also allowed Wilson and Callaghan to develop closer British links to the latter. A visit to Moscow in February 1975 established exchange programmes between the two nations to improve understanding and trust. The meetings took place against a backdrop of change in Europe, as southern European states began to edge away from dictatorships and towards democracy. One of the first to make the transition was Britain's oldest ally, Portugal, where 40 years of dictatorship was brought to an end by the Carnation Revolution in April 1974. In the binary geopolitics of the Cold War the defeat of an avowedly anti-communist dictatorship could be interpreted as a victory for the Soviet Union and the Communist cause. Callaghan and Wilson were keen to emphasise that the Soviet Union should not see the revolution in Portugal as an opportunity to spread its influence to southern Europe. Wilson warned the Soviet leader, Leonid Brezhnev, that Soviet involvement in Portugal would threaten the gains of détente (Dumbrell, 2001, 80).

Wilson's warning came in final negotiations with the Soviet leadership over preparations for the Helsinki Conference on Security and Cooperation in Europe (CSCE), held in August 1975. The Helsinki conference acted as a formal classification of détente, and as such could be seen as an attempt to settle the unresolved disputes arising from the Second World War. There were issues of European security that needed to be addressed: force reduction in Europe; the status of Berlin; and Finland's relationship with the Soviet Union. The FCO saw that the Soviets were keen to make a deal even if this necessitated some movement on the key question of human rights (Beetham, 2006, 29). The Conservative government that oversaw the initial stages of the negotiations for the Helsinki conference could see the advantage of an approach that gave Britain a leadership role and established a position distinct from the US, while burnishing Britain's European credentials.

When Labour inherited the policy they were supportive of an initiative which would both make the government look good and conform to the stated aims of 'socialist internationalism' (Lane, 2004, 154). The agreement in Helsinki was arranged into three 'baskets'. The basket that most concerned the Soviet delegates was the first one, recognising contemporary European borders and pledging that they should not be violated by force. This would mark a significant diplomatic gain for the Soviets, since it provided international recognition for their buffer zone of Eastern European satellite states. However, the same basket also embodied a promise to adhere to human rights and national self-determination, which implied that the Soviet presence in Eastern Europe was illegitimate even if their influence had been benign. Finally, Helsinki included a promise that the implementation of the agreement would be reviewed every three years.

The agreement, when reached, was not greeted warmly in all quarters. The British Ambassador to Moscow summarised it as the 'consolidation and perpetuation of the new territorial and political order in Eastern Europe established by Soviet arms, diplomacy and skulduggery in the years following 1944' (Hamilton, 2006, 18). In retrospect this assessment appears unduly alarmist; after all, most well-informed observers (including the reluctant Churchill) had regarded the dominance of the Soviet Union over Eastern Europe as an established post-war fact. From the British perspective, it was arguably more significant that the Helsinki Accords reiterated standards of human rights, which, while clearly designed as admonishments to the Soviet Union, could also be used as the basis for a criticism of UK foreign policy since 1945 (including its ongoing role in Northern Ireland). After Helsinki, it would be more difficult for British policy makers to ignore moral considerations without convicting themselves of double standards.

Helsinki had a wider significance; indeed, it can be seen as the starting point of a global human rights culture. The review meetings became a forum where the West could 'shame' Moscow into reforming its human rights record. At one review meeting in the 1980s Prime Minister Margaret Thatcher wrote across the top of a ministerial briefing paper: 'This meeting is about human rights and nothing else' (O'Keeffe, 2006, 88). But Helsinki was not just about inter-state point-scoring. The text of the agreement had been published throughout Eastern Europe. In January 1977 a group of Czechoslovakian citizens established a group, Charter 77, which sought to expose human rights abuses. They cited the Helsinki Agreement as their legal guide (Hamilton, 2006, 22). Whatever the skeletons in its own cupboard, Britain had led the way on the propagation of human rights and its influence was not restricted to Europe. Callaghan identified the UN as the most appropriate environment to 'promote the principles of peace and justice and human rights', and he directed the British UN delegation to 'cultivate their connections with the Commonwealth delegations in order to provide greater coordination of Commonwealth policy in that area' (Lane, 2004, 155–6). British aspirations were aided by the 1976 election victory of Jimmy Carter in the US. Reconstructing US foreign policy after Vietnam, Carter emphasised human rights as a key component of his engagement with the world.

Although relations between Britain and the US had been revived by Wilson and Callaghan, this did not always result in policy successes. Both the Ford and Carter administrations worked with the British on possible solutions for the conflict in Rhodesia, but little progress was made. However, Britain had re-established itself as the 'Atlantic intermediary' between Washington and 'Europe' (a role ridiculed by Roy Jenkins as being 'a sort of enlarged Iceland' (quoted in Dumbrell, 2001, 82)). The potential significance of Britain's position became apparent in the year after Helsinki, when the Soviet Union began deployment of an intermediate-range nuclear weapon, the SS-20. This was a significant development in the Cold War arms race. The missiles were delivered from mobile launchers, making their deployment more difficult to detect, and their limited range suggested that they would be reserved for use in the European theatre. The deployment of the SS-20s proved an early challenge to the Carter administration. Much as it wanted to pursue nuclear-arms reduction through the Strategic Arms Limitation Talks (SALT) process, it needed to reassure European allies of its continued commitment to their security. As the US contemplated its response to the Soviet deployment Callaghan acted as a key conduit between 'Europe' and Washington, initially reporting concerns that the German and French governments were losing confidence in the US. Then, when the Carter administration contemplated the deployment of enhanced radiation weapons (or the 'neutron bomb'), a weapons system that killed people but left buildings intact, Callaghan conveyed the 'equivocal responses' of the British and Germans. Both nations were privately relieved when Carter decided against this deployment (Lane, 2004, 163).

The American response to the SS-20s was finally agreed towards the end of Callaghan's premiership. In January 1979 a summit meeting between the leaders of the US, West Germany, France and Britain was held in the French territory of Guadeloupe. The summit had a full agenda, covering the security of Western Europe, the recent revolution in Iran and the possibility of imposing economic sanctions on apartheid South Africa. Another urgent topic was the deployment of cruise and Pershing II nuclear missiles to Western Europe in response to the Soviet SS-20s. The leaders agreed a 'twin track' approach: arms-control negotiations between the Americans and Soviets would proceed, with the ambition of eliminating all intermediate-range weapons from the European theatre. Pending agreement, deployment of cruise and Pershing missiles would go ahead (Dumbrell, 2001, 87). In addition to these negotiations, the British held direct talks with the Americans on a replacement for the British Polaris fleet. The Chevaline system, agreed earlier in the decade, had proved to be a very expensive stopgap, but a long-term renewal of Britain's nuclear deterrent was now required, and the Trident missile system appeared to be the most appropriate choice. Callaghan discussed the new weapons system with Carter, noting that its cost was beyond Britain's means. Carter responded that 'he thought it should be possible to work out satisfactory terms' (Beckett, 2010, 471).

Overall, the summit in Guadeloupe was deemed a success. The US had reaffirmed its commitment to the defence of Western Europe and Britain had secured an agreement on the future of its nuclear deterrent. But this was not how the meeting was remembered in Britain. Following the conclusion of the talks Callaghan and his party moved on to Barbados for a short state visit. The progression of 'Sunny Jim' Callaghan through the sun-soaked Caribbean contrasted with the fortunes of those in Britain who were struggling through a spate of strikes by workers in the public services. When Callaghan returned reporters met him at the airport and questioned him on the 'mounting chaos in the country'. Callaghan dismissed this as a parochial view which would not be recognised by his fellow world leaders. The *Sun* newspaper headlined Callaghan's response as: 'Crisis? What Crisis?'. Guadeloupe became a textbook example of the unintentional perils of international diplomacy, especially when these involve Caribbean resorts in the depths of the British winter. The positive aspects of Callaghan's foreign policy were undermined by the government's limited domestic support and its fragile Parliamentary position. Having brushed off a series of defeats in the House of Commons, it was defeated in a formal vote of confidence in March 1979; two months later it was swept from office in a general election which Callaghan had delayed for too long.

When the record of the Labour governments of 1974–9 is assessed foreign policy emerges as one of the positives compared to the domestic scene of inflation, unemployment, deep cuts in public expenditure and industrial unrest. The Wilson and Callaghan governments had dealt successfully with the debate over membership of the EEC and had re-established Britain's relationship with the US. By the end of their time in office they had settled the immediate future of Britain's nuclear deterrent. The Helsinki Agreement had developed new policy which arguably projected British values behind the Iron Curtain. None of this, however, counted for much in the election of 1979. Britain had just passed through a 'Winter of Discontent' and was associated with 'chaos' and 'crisis'. The Conservative Party election campaign skilfully exploited images of industrial strife. Margaret Thatcher came to office concentrating on the domestic problems that faced the nation: as she put it, 'Take care of the economics . . . and the rest, including foreign policy, will take care of itself' (quoted in Sharp, 1997, 21).

Thatcher's first term

Margaret Thatcher had become leader of the Conservative Party because she was not Edward Heath. The party had grown sufficiently weary of Heath that it was prepared to choose someone who was not only an outsider but also a woman. Over time, Thatcher's gender would be seen as the least radical element of this change. By the end of her premiership even Thatcher's critics conceded that she was a global figure in a way that could not be said of her immediate predecessors. After she left office she continued to speak out on foreign affairs, in front of audiences which tended to be more adoring the further she ventured from Britain. None of this was immediately apparent when she took over the leadership of the Conservative Party in 1975 or even during her first general election campaign as leader. The foreign policy profile that emerged after her general election victory in May 1979 was shaped by Britain's two key relationships: the EEC and the US. By the end of her first term in office she had come to be associated with a less predictable foreign policy issue, relating to some obscure islands in the South Atlantic.

Thatcher and 'Europe'

As we have seen, although Mrs Thatcher was known as a firm (if not exactly fanatical) supporter of British membership of the EEC, her interpretation of post-war history implied a more critical stance. Indeed, elements of her later opposition to the European project could be detected from an early stage. Thatcher sought to distance herself from Heath's 'Euro-enthusiasm'. This was not a rejection of the EEC as such, but rather a reaffirmation of the Tories' traditional support for the 'special relationship' with the US. There was also a gentle scepticism about the future prospects for European unity. Speaking in 1975, she argued that 'the interests of individual nations are not identical . . . Any steps towards closer European union must be carefully considered' (Turner, 2000, 69). But, given the yawning divisions in the Labour Party over European policy in the late 1970s, there was little political advantage to be gained by raising any doubts about the Conservative Party's reputation as 'the natural "party of Europe"'. In the early years of her leadership Thatcher stressed the advantages that EEC membership would bestow on Britain; it 'brought access to an enormous and prosperous market, encouraged inward investment, and enabled Britain to negotiate as part of the world's largest trading bloc' (May, 1998, 68). The Conservatives entered the general election campaign calling for a 'common-sense [European] Community which resists excessive bureaucracy and unnecessary harmonisation proposals, holding to the principles of free enterprise which inspired its original founders'; if membership had yet to pay obvious dividends, this was because of the 'frequently obstructive and malevolent attitude of Labour Ministers' who had alienated their counterparts. Rather than fussing over the question of 'sovereignty' – which Labour explicitly mentioned in its own manifesto – the Conservatives favoured greater coordination of foreign policy between member states.

Labour's ministers may indeed have been 'obstructive' at times, but the main reason why Britain was not deriving economic benefits from the EEC was that it had joined just as post-war economic growth had slowed to a crawl. The renegotiation of Britain's terms of membership by Wilson and Callaghan could hardly resolve this deeper problem. As the election of 1979 loomed the British financial contribution to the EEC grew to a net annual cost of £540 million. Callaghan had announced that he would seek talks on this matter in late 1978, but the task of renegotiating Britain's financial contribution fell to Thatcher. Just before the 1979 general election she had reiterated that Britain under her leadership would be 'resolute' in pursuing and protecting its interests in 'Europe'.

The economic importance of Britain's contribution to the EEC budget was, and remains, very contentious. Even at its highest estimated figure, a net figure of £1 billion in 1980, the budget contributions amounted to just over 1 per cent of total government expenditure. But for Thatcher the issue was symbolically important for three reasons, the first of which had been shared by her Labour predecessors. Membership of the EEC had been presented as a beneficial opportunity, but now it appeared that Britain, despite its faltering economy, was contributing more than its neighbours and getting less back. For Mrs Thatcher, the deficit was all the more galling because it helped to subsidise inefficient agricultural production on the mainland. Just as Wilson and Callaghan had done in 1974–5, Thatcher highlighted the 'distortions imposed by CAP' and set out to change them (Turner, 2000, 89).

Second – to the alarm of many of her colleagues – Thatcher had asserted that a Conservative government would introduce radical reforms. She hoped to establish a new framework for British politics and economics, one that broke away from the Keynesian consensus that had been the dominant British model during the post-war period. The new monetarist orthodoxy which she hoped to establish would be based around control of inflation, lower taxation and a reduced role for the state. As the Conservative manifesto noted, to achieve these aims 'substantial economies' would be sought from government departments. Whether or not it was projected to grow, the EEC budget was outside her exclusive control and therefore objectionable. It would be difficult to impose painful spending cuts at home and not seek 'substantial economies' in the EEC. Finally, the EEC seemed to present an excellent early opportunity for Thatcher to prove her 'resolute' character, demonstrating that a female leader could represent British interests just as firmly as her male predecessors. With its succession of summits, it offered a stage on which Thatcher could assert her international leadership to complement what she hoped would be dynamic domestic leadership.

Thatcher's stated commitment to 'get Britain's money back' brought her into conflict with the President of the European Commission, Roy Jenkins, and with European heads of government who were already learning to dread (and resent) her abrasive approach. From their perspective, 'Britain had known the budgetary implications when it had joined [in 1973]'; although Mrs Thatcher had not been Prime Minister at that time, she had been a member of the Cabinet and had argued for continued membership in 1975. Soon Jenkins was referring the ongoing debates about the budget contributions as BBQ: the Bloody British Question (Geddes, 2004, 79). The frustration and personal ill feeling was mutual, but some observers felt that while other European leaders had been open-minded about

Thatcher at the outset, the Prime Minister had been predisposed to find fault with them. Sir Roy Denman, who had helped to negotiate the terms of Britain's entry into the EEC, thought that Thatcher 'remained the Grantham schoolgirl of the early wartime years. The Germans she detested... The French she despised' (quoted in May, 1998, 67).

Thatcher's engagement with the EEC was in many ways symptomatic of the British failure to see it as a forum for bargaining rather than confrontation. Britain joined the EEC late: it did not shape its institutions and remained ambivalent about engagement with it. British politicians who were forced to undertake fleeting visits to the European institutions found the context uncongenial compared to the zero-sum games they were accustomed to; those who stayed for longer, whether as elected members of the European Parliament (after 1979) or members of the European Commission, usually formed more positive views but only achieved a nationwide profile when they attacked EEC policies. For a naturally combative politician like Thatcher, the EEC was like a vision of hell. She could win outright victories, in theory, if she changed the habits of a lifetime and pretended to sympathise with the views of her opponents; but instead of admitting defeat in the British way, her opponents would claim that they had only given way as a tactical ploy in order to forge a more favourable outcome on a different issue.

The budget negotiations that followed the initial meetings in Strasbourg were often difficult, as it became apparent that the British were prepared to delay European business in pursuit of an acceptable deal. Talks continued but there was little progress. In early 1980 Thatcher went so far as to suggest that the British may withhold their budget contribution altogether. In April 1980, at the Luxembourg Council, British persistence appeared to be paying off, with concessions being offered. But once again they were rejected by Thatcher and further negotiations failed to resolve the issue. Jenkins, the committed supporter of the European project who had broken with his own party to support Heath's policies in the early 1970s, reflected on this process with despair: 'in the course of that argument good relations and her intentions to bring new constructive spirit to Europe, if you like the cause of Conservative Europeanism, perished in the argument' (quoted in Turner, 2000, 92–3). By the end of Mrs Thatcher's first term a final deal on Britain's contribution to the EEC budget had still not been agreed.

Despite the difficult relationship with the EEC, in the 1983 general election campaign the Conservatives still posed as a pro-European party. As usual the manifesto focused on economic arguments: membership of the EEC made Britain part of 'the world's largest trading group... Withdrawal would be a catastrophe for this country. As many as two million jobs would be at risk'. Furthermore, withdrawal would endanger British security; it would be 'a fateful step towards isolation, at which only the Soviet Union and her allies would rejoice'. Thatcher faced a political opposition that had been riven by the issue of 'Europe'. The Labour Party was now offering to take Britain out of the EEC without recourse to a referendum. This position was unacceptable to the repatriated Roy Jenkins, who in March 1981, along with former Foreign Secretary David Owen and other senior Labour figures, formed a new Social Democratic Party (SDP) to compete for the anti-Conservative vote. All that the Conservative Party had to do was navigate between these two European options: Labour's implacable opposition and the strongly positive approach of the SDP and its Liberal allies. If Mrs Thatcher's idea of 'standing up for Britain' was based on a misconception of EEC politics and procedures, it was one she shared with many domestic voters who resented or rejected the idea of post-war decline. Making Britain into an 'awkward partner' might baffle seasoned Euro-watchers, but it made good electoral sense. There was, though, something inherently unstable about the position. At some point the bickering would have to stop, one way or another. In the meantime Thatcher's growing contempt for Britain's EEC partners fostered a gradual change in the outlook of her Parliamentary party, which had always been more pro-European than its grass-roots supporters. Here were the seeds of considerable trouble in future years.

The US and the Cold War

As with the EEC, Margaret Thatcher's engagement with the US represented a continuation of the strategy pursued by Callaghan. Thatcher fully endorsed the 'special relationship' and acclaimed the US as the leader of the free world; she was keen to maintain Britain's nuclear deterrent and happy to cooperate with the US to achieve this; and she sought to maintain transatlantic security ties. In these aims she was little different from previous British Prime Ministers, but, as with the EEC, there was a forceful quality to her statements, of support for the US in this case, that set her apart from her immediate predecessors. Unlike Wilson and Callaghan, there was no need for her to temper her rhetoric in case she alienated neutralists or Soviet sympathisers; unlike Heath, she had no desire to challenge unsubstantiated assumptions about the natural affinity between English-speaking peoples. Thatcher had no doubt that the Cold War world was divided along impenetrable ideological lines, rather than being a new instalment of an old story about conflicting national interests, and wanted to be in the thick of the battle of ideas. In 1976, in one of her first speeches on international affairs, she identified the threat of 'Soviet world domination'. For these comments, the Soviet press did her an inadvertent favour by dubbing her the 'Iron Lady'.

Like her anti-Soviet rhetoric, her admiration of America was reciprocated. Thatcher would recall her early visits to the US as testimony that 'she had been accepted as a leader in the international sphere' (Young, 1991, 120–1). When she finally entered office it was at a time when the US was in need of international allies. Revolution in Iran had deprived it of its most significant supporter in the Middle East, and by the end of 1979 the invasion of Afghanistan by Soviet forces had precipitated a second Cold War after the brief interlude of détente. This was an egregious blunder by the Soviets for several reasons, among which was its apparent confirmation of Thatcher's alarmist rhetoric about Soviet intentions. In fact, compared to its Conservative predecessors, the Thatcher government was ill equipped to make the Soviet threat seem real: if one accepted its argument that state control of industry led to gross economic inefficiency, the Soviet Union should have been on the verge of collapse in 1979, rather than itching to annex another economic 'basket case' like Britain. Nevertheless, when President Carter announced that the US would not be sending athletes to the 1980 summer Olympics in Moscow in protest against the invasion of Afghanistan Thatcher obediently fell into line behind him, but with only limited success. The majority of British athletes attended the games, competing under the banner of the Olympic movement rather than the Union Flag (Controversy 8.1, Chapter 8).

Thatcher's positive relationship with Carter was just a prelude to the most significant international alliance during her time in office. Thatcher had first met Ronald Reagan in London in 1975. At this first meeting, Reagan recalled, the two found themselves 'in great agreement about a number of things that had to do with international situations' (quoted in Young, 1991, 250). The relationship was not just of two political leaders who aspired to high office: it was a meeting of ideological soulmates. The friendship between Thatcher and Reagan was 'intense, and unprecedented in recent history' (Dumbrell, 2001, 89). The connection between the two was based around a shared commitment to change the political and economic trajectory of their respective nations. Through their efforts and those of their conservative allies they pushed through '[d]eregulation, lower tax rates and privatisation' in their respective economies, though even Thatcher was frustrated by Reagan's penchant for budget deficits (Thatcher, 2002, 460). More importantly, they 'saw themselves as engaged in a crusade to rescue their countries from the dead hand of an unrepresentative establishment' (Young, 1991, 254–5). In short, in both of their cases the 'conservative' label could hardly have been more misleading.

The crusade that Reagan and Thatcher embraced went far beyond economic reforms. Thatcher was not indulging in hyperbole when she warned against 'Soviet world domination'. Both she and Reagan believed that the West had been losing the Cold War through the 1970s, and a greater practical and intellectual effort would be required over the coming decade if the advances of Communism were to be reversed. While Reagan and Thatcher both sought to reduce the size of the state, neither wanted to apply the full force of this argument to defence spending. Reagan, in particular, was committed to a significant *increase* in the US military budget, while Thatcher moved ahead with the renewal of Britain's nuclear arsenal.

Reagan espoused a foreign policy doctrine that provided military and financial support to guerrilla forces wherever they were fighting communism in the world. Thatcher made no attempt to conceal her enthusiasm for this approach. During her first visit to see the newly elected President Reagan in Washington in February 1981 the British Foreign Secretary, Lord Carrington, intervened to 'clarify' the Prime Minister's responses to ensure that Britain was not making commitments that it could not honour. Thatcher had suggested that the British might participate in the American Rapid Deployment Force, which could be sent at short notice to conflict zones like Afghanistan or Iran. Carrington found himself having to 'neutralise such rash effusions' (Young, 1991, 252). Fortunately for him, in those pre-Falklands days his party leader was less inclined to challenge the advice of a Foreign Secretary; he was even granted adequate scope to devise a solution to the long-running Rhodesian saga, which was not to the Prime Minister's taste (Case Study 7.2). His successors would not be given a similar licence.

The shared convictions of Reagan and Thatcher enhanced the clarity of their arguments but also gave rise to significant problems. The heightened anti-Soviet rhetoric that Reagan and Thatcher considered to be essential to the robust defence of Western values could often be misinterpreted. Soon after entering office Reagan suggested that it was possible there could be a limited exchange of tactical nuclear weapons in Europe between the US and the Soviet forces. Understandably, talk like this alarmed European partners and made the deployment of a new generation of nuclear weapons to Europe even more contentious (Controversy 7.1). The US's desire to act decisively against ideological foes often meant that its allies were consulted late or after the response had taken place. Thus in October 1983 the US invaded the Caribbean island of Grenada. Grenada was a member of the Commonwealth under the leftist leadership of Maurice Bishop. The regime had close ties with Cuba and as such was regarded with considerable suspicion by the Americans. Bishop had been in power for four years when he was toppled by a military coup. In response, the US assembled an invasion force, ostensibly to rescue American students from the island. Initial suggestions from the US that it might take action were coldly received by the Prime Minister. Thatcher stated that an invasion would:

> be seen as intervention by a western country in the internal affairs of a small independent country, however unattractive its regime. I ask you to consider this in the context of our wider East–West relations and of the fact that we will be having in the next few days to present to our Parliament and people the siting of Cruise missiles in this country.
>
> (quoted in Dumbrell, 2001, 100)

Her objections had no effect, and the invasion went ahead. The British government was forced to make an embarrassed defence in Parliament of its failure to

Case Study 7.2 From Rhodesia to Zimbabwe

Since the white-ruled colony of Rhodesia had made a Unilateral Declaration of Independence in 1965 (Chapter 6) it had been (according to taste) a stain on Britain's conscience, an unmistakable symptom of the country's impotence or a mixture of both. The 'Wind of Change' which, according to Harold Macmillan, had blown through the continent of Africa had bypassed Rhodesia, thanks to a constitution which denied democratic rights to the African majority. Far from inducing an acceptance of reform, British pressure had pushed white Rhodesians towards the unashamedly racist model of government adopted in South Africa. The problem was unresolved when Mrs Thatcher took office, even though Africa had become a major venue for proxy wars between the US and the USSR, and the former was now working closely with Britain in the search for a settlement.

Whatever her private views on race, Margaret Thatcher was not entirely unreceptive to fears about the possible consequences of majority rule in sub-Saharan Africa, especially insofar as this prospect might affect British economic interests. To complicate matters, the Prime Minister of the illegal Rhodesian regime, Ian Smith, had served heroically in the British air force during the Second World War. However, by 1979 Smith's government was under increasing military pressure, confronting several armed movements. Soon after Mrs Thatcher came to power in Britain a coalition government was formed in Rhodesia between Smith's party and 'moderate' representatives of the black majority. However congenial to Mrs Thatcher and the Conservative Party's right wing, this arrangement was never likely to satisfy mainstream opinion within the Commonwealth. In December 1979, at Lancaster House in London, a conference agreed a transitional arrangement under which Britain would oversee a process leading to independence for Rhodesia. The newly independent state – renamed Zimbabwe – had a chequered early history and left the Commonwealth in 2003.

The interim Governor of Rhodesia appointed to guide the country to legal independence was Christopher Soames, the son-in-law of Winston Churchill who had spoken so eloquently of Britain retaining global influence through its membership of three concentric circles. Soames had been Shadow Foreign Secretary from 1964 until he lost his Parliamentary seat two years later. As Ambassador to France from 1968 to 1972 he had played a conspicuous part in the talks which led to Britain's successful bid for EEC membership. As such, when selecting Soames as the frontman in the process which would (hopefully) bring Britain's role in Rhodesia/Zimbabwe to an end, the British government could not have alighted on a candidate whose background and career encompassed so many of the key themes in the country's post-war foreign policy.

Controversy 7.1 Cruise missiles

With the Soviet deployment of land-launched SS-20s in 1976, NATO had lost its previous lead in nuclear weaponry. In response, it was agreed in 1979 that 572 American missiles would be installed in various bases in Western Europe. One hundred and sixty of these missiles – more than in any other country – were to be sited in the UK.

There had always been considerable public opposition to nuclear weapons, whether or not they were under British control. The proposed cruise-missile deployment was particularly divisive, since it could be (and frequently was) argued that they effectively made Britain into a strategic asset for the US military – something not unlike the 'Airstrip One' of Orwellian nightmare. The contrasting viewpoint, of course, was that the missiles would preserve freedom in Western Europe. As such, the issue could be seen as a test of opinion about the 'special relationship' as much as one of public attitudes to nuclear weapons themselves.

From this perspective, the snapshots of opinion at the time make fascinating reading. In October 1981 one poll found a very clear majority (59 per cent to 31 per cent) *against* the deployment (Ipsos MORI, 1983). In the previous month protestors had established a camp near RAF Greenham Common, which had been designated as the first of the proposed missile sites; 'Greenham women' quickly became an additional ingredient in the debate. In 1982 the Labour Party adopted a policy of unilateral nuclear disarmament, covering weapons purportedly under British control as well as the expected American consignment. By 1983 CND, which had declined in popularity and public prominence since the 1960s, boasted more than 300,000 members. Just before the deployment began, in November 1983, more than 3 million people joined protests across Western Europe.

By that time, while British surveys continued to register very significant opposition to the cruise missiles, the gap had narrowed considerably (and, in some polls, disappeared completely). This was partly due to the appointment in January 1983 of the effective publicist Michael Heseltine as Defence Secretary. Also, the missiles probably seemed more acceptable because it was less likely that they would be used (at least intentionally), since the initial tension following the Soviet invasion of Afghanistan had subsided by 1983. Nevertheless, the fluctuations of public opinion relating to cruise missiles can be regarded as a new chapter in an old story, i.e. that a determined government can feel fairly confident of pressing ahead with a policy initiative in foreign or defence policy regardless of public opposition in the expectation that dissent will dwindle in the face of a fait accompli. Lasting

> damage can only arise from clearly perceived failure in these policy fields. In
> the case of the cruise missiles, many will continue to deplore the deploy-
> ment for a variety of reasons; but when they were removed in 1992 the
> Cold War was over, and the Conservative government could argue that the
> missiles had helped to win it.

influence American policy. The Head of the Commonwealth, Elizabeth II, was reportedly not amused.

For critics of the 'special relationship', the events in Grenada only exposed its inherent asymmetry. For others, the continuing British illusion of a partnership of equals could just about survive Grenada, but only because respect for the Commonwealth as an institution had sunk so low by 1983, and the Americans seemed to have intervened against 'bad guys' in a faraway island of which the British knew little. Yet if British reservations had proved ineffectual despite the genuinely 'special' relationship between Reagan and Thatcher, it was difficult to imagine that they would be accorded much respect during international crises which had an even greater bearing on perceived American interests. By contrast, in 1974 the Wilson government had been scrupulous in consulting the US administration while considering its response to the conflict over Cyprus. However, despite the embarrassment of Grenada, the strategic alliance with the US still remained at the heart of the nation's international calculations. The Falklands Conflict, in the year before Grenada, had shown the benefits of maintaining close ties with a global superpower.

The Falklands Conflict

The Falklands Conflict came to be seen as the greatest triumph of Thatcher's period in office: a victory overseas that resulted in domestic electoral dominance for the Conservative Party. But success is rarely complete or unblemished. The war with Argentina was also the result of strategic failure. From a foreign policy perspective, it was indicative of the limitations of Britain's global reach. And despite the imagery of Britain standing alone, it was also an example of Britain's reliance on international support if it wished to act effectively.

When asked by the British government to review the causes for the Falklands Conflict the retired civil servant Lord Franks reached back to 1965 for his starting point. The Falkland Islands were a legacy of the British Empire that were now causing headaches for policy makers in a post-imperial era. The islands were 8,000 miles from the British mainland and difficult to defend. But they were home to a small population with a strongly pro-British sense of identity. At a time when Britain was seeking to restrain its defence expenditure the Falklands remained as an anomalous outpost because the two states that laid claim to it – Britain and Argentina – could not resolve their differences. Franks began his account in 1965 because the UN had first adjudicated on the issue in that year, attempting to balance its desire to see 'an end everywhere [to] colonialism in all its forms' with respect for the islanders' right to self-determination. In other words, two key principles of post-war international relations had clashed head-on. No progress was made on a negotiated solution, but Britain's intelligence services discounted the imminence of an Argentinian military assault on the islands. However, it was impossible to rule out the possibility of 'an unofficial party of raiders' invading the islands. If this happened, an Argentinian government could be forced by public pressure to support it (Franks, 1983, 4–5). So long as the status of the island remained in dispute there was always the danger that Argentina would resort to force of some kind if it did not believe there was a genuine possibility of 'ending colonialism'. As a result, through the 1970s there was a militarisation of the dispute, with Argentina 'resorting officially and repeatedly to military challenges to the British position in the South Atlantic'. Whenever this happened the British 'responded in kind . . . by taking their own military measures and reviewing their military position' (Dillon, 1989, 9–10). The dispute escalated in late 1977 when increased tension in the South Atlantic resulted in the Callaghan government 'deploying a force of sufficient strength . . . to convince the Argentines that military action by them would meet resistance'. A nuclear-powered submarine and two frigates were deployed to the area (Franks, 1983, 10). Negotiations resumed and the threat of conflict receded. Thanks to this timely and decisive action, most Britons remained unaware that the Falkland Islands even existed.

When the problem was inherited by the Thatcher administration the settled policy of the FCO was to be open-minded about the future status of the islands but to insist that any formal transfer of sovereignty to Argentina would be accompanied by a long-term 'leaseback' to Britain. Argentina would effectively be sovereign, but the desires of the islanders would be protected. However, when the islanders were consulted they expressed vehement opposition to this proposal, so the old impasse remained. It may have persisted longer if the Thatcher government had maintained the level of military preparedness shown by its predecessor. Instead, it was announced in June 1981 that the patrol ship *HMS Endurance* would be withdrawn from service. This vessel, based in the South Atlantic, was a tangible sign of continued British commitment in the area. The Conservative government had spared the armed forces from the full force of budgetary cuts applied across the rest of Whitehall, but the Ministry of Defence was not completely immune from the new monetarist strictures. The Defence Secretary, Sir John Nott, was conducting a radical review of the armed forces that sought to reshape the services to best support Britain's role in NATO.

The Royal Navy bore the heaviest costs of the review, and *HMS Endurance* was deemed surplus to requirements.

The withdrawal of *HMS Endurance* was not exactly a cause célèbre for the majority of voters, but it engendered dismay and protest among those whose interests were affected. The Falkland Islands Councils wrote to the FCO, expressing their 'extreme concern' that Britain appeared to be 'abandoning its defence of British interests in the South Atlantic . . . at a time when other powers are strengthening their position in these areas'. The islanders were very effective lobbyists and had accumulated considerable cross-party support in Parliament. Over 150 MPs signed an Early Day Motion protesting against the move; this relatively small but highly vocal group was also active in opposition to any leaseback deal over sovereignty. The Argentine media were not slow to report the changed military environment, noting that Britain appeared to be 'abandoning the protection of the Falkland Islands'. When James Callaghan asked Thatcher about the plans for *HMS Endurance*, she replied that the decision to withdraw 'had been very difficult' but it was the view of the Defence Secretary 'that other claims on the budget should have greater priority' (Franks, 1983, 33–4).

Less than two months after this statement Argentine forces invaded and captured the Falkland Islands in an operation which began with an illegal landing by a group of civilians on South Georgia (the kind of 'freelance' manoeuvre which British intelligence had anticipated). While primary responsibility for the invasion obviously resided with the military junta in Buenos Aires, it was also the result of 'a gross failure of political judgement and leadership by the Thatcher administration' (Dillon, 1989, 226). Taking into account the nature of the Argentine regime at the time, the British government was like a householder refusing to share his possessions with a local burglar while informing him that the back door would be left unlocked in future. By comparison, the fact that the FCO failed to anticipate the invasion should be considered a secondary offence. Nevertheless, Lord Carrington decided to offer himself as a convenient ministerial scapegoat, resigning after facing the wrath of a Conservative backbench meeting.

The British government responded rapidly. Parliament reconvened for a rare Saturday sitting, the day after Argentine forces had captured Port Stanley. As the politicians gathered, the process of putting together a naval task force to be sent to the South Atlantic was already underway. Parliament gave full-throated support to the cause, with Conservative backbenchers saying that the government 'must wipe the stain from British honour'. The Leader of the Opposition, Michael Foot, stated that 'Britain had a moral duty and political duty and every other kind of duty' to expel the Argentine forces (Young, 1991, 264–5). Here foreign policy became less about a calculation of the needs of the nation and how these could be secured through a series of rational decisions and more of a collective howl of rage that Britain had betrayed the clearly declared views of people who wanted to retain their sense of national identity.

The British had been caught off guard by the events in the Falklands, but it would take eight weeks to transport troops and equipment to the conflict zone, offering time for possible international mediation. In particular, the necessary delay offered Nicholas Henderson, Britain's Ambassador to Washington, and Anthony Parsons, Permanent Representative at the UN, the chance to show the true calibre of the country's diplomatic service. Parsons tabled UN Resolution 502, which called for a cessation of hostilities, but also condemned the Argentine action and demanded the withdrawal of its forces.

The invasion of the Falklands had placed the US in an invidious position. The Reagan administration was torn between competing loyalties: on the one hand, there was the 'special relationship'; on the other, there was its long-standing link to Latin America combined with a traditional hostility to 'colonialism' (especially when exercised by the British). Argentina was also seen as a bulwark against communism in South America, although an objective observer would find it hard to imagine how an exchange of the existing right-wing regime for any kind of Communist dictatorship would have made life appreciably worse for the average Argentine citizen. The Reagan administration duly divided, with Defense Secretary, Caspar Weinberger, 'urging support for Britain and the rule of law', while the US Ambassador to the UN, Jean Kirkpatrick, argued that 'Argentina had legitimate claims to Falklands sovereignty'. Almost immediately Weinberger offered military assistance to the British, while refusing any help to the Argentines, undermining the public stance of neutrality that the Reagan administration was hoping to maintain. A senior member of the Royal Navy later remarked that the American military 'went further than politicians would have permitted had they known in time'. Efforts for a mediated solution fell to the US Secretary of State, Alexander Haig, who shuttled repeatedly between the hostile powers, but no agreement could be reached. The British were prepared to talk 'without preconditions' only when Argentine forces had left the islands. The Argentines insisted that they would not leave the islands until they were given assurances on the issue of sovereignty (Dumbrell, 2001, 160–1). When it became clear that this conundrum could not be resolved, and air and sea bombardments of Argentine forces were imminent, the US was forced to choose between its irreconcilable allies.

At the end of April President Reagan formally declared an end to American neutrality, offering material support to Britain and imposing economic sanctions on Argentina. The US offered military equipment, access to facilities on Ascension Island and intelligence support. Publicly, Thatcher continued to explore options for a negotiated settlement, noting that Britain 'could not afford to alienate the United States', but the chances of successful talks receded as the fighting intensified (Dumbrell, 2001, 162). The sinking of the Argentinian ship *Belgrano* and the loss of *HMS Sheffield* in early May hardened opinions on both sides.

Military success for the British was relatively swift, although it came at a significant human price. When Argentine forces surrendered in mid June Thatcher made a sombre announcement to the House of Commons, noting the details of military success while noting the 'deep sense of loss over those who have died . . . that others may live in freedom and justice' (*Hansard, House of Commons Debates*, 15 June 1982, Vol. 25, col. 731). In the months following the conflict it suited the interests of both the United States and Britain to remain diplomatically quiet about their level of cooperation during the conflict. The US wanted to preserve its good relations with Latin America, while the British were happy to play down the role of their allies and be seen once more as a significant global power. As a result, the real lesson of the Falklands – that this was a conflict between two middle-ranking powers, in which the obvious advantages of the aggressor had been nullified because its opponents enjoyed enough logistical support to allow it to exploit the superior skills and morale of its armed forces – tended to be drowned out by a revival of the old Churchillian narrative.

At the centre of this supposedly resurgent global power was Margaret Thatcher. Her resolute approach, which had driven EEC partners to distraction in debates on the British budget contributions, had been deployed to considerable and constructive effect as a wartime leader. Her personal resolution was on display when she announced to the nation that the islands of South Georgia had been recaptured in late April. When asked by a television reporter if she had any further message for the British people she replied sternly: 'Rejoice, just rejoice!' Her ability to translate the Cold War into binary opposites, and to interpret the Falklands from the same perspective, was also demonstrated when she addressed Scottish Conservatives in May 1982: 'The struggle . . . was between good and evil. It went far wider than the Falklands . . . It was a challenge to the West. It must be ended. It will be ended' (Young, 1991, 273).

Conclusions

Mrs Thatcher's combination of resolution and conviction resonated with the public and appeared to mark the close of a difficult historical period for Britain. The 1970s had begun with talk of irreversible decline and the reluctant acceptance that Britain must now seek its future through cooperation within international bodies. But to some observers the Falklands marked a remarkable renaissance. Foremost among those observers, predictably, was Margaret Thatcher. Addressing a party rally in early July 1982, Thatcher unleashed the full force of Britain's post-war narrative:

> When we started out, there were the waverers and the fainthearts. The people who thought that Britain could no longer seize the initiative for

> herself. The people who thought we could no longer do the great things which we once did. Those who believed that our decline was irreversible – that we could never again be what we were.
>
> There were those who would not admit it – even perhaps some here today – people who would have strenuously denied the suggestion but – in their heart of hearts – they too had their secret fears that it was true: that Britain was no longer the nation that had built an Empire and ruled a quarter of the world.
>
> Well they were wrong. The lesson of the Falklands is that Britain has not changed and that this nation still has those sterling qualities which shine through our history.
>
> (www.margaretthatcher.org/document/104989)

Even for the purposes of a party gathering, this was heady stuff. It invited the riposte that when Britain was in thrall to 'the waverers and the fainthearts' back in 1977 its government had dealt decisively with the Falklands issue without any cost in terms of blood or taxpayers' money and without receiving any political credit. The lesson of the Falklands, from this perspective, was that during its decades in the doldrums Britain had been crying out for a bungling government whose mistakes would give it the chance to remember its true self.

In this moment of heightened national pride, Thatcher's devoted followers could convince themselves that the world had been bent into a new shape by the sheer force of a brilliant leader. Yet Britain's post-war foreign policy dilemmas remained largely unanswered. Britain was still a reluctant member of the EEC, looking for assurance to its great ally in Washington and still coming to terms with the problems of a post-imperial world. But this was not the world of Margaret Thatcher. In her world the government elected in 1979 had put an end to uncertainty and decline: 'We have ceased to be a nation in retreat. We have instead a new found confidence – born in the economic battles at home and tested and found true 8000 miles away. . . . Great Britain is great again' (www.margaretthatcher.org/document/104989).

From Falklands fanfare to Maastricht misery, 1983–92

8

Thatcher triumphant

Margaret Thatcher did not enter office with a developed understanding of foreign affairs. Domestic politics was the venue in which the Thatcher revolution would mostly be played out. But the convictions, clarity and obstinacy which she brought to domestic politics helped to build her a prominent international profile. The Falklands Conflict defined her leadership and was a significant part of her legacy; but as much as it defined her, it represented an anomaly. It provided her with a clear and absolute objective: Argentine aggression must not succeed. This meant that the Falklands dispute was far removed from the normal routine of international relations (which, of course, was one reason why it was so badly mishandled, at least initially). A remote group of islands in the South Atlantic could be retaken without threatening the precarious balance between East and West engendered by the Cold War.

Timeline of domestic political developments

May 1983 General election: Conservatives win overall majority of 144
October 1984 Thatcher escapes assassination in IRA bomb attack on Brighton's Grand Hotel
June 1987 General election: Conservatives retain power with majority of 102
September 1988 Thatcher's Bruges speech
October 1990 Resignation of former Chancellor of the Exchequer/Foreign Secretary Sir Geoffrey Howe

> **December 1990** Thatcher forced to resign; John Major becomes Prime Minister
>
> **April 1992** General election: Conservative win fourth successive term of office, though majority falls to 21

After the Falklands were retaken it was easy to predict that British foreign policy would be dominated by Thatcher for the remainder of her premiership. If her first years in office had been marked by a 'more balanced relationship' with her then Foreign Secretary, Lord Carrington, post-Falklands she became more assertive, leading policy from Downing Street rather than deferring to her distrusted neighbours in the FCO (Cradock, 1997, 24). Carrington, the chief political casualty of the war, had been replaced by Francis Pym, who endured a difficult relationship with Thatcher. He had limited enthusiasm for any of her policies, domestic or foreign; and the antipathy was mutual (Young, 1991, 332). Thatcher's strained relationship with political colleagues like Pym contrasted with the close connections that she developed with the British military. The First Sea Lord, Sir Henry Leach, was a case in point. Prior to the conflict in the South Atlantic Leach had been a significant critic of the defence review instituted by Thatcher's government. He was particularly critical of the claims of Sir John Nott that cuts to the budget of the Royal Navy would not undermine Britain's security. But when war in the Falklands began, Leach and his colleagues in the armed forces agreed that Thatcher as 'a leader of the warrior class . . . could not have been improved on'. The military leadership were unused to such decisiveness and fortitude; the Prime Minister had shown herself to 'possess every quality they least expected in a politician' (Young, 1991, 275–9). Thatcher's leadership qualities also won her admirers outside of military circles. In 1984 a foreign policy adviser to Thatcher, George Urban, recorded her impact on a London audience:

> As MT entered the hall everyone got up and stood for 20–30 seconds. That silent tribute was, in my reading, more than good manners . . . It was homage paid to a woman who knows exactly what is ailing Britain and who is analytically rigorous and morally determined enough to impose her remedies. Such characteristics are rare in half-hearted and under-achieving Britain, but when they suddenly appear, and appear spectacularly concentrated in a woman, they attract admiration.
>
> (Urban, 1996, 73)

This description encapsulated the duality of Thatcher's leadership. She came to office possessed of a clear ideological vision of how Britain could be remade economically. This informed her international outlook, defining her closest alliance with the US and later raising doubts about the growth of a 'social Europe' that would, in her view, impair the operation of the market. However, to view Thatcher only through an ideological lens would limit the understanding of her impact on policy. As much as the ideological content it was her personality that drove policy. The description most commonly applied to Thatcher's leadership was that of 'conviction' and her vision 'removed the grey from politics in favour of black and white' (Green, 2010, 2). She might accept tactical compromises more than her critics alleged, but she very rarely changed her mind.

At times Thatcher's stubborn defence of well-defined views paid off. For example, her refusal to back down on the issue of budget reform in the EEC ultimately produced a successful outcome for Britain. The Falklands Conflict had lent itself to the binary divisions that often characterised Thatcher's global vision, but the belief that she knew 'exactly' what needed to be done was also troubling for those versed in more traditional diplomacy. FCO mandarins saw that the Prime Minister's 'assertiveness' could easily develop into 'stridency', and that her unshakable confidence in the justness of the British (i.e. *her*) cause often masked a lack of interest in how others saw Britain: as one close observer put it, 'she had little sense of the forces moving the other side in international exchanges'. This 'lack of imagination' too often resulted in 'one-dimensional policy, the assertion of British claims in a vacuum (Cradock, 1997, 21–2). Her understanding of the world, as for many of her generation, was shaped by a narrative which sought to present the Second World War as a conflict in which Britain had stood alone in the world until America rode in to turn heroic and successful resistance into an overwhelming victory against forces whose worst feature, ultimately, was their tendency to underrate the spirit of the British people. As the world changed, she remained:

> a child of the home front. Early in her premiership, Helmut Kohl became the new Chancellor of West Germany. As a Christian Democrat, Kohl was a natural ideological ally of Thatcher, but at a personal level the two did not connect. Thatcher did not regard the new Chancellor as her intellectual equal, but her prejudices went deeper, remarking to a confident: 'You know the trouble with Helmut Kohl? . . . He's a *German*'.
>
> (Moore, 2015, 22)

Thatcher's attitude towards Germany, and other European neighbours, created considerable difficulties later in her lengthy spell in Downing Street. But in the election year of 1983 she was relatively untroubled. She dominated an election cycle that, in contrast with her first general election campaign, featured significant debates about Britain's role. This was partly a reflection on her first term in office and the impact of conflict in the South Atlantic on her public image. Senior Labour politicians – who knew very well that 'Thatcherite' policies had helped to precipitate the Falklands Crisis and deeply resented her assumed monopoly of patriotism – were unable to counter her narrative of British revival and ended up playing into her hands. The Shadow Foreign Secretary, Denis Healey, accused her of 'glorying in slaughter' during the conflict, and the future Labour leader Neil Kinnock made disparaging remarks about her attitude to the sacrifices of British soldiers. Both were forced to apologise, helping the British public to forget that, in fact, the overwhelming majority of Labour MPs (including their much maligned leader, Michael Foot) had supported the war.

Contrary to popular myth, the 'Falklands factor' did not in itself make Thatcher's second term as Prime Minister inevitable; rather, it gave a triumphalist tone to a victory which owed much to a feeling of economic revival and (more importantly) the divisions between her political opponents (who remained numerous even within her own party). Labour produced an election manifesto that was subsequently described as 'the longest suicide note in history', committing the party to British withdrawal from the EEC within the lifetime of the next Parliament. Running parallel with British exit from 'Europe' would be a shift to a 'non-nuclear defence policy', involving the cancellation of Trident and a refusal to allow US missiles on British soil. Disillusioned Labour supporters could easily be weaned away from their former electoral preference by the Alliance between the Liberals and the Social Democratic Party, which advocated the maintenance of a British nuclear deterrent and continued membership of the EEC. In other respects, however, the Alliance offered moderately 'progressive' policies which diminished its attractions for dissident Conservatives. As a result, Thatcher's party was able to win more seats than in 1979 (397, compared to 339) on a smaller proportion of the popular vote (42.4 per cent compared to 43.9).

Despite this highly significant evidence that the nation was less intoxicated by Thatcher's policies and personality than her grass-roots supporters, the electoral success of 1983 suppressed lingering doubts about her leadership. A senior Conservative Party researcher captured the moment when victory in 1983 had been secured: 'She really did start walking on water. It was wonderful in a way. But the triumphalism horrified me' (Moore, 2015, 63).

The years of 1983 and 1984 marked the zenith of Margaret Thatcher's power. In the domestic arena opposition parties were reduced to Parliamentary impotence, struggling to accommodate themselves to an apparent new 'consensus'. Internationally, Thatcher reached a successful conclusion to the negotiations on the British contribution to the budget of the EEC, and towards the end of 1984 she met the Soviet politician Mikhail Gorbachev for the first time, an event that took on greater significance as the decade progressed. Her close ally in the US, Ronald Reagan, was re-elected for a second-term in November 1984, ensuring the 'Conservative revolution' that he and Thatcher espoused would remain a global phenomenon.

However, the period was not without its difficulties. The invasion of Grenada by the US in 1983 caused great embarrassment to the British government, while the deployment of a new generation of nuclear missiles to Western Europe was greeted with widespread protests (Chapter 7). Nevertheless, Thatcher certainly cashed in on the Falklands factor in her international dealings, recording progress in relation to the EEC and the Soviet Union; but these apparent successes also began the processes that ultimately undermined her leadership and cast doubt on her claim that Britain had enhanced its role within international politics.

Thatcherism in Europe

Although respect is always due to Mrs Thatcher's utterances – even in her enforced and somewhat embittered retirement – it is difficult to accept at face value her claim that she entered Downing Street 'something of a European idealist'. Rather, Thatcher struggled to convince herself that her 'tough talking and hard negotiating' could save the EEC from what she regarded as its worst excesses (Thatcher, 2002, 371). The story of Thatcher's engagement with the EEC during her early years in office can be presented as the erosion of initial optimism by exposure to European institutions and bureaucratic practices. Equally, it can be seen as another staging post in post-war British history, where successive governments have dealt with their European partners from an Anglocentric perspective and been frustrated when this attitude has been greeted with incomprehension or resentment.

Soon after she entered office Thatcher presented her vision of 'Europe':

> We believe in a free Europe, not in standardized Europe . . . We insist that the institutions of the European Community are managed so that they increase the liberty of the individual throughout the continent . . . Whenever they fail to enlarge freedom the institutions should be criticized and the balance restored.
>
> (Thatcher, 1993, 60–1)

This broadly positive pronouncement contrasted with the more practical discussions concerning Britain's relationship with the EEC, which had been taking place since before she took office. In 1978 the Labour government of James Callaghan considered the possibility of British membership of the European Monetary System (EMS), a currency-stabilisation scheme that would attempt to harmonise the exchange rates of the currencies of EEC member states. A successful harmonisation of currencies could be seen as the harbinger for closer economic coordination within the community, and some senior Cabinet ministers were strongly in favour. However, by 1978 even the Labour Party's limited enthusiasm had cooled, and Callaghan, who had been offended by his apparent exclusion from the planning process, decided that Britain should not join the EMS, at least at first. This opened up the possibility of the Conservative Party gaining political advantage from Labour's divisions. Thatcher brought together advisers who outlined two aspects of the scheme that could benefit Britain and a Conservative government. Nigel Lawson, who became Chancellor of the Exchequer after the election victory in 1983, saw that membership could have a disciplinary effect on the British economy, an argument that echoed the beliefs of Thatcher's predecessor, Edward Heath, who believed that the institutions of 'Europe' would buttress capitalism in Britain. Also supporting membership was Geoffrey Howe, Thatcher's first Chancellor, and Foreign Secretary after the election of 1983, who placed the EMS within its wider political context. Howe identified the EMS as a process that would ultimately result in 'economic and monetary union', and membership would be necessary if Britain was to exercise continued political influence in 'Europe' against the dominant Franco-German alliance (Green, 2010, 175–6).

Once in office, Thatcher, like Callaghan, fudged the issue of membership of the EMS. She rejected membership because 'it would weaken the government's control of monetary policy' but intimated that Britain may join in the future and announced the intention 'to swap some of our own reserves in the Bank of England for ecus (the European Currency Unit)'. If the Prime Minister believed that this would augment British influence in 'Europe', she would be disappointed. Later she noted that the technical financial move did not receive a 'visible welcome' from Britain's European partners: 'it appeared simply to be pocketed and then forgotten' (Green, 2010, 179; Thatcher, 1993, 63).

By 1983 the divisions that later caused considerable inconvenience for the Conservative Party were discernible below the surface. Both the Chancellor of the Exchequer and the Foreign Secretary appreciated the economic and political advantages arising from closer links with the EEC, whereas the Prime Minister was becoming more 'sceptical' and resistant to European institutions. These divisions did not, however, prevent Thatcher from securing some of her policy objectives. In June 1984 the European Council met in Fontainebleau and reached agreement on a permanent rebate for the British government to resolve the long-running dispute over Britain's contributions to the community budget (Chapter 7). At the European Council meeting that preceded Fontainebleau, in Athens in November 1983, the impasse over Britain's rebate effectively halted any progress on business. The Athens summit was pithily described by Thatcher as 'a fiasco' (Thatcher, 1993, 338). The British argued that budget contributions should be related to a nation's ability to pay. When agreement was reached at Fontainebleau this key British principle was still not conceded, but the meeting did produce a 66 per cent rebate on Britain's annual budget contributions. Thatcher, grateful for what she had achieved, concluded: 'In every negotiation there comes the best possible time to settle: this was it' (Thatcher, 1993, 545).

The end of the budget dispute allowed the EEC to consider plans for its further development and enlargement. Central to this future development would be the creation of a single market among EEC member states. This proposal (eventually enshrined in the Single European Act of 1986) resembled the Conservative strategy for the British economy in seeking to 'roll back' the economic role of the state and promote market forces. The relatively rapid progress achieved in the adoption of the Single European Act marked a rare moment when Britain played a significant role in the shaping of the European project. But the results were open to interpretation. For supporters of Thatcher's domestic reforms, it appeared that the continent was now moving towards a model that conformed to their understanding of contemporary politics and economics. The 'Europe' of the single market would comprise nation states that retained their independence of action in economic policy within an expanded trading area where the costs of entry into the market were dramatically reduced. Now, in theory, a company in Luton could trade with a company in Lille as easily as it could do business in London. In Thatcher's own words, the single market would fulfil the goals of the original Treaty of Rome as 'a treaty for economic liberty' (Thatcher, 2002, 372).

However, at the same time that Thatcher and her allies were putting the case for community-wide economic reforms, the President of France, François Mitterrand, was advocating institutional changes which he saw as essential counterparts to the single market. Far from endorsing Thatcher's preference for a loose collection of states joined by a common economic market, Mitterrand advocated closer political relations. This, it seemed, was the 'standardised Europe' that Thatcher had cautioned against. Wary of the possible rejection of such a policy by Britain (among others), Mitterrand proposed a phased introduction of this new 'Europe'. In 1984 he raised the possibility of a 'two-speed Europe', allowing states which favoured closer cooperation to leave behind those who were not yet ready (Green, 2010, 178). Mitterrand's proposals for deeper integration implied the promotion of closer monetary union, building on the EMS (which had been established, without British participation, in 1979). Thus the idea of a 'Thatcherised Europe', embodied in the single market, was countered by Mitterrand's federalism. Initially, it was possible to negotiate a compromise which allowed both reforms to proceed, but the seeds of serious trouble had been sown.

Cold War: from thaw to end

In late 1983 the US started to deploy a new generation of intermediate-range nuclear forces (INF) in Western Europe, including the 160 cruise missiles stationed at Molesworth and Greenham Common (Chapter 7). This marked the low point of the renewed Cold War of the early 1980s. In the weeks leading up to this deployment Margaret Thatcher had spoken in the US and addressed the issue of East–West relations. She stated that it was not possible to project Western morality on to the thoughts and deeds of the Soviet leadership. They were, she argued, 'not constrained by our ethics'. Their country resembled 'a modern version of the early tyrannies of history' (www.margaretthatcher.org/document/105450).

Thatcher's words echoed the sentiments of her close political ally Ronald Reagan. Reagan earlier in the year had described the Soviets as 'the focus of evil in the modern world'. The close relationship between the US and Britain during the leadership of Reagan and Thatcher ensured that the President was sure to listen to British argument, but it did not change the underlying dynamics of the Cold War – a 'duopolist' duel in which a third party could hardly hope to effect a positive intervention (Sharp, 1997, 184). Despite the harsher rhetorical line, British policy towards the Soviet Union was barely changed by Thatcher. Britain remained a loyal ally of the US and used its positions within international bodies to make the case for the transatlantic alliance. That Thatcher was more voluble in this support was reflective of her own convictions and of the space opened up in British domestic policy by the non-nuclear policies adopted by the Labour Party. But, as we have seen previously, there were limitations to policy in both directions. While Thatcher was a steadfast Cold Warrior, her support for the US was not automatic even when relations with the Soviet Union were involved. When the US imposed sanctions on the Soviet Union after the imposition of martial law in Poland in 1981, its policy effectively cancelled a wholly European-funded Siberian pipeline project. A single British company, John Brown, lost more from the ending of the pipeline project 'than the entire value of American industrial exports to Moscow' (Sharp, 1997, 256). As Thatcher told Reagan's new Secretary of State, Alexander Haig, 'it affronted the Europeans to be asked to make enormous sacrifices while the US made none' (Dumbrell, 2001, 92).

The Reagan administration might regret these injured feelings but not to the extent of changing either its policies or its overall outlook. In the case of sanctions linked to the situation in Poland, the British and Europeans had only been told of the measures against the Soviet Union five hours before the announcement. A similar approach was followed when Reagan launched his Strategic Defense Initiative (SDI) in March 1983; this time Thatcher was informed only a few hours before the announcement (Moore, 2015, 107). SDI, or 'Star Wars', as it was soon dubbed, was an ambitious project to use new technologies to create a defensive shield which would protect the US from an incoming missile attack. Opposition to the initiative ranged from those who questioned its technical feasibility to the Soviet allegation that it was a deliberate attempt to undermine the existing anti-ballistic-missile treaty.

SDI had major implications for British security, which makes the belated consultation all the more significant. First, if SDI was successful, the US would feel far less vulnerable to 'collateral damage' arising from a war which broke out in Europe (or, indeed, anywhere else). Naturally, it would feel less inhibited about resorting to military action if a serious dispute should arise with the Soviet Union. Second, if the Soviets managed to produce a shield of their own, Britain's nuclear deterrent would no longer serve its original purpose; and, since the Warsaw Pact enjoyed a clear superiority over Western European states in conventional forces, the postwar nightmare of a Red Army advance might become a more realistic scenario.

As the British government responded to the proposals Thatcher remained supportive of Washington. She did not believe the system 'could offer one hundred percent protection', and consequently there was still a role for deterrence (Thatcher, 1993, 466). Discussions about SDI continued in the background long after the initial announcement. Reagan had become personally wedded to the scheme, and it proved difficult for either the Soviets or the Europeans to cool his ardour. At the end of 1984 Thatcher visited Camp David and directly discussed SDI with Reagan for the first time. She sought assurances that Britain's nuclear deterrent would not be undermined by American ambitions for SDI. The Reagan administration was persuaded to sign up to four principles:

> the US, like its allies does not seek superiority over the USSR, would negotiate any SDI deployment as obligated by existing treaty commitments, would do nothing to undermine deterrence, and would engage in arms control talks to reduce existing levels of offensive systems.
> (Thatcher, 1993, 468)

Thatcher recorded with some pride the view of Reagan's Secretary of State, George Schultz, that she 'had secured too great a concession from the Americans' (Thatcher, 1993, 468). Yet although these principles represented a diplomatic success for Thatcher, they also highlighted the weakness of the British position. First, she had been forced to remind her closest ally of the impact that its policy choices would have on Britain; and, second, the continued effectiveness of Britain's deterrent was 'maintained by the USSR's willingness to refrain from deploying the systems which could nullify it' (Sharp, 1997, 132).

SDI was not the only subject under discussion at Camp David. Days before the gathering Thatcher had met a previously obscure Soviet politician called Mikhail Gorbachev, and she was keen to relate her impressions. By the end of 1984 the bellicose language of the Reagan Presidency towards the Soviet Union had mellowed. Early in the year Reagan had spoken of his desire to meet and talk with the Soviets:

> I have openly expressed my view of the Soviet system. . . . But this doesn't mean that we can't deal with each other. . . . The fact that neither of us

likes the other system is no reason to refuse to talk. Living in this nuclear age makes it imperative that we do talk.

(https://reaganlibrary.archives.gov/archives/speeches/1984/11684a.htm)

The softening of the President's tone was welcomed by the British, who were also exploring new relations with the Communist bloc. In February Thatcher visited Hungary, which was edging away from a state-controlled economy and beginning to introduce some economic freedoms. With justice, Geoffrey Howe claimed that 'after a period of relative inactivity in this field, Britain is once again playing a significant role in East/West relations' (Moore, 2015, 226–7).

Whether the Soviet Union was ready to respond positively to these developments was a different question. At the point when the olive branch was being offered by Western leaders the Soviets were dealing with a series of leadership issues. In contrast to the image of Soviet power projected (for different purposes) by governments on both sides of the Iron Curtain, the nation had stagnated in the final years of Leonid Brezhnev. When he died in November 1982 his replacement, Yuri Andropov, initially appeared to offer the prospect of reforms to counter many of the nation's endemic problems. However, his health was already poor, and in early 1984 he passed away, to be replaced by Konstantin Chernenko. Chernenko appeared emblematic of a dysfunctional government; his health was less than robust when he took office, and he made little impact beyond confirming a Soviet boycott of the Los Angeles Olympics in retaliation for the American refusal to take part in the Moscow Games of 1980 (Case Study 8.1). Having met Chernenko at Andropov's funeral, Thatcher implored FCO officials on the flight back to Britain: 'For heaven's sake, try and find me a young Russian' (Moore, 2015, 228).

When Thatcher met Mikhail Gorbachev in December 1984 in London he appeared to fit the profile of the 'young Russian' she was looking for. He was certainly young by the unexacting standard of Soviet leaders, and he was well read and highly articulate, defying precedent by appearing comfortable with Western media. Thatcher enthused that Gorbachev was 'a man she could do business with', and she conveyed that message to Camp David. The notion that an inspired Thatcher plucked Gorbachev from total obscurity is one of the many myths generated by her remarkable career; while he was unknown to the Western public, he was already a rising star of the Soviet politburo, having been identified by Andropov as a future leader. Thatcher's warm endorsement, inspired by some vigorous and mutually enjoyable arguments with Gorbachev, probably helped to convince the US administration to take him seriously. But Thatcher and Gorbachev were knocking at an open door, since Reagan was hoping for constructive talks with the Soviets and would have engaged in dialogue with Gorbachev as soon as he assumed power in March 1985. However, Margaret

Case Study 8.1 Sport, politics and foreign policy

At the start of the 1980s sport had limited financial or institutional significance. As such, it proved a tempting target for politicians wishing to use its popularity to highlight foreign policy goals. The Thatcher governments were not beyond deploying sport as a political weapon, although, as the following case studies show, it was a weapon which the government used selectively.

The Soviet Union

In her first months as Prime Minister Margaret Thatcher faced one of the more difficult policy questions of her premiership: how to respond to the invasion of Afghanistan by Soviet forces. In March 1980 President Carter announced that a threatened US boycott of that year's summer Olympics would proceed, in protest against the Soviet invasion of Afghanistan. Mrs Thatcher was keen to support the US, realising that a sporting boycott could have a greater impact than economic sanctions and 'prevent [the Soviet Union] using the forthcoming [games] for propaganda purposes' (Thatcher, 1993, 88). Thatcher's ministerial colleague Michael Heseltine stated that '[i]f this means we have to embrace the use of sport for the first time as a political weapon, I feel the end would justify the means' (Coe, 2012, 119).

The difficulty for the Thatcher government was that the British Olympic Association was an independent body, receiving no state funding. The decision about British attendance was ultimately the choice of the association and the individuals involved. Nevertheless, pressure was applied by the government. Athletes who worked in the public sector faced difficulties in securing time off work to attend the games. There was growing resentment among the British Olympic community at the prospect of being forced to acquiesce in a boycott at a time when they knew that British companies were still trading with the Soviet Union. Sebastian Coe, who was a world-record holder in middle-distance running and one of Britain's great hopes for the Moscow games, progressed from 'irritation' about the boycott to 'anger' as the games approached. When asked about the prospect of a boycott he told reporters: 'If the government think this is serious, then they should do something about it, but don't just use sport as the fall guy'. This comment allegedly inspired a phone call to Coe's coach, his father, Peter, from Douglas Hurd, then a Junior Minister in the FCO, telling him that he should 'keep his troublesome son in check' (Coe, 2012, 123).

The inability of the government to prevent athletes from competing undermined the British boycott. The British Olympic Association sent a team without official approval, performing under the flag of the Olympic movement while continuing to wear British kits and, when successful, celebrating as British winners.

South Africa

Given the strong sporting culture of South Africa, especially in team events, a refusal to play against their representatives in international competitions was always likely to prove a potent weapon against apartheid, following the UN condemnation of that system in 1962. South African athletes were barred from competing in Olympic Games from 1964. The division of the Southern African communities under apartheid laws excluded non-whites from representing their nation in international sports. This resulted in some moving abroad to pursue their sporting careers, notably the cricketer Basil D'Oliveira, who emigrated to England. D'Oliveira was classified as a 'Cape Coloured' under apartheid, but, living and playing in England, he qualified to play for his new home nation. When he was selected in 1968 to represent England on a tour of South Africa the South African government refused to agree to his inclusion, insisting on an all-white squad. The English cricket authorities cancelled the tour, and by 1971 all other cricketing nations had followed suit, effectively barring South Africa from international cricket.

The final sporting domino was rugby union. Through the 1970s it had become increasingly difficult for touring South African rugby teams to avoid the politics of apartheid, and their tours to Britain and New Zealand were met by sustained opposition. Responding to this grass-roots pressure, the Commonwealth negotiated the Gleneagles Agreement (1977), which called on member nations to do all they could to discourage sporting contact with South Africa.

Among British sportsmen the boycott of South Africa had patchy support. Some agreed with the principle that there could be no engagement with a country which excluded any individual on the basis of race. However, some, echoing the arguments of the Olympic athletes, did not see why sporting men and women should make the sacrifice for foreign policy goals when British companies were still trading with South Africa. In 1982 the South African Cricket Union enlisted a group of English players to take part in unofficial matches in South Africa. The announcement of the cricket tour evoked protests and calls on the government to act. However, the government effectively washed its hands of the process. This refusal to act conformed to the general policy of the Thatcher government, whereby the Prime Minister condemned apartheid but was equally scathing of the demands of anti-apartheid protestors (Green, 2010, 151–2).

The rebel tour of 1982 was a prelude to further problems on the issue of apartheid. These disputes spilled over into the Commonwealth Games of

> 1986 and a boycott that denuded the event of much of its sporting merit. The previous Commonwealth Games, in Brisbane in 1982, attracted participants from 46 different nations. The official motto of these games was 'The Friendly Games', a term originally used to describe the gathering in Edinburgh in 1970. The events in Edinburgh in 1986 were soon dubbed the 'unfriendly games', with only 27 nations participating. Thatcher was unbowed. When the Secretary-General of the Commonwealth, Sonny Ramphal, told her that her games were being 'spoilt' she replied, 'No . . . They are not my games. These are *your* games' (Moore, 2015, 583).
>
> In 1990 another cricket tour was arranged, featuring 16 England players paid directly by the South African government. However, the tour coincided with the release from prison of the ANC leader, Nelson Mandela. Wherever they went the cricketers were met with protests, and the tour ended early. The sportswriter Frank Keating summed up the whole sorry escapade: 'No more inglorious, downright disgraced and discredited team or sportsmen wearing the badge of "England" can ever have returned through customs with such nothingness to declare' (Weaver, 2010).

Thatcher could regard her sponsorship of Gorbachev as additional concrete evidence (following the SDI talks) that Britain's influence 'rivalled anything [it] had enjoyed in the post-Suez era' (Moore, 2015, 249).

A recurring lesson of the Cold War for British foreign policy makers was that – as Dean Acheson had pointed out in 1963 – playing a key role in persuading the two main antagonists to talk never guaranteed a place in the ensuing discussions. Notwithstanding his classical analogies, Harold Macmillan had found in the case of arms control that when the serious talking started the 'Romans' turned a deaf ear to the 'Greeks' (Sharp, 1997, 184–5). In November 1985 direct dialogue began between Reagan and Gorbachev in Geneva and was resumed in Reykjavik a year later. The talks in both cases stalled over Reagan's continued attachment to the SDI programme. However, briefly in Reykjavik the two sides had appeared close to an agreement which would eliminate all nuclear weapons in two five-year periods, beginning with intermediate systems and moving on to long-range missiles. Gorbachev's objections to the SDI programme scuppered the deal, and the summit broke up in a rancorous atmosphere to match the previous fever of expectation (Young, 1991, 479–80). While the world came to terms with the dramatic collapse of the Reykjavik talks, Thatcher could only be horrified by this close brush with success. A deal, after all, would have exposed the willingness of the US President to negotiate away Europe's nuclear forces. As with the initial announcement of SDI, such an agreement would make Europe safe for conventional warfare (Greenwood, 2000, 185–6). Thatcher returned to Washington to reinforce the US commitment to the nuclear defence of Europe and 'to bring Reagan back into the fold'. A subsequent statement confirmed that NATO's future strategy would 'require effective nuclear deterrent ... reductions to nuclear weapons would increase the importance of eliminating conventional disparities'. As well as seeking reassurance for her European partners, Thatcher prodded Reagan into a public commitment to the modernisation of the British nuclear arsenal (Reynolds, 2000, 265–6).

This transatlantic diplomatic mission demonstrated Thatcher's continued influence within Washington, although, like Attlee's flight to see Truman in 1950, it also suggested the limits of that influence. As with the agreement on SDI, she had shown that she could exert pressure on behalf of her favoured policy. But essentially this was a *reactive* power, which was accepted because it reinforced the prevailing mood in Washington; indeed, Thatcher's opposition to the proposed Reykjavik deal was seconded by senior members of the Reagan administration who shared her view that the policy of eliminating all nuclear weapons was potentially dangerous.

During 1988 it became evident to outside observers that the Soviet grip on its Empire was beginning to loosen. In February Gorbachev announced his intentions to withdraw Soviet forces from Afghanistan, infringing the 'Brezhnev doctrine', which decreed that states which adopted 'socialism' would never be allowed to leave the fraternal fold. Inside the Soviet Union the reformist policies of *glasnost* and *perestroika* had unleashed social forces that proved incompatible with continued Communist Party rule. Thatcher had to balance her close personal relationship with Gorbachev with support for movements and reforms in Eastern Europe, which progressed far too quickly for the liking of the Soviet 'old guard' on whom Gorbachev depended. The breakup of the Communist bloc began with Hungary in 1988, where 'round table' discussions resulted in democratic reforms to add to the economic changes that had been instituted in the mid 1980s. In Poland in April and May 1988 a wave of strikes was launched in support of political reforms and an end to the ban on the free-trade-union movement, Solidarity. These protests resulted in talks between the Polish government and the Solidarity leader, Lech Walesa. Thatcher offered her support to Poles demanding change, visiting the country in November 1988 and effectively saying '[p]ursue political as well as economic reform and you will find the West more generous' (Cradock, 1997, 104).

The prospect of a more constructive engagement with the West was also the motivating factor when Hungary eased travel restrictions for its citizens, opening a route which enabled East Germans to exit their socialist homeland for West Germany via Austria. By September 1989 demonstrations were taking place inside East Germany in favour of political reform. When, in early October, Gorbachev made it clear that the Soviet Union would not intervene to shore up the rule of the local Communist leader, Erich Honecker, the possibility of a military response to domestic protests receded. The Berlin Wall was opened in November, effectively bringing an end to Communist rule in East Germany.

The events of 1988–9 were an unequivocal victory for Western politicians, like Thatcher, who had refused to accept post-war 'realities' and lost no opportunity to proclaim their opposition to Communist rule even when it appeared to be entrenched. However, as we have seen, this undoubted personal achievement brought Britain no closer to a well-defined role in international politics, since no objective observer could deny that the US (even under a well-disposed President) would only listen to advice from any ally when it chose to do so. Even this role – as Washington's most faithful lieutenant and occasional purveyor of convenient counsel – was endangered by the end of the Cold War. Although well-placed US decision-makers felt considerable gratitude for services rendered, the removal of the Iron Curtain destroyed the old certainties of international politics; and old alliances, however close, could easily be superseded by affiliations which looked likely to prove more advantageous to the US in the new context. In short, whether the US had ever wanted a 'special relationship' with anyone, the end of the Cold War meant that there were many more contenders for that role.

The Commonwealth

The positive impact of the ending of the Cold War was not restricted to Europe. The decline in East–West tensions was also felt in Southern Africa, where the superpowers ended their habitual sponsorship of proxy wars: conflict eased in Angola and Namibia. These changes increased the chances of a peaceful ending to apartheid rule in South Africa. But before this point was reached Thatcher had once again demonstrated her ability to antagonise opponents and cause problems for British diplomats, this time within the forum of the Commonwealth. It had always been apparent that the Prime Minister did not accord the Commonwealth an exalted place in the hierarchy of international bodies, and in the mid 1980s her irritation grew as it became increasingly vocal in its opposition to Britain's stance towards South Africa.

Contrary to the claims of her critics, Thatcher was not a supporter of apartheid (although her husband, Denis, seemed well disposed towards the system); indeed, she described it as 'contrary to my whole philosophy'. However, as opposition to the government in Pretoria grew in the 1980s, that 'philosophical' rejection of apartheid did not translate into practical endorsement of sanctions (Green, 2010, 151–2). Thatcher and her supporters – who in this case included President Reagan – argued that a policy of sanctions was misplaced in relation to South Africa. Mandatory economic sanctions imposed on the South African government 'would merely confirm [their] sense of isolation and lonely virtue and stiffen their resistance to change' (Cradock, 1997, 146). Rather than the stick of sanctions, Thatcher believed that governments should brandish the carrot of constructive engagement with South Africa. Commenting on the campaigners who had presented their arguments to her, she reflected that 'perhaps because so many of them were socialists [they] never seemed fully to grasp . . . that capitalism itself was probably the greatest force for reform and political liberalization in South Africa, as it was in communist countries' (Thatcher, 1993, 513). Indeed, her advisers believed that a booming economy would 'confer' economic power on the black community in South Africa and, through this, 'political power' (Cradock, 1997, 147).

Whatever the abstract merits of this argument, it obviously lacked the undercurrent of revulsion which marked Thatcher's approach to (pre-Gorbachev) Communist regimes. As such, it met strong opposition from those whose passions were truly engaged. The main South African anti-apartheid force, the African National Congress (ANC), and their jailed leader, Nelson Mandela, wanted tighter sanctions, and their cause won widespread support from other Commonwealth leaders. The security situation within South Africa was deteriorating, and the government declared 'states of emergency' in 1985 and 1986. This only increased pressure for some action, rather than words, from the international community. At the Commonwealth Summit in Nassau in October 1985 the British resisted the proposed sanctions regime, while allowing the meeting to record its criticism of apartheid and of South African aggression against neighbouring states; there were also calls for the release of Mandela and the end of apartheid. Some minor items were added to the existing Commonwealth sanctions regime, but any goodwill generated by this compromise dissipated when it was presented by Thatcher as a 'tiny little' concession. The derisive delivery of these comments, even more than their content, gave the impression that Thatcher opposed harsher sanctions against the apartheid regime because they might actually prove effective. But, as with the EEC, Thatcher had no interest in making friends; on the contrary, being in a 'minority of one . . . was to her a proof of virtue'. The scenario would be repeated, as South Africa continued to resist reform and the calls from Commonwealth nations recurred at each gathering. Further pressure was applied to the South African economy when the US Congress imposed sanctions in 1986, overriding Reagan's veto. Still Thatcher remained staunchly opposed to sanctions, leading to 'concerns that the role of the Queen as the British monarch and Head of the Commonwealth were being brought into conflict' (Cradock, 1997, 150, 153).

How much Thatcher saw South Africa through the prism of the binary divisions of the Cold War is open to debate. A regular feature of her argument against economic sanctions was the fact that the South African economy outperformed its African neighbours; to her mind, it was a bastion of free-market economics in a continent that was dominated by socialist states (Green, 2010, 155). The withdrawal of the Soviet Union from African conflicts therefore offered the promise of progress. With disputes in Angola and Namibia moving towards resolution, radical change in Pretoria would no longer necessarily result in a victory for the 'socialist bloc'. In early 1989 a new reform-minded leadership in South Africa came to power, led by FW de Klerk. Mandela was released from prison in early 1990 and a negotiated end to apartheid rule was agreed. The running sore in Commonwealth relations was thus healed by events inside South Africa; and since the role of sanctions as a spur for change had not been established beyond question, both Mrs Thatcher and her critics could feel vindicated. It was just one part of a more general process of momentous change, with Europe at its heart.

New world order 1: Germany

Lord Ismay (1885–1967), a British soldier who served as the first Secretary General of NATO, is reported to have quipped that the rationale for the newly formed alliance was 'to keep the Russians out, the Americans in, and the Germans down' (Nye, 2002, 33). The division of post-war Germany had effectively kept Germans 'down' in the international arena for over 40 years, but the breaching of the Berlin Wall began to undermine this long-standing settlement. Before the events of 1989 most observers assumed that the division of Germany would prove permanent. Both German states had developed their own identities and their own understanding of their place in European history. When protests began in East Germany demonstrators called for a reformed East German state, rather than reunification. However, once the old order had crumbled, West Germany's Chancellor Helmut Kohl seized the initiative, announcing a ten-point strategy for German unity at the end of November 1989. Kohl had not consulted his Western allies prior to the announcement, but after his statement the question of German reunification had moved from whether or not the two would reunify to how quickly the reunification could be effected. The speed of events in Germany surprised the British government, and for at least one very senior minister the unexpected velocity was highly unwelcome. When asked about the prospects for reunification Thatcher said that she anticipated 'a stately progress' over a period of some ten to fifteen years (Cradock, 1997, 108–9). It soon became clear that this timetable reflected Mrs Thatcher's hopes rather than any rational expectations.

One of the respectable reasons for Thatcher's caution concerning German reunification was its potential to undermine Britain's claim to a 'special relationship' with the US. The dramatis personae of international relations had changed in 1989. President Reagan had left office at the start of the year, and his successor, President George HW Bush, was a very different kind of operator. While appreciative of British support, he was a cool, calculating politician, rather than a swashbuckling radical who allowed his decisions to be coloured by personal friendship as well as ideological considerations. When asked in September 1989 to identify America's closest ally in Europe Bush replied that he should not be forced to choose between friends. This very sensible response was not what Thatcher wanted to hear. Sir Geoffrey Howe observed that for the Bush administration Britain 'was only one of five medium-sized European nations, and by no means the most successful – or influential in continental politics'. Increasingly, the US was seeing "Europe through the prism of Germany" (Dumbrell, 2001, 106). Reunification would only reinforce this tendency, tending further to reduce British influence.

In 1990, while plans for German reunification rushed ahead, Thatcher's foreign-policy adviser at Downing Street, Sir Percy Cradock, noted that 'British policy went astray and we allowed ourselves to be seen as negative' on the matter. For Cradock, this development 'was particularly sad in view of [Britain's] firm public commitment going back some forty years to just that objective' (Cradock, 1997, 110). British opposition to reunification may have been a reflection of British concerns about its changed role in the world, but it also betrayed Thatcher's prejudiced view of Germany. At a private dinner at Downing Street in December 1989 Thatcher made no secret of her real feelings about Germans and her fears concerning German reunification. An informal foreign policy adviser to Thatcher, George Urban, was 'amazed to hear her uttering views about people and countries, especially Germany, which were not all that different from the Alf Garnett version of history'. It was particularly striking that her exposure to international affairs during her time in government had done so little to change views which had been inculcated during her wartime childhood; indeed, subsequent experience seems to have reinforced them. She told Urban that there were events that her generation should never forget: 'We've been through the war and we know perfectly well what the Germans are like . . . and how national character doesn't basically change' (Urban, 1996, 103–4). This was a vivid illustration of Thatcher's curious brand of biological determinism: at various stages of her career she implied that the essential British character was in imminent danger of being undermined, either by mass immigration or by 'socialism' (by which she could mean almost everything to the left of her own beliefs), but she was unable to compute the idea that contemporary Germans might think differently from the people who had inhabited the country during the Third Reich (or, indeed, while Kaiser Wilhelm was on the throne).

If the British were to decelerate (if not derail) the process of German reunification, their obvious obstacle was the fact that events within Germany were beyond their control. The end of Communist rule in East Germany had exposed a regime riddled by ineptitude and corruption. East Germany was in the process of collapse, and significant investment would be required to shore it up and begin the process of reconstruction. The sheer scale of this task was beyond the imagination of most analysts at the time; had Thatcher realised how expensive the process would prove, and the restrictions which this would place on reunified

Germany, her fears might have been allayed. As it was, her main hope for obstruction lay with the Soviet Union. If Gorbachev had signalled that events were moving too fast, the US might have intervened to stall the process. But far from expressing disquiet, the Soviets welcomed a reunified Germany, provided that it was neutral, rather than a member either of NATO or the Warsaw Pact. This would be an unacceptable outcome for the US (and the British), since it would have deprived them of a useful ally (West Germany) while freeing the USSR from a satellite state (East Germany) which had become a serious encumbrance. Ultimately, it was agreed that the reunified Germany could become a NATO member, but no NATO troops would be deployed in the former East Germany while Soviet forces remained in place. Germany would pay for the 'upkeep and eventual rehousing' of the Soviet troops in the three to four years it would take for them to withdraw from the positions they had occupied since the spring of 1945 (Sharp, 1997, 217–19).

When free elections were held in East Germany in March 1990 Chancellor Kohl's Alliance for Germany coalition secured nearly half of the vote. He had been furnished with the electoral mandate required to push through reunification. For the British, these developments confirmed that their attempts to press the pause button on the process had been thwarted. This, however, was not the end of British difficulties. Thatcher continued to voice her concerns that the considerable West German influence over developments within the EEC would be redoubled in the wake of reunification. The language used to highlight this concern often fell below normal diplomatic standards. Nicholas Ridley, a senior government minister and fervent Thatcherite ideologue, was forced to resign after he described European economic and monetary union as 'a German racket designed to take over the whole of Europe' (Lawson, 1990). Ridley's resignation coincided with the leaking to the press of a confidential memorandum from a meeting between the Prime Minister and a group of academics. The gathering, which had taken place in March 1990, had focused on Germany, which had clearly annexed an obsessional place in the Prime Minister's thoughts. The memorandum, written by Thatcher's long-standing foreign policy adviser, Charles Powell, set out an alphabetical list of the abiding characteristics of the German people: 'angst, aggressiveness, assertiveness, bullying, egotism, inferiority complex, sentimentality' (Urban, 1996, 151). The academics present at the event disputed Powell's record, recalling that the negative views of Germany had appeared to emanate exclusively from the Prime Minister herself.

Throughout her career Thatcher had exhibited a relish for 'resolution' and an unwillingness to relinquish unfashionable opinions. This had brought her remarkable (if somewhat deceptive) success in domestic politics; but in international relations, as her time in Downing Street drew to a close, her isolation was unmistakable. The policy towards Germany may, in part, have been influenced by a well-founded fear that a resurgent unified power in Central Europe would reduce British influence over the US and in other quarters; but the evidence that these concerns were reinforced by national prejudice made it much more difficult for British concerns to gain a sympathetic hearing. The ultimate failure of Thatcher's foreign policy was 'rooted in her own particular sense of the past', which depicted Britain as a major global power, facing down foes through sheer force of character, whatever the state of its material resources. This illusion had been sustainable during the Cold War, which prevented it from being subjected to a serious test; but once this period was over, Britain's elected representatives had an opportunity to take the lead in reassessing old rivalries (Sharp, 1997, 224). Instead, Thatcher seems to have taken pleasure from her abrasive encounters with Kohl, treating him as if he and his nation were comic characters rather than influential international actors. Thatcher's Parliamentary colleagues only decided to bring this demeaning episode to an end when it was too late to repair the diplomatic damage; any chance that Britain would act as a trusted coadjutor with Germany in the next phase of EEC development was long gone.

Nemesis

The role of Britain in the world had not really been changed by the end of the Cold War; rather, the pretentions which had been encouraged by the Thatcher/ Reagan interlude were now exposed. The ideological glue that had held British and US foreign policy together during the Reagan years had disappeared, and within 'Europe' ham-fisted British diplomacy had ensured that the reunified Germany would be a more reliable (and powerful) ally for France. The calculations of where Britain would sit within this newly forming global order reverted to the questions that the nation should have addressed at the end of the Second World War. Did it really enjoy a 'special relationship' with the US? Even if the answer to that question was affirmative, was there any national advantage to be derived from being an 'awkward partner' in 'Europe'? Or could British policy makers throw off the shackles of history and forge a positive relationship with the US *and* the EEC?

One of the repeated criticisms of British engagement with the institutions of 'Europe' in the post-war era is that, through some collective myopia, British governments created a vision of how 'Europe' should be and then made no secret of their disappointment when their vision was not matched by the reality. As noted above, Margaret Thatcher was never able to understand other nations' viewpoints; rather, she saw negotiations with her European partners as zero-sum games, in which the representatives of other nation states were always trying to hoodwink the honourable British. The idea that Britain could not be guaranteed to get its way – or, if it failed to persuade its partners, could not quash their deliberations by use of a veto – was all the less palatable since these countries had all experienced defeat, dishonourable occupation or both during the Second World War. Britain's Churchillian time capsule, which preserved the national mindset as it stood in 1945, was capable of captivating the imagination of individuals whose parents had not been alive at that time; it was certainly shared by many grass-roots members of the Conservative Party, young and old. However, as the Single European Act progressed through the British Parliament in 1986, even Eurosceptic MPs allowed themselves to be beguiled by the free-trade element of the legislation and to overlook the implied necessity for a transfer of powers from Britain to the EEC. Trade within the EEC could not be wholly 'free', as it might have been if such an arrangement had been established in the nineteenth century: uniform standards (relating, for example, to food hygiene) would have to be applied in the more squeamish context of the 1980s, and it was logical that relations between the single market and the wider world would now be handled by the EEC rather than by individual nation states.

Unfortunately for the Conservative Party, most of its elected representatives failed to anticipate these predictable by-products of a single market. Once she had been ejected from office, Thatcher felt able to attribute her own failure to the malign intentions of others, criticising European leaders for turning the (welcome) economic reforms of the Single European Act to political advantage. As she put it in her memoirs, 'the idea that these extra powers should be limited to the purpose for which they were actually being given probably never seriously occurred to them' (Thatcher, 2002, 375). Thatcher would come to believe that there was a specific 'purpose' for the single-market reforms, and that this very simple economic goal was exploited by ill-intentioned (i.e. 'socialist') Europeans to pave the way for a 'super-state': 'It simply did not occur to me that they would want to bury the Mother of Parliaments in a United States of Europe' (Moore, 2015, 391).

In 1984 debate was joined on who should become the next President of the European Commission. This was a highly influential role – though not as potent as Eurosceptic newspapers habitually claimed – so it was in the interest of all member states to find a candidate who was amenable to their agenda. The British viewed Jacques Delors, a former Socialist Finance Minister of France, as the most suitable candidate. When he and Thatcher first met she emphasised that he should stick to practical achievable goals rather than allowing 'vague idealism' to distract him. Delors replied that there were two trends in European politics, one envisaging 'practical improvements' and the other agitating for a new treaty to enshrine closer political cooperation (Moore, 2015, 393). President Mitterrand had encouraged the second trend, in which the next step would be the extension of collective rights across member states. After becoming President of the Commission Delors emphasised this development in an address to the British Trades Union Congress (TUC) in 1988. He spoke about the need for a 'social Europe' to complement the creation of a single market. Delors argued that 'it is impossible to rebuild Europe on only deregulation' (Turner, 2000, 121), which the TUC rightly interpreted (and duly acclaimed) as a direct challenge to Thatcherism. Delors' challenge would not go unanswered: Britain's preferred Commission President soon became the chief bogeyman for Eurosceptics in the press and in Downing Street.

The Delors speech transformed the European debate within Britain. His speech to the TUC was an attempt to mobilise support for European institutions among the Labour movement, whose members included many people who continued to regard the EEC as a 'capitalist club'. For Delors, the idea of a 'social Europe' was a progressive cause. The EEC would become the guarantor of workers' rights and working conditions across the continent. In Thatcher's eyes, of course, Delors' successful appeal to Labour merely compounded his original offences. Through the Single European Act, which she had championed, it seemed that Britain was being driven along a path towards ever closer political union, with new restrictions imposed on its businesses and an apparent diminution of its democratic institutions.

Less than two weeks after Delors' intervention, Thatcher offered an alternative vision for 'Europe' in a speech delivered in Bruges. She restated her usual view that Britain was integral to 'Europe' and a protector of liberty in the continent. However, Europe should not (and could not) supersede national identities: it was multifaceted, made up of different nation states with an ingrained sense of self. 'Europe' enhanced its prosperity, security and influence in the world when member states agreed to work together:

> But working more closely together does not require power to be centralised in Brussels or decisions to be taken by an appointed bureaucracy. Indeed, it is ironic that just when those countries such as the Soviet Union, which have tried to run everything from the centre, are learning that success depends on dispersing power and decisions away from the centre, there are some in the Community who seem to want to move in the opposite direction. We have not successfully rolled back the frontiers of the state in Britain, only to see them re-imposed at a European level with a European super-state exercising a new dominance from Brussels.
> (Thatcher, 1988)

Thatcher recorded her surprise at the controversy aroused by the speech. Ardent Euro-enthusiasts – of whom Britain harboured very few specimens – were horrified by her criticism of federalism. More seriously for Thatcher, genuine 'sceptics' – i.e. those who thought that on balance Britain was better off 'in Europe' but reserved judgement on specific EEC proposals – were seriously disturbed both by the tone and content of the remarks. There was, indeed, something rather odd about the presentation of the EEC as a threat to British national identity; if this was as deep-rooted as Thatcher usually asserted, not even the most ruthless totalitarian superstate could hope to efface it. One can only surmise that, despite her defiant rhetoric, Thatcher was uneasy about the prospects for her *personal understanding* of British identity – one which had been fashioned during a war for national survival against powers which were now allegedly conspiring to make British people feel less British. That specific sense of national identity was still very potent but seemed likely to fade with the ageing of Thatcher's own generation. If younger people were less likely to appreciate appeals to the Dunkirk spirit, this was at least partly attributable to the success of the EEC in making war between Britain and Germany (or Italy) seem preposterous.

Oblivious to these idiosyncratic elements of the Bruges speech, Thatcher was buoyed by the support she received from the following month's Conservative Party conference. The Bruges speech highlighted the divisions that had been apparent in the Conservative Party over the EEC since the time of Heath. British cooperation with the European project had been sold on the economic benefits it bestowed; but critics had always asserted that 'Europe' undermined British sovereignty, providing apparent confirmation of the 'defeatist' view that the country was a diminished force in global politics. This was not the Britain of Margaret Thatcher's imagination. In response, Thatcher's political opponents in all parties alleged that an (un)diplomatic approach based on a delusional notion of British power was guaranteed to undermine whatever international prestige the country still possessed. Thatcher's progress around Europe in the wake of Bruges appeared to confirm this. On the night of her speech she had a 'vigorous argument over dinner' with senior Belgian politicians (including the Prime Minister), who recorded their 'stunned outrage' at her unbridled expressions. Thatcher thought that such objections were only to be expected from 'a small country which thought it could wield more power inside a federal Europe than outside it' – another sign that she rejected even the theoretical possibility that the same could be true of a 'big' country like Britain. Moving on to Spain, she encountered similar opposition, which in her view was entirely predictable because Spain's settlement with the EEC was 'so lucrative' (Thatcher, 1993, 746). In her mind, only Britain's motives were beyond reproach – a logic which pointed clearly towards exit rather than positive engagement. The following spring a meeting with the Dutch Prime Minister, where Howe and Lawson hoped some progress could be made on the European Exchange Rate Mechanism (ERM), descended into embarrassment as 'Margaret laid into the Dutch with ferocious gusto' (Green, 2010, 184).

What Delors had planned, and Thatcher rejected with vehemence, was a three-stage process towards closer European cooperation. The first stage would bring all EEC currencies (including those, like Britain's sterling, that had stayed out of the EMS) into the ERM. This technical process would seek to harmonise currency-exchange rates across the continent. The second stage would introduce a social charter, as outlined by Delors to the TUC, along with the development of a European Central Bank to coordinate monetary policy. The process would be completed with virtually fixed exchange rates, leading to a single European currency. The stumbling block to the first stage was Thatcher's rejection of the ERM, as witnessed by the Dutch Prime Minister. Divisions within the Conservative Party were becoming unmanageable, and after the European elections in June 1989 – in which its attempt to persuade voters to eschew a 'Diet of Brussels' failed to enthuse voters – there was growing concern that the European policy of its leader could undermine its future electoral prospects. Nigel Lawson and Geoffrey Howe, two of the most senior members of the government, approached Thatcher and threatened to resign if she did not set out her terms for British adherence to the ERM. Their arguments had remained remarkably consistent throughout the years. Lawson – neither then nor later an advocate of European integration – saw the ERM as a means of imposing discipline on the British economy. For his part, Howe was convinced of the need for Britain to play a constructive role in 'Europe'. The alliance between Lawson and Howe worked in the short term, and Thatcher agreed on conditions for ERM membership. But the compromise had been secured by political blackmail, and it could not last.

Having been treated with something which approached (and sometimes exceeded) contempt by his leader in his role as Foreign Secretary, Howe was demoted in a Cabinet reshuffle in the summer of 1989. Lawson was the first of the conspiratorial couple to leave government, resigning in October 1989. This should have been a crippling blow for the Prime Minister, since Lawson was a key architect of the 'Thatcher revolution' in economic policy and was seen by many as the real hero of the Conservative electoral victory of 1987. In his subsequent resignation speech to the Commons Lawson argued that 'for our system of Cabinet government to work effectively, the Prime Minister must appoint Ministers whom he or she trusts and then leave them to carry out the policy' (Lawson, 1992, 1062–4). The ex-Chancellor was well aware that this had never been Thatcher's invariable approach, but recently she had withdrawn her trust from her most senior ministers; and despite making loyalist noises, Lawson clearly thought that this was unsustainable. His listeners could easily draw the conclusion that the Prime Minister was no longer fit to preside over the Cabinet and represent Britain abroad. However, Thatcher's supporters were able to 'spin' away the full implications of the speech.

Nevertheless, Thatcher's decisive leadership was now replaced by confusion. In October 1990 she attended a European summit in Rome – an event preoccupied with preparations for an intergovernmental conference later in the year on economic and monetary union. Thatcher returned from the Rome meeting and left the House of Commons in no doubt of her continued opposition to closer European cooperation:

> The President of the Commission, Mr Delors, said at a press conference the other day that he wanted the European Parliament to be the democratic body of the Community, he wanted the Commission to be the Executive and he wanted the Council of Ministers to be the Senate. No. No. No.
>
> (*Hansard, House of Commons Debates*,
> 30 October 1990, Vol. 178, col. 869)

Howe had remained in government as Leader of the House of Commons, but Thatcher's latest outburst proved too much even for his elastic endurance. The Prime Minister's statement, he felt, was yet another example of 'Europhobic anti-diplomacy' (Green, 2010, 184). Unlike Lawson, however, Howe was unwilling to leave without spelling out his reasons in phrases that the general public might comprehend. In his resignation statement to the Commons he reiterated his long-standing argument that Britain should be in the ERM because it was beneficial to the British economy and to business. But the stakes were even higher than this:

> The real threat [arising from Thatcher's position] is that of leaving ourselves with no say in the monetary arrangements that the rest of Europe chooses for itself, with Britain once again scrambling to join the club later, after the rules have been set and after the power has been distributed by others to our disadvantage.
>
> (*Hansard, House of Commons Debates*,
> 13 November 1990, Vol. 180, col. 464)

Howe followed up by drawing a somewhat tortuous analogy between Thatcher and a cricket captain who makes it impossible for team members to score runs by breaking their bats. This, rather than the more technical details, was the section of the speech which caught media attention.

Howe's resignation, coupled with two disastrous Parliamentary by-election results, precipitated a leadership challenge against Margaret Thatcher that resulted in her deposition as Prime Minister on 22 November 1990.

Thatcher's downfall was not purely a result of disagreements over the future of the EEC. There were compelling domestic reasons for the Conservative Party to seek a new leader. In democracies even the most successful and visionary leaders eventually exhaust their political capital. While she became the longest serving Prime Minister of the modern era, Thatcher also became a warning to future premiers not to overstay their welcome. But the ending of Thatcher's premiership after disagreement over 'Europe' did highlight a wider truth about Britain's relationship with EEC institutions. When faced with the question of where the future of British foreign policy lay – with the US or with the EEC – it was impossible to give an unequivocal answer in 1990. From a broadly Realist perspective, circumstances should dictate where Britain's interests would best be served, sometimes in 'Europe' and sometimes in Washington. For various reasons, Britain would never be an enthusiastic participant in European institutions, but this did not mean that the British political class and many voters did not see value in maintaining ties with its neighbours. Britain did not particularly like the EEC, but it was fearful of what the world might look like if it was no longer a member. In becoming increasingly 'Europhobic' rather than 'sceptical', in any meaningful sense of that word, Thatcher threatened one of Britain's centres of international influence, and she did so on the basis of a view of Britain's global role which seemed to have been vindicated in the anomalous case of the Falklands but had been sharply contradicted by other episodes like Grenada and Libya (Case Study 8.2) as well as by the incomprehension or outright hostility which Thatcher's defiant rhetoric inspired among other European leaders. The Conservatives – and Britain – needed a leader who seemed capable of recalibrating relations with both 'Europe' and the US.

New world order 2: the Gulf War

Before Margaret Thatcher left Downing Street, in late 1990, she was given one last chance to display her old assertiveness on the international stage. As with the war in the South Atlantic, Thatcher was presented with a foreign-relations crisis that reflected the binary division between 'right' and 'wrong' that had informed her foreign policy pronouncements since her 'Iron Lady' days.

The invasion of Kuwait by Iraqi forces was an anomaly in the modern world. It was rare, since the advent of the UN, for one sovereign nation to invade another. Regardless of ambiguous signals emanating from the US in the days before the Gulf War, the invasion of Kuwait by Iraq represented an unequivocal case of aggression, with a stronger state attempting to subsume its smaller, weaker neighbour. Another anomaly was the fact that action against Iraq could be pursued through the UN. The ending of the Cold War had brought a rare period of harmony to the proceedings of the Security Council, and it was possible for agreement on a military response to be reached without the action being vetoed by one side or the other. Thatcher, who by chance was in the US when the invasion took place, was plunged back into her favourite foreign policy environment, reasserting the close relationship between Britain and the US and making robust statements. Thatcher emphasised two points to President Bush: first, 'aggressors must never be appeased' and, second, as the invasion of Kuwait had opened up the possibility of Iraqi forces invading Saudi Arabia, action must be taken quickly (Thatcher, 1993, 817). President Bush would later recall her instructions to him in a memorable sentence: 'Remember, George, this is no time to go wobbly' (Young, 1991, 574). As so often, Thatcher's decisiveness contrasted with

Case Study 8.2 Libya and the 'special relationship'

The centrality of the 'special relationship' to British foreign policy and its one-sided nature were illustrated once again in early 1986, when the Reagan administration raised the possibility of moving against the Libyan regime of Muammar Gaddafi. Gaddafi was a long-standing opponent of the West, identifying himself at the forefront of the anti-imperialist struggle. More specifically, Gaddafi had long been a thorn in the side of the British as a supporter of Northern Irish republican terrorists. Mutual hostility had deepened in 1984, when shots were fired from the Libyan embassy in London on anti-Gaddafi protestors, killing a British police officer. Following this the British government had severed diplomatic ties with the Libyan government, while remaining cautious about more active measures because of concerns about possible retaliation. Thatcher told Vice President George Bush in the summer of 1985 that it was 'very difficult to do much with [Gaddafi] because he is mad' (Moore, 2015, 515). Yet the issue became more pressing when two bombs were detonated in Rome and Vienna airports towards the end of 1985. Both attacks were linked to Libya, and in January 1986 President Reagan announced that the US would seek to impose sanctions.

In this case Thatcher suspended her usual scepticism about the efficacy of sanctions, but there was concern in London that the US might go further and use military force. Speaking to American journalists after Reagan's statement on sanctions, Thatcher made it clear that the scope for Western action was limited: 'I must warn you that I do not believe in retaliatory strikes which are against international law. . . . Now, I quite agree terrorism is against international law, but I believe that one has to fight it by legal means' (Moore, 2015, 505).

The situation deteriorated further in April 1986, when Libya was identified as the instigator of a bomb attack on a Berlin nightclub, targeting American servicemen. On 8 April President Reagan requested permission to use British airfields to launch military strikes on Libya. The deadline for the reply was given as the following day. At this point the British government hesitated. Three months earlier Thatcher had rejected such a move and now she was being asked to facilitate it. First, the government asked for more information. Howe summarised the questions as: 'what targets? What would be the public justification? Won't this start a cycle of revenge?'. A final question that the British asked was particularly pertinent: 'what about western hostages?'. (Dumbrell, 2001, 102). This related to two British hostages being held in Lebanon, whose lives would be at risk if Libya was attacked. In response Washington clarified its policy, while affirming that the action would proceed.

> Thatcher was now faced with a familiar dilemma for British Prime Ministers, of assessing the importance of the relationship with the US in the UK's foreign policy and for Britain's standing in the world. Other European allies closer to Libya refused the American requests for assistance. Thatcher sought confirmation that the proposed military action could be justified on the basis of 'self defence' as set out in the UN Charter. When this approval was granted she insisted that President Reagan use it as his 'public justification'. Reagan agreed and Thatcher duly acquiesced to the use of British air bases.
>
> When faced with the choice of maintaining the relationship with the US or breaking it, maintenance and continuation was always the likely outcome for the Thatcher government. It was reported that at Whitehall meetings Thatcher interrupted Foreign Office officials raising concerns, 'shrieking about the need to support the Americans and about the need not to be fair-weather friends' (Young, 1991, 476).
>
> The attacks went ahead and a member of the Gaddafi family was killed in the raid on Tripoli. The bombing of Libya aroused considerable international and domestic condemnation, including from within the British Cabinet. A few days after the attacks the bodies of the two British hostages were found in Beirut; an American had also been killed by his captors. Soon more British hostages were taken. An opinion poll taken in the immediate aftermath found 71 per cent of respondents opposed the use of British bases (Moore, 2015, 516). In the medium term, however, the incident (like so many others) merely confirmed the existing polarisation of opinion about Thatcher.

diplomatic attempts to find a face-saving solution for the Iraqi dictator, Saddam Hussein. The latter's coupling of the invasion of Kuwait with the long-standing failure to resolve the Arab–Israeli conflict gave some pause for thought. But Thatcher remained resolute in her argument. When approached by Gorbachev's special emissary on the Gulf, who wanted to find 'some room for manoeuvre' for Saddam Hussein, she retorted that 'Saddam Hussein was a dictator . . . and there could be no deals with such a man' (Thatcher, 1993, 827). For her, the crisis would be over only when Iraqi forces left Kuwait and its government was restored. Her stance through the first weeks of the crisis earned her a scornful rebuke from Saddam, who dubbed her 'an "old hag" with a "canine, harsh voice," who behaved in a "selfish and inhuman way"' (Karsh and Rautsi, 1991, 224).

As Thatcher lamented in her memoirs, she was 'not allowed by the Conservative Party to see through the campaign to throw Saddam Hussein out of Kuwait' (Thatcher, 1993, 822). This task would fall to a new Prime Minister, John Major. Major saw no reason to adjust Thatcher's policy towards the Gulf. Visiting

President Bush in December 1990, he reassured the US of Britain's continued support for the international coalition that was being assembled to expel Iraqi forces from Kuwait. When Major became Prime Minister in late November 1990 the UN Security Council had already agreed Resolution 678, which imposed a deadline on Iraq for the removal of its troops from Kuwait. In the absence of a negotiated resolution, it seemed inevitable that conflict would begin in mid January.

Britain's contribution to the multinational coalition was just over 50,000 troops from all of Britain's forces, who would operate under US tactical command. Major (who was born in 1943 and thus carried little of the Churchillian baggage which coloured Thatcher's outlook) proved to be an effective wartime leader, offering a more consensual approach than his predecessor while also asserting his authority: 'Unlike Thatcher, he did not pretend that he was a general. He took care to be bipartisan' (Seldon and Baston, 1997, 155).

The British, along with other members of the multinational coalition, played a subsidiary role to the US. In the lead-up to the conflict, and in its aftermath, President Bush talked of the emergence of a 'new world order'. The ending of the Cold War, it was thought, would usher in a new global context, enabling the UN to 'police the world', protecting the weak from the powerful. The new world order would be governed by international law and respect for human rights. This optimistic rhetoric to some extent cloaked the actual world order that was given tangible form in the Kuwaiti desert and the cities of Iraq. The Gulf War provided concrete confirmation of the US's military reach and superiority as an unrivalled superpower. After the outbreak of hostilities continuous media reports from the front line demonstrated the technological superiority of the US; and although British service personnel made a notable and often heroic contribution, no rational observer could be left in any doubt that the US provided the decisive firepower, demonstrated in vivid television coverage.

From the British perspective, one aspect of the war over Kuwait is too easily overlooked in hindsight. In preparing for the conflict, the British had readied themselves for significant casualties. But the reality of the new world order appeared to be that victory could be achieved for technologically advanced militaries with a limited loss of life. This consideration, coupled with the changed international environment, made the prospect of policing the world superficially more attractive for Britain as well as the US. As the fighting in the Gulf War came to an end, a new role for the British appeared to be emerging – that of a nation which was willing to take a prominent role in any conflicts which were likely to emerge in the post-Cold War era, confident that the price in terms of British lives and economic outlay would be justified by the (inevitable) outcome. The first test of this approach came soon after the end of fighting in Kuwait.

If the victory in Kuwait had proved to be militarily straightforward, the aftermath inside Iraq was highly complex. Rather than enforcing regime change in Baghdad,

Bush and his advisers decided to halt their advance into Iraq and allow the people of the country to dispose of Saddam if they so wished. Popular uprisings against the dictatorship duly took place in the south and the north of the country. In the south Iraqi forces which had survived the Gulf War and remained loyal to Saddam put down the uprising with great brutality. This task completed, they turned their attention to the Kurdish community in northern Iraq. The Iraqi Kurds had previously been targeted by Saddam's forces, which had used chemical weapons against the civilian population. As Iraqi forces moved north the Kurdish cities emptied, their inhabitants fleeing into the mountains or attempting to cross into Turkey and Iran to save themselves from the oncoming troops. Even more embarrassing for the British and the Americans who had offered explicit encouragement to this revolt, their victorious forces were 'on the spot, [but] were compelled to watch helplessly as Saddam's troops brutalized large sections of the Iraqi population' (Cradock, 1997, 181).

This was not the new world order that President Bush had hailed. While full-scale intervention into Iraq was beyond the scope of the resolutions already agreed by the UN Security Council, John Major sought to find 'a middle way . . . between the prohibition of Article 2(7) of the UN charter, forbidding all interference in a country's internal affairs, and humanitarian imperatives' (Cradock, 1997, 181). Major promoted the idea of 'safe havens' for the Iraqi Kurds, in the hope of protecting them in their own enclaves. A limited intervention by coalition forces based in Turkey encouraged the Kurdish population to return to their homes, and Iraqi troops halted their advance in the north. The wording for UN Security Council Resolution 688, drawn up by the British and the French, referred to Iraq's responsibility to desist from human rights abuses against its own people. As such, it 'challenged dominant understandings of the sovereignty rule that had hitherto prohibited' intervention. In short, the creation of safe havens for the Kurds marked the emergence of a new international norm (Wheeler, 2002, 169). Major had pushed the policy of safe havens because he was concerned that the images emanating from Iraq would undermine domestic support for the war. The policy, then, could be regarded as a short-term fix – the kind of manoeuvre at which Major excelled – but it nevertheless set a precedent of lasting significance.

The new world order that followed the Cold War would be formed without the influence of the Soviet Union – indeed, the disappearance of the latter as a major force in world politics was the key factor which promoted talk of such an 'order' in the first place. Gorbachev had clung to power throughout the upheavals in Eastern Europe and the reunification of Germany. But, contrary to his hopes, the reform process he had started did not result in a rebirth of the Soviet Union and its values. A military coup was launched in August 1991, but it soon collapsed. Gorbachev, who had been placed under arrest in his Crimean holiday home, was saved by the intervention of the President of the Russian Republic, Boris Yeltsin. Power had slipped away from Gorbachev and from the governing institutions of the Soviet Union. At the end of 1991 it was replaced by a 'Commonwealth of Independent States', which was dominated by the Russian Republic. As in the case of Communist Eastern Europe, the Soviet Union passed into history with few mourners.

The end of the Cold War did not usher in a period of peace – far from it – but there was no single defining antagonism as there had been for the previous 45 years. In this new environment the armies of the Western world and their governments rethought their security. Major's middle way between absolute sovereignty and individual human rights became a new template for military action. The new world order did not match the rhetoric of President Bush or the speculations of the academic and government adviser, Francis Fukuyama, who wrote about the hegemony of Western liberal ideals (Fukuyama, 1989, 1992). But after the Cold War humanitarian goals were accorded a new priority among politicians and military strategists. Britain had already played a significant role in this development, and it would become even more prominent under Major's successor, Tony Blair.

The boy from Brixton

Unlike the Conservative Party grandees he defeated to become party leader, John Major was a man from a modest background who appeared to embody the emergence of a 'meritocratic Britain', where the best could rise to the top irrespective of background. Major appeared to be an agreeable (if unexciting) individual, whose style was a sharp contrast from Thatcher's hectoring stridency. As a result, when Britons voted in the 1992 general election they could feel that they were voting for change, even if they returned the Conservatives to office for the fourth consecutive time. Major's party duly won, against the expectation of the pundits and pollsters.

But although Major offered a new narrative for the Conservative Party, he was saddled with the legacy of Thatcher's leadership in foreign and domestic policy. His success in the 1990 leadership election was, in part, due to the support he received from Thatcher as her anointed successor. But this created a dilemma for the new Prime Minister. He owed his position in Downing Street to the need for the government to shift away from the policies which had undermined Thatcher (most notably, the much resented Community Charge or 'Poll Tax'). Yet if he moved too quickly and too far from her legacy, he risked antagonising the very supporters who had brought him to office. The Gulf War had demonstrated that he could rise to the challenge of an international crisis and build a working relationship with the US; but a more difficult problem was how to resolve the conflicts in the Conservative Party over 'Europe'.

After the antagonism that marked Thatcher's third term in Downing Street, Major offered himself up as a 'Europragmatist', convinced of the benefits of

British membership but not prepared to embrace a federal Europe (Seldon and Baston, 1997, 164). The difficulty for Major, and indeed any British Prime Minister following this strategy, was that such an approach still left Britain on the outer ring of the European debate whenever closer cooperation was discussed. Major could, and did, change the tone of the debate. His more consensual approach was a relief to Britain's European partners after Thatcher's unrelenting pugilism. He sought out Chancellor Kohl and attempted to mend relations between Britain and Germany. The French newspaper *Le Monde* commented that '[i]nterventions, tirades, arguments and foot-stamping are a thing of the past. In its place there arrived the smiling softly spoken, amicable new British premier' (Seldon and Baston, 1997, 165). But despite the emollient tone at the top, the Conservative Party could not resolve its own internal differences on European policy. Thatcher's downfall might have been triggered by her hostility to the EEC, but her views enjoyed strong and swelling support from grass-roots party members, backbench Conservative MPs and even government ministers. The party had become culturally Eurosceptic, making it difficult to see how Major could possibly realise his initial stated intention of taking Britain closer to 'the heart of Europe'.

If Major had presided over a period of stagnation within the EEC, his experience in Downing Street would have been very different. As it was, the new impetus towards political integration, stemming from the Single European Act, led to the proposal of significant constitutional changes. The ensuing Maastricht Treaty haunted Major's second term in office; but when the agreement was initially made, in December 1991, he could feel considerable satisfaction in a negotiating feat which vindicated Thatcher's unexpected (1989) decision to appoint him Foreign Secretary in succession to Geoffrey Howe. He had secured an opt-out for Britain from Economic and Monetary Union (EMU), meaning that the country's membership of what became the European Union (EU) would not be conditional on accepting a single currency. Instead, Britain retained the right to retain sterling until a later date, if this was considered to be beneficial for the British economy. In addition, Major also opted out of the Social Chapter, the common framework for workers' rights and protection that had so upset Thatcher when proposed by Jacques Delors. The initial press reaction to the agreement was favourable, not least because (in a fateful moment) Major and his advisers decided to emulate the 'us against them' language favoured by the tabloids and crowed that the result meant that the brave Brits had secured 'game, set and match'.

Nevertheless, the government could anticipate impassioned opposition to the Maastricht terms from within its own ranks. Although the treaty was signed in February 1992, rather than seeking ratification at the earliest opportunity and running the risk of exposing Conservative divisions, the party's business managers concluded that it would be preferable to delay this process until after the impending general election. There was a mini rebellion when the treaty was initially discussed in Parliament, but in the short term the strategy paid off, and when the election was held in April 1992 the European issue inflicted little damage on Major or his party.

Thatcher, however, had no intention of reflecting in tranquillity on her time in office. Before the election she voiced her doubts concerning the treaty, arguing for a looser model of European cooperation. Later she asserted that although Britain had opted out of the single currency, other member states were steaming ahead with a project which could only end with the establishment of a federal 'superstate'. The fact that Maastricht inaugurated the EU in place of the former structure of 'communities' did indeed suggest that the federalist agenda had picked up momentum in the wake of the Single European Act. Furthermore, Maastricht had established 'a European citizenship and a common defence policy' and a Committee of the Regions, which, in Thatcher's eyes, was an attempt 'to undermine the sovereignty of nation states from below' (Thatcher, 2002, 377). But with Major confirmed as Prime Minister, after winning an election that many in his own party believed he was destined to lose, it appeared that his position had been strengthened. The problem for Major was that although he had prevailed in the election with a record tally of votes, the first-past-the-post electoral system had left him with a greatly reduced Parliamentary majority. This had the potential to make the ratification of the Maastricht Treaty more difficult than it would have been before the election; and Eurosceptic Conservatives ensured that this potential was fully realised. Their resolve was bolstered by Lady Thatcher's energetic interventions but also by unexpected developments within other member states.

Arguably, the British government should have followed the 1975 precedent and made its new deal the subject of a referendum. This argument seemed even stronger a quarter of a century later, when British citizens were belatedly given a vote on their country's relationship with the EU and seized the opportunity to vent their varied frustrations. While Major stuck to the orthodox British path of Parliamentary ratification, other European states called referendums in accordance with constitutional practice. In June 1992 the first Maastricht referendum was held in Denmark, resulting in the rejection of the treaty by a small margin. It was the call to arms which Eurosceptics in the Conservative Party had been waiting for. The Danish people had shown that they would not be passive recipients of advice from governing elites, whether in Copenhagen or in Brussels.

Major was now faced by vociferous demands for a British referendum on the treaty. He rejected them, appealing to the same principle of Parliamentary sovereignty which Mrs Thatcher had used back in 1975 when she argued that Labour's referendum was unnecessary. Things had changed rather radically since then; among other things, the press was now violently Eurosceptic, enhancing the feeling among Conservative MPs that they were 'speaking for Britain'.

An Early Day Motion calling for the government to make a 'fresh start' on 'Europe' was widely supported by Conservative MPs. It was estimated that 'perhaps two-thirds of backbenchers, and a half of government' were opposed to Maastricht (Seldon and Baston, 1997, 295). Major's difficulties with 'Europe' only deepened, as Britain was forced to leave the ERM in September (Chapter 9).

The decade between the Falklands War and Britain's exit from the ERM was dominated by the ending of the Cold War and the demise of the Soviet Union. The central foreign policy and security question of the years since the Second World War had been resolved. The denoument came unexpectedly and exposed the ambiguity of Britain's international role. Margaret Thatcher had offered an assertive domestic and foreign policy, but the proclamation of a restored 'Great' Britain masked the reality of a power which was still in relative decline and handicapped, rather than helped, by an exaggerated self-estimation which politicians did nothing to correct. This tendency was most noticeable in 'Europe', where Britain failed to establish a constructive role for itself under either Thatcher or Major.

Conclusions

This eventful period left two legacies of lasting importance for British foreign and defence policy. First, the crafting of a safe haven for the Iraqi Kurds in the aftermath of the Gulf War influenced military deployments over the following decades. British military personnel and civilians found themselves despatched to Bosnia, Kosovo, Sierra Leone, Afghanistan and, once again, Iraq in the decade and a half that followed the Gulf War. Sometimes they went in a war-fighting capacity, but predominantly they were attempting to provide humanitarian aid or to stabilise nations recovering from conflict. The justifications that were used in respect of safe havens in northern Iraq in 1991 would be repeated for later conflict zones, and through this Britain established a new image for its security and foreign policy. This was consonant with a narrative concerning Britain's role in the world, i.e. that whatever the stains on its record from imperial times, it now recognised moral obligations and saw the pursuit of these ends as a key facet of the 'national interest' – which had rarely been aired during the Thatcher years (except as a rhetorical stick to wield against the Soviet Union). With the dismantling of the 'evil empire' and the replacement of Thatcher by less abrasive leaders, the narrative could be developed and even acted upon.

The second legacy related to Britain's relationship with 'Europe'. The Single European Act can be viewed as both the best example of positive engagement and the beginning of estrangement. Thatcher was a key proponent of the European single market, but her furious rejection of the way in which the Single European Act was exploited to serve a federalist political agenda ultimately turned her party away from its previous support for the European project. Even if Lady Thatcher had lapsed into unwonted diplomatic silence and left her record to speak for itself, her legacy would have been difficult enough for her successors to manage after 1990. As it was, her continuing presence as a living icon for the great-power narrative helped to create a public mood which thwarted any attempt to construct a more viable alternative.

Ethics and interventions, 1992–2001   9

Introduction

Arthur Balfour – Foreign Secretary from 1916–19 and author of the notorious 1917 Declaration (Chapter 3) – once declared that he would rather consult his valet than take advice from the Conservative Party conference. Balfour found it impossible to sustain this haughty attitude in practice; and since his time Foreign Secretaries have had no choice but to recognise the importance of a broadly supportive framework of domestic opinion, within their own parties and the electorate more generally. To take the most obvious examples, the retreat from Empire and the negotiation of membership of the EEC were operations which were conducted in a manner which took account of likely reactions from MPs and voters.

> **Timeline of domestic political developments**
>
> **September 1992** Britain forced to withdraw from Exchange Rate Mechanism (ERM) of European Monetary System
> **July 1994** Tony Blair becomes Labour Party leader
> **June 1995** John Major resigns as Conservative Party leader to force his critics to 'put up or shut up'; stands for re-election and wins unconvincingly
> **May 1997** General election: landslide Labour victory; overall majority of 179
> **April 1999** Blair's Chicago speech on principles of 'liberal intervention'

In its dealings with the world beyond Europe, the second Major government was similar to its post-war predecessors. Its record was criticised in Parliament and in the press, and in respect of international crises, like the conflict in the Balkans, its policy was shaped to a considerable degree by its perception of public opinion. However, British diplomats continued to feel that public opinion was one among numerous policy influences, in which their own responses to the situation in various countries mattered a great deal. Policy towards 'Europe' was a very different matter. Here, between 1992 and 1997 the government itself was seriously divided; and the Prime Minister was unable to pursue his preferred policy line because of obstruction from a relatively small Parliamentary faction, whose position was supported by powerful voices in the media.

Major's Maastricht misery

As we have seen, the Conservative victory in the general election of 1992 was decisive in terms of the votes it received (more than 14 million), but the party suffered a net loss of 40 seats compared to the previous contest of 1987, and its overall Parliamentary majority was cut to 21. In other words, if just 11 Conservative MPs felt strongly enough to oppose Major's policy towards the EU, the government could be outvoted in the House of Commons.

Even before the 1992 general election Major had delayed Parliamentary ratification of the Maastricht Treaty in case it exposed the divisions within his own party. After the election, events elsewhere ensured that Major's precarious Parliamentary position would be subjected to the maximum strain. In June 1992, by a margin of less than 50,000, Danish voters rejected the Maastricht Treaty in a referendum. A similar poll was scheduled to take place in France in September; global markets were unsettled by rumours that this might also have a negative outcome. The general uncertainty encouraged speculators to focus on the values of various currencies which had joined the European Exchange Rate Mechanism (ERM). The Italian lira came under pressure and was duly devalued despite government support. The British pound sterling was the next in the firing line.

The lesson of the lira might have suggested that it would be worse than futile for the UK government to resist the message of the markets. A devaluation of the currency might even generate some economic benefits, making British manufactured goods more competitive and allowing a reduction of interest rates. However, Major himself had advocated membership of the ERM during his brief spell as Chancellor of the Exchequer in 1990, so the maintenance of the value of the pound at the agreed level was a matter of personal prestige. In addition, Britain had just taken its turn to adopt the Presidency of the EU (which rotated among member states every six months); to say the least, this would be an inopportune moment for the markets to pass a tacit vote of no confidence in the country's economic management. Finally, successive devaluations of the pound sterling had been greeted in the British media as national humiliations, which tended to be followed quite swiftly by election defeats for the party which happened to be in office at the time. The howls of British anguish ultimately arose not from an 'objective' assessment of the nation's economic needs at any given time, but rather from perceived affronts to the post-war narrative of Britain's continuing great-power status. Before the ERM crisis of 1992 John Major had proved unwilling to accept that story as the guiding principle for government decision-making. However, in September 1992 he suddenly seemed far more susceptible to its persuasive power – not least because the country which was best-placed to alleviate pressure on the pound sterling happened to be Germany, which had established high interest rates in response to its own domestic economic situation, in the wake of reunification. Despite Major's attempts to build a constructive relationship with Helmut Kohl, the German Bundesbank was under a constitutional obligation to conduct monetary policy in accordance with national priorities, and duly refused to cut its interest rates in order to help the British.

Unable to sustain the value of the pound despite considerable expenditure and several panic-induced interest-rate rises, the government admitted defeat on the morning of 16 September 1992. In economic terms, 'Black Wednesday' (as it soon became known) was actually beneficial to Britain. It was, however, a disastrous blow to John Major's authority. Having posed as a refreshing alternative to Mrs Thatcher's autocratic style, he was now easily portrayed as an inadequate Prime Minister who allowed other European leaders to use him as a doormat. In these circumstances it was only natural for a Conservative Party leader with an interest in self-preservation to revert to the seemingly successful formula of his predecessor. Whatever else it might have done, Black Wednesday turned John Major from a Euro-friendly political leader into someone whose default response to any dilemma within the EU was to assert 'British interests' (as his increasingly Europhobic party perceived them) in the hope that this pugnacious stance would generate sufficient positive publicity to efface the memory of September 1992.

Among its other consequences, Black Wednesday was a serious setback to Major's hopes of securing Parliamentary approval for the Maastricht Treaty. Parliamentary proceedings, which had been suspended in the wake of the Danish referendum, resumed in November 1992 after a government motion to that effect had passed by just three votes. Backbench Conservatives tabled numerous amendments, delaying the passage of the bill until July 1993. But Major's ordeal was not over, since the legislation included a clause which ensured a Parliamentary debate on the treaty's Social Chapter, from which Britain had been allowed to opt out. After the debate, on 22 July, a government motion was defeated by eight votes. Major prevailed in a vote of confidence the following day, but the man who had allegedly won game, set and match at Maastricht was now firing every shot into the net or over the baseline. Black Wednesday had permanently tarnished his reputation for economic competence, and the Maastricht debates made him look incapable of managing his party. On 23 July, after winning the vote of confidence, he told a reporter that he only refrained from sacking disloyal members of his Cabinet because he did not want three more 'bastards' causing trouble on the backbenches.

Mad cows

Major's new stance towards Britain's European partners was, on the face of it, not entirely devoid of promise; he could claim that he was merely reverting to the uncooperative stance of all his predecessors since Edward Heath. However, in the years since Mrs Thatcher had offended the sensibilities of European leaders by demanding her country's money back European diplomacy had become much more demanding for a Conservative Prime Minister. On the one hand, the EEC which had finally agreed to a compromise with Mrs Thatcher was now a far more confident EU, talking of a multi-speed 'Europe' in which recalcitrant countries like Britain could be left behind, at considerable cost in terms of future influence. On the other, thanks at least in part to Lady Thatcher's unbridled verbal interventions since 1990, an increasing proportion of Conservative MPs and grass-roots supporters was now promoting policy positions based on a mixture of free-market economics and national assertiveness – a combination which was difficult to sustain under rational scrutiny but which amounted to an intoxicating brew when turned into simplistic soundbites by tabloid newspapers. In short, having decided to abandon his emollient attitude towards 'Europe', Major found himself trying to land a simultaneous blow on targets which were rapidly moving apart – 'Eurocrats', who were too complacent to be intimidated by British bluster, and Conservative Eurosceptics, who could no longer be appeased by anything short of a direct threat to leave the EU.

Given his domestic weakness Major was ill equipped for any serious confrontation; to the European allies he had alienated, he was like Margaret Thatcher without the handbag. All too obviously, that deadly accessory was still in the hands of its original owner, who was wielding it against her successor with increasing savagery. In 1994 Major was forced to abandon an attempt to revise the EU's voting procedures to make it easier for Britain to block proposed legislation, and he vetoed one candidate for President of the EU Commission only to hand the job to another (Luxembourg's Jacques Santer) who was at least as equally determined to promote a federalist agenda. After eight Conservative MPs defied the government in a vote on the EU budget Major tried to impose some discipline by depriving them of the party whip. This merely elevated them to the status of martyrs, and a ninth MP resigned the whip in sympathy.

In June 1995 Major resorted to the ultimate gamble, resigning as party leader (though not as Prime Minister) in the hope of persuading critics of his European policy to 'put up or shut up'. Unexpectedly, a challenger did emerge from the

Cabinet ranks – John Redwood, a cerebral Eurosceptic with limited charisma. Major won the ensuing leadership election by 218 to 89 votes, and his allies tried to present this as a remarkable endorsement. Those with a true appreciation of the contest could only regard it as a further blow to his authority.

However, Major had yet to reach the dregs of his European cup. Rightly alarmed that the cattle disease Bovine spongiform encephalopathy (BSE) could spread to humans through infected meat, in 1996 (ten years after the disease had first appeared in the UK) the EU banned the export of British beef. While BSE was not confined to Britain, the outbreak was far more serious there than in other European countries, at least in part because of inadequate oversight of animal husbandry. Far from acknowledging that the EU was taking (somewhat belated) action in response to a potentially catastrophic threat to human health, Major tried to blackmail his supposed partners by obstructing the EU policy-making process until the ban was lifted. This was not just a case of shooting the messenger; rather, Major was standing at the scene of a serious accident and training machine guns on the arriving ambulance crew. Predictably, his gambit misfired and Britain was forced to resume its strategy of reluctant cooperation with EU institutions.

With each successive episode of unavailing protest against EU decisions, Major provided unwitting authorisation to the Eurosceptic position, which already enjoyed ample support from the tabloid press and from Lady Thatcher. Unfortunately, his most senior (and most reliable) Cabinet colleagues were throwbacks to the time when the Conservatives had been happy to accept the (somewhat misleading) title of 'the party of Europe'. Indeed, up until the 1997 general election defeat, which put Major out of his protracted misery, the Chancellor of the Exchequer Kenneth Clarke and the Deputy Prime Minister Michael Heseltine were arguing that Britain should join the projected European single currency. Long before this, however, Britain's European partners had begun to crave a change of government. In the 1997 general election campaign Major ended up pleading with the warring factions within his party to give him some respite in order to focus his energies on the fight against the Labour Opposition; true to form, his appeal fell on deaf ears.

'Punching above our weight'

Away from 'Europe' Major's foreign policy record was more respectable; but there was still some trace of a pattern in which the Prime Minister faltered after a decent start. Relations with the US, for example, were soon placed on a more sustainable, businesslike footing after the unwholesome intensity of Reagan–Thatcher. In George H Bush, Major found a pragmatic operator of a similar stripe. By the time of the 1992 British general election it was widely felt that the UK had shored up its position as the key European ally of the US.

However, in November 1992 Bush was defeated by the Democrat Bill Clinton – another politician who was unencumbered with heavy ideological baggage but who was very different from Bush in terms of background and personal characteristics. It emerged that British Conservatives – now perceiving themselves as part of a transatlantic tribe of anti-progressives – had assisted the Bush campaign, and that this help had extended to a civil-service trawl through UK records in the hope of finding evidence that Clinton had misbehaved during his spell as a Rhodes scholar at Oxford during the 1960s. It was impossible to imagine similar services being offered by the Conservative Party of Harold Macmillan to help the Republican Richard Nixon beat the Democrat John F Kennedy in 1960. But if such a thing had occurred, there would have been good reasons for Kennedy to swallow his resentment since warm relations with Britain were so clearly beneficial to American policy. By 1992 it was not difficult for Americans to regard Britain as an expendable ally, whose diplomatic slights would be resented and punished.

Although Clinton chose not to make too much of this ghastly blunder, a White House foreign policy adviser claimed that 'Clinton hates Major' (Baylis, 1997). After this unpromising opening the relationship between the leaders could never go beyond conventional cordiality. However, cooperation with other US officials proceeded without noticeable interruption, at least partly thanks to the diplomatic skills of Major's Foreign Secretary, Douglas Hurd. The product of public school and Oxford, Hurd had worked in the Foreign Office before standing for Parliament. He was a skilled linguist and a former aide to Edward Heath – attributes which had a roughly equal propensity to stir Margaret Thatcher's suspicions. As a result, Hurd's promotion to his natural berth as Foreign Secretary had to wait until Thatcher had drained the pool of rival candidates (plumping for John Major as successor to Sir Geoffrey Howe in 1989 as her last hope of thwarting Hurd).

Despite their sharply contrasting backgrounds – and the fact that they had been rival candidates to succeed Thatcher in 1990 – Major and Hurd quickly established a relationship of mutual trust. In January 1992, while the government was basking in Major's early successes in the Gulf and at Maastricht, Hurd wrote an article for the *Daily Telegraph* in which he claimed that:

> In recent years Britain has punched above her weight in the world. We intend to keep it that way. Britain plays a central role in world affairs. We owe this in part to our history, but we continue to earn it through active diplomacy and a willingness to shoulder our share of international responsibilities.
>
> (quoted in Wallace, 1994, 292–3)

The 'punching above our weight' remark has become something of a cliché in discussions of Britain's role in international affairs. In its true context it could be seen as an attempt by a skilled wordsmith to encapsulate Britain's position in a morale-boosting way which also conveyed a coded warning to the Treasury against cuts in the FCO's budget. However, in the boxing world contestants who punch above their weight tend to end up on the canvas, regardless of nimble footwork or well-aimed jabs. It was certainly open to sceptical readers of Hurd's article to suggest that it was time for Britain to give up an ultimately pointless attempt to defy its physical limitations. In his article Hurd explicitly accepted that Britain's 'central role in world affairs' was a product of the past. Why try to maintain this role, which entailed considerable expenditure on the upkeep of grand embassies and their associated staff?

From the perspective presented in this book, Hurd's article is noteworthy as an attempt to reconcile the main post-war narratives relating to British foreign policy. On the one hand, 'punching above our weight' is an explicit acceptance of the country's decline since 1945; it would never have occurred to Ernest Bevin, for example, to concede that other states were weightier. One might have expected Hurd to put a positive spin on Britain's new role as a European power, especially since he was a 'Heathite' who had been repulsed by Thatcher's Euroscepticism. However, even Hurd could not withstand the potency of the Churchillian great-power argument. Britain, it transpired, had a *duty* to persevere with its global role; and it deserved to do so because power should not be measured in crude material terms. Morality matters too; and this factor ensured Britain's continuing place at diplomacy's 'top table'.

Bosnia

Hurd announced his resignation from the government in July 1995, on the day after John Major triggered a Conservative leadership contest (see above). By that time, Major's government had been poleaxed by dissident MPs, who, thanks to the small Parliamentary majority secured in 1992, genuinely *did* punch far beyond their weight.

Hurd's departure also coincided almost exactly with the worst war crime committed in Europe since 1945, when an estimated 8,000 Muslim men and boys were butchered in the Bosnian town of Srebrenica, which was supposed to be under UN protection. This was one of many atrocities in the ongoing conflict within the former Yugoslavia, which had begun to splinter in 1991. The subsequent international outcry – seconded energetically by Lady Thatcher – precipitated NATO air strikes against Bosnian Serb forces, which had pursued a policy of 'ethnic cleansing' in pursuit of their goal of incorporating Bosnia within an enlarged Serbia. The strikes soon brought an end to the conflict, and a ceasefire was agreed in October 1995, followed by a treaty signed in Paris in December.

Britain's initial response to the crisis in the former Yugoslavia was widely criticised as inadequate, in keeping with its hesitant performance during the preceding crisis in Croatia, where Germany took the leading role. Major and Hurd accepted the case for humanitarian assistance to the predominantly Muslim Bosnian government but based their approach on the need to *contain* the conflict, rather than supporting initiatives aimed at bringing it to an end. Indeed, they strongly opposed the lifting of an arms embargo, even though the Bosnian Serbs were much better equipped than Muslim forces. In particular, the British government resisted the American proposal ('lift and strike') to supply the Bosnian army with weapons and attack the Serbs from the air. The British felt that the war could not be ended without the commitment of ground troops, which none of its NATO allies was prepared to countenance; meanwhile, its own forces conducting humanitarian missions in Bosnia would be in serious jeopardy.

In his memoirs Major continued to argue that British policy had been vindicated. The air strikes had only brought peace, he felt, because by September 1995 other factors had fallen into place (including the availability of a viable plan for a post-war settlement). 'It is bizarre', he wrote, 'that in the popular imagination British policy was seen as a callous washing of hands in the face of the nightly suffering of the innocent on the nation's television screens' (Major, 1999, 545, 547). His reference to television coverage, however, only explained why his cautious policy had attracted so much criticism.

Rather than being hard-hearted or unduly calculating, Major and Hurd are more appropriately indicted for standing out against some key assumptions arising from the idea of a new world order, reinforced by images from the 1991 Gulf War which showcased the terrific power (and apparent precision) of air strikes to a global television audience. From this perspective, it was easy to assume that aggressors in any part of the world could be repulsed by the use of 'smart' weapons, deployed by service personnel who were too distant from the conflict zone to fear retaliation. In other words, it now seemed possible to wage 'war without tears' (at least on the interventionist side). In addition to such complacent assumptions, Major and Hurd had to confront the implications of 'the CNN effect', which meant that heinous war crimes could be reported almost instantly and through vivid electronic imagery. In combination, these developments increased the likelihood that British decision-makers would come under pressure to intervene in international conflicts – and that the public mood would change overnight if the 'wrong people' – civilians or UN peacekeepers – became victims of 'surgical strikes'.

Superficially, at least, it could be argued that Major and Hurd had tried to implement a Realist strategy in response to the Bosnian crisis and had come to grief because (like academic analysts who adopt a Realist outlook) they had been insensitive to public opinion at home and abroad (Chapter 1). As usual, the true picture is more complicated (Controversy 9.1). In fact, both Hurd and

Controversy 9.1 Realism and British policy towards Bosnia

In his memoirs John Major wrote that:

> Our policy had to be dictated by two concerns: to save as many lives as we could while the slaughter continued, and to do all in our power to limit the conflict. . . . At the time, many politicians and commentators argued that this decision was mistaken, that Britain had no strategic interest in Bosnia. I disagreed. I had no doubt that there were sound policy reasons to justify sending in our troops.
>
> (Major, 1999, 535)

For scholars of international relations, this is a fascinating passage. From a broadly Realist perspective, it is noteworthy that Major asserts the importance of Bosnia to Britain's strategic interests. However, as Chapter 1 shows, Realists regard ethical considerations as secondary (at best) in the making of foreign policy. Yet Major seems to have had a different order of priorities; even if humanitarian concerns were not his *primary* motivation, they were on a par with other 'sound policy reasons' which justified intervention. One might wonder whether Major's calculations would have been the same without the CNN effect – a suspicion which is deepened by British policy during the Rwandan genocide (see p 250), which did not command much media attention until the worst of the slaughter was over. Nevertheless, on his own testimony Major seems to have accepted that the situation in Bosnia affected Britain's national interest at least in part because of the moral concerns it raised, and this attitude is very difficult to square with academic understandings of Realism.

In his memoirs Douglas Hurd quotes an undated memorandum to the Prime Minister (presumably written some time in 1994) in which he argued that 'more than any country, at some cost to our reputation, we have been the realists in this. We should continue to insist on realistic objectives and timetables' (Hurd, 2003, 467). This is another thought-provoking passage for theorists of international relations. Although Hurd's approach to the Balkan crisis is often interpreted (and criticised) as a manifestation of Realism, it seems odd that a Realist of this kind would persist in a policy line 'at some cost to our reputation', since the maintenance of an unclouded reputation is an obvious Realist objective unless the issue has a direct effect on national survival (which was clearly not the case in respect of British policy towards Bosnia).

On reflection, it appears that in this memorandum Hurd was using the words 'realists' and 'realistic' in their more common, non-academic sense, i.e. he was trying to reassure Major that British policy had been guided by a careful calculation of the various goals that could be achieved (including humanitarian ones), rather than by wishful thinking. As such, Hurd's memorandum to Major can be translated as a way of saying that 'in this crisis, Britain is actuated by a mixture of motives, which include the possibility that national security might be affected as well as humanitarian concerns. More than any other country, we have been consistent in proposing and opposing measures which seem most likely to promote these objectives'. This coincides with Hurd's own evaluation of British policy towards Bosnia as an attempt to 'balance' the promptings of 'Realism' and 'idealism' (Hurd, 1997, 127). This, though, was written before the intervention in Kosovo (see pp 263–7), which reinforced the impression that diplomacy backed with a concrete threat of military action would have saved thousands of Bosnian lives.

After quoting from his 1994 memorandum, in his memoirs Hurd notes that 'part of realism was maintaining the Atlantic Alliance, and that meant keeping our disagreement with the Americans within bounds' (Hurd, 2003, 467). In this passage Hurd seems to be using the word 'realism' in its academic sense, i.e. that Britain's national interest, narrowly conceived, is best served by 'maintaining the Atlantic Alliance', even if in specific instances US policy happens to be wrong-headed. But if Hurd really accepted the highly questionable view that keeping in step with the Americans should be an overriding priority for British Foreign Secretaries, he was taking a considerable risk in opposing the preferred US option of 'lift and strike', especially when other European powers could be expected to take advantage of any cooling in the 'special relationship'. Fortunately for Hurd, although he accepts in his memoirs that Bosnia created 'strains' in the alliance, 'the leaders on both sides of Atlantic kept them under control' (Hurd, 2003, 467).

Major were taking a close interest in public opinion and were well aware that they were out of step. As early as July 1992 Hurd reflected in his diary on 'a deeply gloomy day. The clamour and emotional pressure for intervention growing fast here and especially in the US. Our prudent stance looks feeble and inhumane' (Hurd, 2003, 454–5). Presumably, Hurd was unaware that he had echoed almost exactly a passage in another diary – this time the fictional one of James Hacker, the central character in the satirical television programme *Yes, Prime Minister*, who had mused that 'It doesn't do the government any good to look heartless and feeble simultaneously' (Lynn and Jay, 1986, 212). As Hacker and Hurd both knew, domestic perceptions mattered, whether accurate or not. It also mattered that on this occasion the US and the British government had disagreed, and that the crisis had ended in a way which suggested that the senior partner should pay less heed to Britain's advice in future.

Hurd also faced bitter criticism for his stance towards Rwanda, where around 800,000 members of the minority Tutsi population were slaughtered by the Hutu majority between April and July 1994. On this occasion Britain's failure to act was less easily defended, which probably explains why the country's name does not feature in the index of John Major's memoirs. Blanket television coverage rammed home the geographical reality that Bosnia was situated on Europe's doorstep; but if reporters were not physically present, Western policy towards Rwanda could be (and was) justified on the lines used by Neville Chamberlain in relation to Czechoslovakia, that the Tutsi were a faraway people of whom little was known. However, members of the British Intelligence community were aware of dangerous tensions prior to the Rwandan massacre; and if it was really true that Britain 'punched above its weight' as a member of the UN Security Council, it could have done something to prevent this from becoming one of the most discreditable episodes in UN history (including attempts to deny that butchery on this scale could be defined as 'genocide', an exercise in verbal pedantry which was obviously prompted by a shared concern among members of the international community for the avoidance of intervention). It would be wrong to single out Britain in this dismal story, although it is entirely proper to note that its role was characterised by a singular lack of heroism.

Dams and lies

In his memoirs Hurd admits to feeling 'deeply dismayed' in April 1994, when the Rwandan massacres began (Hurd, 2003, 495). However, he was not referring to Rwanda but to the news that the government's decision to confirm funding for the construction of a dam in Malaysia might be open to legal challenge. Work on the dam, at Pergau in Kelantan state, had begun in 1991, with the British multinational company Balfour Beatty taking a leading role. The UK government's contribution to the costs was £239 million, initially allocated from the Overseas Development budget. However, when the deal was negotiated between Margaret Thatcher and the Malaysian Prime Minister Mahathir the latter agreed to purchase British-made defence equipment.

Confronted by concerns about the cost of the deal in 1991, Hurd (with Major's approval) decided that Britain could not withdraw the funding without significant loss of face. Hurd was unaware of the apparent link with defence sales, but he would have been rather naïve – not a trait readily associated with seasoned diplomats – if he had felt that Thatcher's government would have made such a generous contribution without some quid pro quo. The concerns expressed in April 1994 turned out to be wholly justified: a subsequent judicial review held that Hurd's decision to proceed with the funding had been illegal, since it was not intended to assist the Malaysian people on either humanitarian or economic grounds.

Hurd's memoirs betray his lasting discomfort concerning Pergau; he contrives to discuss the affair without reminding the reader of the enormous sum involved. It was not very consoling that, ultimately, this was an instance of 'blowback' from the Thatcher years, during which the British armament industry was the recipient of numerous contracts secured on dubious terms. In 1996 another judicial review, headed by the respected Lord Justice Scott, published its findings. This brought a close to an ignominious saga which (like Pergau) originated in 1988.

The subject of Scott's review was the export of sophisticated machine tools to Iraq by a Coventry-based firm, Matrix Churchill, which had itself been purchased by the Iraqi government. Equipment which might be used by Iraq for the production of weapons had been subject to export restrictions – until the fateful year of 1988, when the government relaxed its guidelines without taking the trouble to inform Parliament. In the wake of Iraq's invasion of Kuwait certain government departments were less inclined to take a laissez-faire approach to the export trade with Iraq; and the directors of Matrix Churchill were duly prosecuted by Customs and Excise. The trial collapsed when government collusion was exposed, leading to the establishment of the Scott inquiry.

Compared to the petty corruption of the Pergau Dam affair, 'arms to Iraq' amounted to a deadly indictment of the Thatcher government's habitual tendency to prioritise short-term economic goals, whatever the cost in terms of British foreign policy or indeed the safety of British citizens who might be exposed to danger in future conflicts. As Scott pointed out, the issues went to the heart of the conduct of British government – particularly in relation to the crucial principle that the government should be held to account for its decisions. In this instance Parliament had not been informed of revised policy guidelines – indeed, when the issue was raised MPs had been *misinformed*. Regrettably, though, if the scandal had been exposed back in 1988, it would probably have passed without media comment, since Iraq was not regarded as a significant threat to British interests at the time and (despite his penchant for slaughtering his own citizens) Saddam Hussein had yet to be demonised. By 1996, although some ministers who had been involved in the deception were still in office, the person who had presided over the original misdemeanours was out of office and devoting her energies to a lucrative series of speaking engagements. Nevertheless, a brilliant speech by Labour's Shadow Foreign Secretary, Robin Cook, ensured that the Scott Report took a prominent place in a more general indictment of the Major government, which long before 1996 had cemented an indelible reputation for political ineptitude and public misconduct. The government won the Parliamentary vote after the debate on 'arms to Iraq'; but when the public was polled at the end of February 1996 only 8 per cent believed that the government had handled the Scott Inquiry well, against 69 per cent who thought it had performed badly (Riddell, 1996).

In 1994 the eminent academic William (later Lord) Wallace had presented a preliminary verdict on the Major government. In his view, it 'had no foreign policy; no sense of Britain's place in the world or how best to use diplomacy to achieve national objectives' (Wallace, 1994, 299). Britons who were hoping for clarity in these crucial respects could only share the feelings of many people working within the EU, who longed for a change of government at the next British general election in the expectation that 'things can only get better'.

Labour, 1983–92

The general election of 1983 represented the nadir of the post-war Labour Party. Under the leadership of Michael Foot and armed with a radical manifesto, the party polled only 27 per cent of the national vote, placing it just ahead of the alliance between the Liberal Party and the newly formed Social Democratic Party. Unusually for a general election campaign, foreign policy issues had featured prominently in pre-election debates, focusing on Labour's most eye-catching proposals – the elimination of Britain's nuclear arsenal and withdrawal from the EEC.

Labour's defeat in 1983 was so crushing that the party was still nursing the wounds 11 years later, when Tony Blair became leader. The policy of withdrawal from the EEC had been jettisoned almost immediately after the election by Labour's new leader, Neil Kinnock. However, the commitment to nuclear disarmament was retained. While electorally it appeared to alienate some voters within the Labour movement, it remained a key and popular pledge. Kinnock was especially keen to demonstrate that the policy would not harm the 'special relationship'. To bolster his image and the credibility of his policy Kinnock travelled to Washington in early 1987 to meet President Reagan to explain Labour's position. A disastrous visit ensued, during which Reagan broke with diplomatic protocol to criticise Labour's defence policy in order to assist his friend Margaret.

During the election campaign of 1987 Kinnock was questioned on how Britain would defend itself without nuclear weapons. His response was portrayed by political opponents and a hostile print media as a recommendation of 'guerrilla warfare' against an occupying power. A second overwhelming election defeat meant that even the most ardent proponents of nuclear disarmament were forced to recognise that the policy was a liability. The commitment was eventually dropped in 1989 – ironically, just at the point that the Soviet Union ceased to be a military threat.

In the next general election campaign (1992) Labour argued for the maintenance of Britain's nuclear arsenal and supported its continued membership of the EEC (shortly to become the EU). These new policies promised to neutralise what had previously been electoral weaknesses for Labour, but the potential benefits were minimal since the party merely seemed to be playing catch-up with the Conservatives. In any case, foreign policy was only a significant electoral consideration when there was a sharp contrast between the platforms of the rival parties (as in 1983 and 1987).

The Blair era

Neil Kinnock resigned immediately after the 1992 general election; his successor, John Smith, was a more reassuring character who (unlike Kinnock) had served as a minister (from 1975 to 1979, with full Cabinet rank for the last few months of the Callaghan administration). Polling evidence suggests that Smith would have won the general election of 1997 comfortably; but he was a proponent of gradual change within the Labour Party, whereas his successor was an unflinching radical. When he was elected Labour leader in 1994, after Smith's premature death, Blair was 41 years old. He had been elected for the first time in the notorious 1983 general election but was unencumbered by the legacy of Labour's perceived failure. When it came to international relations and foreign policy Blair benefited from trends that favoured the Labour Party: the fallout from the ERM crisis allowed Labour to win a hearing for a more constructive approach towards 'Europe', and the *froideur* between Major and President Clinton allowed Blair's Labour Party to pose as the true guardians of the 'special relationship'.

Blair emerged as a significant political figure at a time when Britain's relationships with 'Europe' and the US seemed ready for reconfiguration in the context of a changing world order. The ending of the Cold War had freed the Labour Party from one of its persistent electoral handicaps – the sense that it was not sufficiently forceful in confronting the Soviet Union. The collapse of the familiar foe tempered some of the criticisms aimed at the Labour Party, while also reducing the electoral salience of defence issues. It seemed that Britain would engage in wars of choice in the future, rather than wars of survival. The British military could be reformed in an appropriate fashion. When the Major government commissioned a defence review in 1990 the resulting report, *Options for Change*, argued that a reduction in defence spending was possible. Debate on defence was now framed around the size and uses of an anticipated 'peace dividend'. Despite conflicts which demanded a significant military commitment – notably the Gulf War in 1991 – the defence budget began its gradual projected decline from 4 per cent of GDP in 1990 to less than 3 per cent by 2000. Given the unexpected liberation from the threat of nuclear annihilation, the Labour Party suddenly enjoyed the option of a return to its policy of nuclear disarmament. However, this was eschewed by the party, which, perhaps understandably, was obsessed with the need to avoid another repetition of previous defeats rather than thinking creatively about the future.

Bill Clinton's victory over George Bush in the 1992 US Presidential election was a significant fillip for Labour, suggesting that 'progressive' forces could thrive in the post-Soviet new world order. The final advantage for the Labour Party arose from Britain's uncertain engagement with 'Europe'. Since 1983 there had been a thawing of relations between Labour and the EEC, in sharp contrast to the growing antagonism on the Conservative side. The switch from a policy of withdrawal to one of more than grudging acceptance was assisted by the appointment of the French Socialist Jacques Delors as President of the European Commission, and Delors' speech to the 1988 TUC conference threatened to turn a token kiss on the cheek into a full-on embrace. In the space of a decade the two main political parties in Britain had switched sides on the European debate; Labour appeared genuinely united behind a positive view of the EEC, while the Conservatives were giving the appearance of a bickering rabble.

The ethical dimension

The election of 1997 transformed the political landscape in Britain, almost, on this rare occasion, justifying the constitutional cliché that a government had secured a 'mandate' for its policy programme from the British people. Blair's New Labour secured an overall Parliamentary majority of 179 seats – the biggest majority held by any government since Baldwin's 1935 coalition.

While critics predicted that, in terms of domestic policy, Blair would merely be a more telegenic version of John Major, Robin Cook, the new Foreign Secretary, lost no time in putting his mark on his new workplace. Within two weeks of the election Cook had launched a new mission statement, establishing the parameters of New Labour's approach to foreign policy. Viewing the interdependent global order, Cook pronounced the priorities of 'security, prosperity and quality of life'. In sharp contrast to the Realist outlook of Douglas Hurd, Cook argued that the political values that shaped domestic policy should be replicated in the making of foreign policy: as he put it, 'political values cannot be left behind when we check in our passports to travel on diplomatic business'. Any foreign policy that Cook endorsed would promote British values:

> Our foreign policy must have an ethical dimension and must support the demands of other peoples for the democratic rights on which we insist for ourselves.

(Cook, 1997)

Ethics and interventions, 1992–2001　**255**

The statement provoked widespread comment which was not invariably favourable. Cook was certainly not the first Foreign Secretary to enter office with high ambitions, but, as the *Economist* noted, the professionals were sceptical of 'the intrusion of morality into the hard business of foreign policy' (*Economist*, 1997). From their perspective, it seemed inevitable that the idealism of human rights promotion and arms embargos would soon be overtaken by 'events'. But in the early days of the new government it appeared that a number of circles could be squared. Crucially, far from having to contemplate a self-imposed choice between 'Europe' and the US, there was every chance that the new government could maintain good relations with both.

Robin Cook's mission statement reasserted a British commitment to the North Atlantic Alliance and made positive noises about the role that Britain could play in 'Europe'. By the end of May, changing the natural order of things, US President Clinton visited the new British Prime Minister, apparently on the assumption that this would help his profile back home.

While Blair's honeymoon with the British electorate lasted much longer than usual, Cook's attempt to give a new priority to ethical considerations quickly foundered. The first mishap came with the sale of military aircraft to Indonesia, a country ruled by a military dictatorship with a history of human rights abuses. The £160m order for sixteen Hawk fighter aircraft from British Aerospace had been agreed by the previous government. In July 1997, after consultation, the FCO stated that legal obstacles had prevented them from revoking the export licence. The new Foreign Secretary did not block the deal, but the government reaffirmed its opposition to the sale of equipment which could be used for repressive purposes. The reversal for Cook on Indonesia highlighted that the ethical dimension of foreign policy could easily conflict with other government priorities, notably the anxiety to protect the British arms industry, which was responsible for over 350,000 jobs and 3.3 per cent of Britain's total exports of finished manufactured goods. It was an effective economic sector with well-established Whitehall contacts. Indeed, in the case of Indonesia alone, between the election of the Labour government in 1997 and the imposition of an EU arms embargo in 1999, a further 111 arms-export licences were granted by the UK government (*Economist*, 1999). Cook and his supporters could argue that he had spoken of an ethical *dimension* to foreign policy, which was not the same as a promise to eschew *all* other considerations. However, the government's hyperactive spin doctors had given the impression that moral concerns would now be uppermost, implying that this government would be far more virtuous than its tawdry predecessors. Whatever it did for Britain's international image, the episode undoubtedly diminished Cook's public standing and reduced his authority within a government riven by personal rivalries.

The first weeks of the new government were marked by a more momentous development which illustrated the difficulty of including a significant ethical dimension in foreign policy. On 1 July 1997, after a rather bathetic ceremony, the British ceded to China control of their prosperous Hong Kong colony. This was not a decision which could be attributed to the Labour Party, in either its 'old' or 'New' manifestations; the key development was a deal negotiated in 1982 by Mrs Thatcher and the Chinese government and enshrined in a Joint Declaration between the two governments in December 1984. Mrs Thatcher had entered the talks with reluctance, not least because of the apparent contrast between her approach to Hong Kong and her refusal to negotiate with Argentina during the Falklands Crisis. There was, in fact, a significant difference in the legal situation, since the Hong Kong colony (consisting of Hong Kong Island and Kowloon) was only viable thanks to the inclusion of the 'New Territories', which Britain acquired in 1898 on a 99-year lease. Even so, if China had been comparable to Argentina in its military capacity, the future of Hong Kong might have been a more problematic political issue. As it was, China held all the cards in the 1982 talks, and it was testimony to the skills of British diplomats (as well as the flexibility of their interlocutors) that, rather than proposing to absorb Hong Kong as if it had never been detached from their country, the Chinese recognised its distinctive developmental path in line with Deng Xiaoping's slogan 'one country, two systems'.

However, although it was wise to negotiate the basis for a handover well in advance, the agreement of the Joint Declaration left more than a decade before the Chinese took over in Hong Kong – allowing ample opportunity for discomfiting developments. The death throes of Soviet Communism were not necessarily a serious setback for the Chinese regime, whose relations with its supposed ideological ally had been equivocal at best. However, Mikhail Gorbachev's attempt to 'modernise' the Soviet system had foundered because of the difficulty of negotiating a course which would permit an element of economic liberalism without endangering the rule of a single party. China had embarked on a similar path, and many of its citizens accepted the argument (familiar among Western liberals) that economic and political freedom were inseparable. In April 1989 – weeks in advance of a scheduled visit by Gorbachev himself – up to 100,000 students marched on Beijing's Tiananmen Square to demand political reforms. The government response was initially ambiguous, but martial law was declared on 20 May 1989, and on 3 June soldiers began to fire on the protestors. The final death toll is disputed, but most reliable estimates indicate that thousands, rather than the officially admitted hundreds, were killed.

For the West – and for the British in particular, given the impending Hong Kong handover – the Tiananmen Square massacre ushered numerous chickens home to roost. Had the repression been authorised by a favoured anti-communist regime during the Cold War – for example, had it been instigated by Mrs Thatcher's close personal friend General Pinochet of Chile – the British government would have treated it as something like a tragic traffic accident. Public expressions of concern would have been issued alongside more 'understanding' private messages. Since this was China rather than Chile, Lady Thatcher expressed her 'revulsion and outrage', but the government confirmed that the Hong Kong timetable would not be affected.

The awkward truth for the British was that, in the eyes of the Tiananmen Square demonstrators, the prevailing political system in Hong Kong was scarcely preferable to that of one-party China. The practice of ruling the colony without consulting its citizens was reflected in Mrs Thatcher's negotiations of 1982, in which the people of Hong Kong were not represented. Belatedly, the British came to the view that it would have been advisable to let democratic institutions take root in Hong Kong well in advance of the handover; when they had enjoyed the opportunity, however, they had let it slip precisely because, like the Chinese, they had preferred to keep decisions within a (very) confined circle. In the years between Tiananmen Square and 1997 the last Governor of Hong Kong, the ex-Conservative minister Chris Patten, tried to make up the lost ground, only to be subjected to personal abuse by the Chinese, who were well aware that (like the British in general) he was acting in accordance with an ethical narrative of Britain's imperial role, which bore an uneasy relationship to the practical record.

Tony Blair was present for what Prince Charles scornfully dubbed as the 'Great Chinese Takeaway'. To the relief of officials, even in private discussions with Chinese leaders he emphasised that the handover provided an opportunity for a 'new start' in the relationship between Britain and China and made only 'a very brief mention of human rights' (Campbell, 2011, 77).

Blair in office: the domestic and European balancing act

The ability of British premiers to influence international agendas in the post-war period relies on a combination of factors, not least of which is their relative domestic strength. Margaret Thatcher, throughout her premiership, commanded comfortable majorities in the House of Commons, providing her with a solid base from which to engage with international relations. In turn, Thatcher used the international arena to burnish her domestic image. The electoral landslide of 1997 provided Tony Blair with a similar platform to build his international image but, as with Thatcher, domestic politics was an ever present consideration.

Blair had taken full advantage of Conservative divisions over 'Europe', arguing that the Major government had thrown away the chance to take a positive role. Under more vigorous leadership Britain would engage and help reform the EU. For example, Labour committed itself to signing up to the Social Chapter of the Maastricht Treaty. This was an endorsement of the 'social Europe' that

Jacques Delors had used to bridge the divide between Brussels and the British Labour movement in the late 1980s. However, Major's difficulties over 'Europe' were not entirely the product of his own ineptitude or even of a Conservative propensity for deadly infighting. The British public appeared resistant to the benefits of the EU, particularly its plans for a single currency; and this mood was cultivated by sections of the press which had various self-interested motives for promoting Europhobia. Having courted media proprietors (notably the Australian-born US citizen Rupert Murdoch) so assiduously since 1994, Blair was reluctant to risk losing their goodwill over an issue which was likely to tax even his legendary powers of persuasion. Therefore New Labour attempted to navigate a 'Third Way' between the scepticism of the Conservative Party and the general positivity offered by Britain's other significant political force, the Liberal Democrats.

Thus, in its 1997 manifesto, New Labour promised that in adopting the Social Chapter it would 'promote employability and flexibility, not high social costs'. This caveat indicated that Blair sought a leading role within the EU while stopping short of a full-hearted endorsement of the European project. The election campaign took place less than two years before the scheduled introduction of a single European currency. From the wording of the manifesto, and comments during the election campaign, it was clear that Britain would not be joining the first wave of nations signing up to the single currency, due to be introduced on 1 January 1999. Not ruling out future adoption of the euro, and indeed pledging that a New Labour government would play a full role in planning for the new currency, the manifesto also followed the Conservatives in promising that no decision would be taken without a referendum. This carefully crafted position could not disguise the real meaning of New Labour policy: the initial phase of the most significant project in the history of European cooperation would go ahead without the British.

Blair was instinctively pro-European. Even when the official policy of the Labour Party had advocated withdrawal from the EEC, Blair had spoken in favour of Britain maintaining its membership (Seldon, 2004, 81). He entered office with the backing of a large Parliamentary majority that supported closer ties with European institutions. But the decision to join a European single currency was not straightforward. Apart from widespread opposition within the public and the press, there were also practical questions to address. The manifesto commitment that a referendum would ultimately decide if Britain joined entailed a delicate tactical calculation. Any referendum would have to take place after a subsequent general election to avoid it becoming a plebiscite on the government of the day, rather than the issue at hand. There was also a technical calculation, which limited the scope for immediate action, since expert opinion judged that the British economy was not 'in convergence' with the European states joining the euro in the first wave. Then there were the practical considerations of what would be required for Britain to change its currency. This final fact alone made adoption of the euro in 1999 highly unlikely. Taking all these factors into account, the earliest realistic date for a referendum on the euro would be after a general election held either in 2001 or 2002.

The prospect of Britain joining the European currency during New Labour's first term was ended in October 1997, following a chaotic period of contradictory 'official' briefings by rival teams of spin doctors. The Chancellor of the Exchequer, Gordon Brown, had been broadly in favour of euro membership, but the experience of office induced second thoughts. The adoption of the euro would ultimately mean a transfer of economic powers away from London, something that any Chancellor was unlikely to relish. Brown, whose influence over domestic policy extended far beyond the Treasury's usual remit, was in no hurry to divest himself of his dominant position. While Brown was growing more sceptical about the euro Blair had remained positive, and Robin Cook had also begun to appreciate the advantage of closer ties with 'Europe'. A compromise was necessary, ruling out euro membership in the short term while allowing Blair to reassure his EU colleagues that Britain would not revert to its former role of an 'awkward partner'. Presenting the agreed policy to Parliament, Brown described the decision on the euro as 'the single most important question the country is likely to face in our generation'. He established five economic tests that would have to be satisfied before Britain could contemplate holding a referendum on the single European currency. While effectively ruling out membership for the current Parliament, Brown's tests had been designed to keep the issue under the Treasury's control, making the Chancellor, rather than the Prime Minister (let alone the Foreign Secretary), the ultimate arbiter of this key policy decision. Brown was like a university lecturer who reserves the right to reinterpret the wording of his own exam questions in order to ensure that his students either passed or failed. It was not fanciful to depict Tony Blair as the unfortunate student whose career prospects could be helped or blighted according to Brown's fluctuating mood. As a senior official subsequently reflected: 'I don't think any of us realised at the time, that October would be such a profound turning-point in the whole Euro story' (Seldon, 2004, 327).

With hindsight, if New Labour was to tackle the euro issue it would have been better to start work without delay. In the first months of the new government, Blair commanded unprecedented levels of support. In September 1997 his approval rating was recorded at 93 per cent, making him the 'most popular democratic politician in history' (Castle and Routledge, 1997). It could not last, but this would have been the time to push the case for 'Europe'. As it was, with membership of the currency ruled out, Blair sought other routes to European influence, particularly in the area of defence and foreign policy. At Saint-Malo in December 1998 the French and British governments signed a Joint Declaration on European Defence, committing the EU to develop a military capability which would operate in circumstances where NATO intervention was inappropriate. The Saint-Malo agreement held out the prospect of closer European cooperation in a sphere where the UK could play a very prominent role. However, the security developments in the years immediately following 1998 offered little opportunity for the new capability to be utilised.

Overall, with regard to 'Europe' the record of New Labour's first term resembled that of the Major government between 1990 and 1992. In both instances the Prime Minister made positive noises about integration, but these stated intentions were thwarted by circumstances. The obvious difference was that John Major led a deeply divided party, whereas there were few dissenters in Labour ranks, and even if they had been more numerous, they could not have endangered Tony Blair's gargantuan Parliamentary majority. With this context in mind, Blair can actually be seen as a more recalcitrant partner than Major. The latter secured an opt-out on the single currency at Maastricht, and, despite his obvious advantages during his first term, Blair acted on it by retaining the pound sterling. New Labour did accept the Social Chapter, which Major had rejected, but that decision was unproblematic because it enjoyed considerable support from Labour voters (and the trade unions), whereas Major's backbench tormentors would have opposed it on ideological grounds even if it had not emanated from Brussels. As if to compensate for their acceptance of 'social Europe', Blair and Brown lost no opportunity to deliver unwelcome sermons on the superiority of thinly regulated Anglo-American capitalism – a line of argument that was at least as irritating to European audiences as John Major's 'us against them' rhetoric. Against this background, Saint-Malo looks like a radical attempt by Blair to exploit his popularity at home in order to promote integration; equally, though, it can be interpreted as a (belated) move to shore up European security after the end of the Cold War, amid well-founded expectations that the US would now shift its attention to other global theatres. Certainly, Saint-Malo suggested that Blair's Britain was sidling towards the acceptance of a European 'destiny'. But the impression that the UK was finally finding a role remained vulnerable to 'events' – and in Blair's second term these came thick and fast.

Bridging the Atlantic

While Blair's ambitions in 'Europe' were obstructed by various factors, prospects for an improved relationship with the US were promising. The terminology of the 'special relationship' that seemed so inappropriate in the Major years was resuscitated by the shared ideological vision and apparent personal chemistry of Clinton and Blair. When Blair visited Washington in 1996 the New Labour leader rapidly established a rapport with Clinton in discussions which focused on political strategy more than traditional foreign policy (Riddell, 2003, 68). Apart from the natural inclination of British political elites to take much greater interest in American politics than those of neighbouring European states, Blair found in Clinton someone who was equally keen to establish a reputation for 'progressive' thinking. It was an unsettling shift, from the right-wing crusaders Reagan and Thatcher to the new firm of Blair and Clinton, purveyors of high-sounding rhetoric from an imprecise position on the centre-left. But whatever their Third Way really amounted to, the fact that they both supported the slogan provided a promising basis for cooperation.

For Blair, the Third Way had an obvious application to foreign policy; it meant that instead of having to choose between the US and the EU, Britain could be best friends with both. In London in 1997 Clinton felt emboldened to articulate the position of most (if not all) of his post-war predecessors: 'It is good for the US to have a Britain that is strong in Europe and strong in its relations with the US'. Blair often returned to this theme, declaiming in January 2003 that:

> there is no greater error in international politics than to believe that strong in Europe means weaker with the US. The roles reinforce each other. . . . [Britain] can indeed help to be a bridge between the US and Europe and such understanding is always needed. Europe should partner the US not be its rival.
>
> (Blair, 2003)

It all sounded very sensible, but as in other areas it proved more difficult to match rhetoric with reality.

The first test of Blair's balancing act came soon after his 1997 election victory. Since August 1990 Iraq had created its own subset of foreign policy issues for the UN and the permanent members of its Security Council. The ambiguous denouement of the Gulf War in 1991 had left Saddam Hussein in power in Iraq, badly damaged but potentially even more dangerous as a result. Anticipating this eventuality, the ceasefire agreements, codified in UN Security Council Resolution 687, had called on Iraq to:

> accept the destruction, removal, or rendering harmless, under international supervision of . . . [a]ll chemical and biological weapons and all stocks of agents . . . [and] all ballistic missiles with a range greater than 150 kilometres.

In addition, Iraq would 'agree not to acquire or develop nuclear weapons or nuclear-weapons-usable-material' (www.un.org/Depts/unmovic/documents/687.pdf). Once Iraq had met these requirements, the UN sanctions regime, established after the invasion of Kuwait, would be lifted. What appeared straightforward in the aftermath of the defeat of Iraqi forces in 1991 became an ongoing struggle which outlasted the decade. As Saddam Hussein reasserted his rule, he embarked on an elaborate game of cat and mouse. The Iraqi authorities would announce compliance with UNSCR 687 and demand the lifting of sanctions, only to be countered by new evidence highlighting that the Iraqi weapons programme was more advanced than previously believed and/or that Iraq was falling far below the standards of transparency specified by the wording of the UN resolution. Iraq gained support from states around the world by highlighting the humanitarian consequences of the UN sanctions regime. By the time that Blair entered Downing Street both Russia and France were lobbying for the easing of sanctions, whereas the US had indicated that they would not be lifted while Saddam Hussein remained in power.

The situation came to a head in November 1997, when UN weapons inspectors were expelled from Iraq. Blair was strong in his condemnation, attacking Saddam Hussein in a form of words that would become familiar over the next five years: 'He has deceived people, used chemical weapons on his own people, and invaded other countries without any possible justification'. Blair went on to say that Hussein had to 'be made to back down . . . because, if he does not, we will simply face this problem, perhaps in a different and far worse form, in a few years' time' (*Hansard, House of Commons Debates*, 19 November 1997, Vol. 301, col. 323). While Blair continued to urge a diplomatic solution, future schisms between the permanent members of the UN Security Council were already emerging, challenging Blair's aspiration of acting as a bridge between 'Europe' and the US.

Despite a deal, brokered by the Russian Federation in late November 1997, that allowed weapons inspectors to return to Iraq, the crisis was postponed rather than resolved. The following year was marked by further disputes between the Iraqi government and UN weapons inspectors over access to sites and information. Early in 1998 the US indicated that progress on weapons inspection might require the use of force to convince Saddam Hussein that the international community was serious about compliance. If military action took place, it would do so with support from the British government even if 'a further UN resolution was "unachievable"' (Seldon, 2004, 388). When Blair addressed the House of Commons in February 1998 he reaffirmed his loathing for Saddam Hussein – 'an evil, brutal dictator' – and warned that '[y]ou can achieve much by diplomacy, but you can achieve a lot more when diplomacy is backed by firmness and force' (*Hansard, House of Commons Debates*, 24 February 1998, Vol. 307, col. 175).

Relations between the UN and Baghdad finally broke down at the beginning of November 1998, when Iraq halted cooperation with the weapons inspectors. At this point the US committed itself to military action, citing UNSCR 678, the resolution that had authorised the use of force in the Gulf War of 1991, as the legal basis. Blair supported this move. On 14 November he authorised 'substantial military action' by UK forces for the first time in his premiership. At the last minute an intervention by UN General Secretary Kofi Annan halted a joint US–UK strike against targets in Iraq. But this time, unlike the previous year, the postponement was of brief duration. UN weapons inspectors withdrew from Iraq, and on 16 December Operation Desert Fox began. A four-day intensive bombing campaign targeted Iraqi sites linked to its WMD programme.

Through Operation Desert Fox, Blair had confirmed his willingness to use military force in pursuit of foreign policy goals. While the US administration welcomed this return to business as usual, the European reaction was more nuanced. The German Chancellor, Gerhard Schröder (another member of the Fellowship of the Third Way), blamed the need for military action on the intransigence of Saddam Hussein; but the French offered a more guarded commentary, deploring 'the spiral which led to the American military strikes against Iraq and the serious humanitarian consequences they could have for the Iraqi population' (Youngs and Oakes, 1999, 34). The notion that Britain could serve as a bridge between 'Europe' and the US had not been discredited, but it was soon subjected to another test, which raised questions about the US commitment to Europe.

Kosovo

If Operation Desert Fox had emerged from the inconclusive Gulf War, Blair's next foreign policy challenge arose from unfinished business in the Balkans. The disintegration of Yugoslavia had overshadowed European politics in the 1990s, and at the close of the decade its final conflict played out where it had begun a decade before, in Kosovo. As the events unfolded through the early 1990s European governments, the US and UN had all struggled to cope with the complexity of the conflict, most especially the Bosnian civil war, which contained multiple frontlines and a shifting array of military alliances. But some events brought clarity out of complexity, most notably the massacre of civilians in Srebrenica in 1995. While Blair had maintained his focus on domestic politics, he voiced private concerns about Britain's inactivity over Bosnia (Seldon, 2004, 392).

When Blair became Prime Minister the situation in the Balkans had been simplified to an extent, with the Bosnian conflict now approaching a resolution. Furthermore, although ethnic nationalism had been defeated in Bosnia, the conflict had shown its propensity to inspire a level of barbarity which Europe had not witnessed since the Nazis. The conflicts in Croatia and Bosnia had brought the term 'ethnic cleansing' into common usage, and the tragedy of Srebrenica was a forceful argument for politicians to take prompt and resolute action to avert a repetition. In addition, for the US and 'Europe', the example of the Bosnian war had shown that a bombastic leader – the Serbian Slobodan Milosevic – could be forced to retreat and negotiate through a judicious blend of diplomacy and military force.

By 1998 Milosevic was a diminished figure. The Dayton Agreement which followed the Bosnian conflict had disabused those who dreamed of a greater Serbia. Rather than representing expansionary objectives, Kosovo was a region *within* the Serbian republic. While it had played a significant part in the history of Serbian nationalism, in its modern incarnation it was home to a majority ethnic Albanian population. The Yugoslavian authorities had recognised this when they granted Kosovo a considerable degree of autonomy in 1974. But while this policy may have seemed enlightened, it failed to meet the demands of the majority population who wanted a republic on a par with those enjoyed by the Croats and Bosnians. It also stoked the resentment of the Serbs in Kosovo, who believed they were becoming second-class citizens within their own Serbian republic (Youngs and Dodd, 1998, 10). Milosevic had capitalised on these grievances to build support for Serbian nationalism. Having gained the presidency of Serbia, he soon moved to extinguish Kosovan autonomy and reassert control over the region.

As the rest of Yugoslavia fractured, Kosovo also began dividing on ethnic lines. In 1996 the Kosovo Liberation Army (KLA) emerged as the self-styled defenders of the ethnic Albanian community, targeting Serbian security forces. Kosovo moved closer to full-scale conflict through 1998 as the KLA increased its activity, fighting for and holding territory. The Serbian government responded with heavy-handed security measures, and soon civilian casualties were being reported. The international community, discerning a pattern of events that was all too reminiscent of Bosnia, started to mobilise. The UN agreed a trade and arms embargo while the Clinton administration engaged in direct diplomatic talks with Milosevic. Hopes of a peaceful resolution were checked by a new Serbian security offensive against the KLA in late May 1998, provoking an exploration of various interventionist options. George Robertson, Britain's Defence Minister, warned that 'President Milosevic should be under no illusions' about NATO's resolve (Youngs and Dodd, 1998, 26). The diplomatic road was still open, depending, crucially, on Russian mediation. This appeared to be working when talks between Russia's President Boris Yeltsin and Milosevic in mid June made progress, once again suggesting that conflict could be avoided by concerted diplomacy backed by a credible threat of force.

Through this period the British government had applied diplomatic pressure on Serbia and planned for military action through NATO. The diplomatic promise of 1998 began to fade by the end of the year, when fighting between the KLA and Serbian forces resumed. The conflict now repeated some of the familiar images of the previous tragic events in Yugoslavia, with media exposure of ethnic killings and refugees fleeing the war zone. The member states of the EU which had already absorbed refugees from the Bosnian conflict viewed the potential for a new exodus with concern. Once again the diplomats were engaged, but this time with the explicit understanding that NATO air strikes would be launched against Serbia if the violence could not be brought under control. In Rambouillet Britain and France chaired discussions between the Serbs and the Kosovars. The proposed settlement would disarm the KLA. In return the Serbian security forces would have to withdraw from the region and its autonomy would be restored. This agreement would be secured by NATO peacekeeping forces.

The British and French were helped in this process by the US, which persuaded the KLA to sign up to the deal in order to heap the pressure on Milosevic. However, this tactic failed. The proposed deal threatened to destroy the President's standing within Serbia, after his impassioned pledges to protect the Serbian population of Kosovo. In the absence of an agreement at Rambouillet NATO air strikes began on 24 March 1999.

Speaking on the eve of the conflict, Blair framed this upcoming military action as a humanitarian mission. Resorting to military force did not signal an abandonment of the ethical stance that New Labour had proclaimed on arriving in office. Quite the contrary: the primary reason for British involvement was 'to avert what would otherwise be a humanitarian disaster'. Blair emphasised that the British government promised to protect the people of Kosovo from further Serbian repression: 'To walk away now would not merely destroy NATO's credibility; more importantly, it would be a breach of faith with thousands of innocent civilians whose only desire is to live in peace, and who took us at our word' (*Hansard, House of Commons Debates*, 23 March 1999, Vol. 328, col. 162). While Blair warned the British public of the risks and potential casualties for British forces, the early stages of the Kosovo war followed the template of Operation Desert Fox and the 1995 air strikes against the Bosnian Serbs. However, in Kosovo NATO planes could not use their laser-guided munitions because of heavy cloud cover; Serbian forces proved more difficult to locate than war planners had hoped; and, most damning, for a war being fought for humanitarian values, the air strikes actually increased the pace of ethnic cleansing within Kosovo. Far from backing down, Milosevic had been emboldened by the air war, ensuring that every stray missile and civilian casualty was built into a media narrative to counter the efforts of NATO spin doctors.

As the prospect of a limited conflict faded, Blair became increasingly concerned that there was a real prospect the air strikes would fail. Apart from threatening the credibility of NATO, this could also undermine his leadership at home. Blair began to explore the possibility of deploying ground troops to support the air campaign, and military planners set to work on the logistics. In mid-April 1999 Blair travelled to Brussels to meet General Wesley Clark, the NATO Supreme Commander. Blair pushed Clark on whether the war was winnable without ground troops, and Clark could offer no guarantee. Clark saw that Blair regarded the conflict in Kosovo as 'more significant to the Europeans than to Washington' and that Blair was 'representing Europe' (Riddell, 2003, 104–5). Blair had already started to lobby Clinton on the need for ground troops, but Washington appeared unconvinced, and cracks began to appear in the close relationship between the two political allies.

Blair visited Washington in late April 1999 for a formal NATO meeting to mark the organisation's 50th birthday. Prior to the gathering he gave a speech to the Economic Club of Chicago. The speech, entitled 'The Doctrine of the International Community', was soon dubbed the 'Blair doctrine'. In Kosovo Blair was faced with the dilemma of deciding the circumstances which could justify military intervention within another state. Reflecting on events in Kosovo, Blair presented a set of five considerations for the international community:

> First, are we sure of our case? . . . Second, have we exhausted all diplomatic options? . . . Third, on the basis of a practical assessment of the situation, are there military operations we can sensibly and prudently undertake? Fourth, are we prepared for the long term? In the past we talked too much of exit strategies. But having made a commitment we cannot simply walk away once the fight is over; better to stay with moderate numbers of troops than return for repeat performances with large numbers. And finally, do we have national interests involved?
>
> (Blair, 1999)

The speech did not in itself break new ground, but it clarified Blair's assessment of the contemporary world in which isolationism was not an option.

> We are all internationalists now, whether we like it or not. We cannot refuse to participate in global markets if we want to prosper. We cannot ignore new political ideas in other countries if we want to innovate. We cannot turn our backs on conflicts and the violation of human rights within other countries if we want still to be secure.
>
> (Blair, 1999)

It was a world that would intermittently throw up crises and humanitarian disasters. The international community had a responsibility to act, through military force if other methods of persuasion proved ineffective. This commitment could not be made without some consideration of the national interest, but if undertaken, the interventions would have to be long-term engagements rather than short-term fixes. Blair argued that Kosovo did constitute a national interest for Britain, as failure there would destabilise southern Europe. While arguing that intervention in Kosovo was justified on his Chicago principles, he recognised that the air strikes had not received UN endorsement. Therefore he suggested that a priority for the international community after Kosovo would be reform of the UN Security Council structures, to avoid it being bypassed in the future. Legal advisers in the FCO, who had not seen the speech before its delivery, were concerned about the implications of the 'Blair doctrine' in relation to international law and the UN (Seldon, 2004, 399). It was also notable that the UK Prime Minister, rather than the US President, was making a public attempt to delineate a framework for action by the 'international community' – and in a speech delivered in Clinton's own country.

The divisive issue of ground troops had been left off the agenda of the NATO meeting in April 1999, but it did not go away, and the British government kept pressing the US. By mid May, this had developed into a row between the two allies. Clinton was angered by criticism of his leadership in the British press – taking at face value Blair's claim to have mastered the media – and he was critical of what he believed was British 'grandstanding' (Seldon, 2004, 403). The US were resentful of the British attempt to bounce them into a commitment to ground forces that would fall disproportionately on them, despite British offers of a significant troop deployment. The bombing campaign was still underway, and the US explored diplomatic channels through the Russian government. By early June there was a diplomatic breakthrough with Milosevic after the Russian government had made it clear that it would not block a NATO intervention in Kosovo and that if Serbia did not withdraw its forces from Kosovo military action would continue. Having withstood ten weeks of bombing and now facing a serious escalation and the prospect of an operation on land, Milosevic's options were narrowing. A deal was reached for the withdrawal of Serbian forces from Kosovo, and the NATO bombing campaign ended on 9 June. UN Security Council Resolution 1244 authorised the deployment of NATO forces to Kosovo to oversee the return of refugees. NATO had prevailed in its conflict with Milosevic and both the UK and the US could claim vindication. For Blair, raising the possibility of ground troops had convinced Milosevic that NATO would not be backing down and that a deal would have to be made. For Clinton, the issue of ground troops had been a distraction, and the crucial factor was the adroit use of Russian mediation.

Kosovo was a defining moment for foreign policy during Blair's first term. While Operation Desert Fox had provided him with an international stage, he had obviously played a subservient role to the US. Kosovo raised his profile further, and his Chicago speech reflected a desire to take a global lead in the development of a principled justification for the use of force. If the 'Blair doctrine' had been inspired by reflections on Kosovo, it seemed to be verified by a subsequent intervention, this time in the West African state of Sierra Leone, a colony which had become independent in 1961 but had retained strong economic links with Britain. Sierra Leone had been affected by civil unrest since the early 1990s, and in 2000 it seemed possible that the democratically elected government would be overthrown for a second time, despite the presence of UN peacekeepers.

British forces were despatched and transformed the situation, in an operation which was a classic of its kind – successful and swift and involving heroic actions without significant casualties on either side. The congruence between Britain's role and the five Chicago principles was striking, including the commitment of 'moderate numbers of troops' – mainly for training purposes – to prevent the need to 'return for repeat performances'.

From being a novice Prime Minister with very limited foreign policy experience, Blair had now eclipsed his Foreign Secretary and exceeded even Mrs Thatcher's tendency to dominate foreign policy from Downing Street. But Blair's leadership ambitions left him exposed in Europe, where there had been no consensus on the deployment of ground troops in Kosovo, and they had damaged his relations with Washington. The question that this raised – and that remained throughout Blair's time in office – was how much influence did this high-profile role actually bring, in view of the yawning disparity in hard power inherent in the 'special relationship'?

The relationship between Tony Blair and Bill Clinton, which had promised a lasting renewal of the 'special relationship', came to an official close in January 2001. Clinton had served the two terms of office allowed by the US constitution; Blair was facing a second election in which victory was virtually assured, and there seemed to be little to stop him going for a hat-trick. Whatever the personal differences between the two over Kosovo, they were still united by the Third Way mantra. A year after he left office Clinton addressed the Labour Party conference to confirm that he remained committed to New Labour. His reassurance to the Labour delegates was, however, twofold. He told the gathering that they should reconsider their traditional misgivings about the continued close relationship between their two countries, and that they could trust Blair to be a moderating influence on the new man in the White House – the Republican George W Bush.

'Not in my name', 2001-7

10

Introduction

For decades, the Suez Crisis of 1956 was generally regarded as Britain's biggest foreign policy mistake since Neville Chamberlain's 1938 flight to Munich (Chapter 3). In itself, the Blair government's decision to commit British forces to the 2003 American-led war in Iraq seems less momentous, since Suez was a spectacular demonstration of Britain's reduced role, while Iraq can be seen as a repetition of the same lesson, i.e. that the country was unable to embark on significant foreign policy initiatives without American acquiescence. However, the domestic political impact of Suez was short-lived. In contrast, Iraq was still casting a shadow over British politics more than a decade after the war; and, internationally, there was a lasting reputational impact. If the full implications of Britain's involvement in the Iraq War of 2003 have still to be worked out, it cannot be understood without reference to earlier events. The terrorist attacks of 9/11 on various targets in the US – notably, the World Trade Center in New York and the headquarters of the Department of Defense – dramatically altered the global political climate. Apart from the resulting wars, in Afghanistan as well as Iraq, 9/11 brought issues relating to domestic and international security into sharp focus, making them a constant concern for citizens across the world as well as professional policy makers.

The concentration of this chapter on the War on Terror risks giving the impression that the 'normal' routine of British foreign policy was suspended for the rest of Blair's premiership. This, of course, is not the case, although the legacy of 9/11 was registered at least to some extent in all of Britain's external relations (particularly in respect of the EU). Using Britain's response to 9/11 as the central theme of the chapter allows us to examine key issues which recurred throughout the decades after 1945. In particular, the episode provides insights into the nature of the 'special relationship', raising the question of whether this concept served tangible British foreign policy goals or had come to be treated as an end in itself. Second, it allows us to consider the nature of the foreign policy decision-making process in a mature liberal democracy, whose leaders at the time of the Iraq War had described themselves as 'servants of the people'. Finally, decisions taken by key policy makers invite analysis in relation to the various theoretical approaches to international relations, building on our survey in Chapter 1.

Timeline of domestic political developments

June 2001 General election: Labour wins another landslide (overall majority 166), but voter turnout less than 60 per cent

18 March 2003 House of Commons approves impending attack on Iraq by 412 votes to 149

July 2003 Suicide of weapons expert Dr David Kelly

January 2004 Publication of Hutton report into Dr Kelly's death; this exonerates government and lambasts the BBC

May 2005 General election: Labour wins again, but majority down to 66

July 2005 On successive days London wins right to hold 2012 Olympic Games and 52 people killed in terrorist attack on capital's transport system

December 2005 David Cameron becomes leader of the Conservative Party

June 2007 Blair resigns as Prime Minister and is succeeded by Gordon Brown

---

9/11

At 8.46 on the morning of 11 September 2001 American Airlines Flight 11 crashed into the North Tower of the World Trade Center in New York. Seventeen minutes later, United Airlines Flight 175 was flown into the South Tower, while at 9.37 American Airlines Flight 77 crashed into the Pentagon. United 93, an American Airlines flight from Newark International Airport, New Jersey, to San Francisco International Airport, California, was also hijacked, by a group which intended to attack the White House. The latter mission was thwarted, but by 10.28 both towers of the World Trade Center had collapsed. The four attacks resulted in almost 3,000 deaths, including a total of 19 hijackers.

Those who remember that day do so vividly, thanks to the broadcast images. The weeks after the attacks were shrouded in uncertainty and fear. It soon became apparent that Al Qa'ida, a network of operatives led by a Saudi billionaire, Osama bin Laden, was responsible for the attacks; well-informed observers were able to make this connection instantly, since bin Laden's followers had made a previous attempt on the North Tower of the World Trade Center with a truck bomb in February 1993. Masterminded by Khalid Sheikh Muhammed, a Pakistani national, the 9/11 attacks were carried out by individuals from Saudi Arabia, the United Arab Emirates, Egypt and Lebanon. They were motivated by opposition to American foreign policy in the Middle East, which had resulted in the long-standing presence of US forces in Saudi Arabia and unwavering support for the state of Israel.

The events of 9/11 evoked global condemnation and an outpouring of sympathy for the victims (of various nationalities) and in particular for the US. In Britain Tony Blair was quick to respond, telling Britons that:

> We've offered President Bush and the American people our solidarity, our profound sympathy, and our prayers. . . . this is not a battle between the United States of America and terrorism, but between the free and democratic world and terrorism. We therefore here in Britain stand shoulder to shoulder with our American friends in this hour of tragedy, and we like them will not rest until this evil is driven from our world.
>
> (Blair, 2001)

In New York on 12 September 2001 the UN Security Council unanimously adopted Resolution 1368, which condemned in the strongest possible terms the acts of the previous day on the south side of the same city. Even countries considered to be hostile to the US, such as Iran and North Korea, joined the chorus of condemnation, although Iraq's leader Saddam Hussein imprudently argued that America had brought the attacks on itself.

In the weeks after the attacks world leaders flocked to New York and Washington to pay their respects and to demonstrate their support for America. In a New York memorial service shortly after the attacks the British Ambassador to the US, Sir Christopher Meyer, read an address on behalf of the Queen. It included the memorable sentiment that 'grief is the price we pay for love'. This eloquent message was seconded by British politicians and officials, who sought to stress the proximity of London and Washington. The burgeoning personal relationship between Blair and Bush in the wake of 9/11 took many observers by surprise; yet Blair's ideological commitments were not so strongly defined to rule out the possibility of cooperation with any US President, Democrat or Republican. Bill Clinton had advised Blair to establish cordial relations with his Republican successor, but it is unlikely that Blair needed much encouragement in this respect. Whatever else it did, 9/11 gave Blair an outstanding opportunity to keep the 'special relationship' as warm as it had been while Clinton was in the White House – if not to make it even closer.

The first time Blair spoke to Bush after the attacks, the two agreed on the importance of a diplomatic response. Jack Straw, who had replaced Robin Cook as Foreign Secretary after the 2001 general election, stressed that the best role for Britain was 'to stay close and try to exercise influence privately' (Campbell, 2012, 563). To the chagrin of the FCO, this crucial task was mainly entrusted to Blair's foreign policy advisers. A key member of the Downing Street team, David Manning, took soundings in Washington and reported back in terms which echoed Blair's existing approach: 'At the best of times, Britain's influence on the US is limited. But the only way we exercise that influence is by attaching ourselves firmly to them and avoiding public criticism wherever possible' (Kampfner, 2003, 117). Jack Straw had already established an excellent relationship with his American opposite number, Colin Powell. But Powell, despite (or perhaps because of) the respect he commanded in the US and beyond, was outside the charmed circle of 'neo-conservatives' which had begun to drive his country's foreign policy. The US State Department, and the UK's FCO, were little more than spectators after 9/11 – indeed, they enjoyed something less than the influence usually allowed to spectators, since their institutional roles prevented them from jeering disputed decisions. They could only applaud politely when other people's plans seemed to produce positive results.

All too aware that an inexperienced US President was under increasing pressure to respond to the worst attacks on the US since Pearl Harbor, Blair and his advisers were eager to cement the diplomatic consensus which had formed in response to 9/11. As Alistair Campbell's diaries record, Blair:

> felt that the US would feel beleaguered and angry because there was so much anti-Americanism around . . . We had to start shaping an international agenda to fill the vacuum.
>
> (Campbell, 2012, 561)

Blair's concerns were borne out by subsequent developments, which suggested that although Bush was grateful for international support, he was determined to show that America needed no material assistance. As Alistair Campbell noted, Blair felt that the Americans 'were looking inwards when they should be looking outwards' (Campbell, 2012, 566). Blair seized the initiative by orchestrating a face-to-face meeting with Bush, neglecting diplomatic protocol and frustrating the British ambassador. This occasion seems to have created (in Blair, at least) the sense of personal friendship which injected an additional consideration into a British decision-making process which already seemed difficult to reconcile with a careful evaluation of national interests. According to Campbell's diaries, Blair's chief anxiety was to ensure that the British electorate could be persuaded to share his own, idiosyncratic perspective: 'TB talked about the need to be sure of his ground, that we needed public opinion with us the whole time' (Campbell, 2012, 574).

Britain, Afghanistan and Operation Enduring Freedom

UN Resolution 1368 called on members to respond to the attacks. However, although it was clear that Osama bin Laden and his Al Qa'ida organisation were responsible, an appropriate response was less easily discerned. The group was based in Afghanistan, having been offered safe haven by the Taliban, yet drew membership from across the Muslim world. While transnational terror groups were not entirely new, the scale and sophistication of the 9/11 attacks presented an unprecedented threat, demanding a radical reimagining of the strategic and security environment.

In his 1999 Chicago speech – and in decisions relating to Kosovo and Sierra Leone – Tony Blair had argued, in effect, that the presumed sanctity of international boundaries should be set aside when brutal governments were creating 'humanitarian distress' among their own citizens. In a sense, 9/11 represented a distorted image of his vision – it was an attack planned across national boundaries, perpetrated by individuals of various nationalities. It was thus unsurprising that, among his other reactions, Blair interpreted the 9/11 attacks as an opportunity for the international community to reshape the global order. In particular, Blair hoped that states could be brought together in the face of this new global terrorist threat to make a reality of the new world order hailed by George H Bush, facilitated by international organisations such as the UN.

In pursuit of this goal Blair embarked on a 'diplomatic odyssey' to cultivate support from key global actors. Blair was a firm believer in his powers of personal persuasion, at home and abroad. Initially, his dynamic approach yielded a number of diplomatic successes, notably with Vladimir Putin, the President of Russia, and General Musharraf, the military leader of Pakistan. Blair also called France's Jacques Chirac, the German Chancellor, Gerhard Schröder, and Guy Verhofstadt of Belgium (the country which currently held the rotating EU Presidency). It was as if Blair had appointed himself (with something more than American acquiescence) as the agent of coordination within the great coalition of nations which had been conjured into existence by 9/11. It was a role which would have intoxicated a more self-effacing individual than Tony Blair. At least in part, it seemed also to vindicate his conviction, expressed at Chicago, that Britain was ideally placed to act as a catalyst for a new era of international cooperation. It was also natural for Blair to suppose that his earnest voice, rather than Bush's bellicose utterances, would prevail in ensuing developments.

Even in this early phase of their relationship, there were signs that Blair's self-adopted role of George Bush's 'ambassador-at-large' would cause difficulties. One major problem in the autumn of 2011 was the possibility that the Israeli Prime Minister, Ariel Sharon, would attempt to draw parallels between the Palestinian leader Yasser Arafat and Osama bin Laden. Blair sought to use this crisis as an opportunity to make some progress over Palestine, which would have the additional benefit of forestalling criticism from Arab leaders. However, this objective met an obstacle in the young Syrian President, Bashar Al Assad, who used a joint press conference to condemn the US-led military action in Afghanistan for its collateral damage. On the same trip Blair was turned away from a meeting with the then Crown Prince Abdullah of Saudi Arabia, on the grounds that it was too sensitive for him to be seen at that time.

A 'normal' political leader would have been deterred by such rebuffs. However, only an individual who genuinely saw himself as an apostle of international amity would have undertaken these missions in the first place; and such a person would be unlikely to detect signs that he might be straining his diplomatic credibility. Blair's self-confidence seems not to have been affected. The weeks after 9/11 were challenging for all those involved, many of whom (like Blair's media advisor Alastair Campbell) lacked foreign policy experience and seemed too ready to assume that their ability to spin dubious domestic outcomes as if they were unqualified successes could be transferred painlessly to the international sphere. Throughout this period Blair relied heavily on a small coterie of advisers who were loyal to himself and thus unlikely to act as constructive sounding boards. In contrast, between the 9/11 attacks and the beginning of operations in Afghanistan Blair met his Cabinet only twice.

Despite intense international pressure, the Taliban regime in Afghanistan rejected Washington's demands for Osama bin Laden to be handed over and for the dismantling of terrorist training camps. Operation Enduring Freedom was duly launched by the Americans on 7 October, with almost universal support from the international community. Given the proximity of London and Washington in the aftermath of the 9/11 attacks, British involvement in military action in Afghanistan was a formality. Thus 162 years after the outbreak of the First Anglo-Afghan war British forces returned to Afghanistan. Australia also sent troops for the initial assault, and other countries (including Canada, France and Germany) made later contributions. The military operation was further strengthened by cooperation with the Northern Alliance, a collection of powerful Afghan warlords who had been opposed to Taliban rule.

On 13 November, less than two months after the onset of Operation Enduring Freedom, Kabul fell to coalition and Northern Alliance forces. Knowing the fickle nature of public opinion – and, despite his general lack of historical knowledge, having some awareness of the hazards involved in an invasion of Afghanistan – Blair had been impatient for a quick end to the conflict. In December 2001 the UN Security Council agreed Resolution 1386, authorising the creation of an International Security Assistance Force (ISAF) to help restore governing institutions to Afghanistan, train its security forces and oppose residual elements of the defeated Taliban regime. Rather than being dominated by the US, this was primarily a NATO operation, with assistance from other countries. Britain's contribution was focused on Helmand province in the south of Afghanistan.

In the immediate aftermath of 9/11 the US had invoked Article 5 of the North Atlantic Treaty – the first time that this had been done – and thus could have asked all its NATO partners to join the invasion on the grounds that this would be a response to an attack on a member state. However, from the outset it was clear that the US administration had no interest in delegating or sharing direction of the main campaign against the Taliban. At most, the Bush administration was grateful to its allies for moral support, but they were sure that they could handle the situation on their own and would only ask for material help in the unlikely event that it was needed. It was also possible to suspect that, given their understandable desire to avenge 9/11, the Americans would place less emphasis on the constructive elements of Blair's Chicago speech, i.e. the need for long-term commitments to 'failed states'. In fact, the US did make a significant contribution to ISAF. However, it showed itself to be uneasy about the purpose of the operation and frustrated by its multinational nature.

As early as January 2002 Blair reassured Hamid Karzai, the leader of an 'interim' Afghan government, that although the country faced 'a huge task of reconstruction' Britain would not back away:

> Afghanistan has been a failed state for too long and the whole world has paid the price – in the export of terror, the export of drugs and finally in the explosion of death and destruction on the streets of the USA. It is in all our interests that Afghanistan becomes a stable country, part of the international community once more.
>
> (Watt, 2002a)

These sentiments were probably reassuring to the fragile new regime in Kabul, and it is testimony to Blair's sincerity that he had flown to Afghanistan at considerable risk to himself and to his wife Cherie. However, the speech would have been more effectual if it had been delivered by George W Bush, rather than the Prime Minister of a country whose contribution to the war against the Taliban had been relatively small and which could hardly hope to restore 'stability' to Afghanistan unless the US was wholeheartedly committed to the same goal. The fact that Blair felt compelled to undertake the perilous journey to Kabul in the New Year of 2002 suggests either an inflated estimation of Britain's (and his own) importance or a realisation that, without prompting, his ally in the White House would lose interest in the recipe of national reconstruction after breaking the eggs – or, indeed, a blend of both. On any reading, Blair's intervention suggested that there were serious lessons to be learned from Afghanistan, and that subsequent interventions initiated by America should only be endorsed after serious consideration (Box 10.1).

> **Box 10.1 Tracking public opinion**
>
> In the months after the invasion of Afghanistan the British public was largely supportive of the Prime Minister and his policy. In an Ipsos MORI survey conducted on 14 September 83 per cent of those asked expressed approval for Tony Blair's response to 9/11 (Ipsos MORI, 2001a). A month later, another Ipsos MORI poll found that 71 per cent backed the decision to join the US in the invasion of Afghanistan (Ipsos MORI, 2001b). However, within a year, the British public's initial enthusiasm had declined sharply. Support for Blair's response to 9/11 was now little over a third of those surveyed, while just over half now explicitly disapproved. Bush's approval ratings in Britain suffered a similar slump.
>
> The decline was understandable given the continuing instability in Afghanistan and a loss of British lives which, by 2010, had exceeded those killed in the Falklands campaign (eventually more than 450 were killed, with more than a thousand wounded). By April 2014, as British troops withdrew from Helmand province, a YouGov survey found that only a quarter of the public supported an action which had begun with such overwhelming support (YouGov, 2014).

The Iraq War

In his State of the Union address of 29 January 2002, Bush stated that the operation in Afghanistan was just one part of a War on Terror:

> Our response involves far more than instant retaliation and isolated strikes. Americans should not expect one battle, but a lengthy campaign, unlike any other we have ever seen. It may include dramatic strikes, visible on TV, and covert operations, secret even in success. We will starve terrorists of funding, turn them one against another, drive them from place to place, until there is no refuge or no rest. And we will pursue nations that provide aid or safe haven to terrorism. Every nation, in every region, now has a decision to make. Either you are with us, or you are with the terrorists. From this day forward, any nation that continues to harbour or support terrorism will be regarded by the US as a hostile regime.
>
> (Bush, 2002)

Bush's speech identified an 'Axis of Evil', comprising North Korea, Iran and – especially – Saddam Hussein's Iraq. It had a profound and lasting impact on approaches to global security. The powerful rhetoric of either being 'with us or with the terrorists' drew battle lines which proved to be divisive and controversial when US attention turned from Afghanistan to other targets.

The second phase of the War on Terror was dominated by the invasion of Iraq, which began in March 2003. While the international community was largely supportive of Operation Enduring Freedom in Afghanistan, the move towards military action in Iraq provoked strong criticism from numerous sources, including large-scale demonstrations in the UK and elsewhere.

In July 2002, eight months before the invasion, Blair wrote to Bush about the possible consequences of going to war in Iraq. The note opens with the phrase 'I will be with you, whatever'. After its publication, along with other papers released as a result of the Chilcot Inquiry, the memorandum was widely interpreted as proof that Blair had committed Britain to the impending war, regardless of any attempt to reach a peaceful settlement of the dispute between Iraq and the international community. In fact, the only reasonable interpretation of reliable documentary evidence is that the US administration had no doubts concerning Blair's support for action in Iraq much earlier than the date of his memorandum – indeed, even before his notorious stay at President Bush's Texas ranch in April 2002.

Blair was acutely conscious of the need to present his policy towards Iraq as a justified response to a general threat, rather than the product of his desire to keep in step with a US administration which was obviously preoccupied with perceived American interests. This case depended on concrete evidence of Saddam Hussein's possession of WMD and his attempts to develop this programme further. To this end, two dossiers were compiled and published by the British government, in September 2002 and February 2003 (Controversy 10.1). Even at the time the latter document raised more questions than it answered; much of its content was shown to have been copied from a doctoral thesis, even to the extent of reproducing the original typing errors. The Chilcot Inquiry into the Iraq War revealed how evidence used to justify military action had been based upon the 1996 action film *The Rock*. This was doubly unfortunate, since it demonstrated that Blair and his supporters within the government machine were only interested in 'evidence' that assisted their purpose, and were not very choosy about their sources, as well as being a slap in the face for the British intelligence services whose own information had clearly proved inadequate.

Even those who remained unconvinced that action against Iraq was a key national interest for Britain might be swayed if it could be shown to arise from a sense of international responsibility, thanks to UN authorisation. Blair used his influence with Bush to get the US to work through the UN in September 2002, but the Security Council could not agree on a resolution that would offer support for the deployment of 'all necessary means' to resolve the issue of Iraq's weapons programme (Seldon, 2007, 104–5). This left Blair with a weaker hand to play as he sought to convince both the public and members of his own government of the case for supporting an invasion of Iraq. If the war went ahead, it

Controversy 10.1 The 'sexed up' September dossier

In September 2002 a dossier was produced that incorporated the previous year's intelligence on Iraq. The genesis of the dossier can be traced back to early 2002 and the need to 'put more evidence in the public domain' (House of Commons Foreign Affairs Committee, 2002). The document was created by the FCO, before being passed to the Joint Intelligence Committee (JIC), which supplemented it with evidence from other sources.

It made several claims about Saddam Hussein's WMD capabilities, including:

- that Iraq had continued to produce chemical and biological agents;
- that the Iraqi nuclear programme was seeking 'an indigenous ability to enrich uranium to the level needed for a nuclear weapon';
- that there were military plans to use these agents, which could be deployed within 45 minutes of an order to use them;
- that mobile military laboratories had been developed.

As Tony Blair wrote in his foreword:

> It is unprecedented for the Government to publish this kind of document. But in light of the debate about Iraq and Weapons of Mass Destruction (WMD), I wanted to share with the British public the reasons why I believe this issue to be a current and serious threat to the UK national interest.
>
> (Blair, 2002)

In fact, back in November 1997 Blair had told the Liberal Democrat leader Paddy Ashdown that he had seen intelligence reports on Iraq which were 'pretty scary'. They showed that Saddam Hussein was 'very close to some appalling weapons of mass destruction . . . We cannot let him get away with it'. Ashdown had replied that such material should be 'put into the public domain as soon as possible'. Blair agreed and said that he had suggested this to President Clinton (Ashdown, 2001, 127).

The fact that the exchange between Blair and Ashdown was made public before the removal of Saddam – indeed, in advance of the appearance of the September dossier – makes this an intriguing piece of evidence. Among other things, it suggests that in 1997 Blair was already thinking along the lines which inspired the Chicago speech of 1999, in which he argued that 'If we leave an evil dictator to range unchallenged, we will have to spill infinitely more blood and treasure to stop him later'. This was clearly a reference to Saddam Hussein as well as to Serbia's Slobodan Milosevic. Second, the suggestion that the British government could not publish its intelligence on Iraq – or, at least, preferred not to do so without American agreement – is an interesting reflection on the nature of the 'special relationship' at work within the intelligence community as well as at the political level. If the information on WMD had been gathered as a result of cooperation between the British and the Americans, it would remain secret unless both governments authorised its release. Secrecy, of course, has proved an irresistible tool for all governments and can be accepted as a regrettable necessity for liberal democratic regimes which claim to be working on behalf of their people. However, if such a government is hoping to introduce a new principle of international relations, justifying armed interference in other countries, there is an obvious temptation for it to move from a culture of secrecy to one of *selective* transparency, i.e. to ensure that information reaches the public domain if – and only if – it suits a predetermined purpose.

In 1997 decision-makers in the UK and the US decided against the publication of intelligence on Iraq. By 2002, however, their mood had changed; and instead of keeping 'pretty scary' information to themselves they wanted it to be known as widely as possible. In itself, that sudden impulse for full disclosure rendered the information suspect. Were the intelligence services being encouraged to report anything 'scary', however flimsy the evidence? Even if the intelligence gatherers were providing the full picture, were their findings being sifted in order to build a partial picture for public consumption? Against this background, it was not surprising for observers to suspect that the material included in the September dossier had been distorted – or, in the phrase which soon became associated with the dossier, 'sexed up'.

In a liberal democracy it ought to be a minimum requirement that foreign-policy decisions are 'evidence-based'. The private exchange between Blair and Ashdown suggests that in 1997 Blair really *was* impressed by the evidence that Saddam posed a potent threat to countries in the region. There is good reason to suspect that over the next five years the emphasis shifted, so that instead of making foreign policy decisions on the basis of intelligence, Blair and his allies were interpreting intelligence from the perspective of a decision which had already been taken.

would do so without new backing from the UN; instead, its legal basis would be drawn from the resolutions agreed at the end of the Gulf War in 1991.

Despite agreeing to follow 'the UN route', the Bush administration had left Blair in no doubt that it would go ahead even if it encountered obstructions.

Blair himself had already shown a readiness to act without specific UN authorisation; his Chicago speech of 1999 – which argued for reform of the UN Security Council – had been delivered against the background of an intervention in Kosovo which had been launched without an explicit resolution. If the UN could not be persuaded, Blair could still hope for support from the British Parliament, where his party enjoyed a commanding majority. Creating a new constitutional precedent, Parliament was invited to vote specifically to authorise British participation after a debate on 18 March 2003. Making the case for British involvement, Blair returned to themes of Operation Desert Fox (1998), where military action had taken place because Clinton and Blair had not believed the evidence presented to them by the Iraqi authorities. Nothing in the intervening years had altered Blair's perception of Saddam Hussein, and the notion that Saddam had 'decided unilaterally to destroy' his weapons programme was held to be 'palpably absurd'.

The second component of the government's case for war was the need to neutralise the Iraqi WMD programme and prevent weapons from reaching the terrorist groups responsible for the outrages of September 2001. In an interdependent world, Blair argued, 'Confidence is key to prosperity' and '[i]nsecurity spreads like contagion'. The greatest sources of insecurity in the world were dictatorial regimes which possessed WMD and terrorist groups propagating a perverted form of Islam. At present the link between the two was 'loose', but it was 'hardening'. The unchecked development of weapons programmes raised the prospect of a terrorist grouping gaining access to a nuclear device – something that could not be contemplated. Finally, Blair restated the appalling human rights record of Saddam Hussein's regime. Iraq had been a wealthy country, but the money it received from oil had been squandered by wealthy elites. The basic freedoms that were afforded to people across the world were denied to Iraqi citizens. If Saddam Hussein remained in power the Iraqi people would stay imprisoned: 'the darkness will close back over them again' (*Hansard, House of Commons Debates*, 18 March 2003, Vol. 401, col. 762).

In framing his argument for British intervention, Blair had to take account of a withering critique of his policy delivered the previous day by the former Foreign Secretary, Robin Cook. Cook, who had remained in the Cabinet as Leader of the House of Commons after his 2001 sacking from the FCO, had endorsed military action against Iraq's WMD programme in the past, but the circumstances had changed and he could no longer support government policy. On the eve of the Parliamentary debate on Iraq Cook resigned his Cabinet post, after telling Blair, 'Next time don't get so committed that you can't draw back' (Cook, 2003, 324). In his resignation statement, delivered to the Commons rather than directly to the press, he insisted that the 'threshold for war should always be high'. The unseemly rush towards conflict was closing off the possibility of the UN weapons inspectors completing their task of disarming Iraq without bloodshed.

Cook thought it unlikely that Iraq had WMD, 'in the commonly understood sense of the term – namely, a credible device capable of being delivered against a strategic city target'. While few denied that Saddam Hussein was a 'brutal dictator', there was no evidence that he was 'a clear and present danger to Britain'; indeed, 'it is only because Iraq's military forces are so weak that we can even contemplate its invasion' (*Hansard, House of Commons Debates*, 17 March 2003, Vol. 401, cols 726–7). Ironically, Cook, the chief advocate of an ethical dimension to Britain's foreign policy agenda, was presenting a case against war which owed much to the supposedly amoral Realist perspective on international relations (Chapter 1).

True, Cook argued that '[o]ur interests are best protected not by unilateral action but by multilateral agreement and a world order governed by rules'; but the gist of his speech was that if the UN really *had* authorised action, its members would have been making a mistake because they would have been serving (perceived) US interests rather than their own. As it was, when Cook, along with Blair, had argued for decisive action against Serbian expansionism, he had done so without the agreement of the UN Security Council; but Britain was supported by NATO, by the EU and 'by every single one of seven neighbours in the region'. While Blair stuck doggedly to his argument that British justification for action against Iraq was not 'regime change', it appeared clear to Cook that this was precisely the motivation for US policy; and that even if Blair sincerely believed his own rhetoric, he was fooling himself if he thought that he could revise the predetermined American agenda.

In his July 2002 note to Bush, Blair had reminded his friend of the importance of public opinion, and that:

> opinion in the US is quite simply on a different planet from opinion here, in Europe or in the Arab world. In Britain, right now I couldn't be sure of support from Parliament, Party, public or even some of the Cabinet.

Cook's parting shot could have been a devastating blow to Blair's standing in all four of these constituencies. But whereas on paper his speech is more impressive than other resignation statements (e.g. Sir Geoffrey Howe's (1990) and even Nigel Lawson's forensic indictment of Thatcher's style of government in 1989), and indeed stands comparison with any Parliamentary speech of the post-war era, it was never likely to induce a rethink of policy, let alone a change of Prime Minister. Ultimately, when the House of Commons voted, Blair's fears proved unfounded: an amendment asking for a delay was beaten by 396 to 217, after which the government's policy was approved by a much wider margin (417 to 149).

Regrettably for Parliament's reputation, on this occasion it fell far below its representative role and confirmed the suspicions of those who regarded it as an unsuitable venue for foreign policy decision-making. Many Conservative MPs supported the government in the mistaken view that this would prove they were sufficiently open-minded to put country above party (as Conservative strategists soon realised, their calculations had been wrong on both counts). As for Labour MPs, a handful might have been convinced by Blair's arguments; but it is highly likely that most (if not all) of these would have voted against the war if it had been proposed by a Conservative Prime Minister. Having rewarded Cook's resignation speech with a standing ovation (against Parliamentary precedent), the majority of his colleagues voted against his argument, mainly because they did not want to bring down a Prime Minister who had delivered two election victories but also because an effective revolt would have made Cook the obvious replacement, and he was not a popular choice as an alternative leader. As the backbench MP Chris Mullin wrote in his diary, Cook 'is perceived by many as arrogant and has relied on intellect rather than charisma for his mastery of the House' (Mullin, 2010, 383). Coming from someone who decided (despite intense pressure from government whips) to vote against the war, this is telling testimony. In a mature liberal democracy, it would be reassuring to think that politicians should command the support of legislators through their 'intellect rather than charisma'. Yet in the matter of Britain's involvement in Iraq, which even on the most optimistic view would prove fatal to thousands of people abroad and at home, Mullin accepted that charisma would prevail over intellect. Even if one accepts that the Commons took the right decision on 18 March 2003, the best that can be said is that it made the right choice for inappropriate reasons.

The invasion of Iraq began with coordinated bombing raids on 20 March 2003. British troops were a significant component in the invasion force, capturing the southern city of Basra. As the fighting came to an end in early April there was a predictable surge in public support for military action, but even at its lowest point dissent did not drop far below a third of British voters, and the failure to uncover conclusive evidence of an advanced Iraqi WMD programme made it easier for Britons to confide their suspicion that they had been presented with a false prospectus for war.

In the aftermath of the invasion a number of inquiries were launched to ascertain the real reason for Britain's decision: the Hutton Inquiry following the suicide of government scientist David Kelly (Controversy 10.2); the Butler Review on the intelligence failures relating to Iraq's WMD programme; and, ultimately, the Chilcot Inquiry, which was established by Gordon Brown in 2009 in an attempt to distance his own administration from Iraq. Jeremy Corbyn, the leader of the Labour Party when the Chilcot Inquiry was published seven long years later, claimed that Parliament was 'misled', although the inquiry found that the Cabinet was not. There was, however, considerable suspicion about the role of the government's chief law officer, the Attorney-General, Peter Goldsmith, who initially expressed doubts about the legality of the war and subsequently changed his mind.

Controversy 10.2 The Hutton Inquiry

On 17 July 2003 Tony Blair delivered a speech to both Houses of the US Congress. He had just been awarded the Congressional Gold Medal, and he was given a rapturous reception as he acclaimed Britain and America as bearers of 'the universal values of the human spirit'.

Within a few hours Blair's sense of moral superiority had been unsettled by news that Dr David Kelly, an expert on munitions who had been working within the Ministry of Defence, had been found dead. Kelly had been unmasked as the source for a claim, made in a BBC radio report, that the government had probably known in advance that Iraqi forces were not capable of threatening British troops within 45 minutes of an order being given. This had been a key feature of the case for war, which Blair had presented to Parliament and the British people. After being named, Kelly was made to appear before the Commons' Foreign Affairs Select Committee, where he endured a searching examination. He had also been badgered by the media. Two days after the committee hearing he (apparently) took his own life.

The government immediately set up an inquiry under the senior judge Lord Hutton, who initially was hailed as a fearless inquisitor who would deal impartially with established facts. However, the government had learned from the unfortunate experiences of the Major years. Hutton's terms of reference were circumscribed; and, in any case, it turned out that he had little taste for troublemaking. The televised proceedings provided plenty of drama, and the eventual report created a sensation of a kind – but not the expected one, which would have included ministerial resignations and maybe even the departure of Blair himself. Instead, the resignations took place within the BBC, which Hutton had criticised at every opportunity while leaving the government unscathed.

Naturally, the public reaction was a mixture of anger and astonishment, and the report was widely regarded as a blatant whitewash. However, there is a sense that the inquiry had been framed even by reputable media outlets (notably, the BBC itself) in a misleading way. Public expectations resembled the mood before a trial for murder, including evidence which identified specific culprits. While David Kelly's fate was a human tragedy, it is arguable that something more important than the death of an individual was involved in the Hutton Inquiry, and that it should have been an inquest into the demise of liberal democratic government based on procedural rules and accepted standards of government integrity. On this score, the subsequent Butler Review (2004) and

> the Chilcot Report (2016) were sufficiently damning, but less headline-grabbing than Hutton's findings because their conclusions reflected on an overall system of decision-making rather than producing irrefutable evidence of individual guilt.
>
> Perhaps the most appropriate perspective on this tawdry affair should be derived from the Blair government's treatment of the BBC compared to tabloid newspapers like the *Sun*. Undoubtedly, the BBC had many faults, but in its coverage of the Iraq War these arose from an overzealous desire to expose malpractice in order to hold the government to account. By contrast, tabloid newspapers are prepared to falsify and fabricate in the quest for profit. Although the initial BBC report could have been worded more carefully, its defects were irrelevant compared to the wider point being made, i.e. that the public should be furnished with accurate information in advance of a conflict in which innocent individuals will die, and that spin doctors (whether or not they have a background in tabloid newspapers) should play little or no part in the provision of this information. State funding for an institution like the BBC is difficult to support in a liberal democracy: it depends on a feeling that this is a better basis for impartial reporting than financial dependence on rich individuals like Rupert Murdoch (owner of the *Sun*), who are likely to encourage a particular editorial line. During the Iraq War there was a strong feeling that unelected members of Blair's team regarded the BBC as uniquely vulnerable to bullying because of its dependence on state funding – and that the Hutton Inquiry provided them with some vindication.
>
> Meanwhile, far from being subjected to pressure, 'reliable' media outlets like the *Sun* newspaper continued to be fed with privileged information – including leaked (and suitably 'spun') findings of the Hutton Inquiry itself.

Those who disagreed with the decision to go to war tended also to criticise the way it had been reached. Clare Short, the Secretary of State for International Development, who left the government in May 2003 after allowing herself to be persuaded not to resign alongside Cook, suggested that:

> Alastair Campbell ... Jonathan Powell, Baroness Morgan, Sir David Manning, that close entourage. ... That was the team, they were the ones who moved together all the time. They attended the daily 'War Cabinet'. That was the in group, that was the group that was in charge of policy.
>
> (House of Commons Foreign Affairs Committee, 2003, 43)

This sentiment was echoed by Sir Christopher Meyer, the British Ambassador to the US, who later noted that:

> between 9/11 and the day I retired at the end of February 2003 I had not a single substantive policy discussion on the secure phone with the Foreign Office. This was in contrast to the many contacts and discussions with No. 10.
> (Meyer, 2005, 190)

The Chilcot Inquiry identified a lack of formal ministerial oversight both in the lead-up to the war and its aftermath.

It also seems unlikely that the Cabinet was closely consulted by Blair during the planning stages of a subsequent diplomatic coup, which briefly revived the notion that the Iraq intervention had been beneficial to British interests. In March 2004 the Prime Minister shook hands with the Libyan dictator, Colonel Muammar Gaddafi, who in the previous December had renounced the idea of equipping his regime with WMD. Almost simultaneously it was revealed that the Anglo-Dutch energy company Shell had entered into a contract worth more than half a billion pounds to search for gas reserves off the Libyan coast. Other elements of the deal involved progress in investigations relating to the murder of PC Yvonne Fletcher outside the Libyan Embassy in London in 1984, and the future of Abdelbaset Ali Mohmed al-Megrahi, the Libyan intelligence operative who had been sentenced to life imprisonment after being convicted of involvement in the 1988 bombing of Pan Am Flight 103, which came down over the Scottish town of Lockerbie.

Given the previous record of the two leaders who hailed the prospect of a new, cooperative relationship as they stood together in a Bedouin tent near the Libyan capital of Tripoli, students of IR theory could be forgiven for consigning their textbooks to the nearest recycling depot. The sudden rapprochement was not simply a case of 'letting bygones be bygones'; rather, given that Gaddafi had promised to stop developing WMD without forswearing his well-established habit of brutalising Libyan citizens in more 'traditional' ways, it suggested that the ethical dimension to British foreign policy would now include a willingness to look aside while dictators who were not quite dangerous enough to be placed within the exclusive Axis of Evil continued to indulge themselves in the arbitrary selection of targets to be tortured and/or murdered. It was as if the 'idealist' Blair of the Chicago speech had suddenly stumbled upon the works of Niccolo Machiavelli and decided to try his hand at Realism, with predictably limited success (Chapter 1).

Public opinion

While there was considerable support for British involvement in Operation Enduring Freedom, military action in Iraq was always more controversial. In early 2003

61 per cent of respondents to an Ipsos MORI poll said they would support British forces participating in American-led military action in Iraq – a significant proportion but a fall of ten percentage points since the September dossier. More than three quarters expressed opposition to military action without explicit UN approval (Ipsos MORI, 2003a).

Public misgivings about the prospect of war were given vivid expression on 15 February 2003, when an estimated one million people joined a protest march in London. Whatever the true attendance, the visual impression of opposition was remarkable. It was the largest demonstration in British history, building upon a series of smaller protests across the UK in the previous six months and forming part of an international movement covering around 600 cities; indeed, there were more demonstrators in Rome and Madrid than in London.

Whether or not the London demonstrators were speaking for a majority of Britons when they expressed their opposition to war in Iraq in the phrase 'not in my name', opinion swung against them once British forces had been committed to action; indeed, there was the usual marked tendency for members of the public (and some media outlets) to regard continued dissent as unpatriotic. As a result, the 21 surveys conducted by the polling organisation YouGov between March and December 2003 found an average of 54 per cent in favour of intervention (YouGov, 2015).

It is not uncommon for people to forget what they really felt during times of crisis. Many of those who had regarded the protestors of February 2003 with contempt subsequently imagined that they had been marching beside them in spirit. Surveyed in early 2007, less than a third of the public (29 per cent) believed the British and US had been right to invade Iraq; 60 per cent now regarded the intervention as a mistake. When asked if the invasion of Iraq had made them feel safer, only 5 per cent answered in the affirmative, while more than half felt less secure (BBC, 2007). The poisonous legacy of Iraq became increasingly dangerous to New Labour (as well as to Blair himself) when David Cameron replaced the fervently pro-American Michael Howard as Conservative leader after the 2005 general election. Cameron had supported the war, and (true to his self-proclaimed status as 'heir to Blair') used the familiar New Labour argument that politicians have to take tough decisions which are right, even if this impairs their short-term poll ratings. Helpfully for Cameron, the decisive shift in public opinion coincided with his growing conviction that, in invading Iraq, Blair had taken a tough decision which was wrong. Unlike Howard, he was flexible enough to make it look like an exclusively New Labour misadventure by the time that, as Prime Minister, he took responsibility for winding up the main British contribution in Iraq and Afghanistan.

'Europe'

The decision to go to war in Iraq also had a profound impact upon Britain's position in 'Europe'. In Blair's first term this had been relatively strong, despite the decision to delay joining the single currency and occasional irritations over Britain's championship of 'light-touch' economic regulation (Chapter 11). The British public, however, remained sceptical about the European project and Blair seemed disinclined to exert his legendary powers of persuasion in a concerted drive to generate more positive feelings.

In its 2001 manifesto New Labour explicitly set out a vision to 'take Europe forward, to meet British needs'. The manifesto argued that 'if Britain is stronger in Europe, it will be stronger in the rest of the world'. However, the developing War on Terror changed all this, rendering Blair's Atlantic bridge obsolete for foreign-policy purposes. France and Germany were opposed to military action, with President Chirac pledging to veto a second UN resolution. In response, the Bush administration displayed a degree of contempt for 'old' Europe which it had been careful to conceal during the Cold War. As so often in Britain's post-war history, it seemed that it was faced with a choice between being a 'good European' or continuing the 'special relationship' – and, despite his diplomatic efforts, there was no doubt which side Blair preferred.

The impression that Blair's premiership had brought further estrangement between the UK and 'Europe' was enhanced by the growing gulf between member states which had adopted the euro and those, like Britain, which had not. In June 2003 the Treasury announced that it was still premature for Britain to join the eurozone, since the five tests set out by Gordon Brown had not been satisfied. While the UK continued to play an important role in decision-making – even in economic matters – its exclusion from discussions relating to the currency symbolised and cemented its distance from 'the heart of Europe'. Above all, the notion that Britain's best hope to exercise influence was to disrupt the alliance between France and Germany now seemed increasingly tenuous.

This was not an ideal context for Britain's engagement with the process, instigated in 2001, of drawing up a European constitution. This was deemed necessary because the EU was due to expand to 25 member states in 2004, requiring reform of key procedures (in particular the rules applying to qualified majority voting in the Council of Ministers). However, for some observers, the prospect of a constitutional convention evoked the spirit of Philadelphia and the Founding Fathers of 1787. Such an event could mark a decisive moment in the process of European integration.

The Constitutional Treaty, which was signed by all 25 member states in October 2004, was certainly not the stuff of Eurosceptic nightmares. For example, there would be a single spokesperson on foreign policy, but he or she would only act on instructions arising from talks between the individual member states. There would also be a President of the European Council, in place of the existing arrangement where the position rotated between the member states. However, the person chosen would serve for a maximum of five years and, again, would have quite limited scope for independent action. The EU's areas of policy competence were expanded but not significantly; and the British made clear their reservations about a proposed Charter of Fundamental Rights. In most member states the draft constitution was criticised because it seemed to offer too many concessions to British sensitivities on a range of key issues (Riddell, 2005, 375).

In itself, the expansion of the EU to 25 members was a success for Britain, which had consistently pressed for enlargement. However, the thinking behind this stratagem was that a larger EU would be less susceptible to centralising tendencies: the more members, the more difficult it would be to reach agreement on any controversial matter. The constitutional process could thus be regarded as a cautionary tale, teaching Britain to be more careful what it wished for. Even before the final text of the original Constitutional Treaty was agreed, Blair announced that Britain would follow several other nation states in holding a referendum prior to ratification. Although this gambit dismayed Blair's pro-European colleagues, a referendum could have given him the chance to sell 'Europe' to the British people, rushing around the country delivering sermons to the stubbornly unconverted. The opportunity never knocked. Within a few days in May–June 2005 the French and the Dutch rejected the Constitutional Treaty in their own referendums. The fully fledged constitution – which, in typical EU style, was expressed in words which implied that all European citizens shared a common federal dream – was duly replaced by a humble treaty (the Treaty of Lisbon), which contained many of the same proposals but lacked the awe-inspiring majesty of the original. This was ratified by Britain without a referendum after Blair's departure from Downing Street.

Labour's third term

Blair was returned to office for a third and final time in May 2005. Once again, his party secured a large majority – 66 seats – but this could not conceal a sharp decline in Labour support. As usual, few voters regarded foreign policy as a key consideration when making their choices. Nevertheless, it was obvious that Iraq had done lasting damage to Blair's image, and the Liberal Democrats, who won a record tally of 62 seats, clearly benefited from the disillusion of many erstwhile Labour supporters. Prior to the election, Blair announced that it would be his last as Prime Minister; if re-elected, he would complete a third term, without contemplating a fourth. After the election he could turn his thoughts to two significant dates in the first days of July: the gathering of the G8 group of leading industrial nations in Scotland and the vote of the International Olympic Committee (IOC) to choose the host city for the 2012 summer games.

The events provided an opportunity for the government to reconnect with some of its first-term themes. The meeting of the G8 at Gleneagles was a chance for Blair to re-emphasise the ethical dimension to foreign policy, which had been obscured by the post-9/11 security agenda. The candidacy of London to be the Olympic venue for 2012 recalled Blair's early rhetoric, when he had talked about Britain becoming a 'young country' projecting an image of modernity and multiculturalism around the world. After eight stressful years in office Blair had lost the youthful look which had inspired his original nickname of 'Bambi'. However, the possibility of hosting the Olympics could boost national morale and refute the idea that Britain's soft power had been dissipated by its role in the Iraq War.

The planning for the G8 had started prior to the election. Blair set ambitious targets for the meeting, focusing on climate change and development in Africa. This was always going to be a difficult agenda to agree with the US because of the widespread scepticism in the Republican Party about the scientific evidence that human activity was responsible for changes in the global climate. As such, while the subject was raised in pre-G8 meetings in Washington, the greatest emphasis was placed on reaching agreement on Africa. For Africa, which in his speech to the 2001 Labour Party conference Blair had described as 'a scar on the conscience of the world', there was a two-part policy: debt forgiveness for the poorest nations on the continent coupled with a pledge by the G8 to increase development aid to the continent to $50 billion by 2010.

This additional funding would be aimed at improving governance, education and healthcare for the poorest. To support this policy pledge the government mobilised civil society, co-opting the Make Poverty History campaign that had emerged out of the work of church groups and aid organisations in the UK. The weekend before the gathering a rock concert was held in Hyde Park and broadcast around the world. Organised by individuals involved in the landmark 1985 Live Aid concert, the Live 8/Make Poverty History event called on world leaders to grasp the nettle and agree a deal for Africa. The Gleneagles G8 did produce an agreement on Africa, along with a compromise on climate change that could be endorsed by the Bush administration.

Blair did not attend the concert in Hyde Park as he was on his way to Singapore to campaign on behalf of the London Olympic bid. This was the culmination of a two-year process. London had started as an outsider but now appeared to be reeling in the front-running French, who were promoting the claims of Paris. There were arguments against Blair's attendance in Singapore. If the London bid failed it might undermine his authority at the crucial G8 gathering. However, the organisers of the London bid thought Blair could make the difference, and so he travelled across the world to lobby on their behalf. They made an ill-assorted bidding team: the Prime Minister, the former Olympian turned Conservative politician Sebastian Coe and the left-wing London Mayor, Ken Livingstone. However, the unlikely combination worked. Coe was in awe of Blair's skills of persuasion, as the Prime Minister converted a large number of IOC delegates to support the British bid. Coe felt that, 'if anybody was put on the planet to do this, it was him. As for those conversations, it was like watching a surgeon at work' (Coe, 2012, 364).

When it was announced that London had beaten Paris to host the games, French commentators were quick to criticise Britain's lobbying style. However, the efforts in Singapore and Gleneagles demonstrated that Britain retained significant soft power, capable of making a positive global impression in creative sectors, be it the arts, music or sports, and possessing institutional and diplomatic power that could be projected through bodies like the IOC. If this was a moment to reflect on what British foreign policy could have been, had 9/11 not taken place, it was tragically short-lived.

Terrorism in London

The morning after the announcement that London would host the 2012 Olympics, a coordinated attack was launched on central London by four suicide bombers. Fifty-two people were killed and 770 injured. Two weeks later another mass bombing was attempted, as five terrorists set out with devices across London. This attempt failed, and in an atmosphere of heightened tension a Brazilian man was shot and killed at Stockwell tube station by police officers in the mistaken belief that he was about to launch another attack.

In the aftermath of the attacks in London some were quick to apportion blame. George Galloway, a former Labour MP who had been elected as a member of the anti-war Respect party in 2005, claimed that the attacks on London were 'the price for war on Iraq'. The leader of the Liberal Democrats, Charles Kennedy, was more circumspect, not seeing a direct 'causal link' between the two but recognising that conflict in Iraq could be utilised by terrorists 'to increase resentment and as fodder for recruitment'. A year later the official government report into the events of July 2005 sought to determine the motivation of the bombers. The 'best indications' were found in the 'martyr's video' left by Mohammed Sidique Khan, the group's leader:

> Your democratically elected governments continuously perpetuate atrocities against my people all over the world. And your support of them makes you directly responsible, just as I am directly responsible for protecting and avenging my Muslim brothers and sisters. Until we feel security, you will be our targets. And until you stop the bombing, gassing, imprisonment and torture of my people we will not stop this fight. We are at war and I am a soldier. Now you too will taste the reality of this situation.
> (House of Commons, 2006, 19)

While debates about 'radicalisation' are complex, it would be foolhardy to reject the connection between intervention in Iraq and a serious new dilemma for the British state.

Blair's end

The last months of Blair's premiership were, perhaps appropriately, characterised by undignified faction fights between the Prime Minister's supporters and those who had been working to dislodge him since 1994, when he, rather than their own favourite, Gordon Brown, seized the Labour leadership. The policy differences between 'Blairites' and 'Brownites' were more profound than the disputes between Lewis Carroll's Tweedledum and Tweedledee – but only slightly. The real basis was a personal antipathy between the two principals, which grew increasingly difficult to conceal. Like Winston Churchill contemplating the succession of Anthony Eden, Blair postponed his retirement at least in part because of doubts concerning the aspirant's aptitude for the job. But other motives were at work – in Blair's case, presumably, a desire to depart amid cheering crowds rather than a throng of protestors denouncing him as a war criminal.

The pace of events quickened after May 2006, when Labour's poor performance in local elections prompted Blair to reshuffle his ministerial team. He decided to move Jack Straw from the FCO, apparently because he thought a five-year stint was sufficient. Straw's successor, Britain's first female Foreign Secretary, Margaret Beckett, seemed 'stunned rather than elated [by] the promotion'; for his part, Straw was dismayed (Blair, 2010, 594). If Blair's assessment of these reactions is accurate, it confirms the impression that the period since Straw became Foreign Secretary in 2001 had denuded the FCO of the residual prestige, in Whitehall and beyond, which had been guaranteed to make an incoming minister the happiest person in London.

Weeks later conflict broke out in the Middle East between Israel and the Hezbollah group of Shia militants, backed by Iran. In July 2006 Hezbollah launched attacks in which several Israeli soldiers were killed; Israel, in typical fashion, retaliated with air strikes, followed by a ground incursion across its border with Lebanon. Public opinion in Britain (and in Europe more generally) has been tolerant of 'robust' Israeli responses to attacks on its territory, presumably because (for various geographical and historical reasons) Israel has good reasons to feel vulnerable. On this occasion, however, there was a widespread view that Israel had exploited its military advantages to the extent that it no longer seemed the 'underdog'. Overall, the month-long conflict is estimated to have killed more than a thousand Lebanese citizens and Hezbollah operatives, against fewer than 200 Israelis.

True to form, Blair resisted pressure from his own party and refused to call for Israeli restraint. After his departure from office he tried to rationalise his position, with results which were equally tortuous and tenuous (Blair, 2010, 397, 399, 596). On the flight to another of his notoriously luxurious holidays, Blair reflected on the new evidence of his alienation from informed public opinion in Britain. Having once basked in public approval for every decision he took, he now reassured himself that he must be right because his decisions were unpopular (Blair, 2010, 603).

However, after hearing his response to the clashes between Israel and Hezbollah, the Labour Party had decided that it had lived with this kind of logic for long enough. Blair was allowed to notch up ten years in Number 10 but was finally compelled to change his residence on 27 June 2007.

However, far from giving himself up entirely to the lucrative speaking tours which pad out the pensions of ex-premiers, Blair still felt that he could be a positive influence on the global stage. Within hours of his resignation he was appointed Middle East Peace Envoy on behalf of the UN, the EU, the US and Russia. This mission brought to mind a comparison with the Emperor Caligula's decision to make his horse a Senator, which had been used to ridicule Harold Macmillan's appointment of Lord Home as Foreign Secretary back in 1960; but Caligula's horse had not previously exhibited a tendency to apply double standards in relation to disputes within the Roman Empire. Blair gave up the role eight years later; as could easily have been predicted in advance, any progress he had made fell into the 'imperceptible' category.

Two years later Blair was once again at the centre of a flurry of speculation. The EU's Lisbon Treaty, which replaced the still-born constitution, had enhanced the role of President of the European Council (though not as much as Eurosceptics tried to argue; see above). As EU member states prepared to make the first Presidential appointment, Blair was strongly tipped. David Miliband, Britain's Foreign Secretary since Blair's resignation, lobbied on behalf of his former leader, arguing that 'Europe' needed 'someone who, when he or she lands in Beijing or Washington or Moscow, the traffic does need to stop and talks do need to begin at a very, very high level' (www.telegraph.co.uk/news/worldnews/europe/eu/6430574/David-Miliband-backs-Tony-Blair-as-EU-president.html).

Blair's candidacy was supported by the French President, Nicolas Sarkozy, but the German Chancellor, Angela Merkel, was far less keen. Blair would have been a problematic President irrespective of the personal qualities or baggage that he brought with him. Rather than seeking a leader who could 'stop the traffic' – or, according to his numerous critics, cause a series of unpleasant accidents – EU leaders were looking for a candidate who would not rock the boat even if he was sponsored by a torpedo manufacturer. For Merkel, there were specific problems – the legacy of bitter disagreements over Iraq and Blair's failure to coax Britons into accepting the single currency. The Belgian Christian Democrat Herman Van Rompuy was duly appointed instead. At least the Eurosceptic press chose to present the decision as a personal affront to Blair, rather than yet another slap in the face for Britain.

Conclusions

Margaret Thatcher once nominated the creation of New Labour as her greatest achievement; and Tony Blair certainly proved to be a more faithful follower than

John Major. Unlike Major, Blair was a Cold War warrior in domestic politics, with an unquenchable hatred of 'socialism' or anything that resembled it. While Major had reacted against Thatcher's 'presidential' approach to government, Blair embraced it and pushed it much further. Like Thatcher – but again in contrast to Major, who at least had gained a glimpse of life inside the FCO – he entered office with no experience of foreign policy and nugatory knowledge or understanding of history. He rightly perceived that Thatcher had made an avoidable mistake by antagonising Britain's European partners. Nevertheless, he ended up doing the same thing, while lacking Thatcher's excuse of being the product of the wartime generation and thus the bearer of some ineffaceable prejudices.

Blair, however, was profoundly affected by a war – in his case, the Cold War. Born in 1953, he was in his tenth year at the time of the Cuban Missile Crisis, and the ill-fated US intervention in Vietnam had provided the political context of his formative years. Nevertheless, Western liberalism had apparently held its own during the darkest days, and as a young MP who was first elected in the immediate aftermath of the Falklands War he could appreciate the importance of the 'special relationship' in both spiritual and material terms.

Blair, in short, believed that he could transcend Britain's post-war dilemma and give the impression of committing his country both to 'Europe' and the US, despite his obvious preference for the latter over the former. As we have seen, the adoption of this position was what some people might call a 'no-brainer', especially for someone who was cushioned against the continuing political potency of the post-war narrative by an overwhelming Parliamentary majority. In the circumstances of 1997 he could improve on Thatcher's record by sounding positive about European integration, on the assumption that this would proceed upon lines which were acceptable to America. This would entail a reduction in the kind of economic intervention which the US disliked, i.e. the creation of a genuinely free-market EU, as well as the development of increased cooperation in the field of defence, which would allow a reduction of US commitments in Europe.

Blair's strategy was working reasonably well – apparently surviving the switch from a Democrat to a Republican in the White House – until terrorist hijackers launched the 9/11 attack. Blair grabbed this opportunity to demonstrate Britain's commitment to the 'special relationship', which had flagged a little under Clinton and could not be guaranteed to survive the Presidency of George W Bush, whose father had flirted with Germany. Blair's over-excitement was more understandable, since, apart from the opportunity it presented for him to outshine other US allies on the oratorical front, 9/11 opened the possibility that America would act in accordance with the interventionist doctrine he had promulgated at Chicago two years earlier.

Unfortunately for Blair, his supportive gestures after 9/11 proved too intoxicatingly successful for him to reflect on two immediate problems. First, could he be sure that other European leaders were equally anxious to hand George W Bush a blank cheque to prosecute a War on Terror, wherever that might lead? During the Cold War, Western European countries had generally complied with American wishes; but in the post-Soviet age they might feel able to be offer more selective support. The downfall of the Soviet Union and the collapse of its satellite states might have given them a new freedom to consult their own national interests before taking foreign policy plunges. It seems that, when making his own calculations, Tony Blair gave insufficient attention to this possibility – or, rather, that he assumed they would follow his own example, and behave as if the interest of their countries lay in unthinking obedience to the American line.

As we have seen, there is evidence which strongly suggests that Tony Blair favoured regime change in Iraq long before 9/11. On the balance of probability, this arose chiefly from a moral distaste for Saddam Hussein's tyrannical rule more than any perceived threat to British interests; after all, Saddam's attempt to establish a cult of personality was one of the few remaining replicas of the Soviet style which had outlived the Cold War. Yet in order to gain acceptance from a largely inert British public for an onslaught on Iraq on a scale which would eject Saddam from power, Blair knew that he would have to provide evidence of a tangible threat to British interests. Indeed, on the basis of his 1999 Chicago speech, Blair himself would have needed something more than a moral justification if he was to join the American attack. In terms of IR theory, Blair wanted to go to war on Liberal grounds, but he had to reckon with a British public which was more likely to be impressed by evidence which would convince a Realist. Thus it was necessary to produce documentary evidence (in the form of the dossiers) to give concrete support for a position which Blair had already accepted. But since those dossiers contained material which was based on dubious 'intelligence', Blair's hopes ultimately hinged on the old adage that 'nothing succeeds like success'; if Saddam could swiftly be toppled and a democratic regime installed in his place no one would inquire too closely into the process which led to war. For Blair, it would be like Kosovo and Sierra Leone, albeit on a grander (and more risky) scale.

Blair's motives, however, will remain a topic of debate for as long as the Iraq War is remembered in Britain. Even if one accepts that he committed Britain to the intervention chiefly because of moral considerations, there is also the possibility that he was reinforced in that view because he genuinely thought that Britain's national interest lay in backing the US administration of the day in pursuit of what it perceived as *its* interests. Undoubtedly, his personal judgement was affected by a sense that, in articulating the American position after 9/11, he was outdoing Churchill and Thatcher as an exemplar of the 'special relationship', whether or not it turned out that he had only exploited a brief interlude of shared peril and sacrifice. Probably the safest conclusion is that after 9/11 Blair quickly realised that Bush wanted to settle scores with Saddam and did not enquire too closely into his motives because the prospect of intervention made such good sense to him: it would rid the world of a hateful dictator as well as shoring up the 'special relationship'.

Whatever the best way of explaining Blair's policy in terms of IR theory, it seems difficult to dispute that it failed both the Liberal test (of making the world a better place) and the Realist one (of advancing Britain's national interests). For obvious reasons, Blair (and a surprising number of his former ministerial colleagues) continued to argue that Saddam's removal had been (in the language of *1066 and All That*) a 'Good Thing'. The difficulty for his critics was (and is) that the task of refuting him invites a profitless plunge into the shoreless sea of counterfactuals. One can, at least, concede that toppling Hussein *might* have made Iraq (and the world) safer *if* it had been conducted by competent leaders who guessed in advance that the dismantling of the Iraqi army and key administrative structures might not be sensible.

As far as direct British interests are concerned, it would only have been natural for Blair to expect some 'trickle-down' benefits from the oil-soaked banquet anticipated by the neo-conservatives in the Bush team. Probably, he also assumed that British forces would acquit themselves with typical courage and efficiency, enhancing the country's military prestige. There was, though, no economic pay-off; and although British troops did indeed perform many tasks with distinction, their substandard equipment drew attention to Britain's meagre resources, while some of their activities generated allegations of brutality. Damning reports of British complicity in US 'rendition' and torture programmes also damaged perceptions of Britain globally, although the implications for the country's sovereignty were probably missed by most of the people who suffered from the common delusion that violations of British constitutional and legal norms could only emanate from the EU. In Iraq itself Britain's role in the Middle East had attracted mixed reviews from the time of the Sykes–Picot agreement of 1916, if not before. Its reputation within the region as a whole was certainly not enhanced by the American-led intervention, although its relationships with various unsavoury regimes were not seriously affected. These had limited potential to cause embarrassment, because other leaders had not been demonised as Saddam had been; nevertheless, there was a potential for embarrassment here which Blair bequeathed to his successors.

The main downside for Britain, however, arose from the consideration which had helped to persuade Blair to embark on the adventure in the first place – that is, the need to reinforce the 'special relationship'. Blair himself, and by extension Britain as a whole, was widely regarded as acting like a 'poodle' to Bush and the US. At the G8 Summit held in St Petersburg in July 2006 Bush greeted his faithful friend with the salutation 'Yo, Blair, what are you doing?'. In his memoirs Blair expressed wonderment that Britons regarded this style of address as an insult to their country. It was, in fact, a sign of the 'total intimacy' between the two – it was 'a joke; but unfortunately only I got it!' (Blair, 2010, 595–6). It is unlikely that any of Blair's predecessors would have sniggered if a US President had accosted them with the words 'Yo, Attlee', or even 'Yo, Thatcher' (although if John F Kennedy had said 'Yo, Macmillan', the latter might have written in his diary that 'one was flattered by the implication that we Greeks are equally conversant with the kind of jargon adopted by contemporary Roman adolescents'). What Blair failed to appreciate was that his critics regarded the 'total intimacy' as demeaning in itself and thus something of a joke at Britain's expense. Certainly, those who clung to the view that Britain had acted honourably with regard to Iraq, only to be let down by bungling Americans, would not be impressed by evidence that the two leaders were still on such jocular terms after so many misadventures.

While some of his critics insisted that Blair was guilty of war crimes, it was open to others to echo Napoleon's colleague, who after one of the Emperor's maladroit decisions exclaimed that 'it's worse than a crime, it's a mistake'. This chapter has focused heavily on Tony Blair, for the adequate reason that after 9/11 this Prime Minister took a conscious decision to shunt the FCO professionals into the sidelines and (even more than Thatcher in her later years) assume direction of foreign policy decisions. It remained to be seen whether his successor, Gordon Brown, would profit from the numerous lessons inadvertently taught by Blair since that fleeting interlude after 9/11, when he may have convinced himself that through sheer eloquence combined with moral example he had taken on the leadership of the free world.

Heirs to Blair and 'Brexiteers', 2007–17

11

Introduction

The relationship between Tony Blair and Gordon Brown, which dominated British politics between 1997 and 2010, was dogged by two major misunderstandings. The first was created by the protagonists themselves at a meeting before the party's 1994 leadership election. Brown had been persuaded not to stand, despite his superior claims on paper. He was convinced after the meeting that Blair had promised to step down as party leader after a limited period and would do his best to ensure that Brown would succeed him. All one can say about this much debated incident is that a promise of that kind could hardly be considered to be binding regardless of circumstances – which, indeed, would have been absurd in a country where political fortunes could be transformed in the course of a few hours – and that Blair acted in future as if the 'deal' had been a guarantee that Brown would enjoy considerable influence over domestic policy, rather than an agreed leadership transition.

The second misunderstanding affected media pundits and Labour supporters who were not close associates of either Brown or Blair. These observers tended (especially after New Labour took power in 1997) to relate the ill-concealed estrangement between the party's dominant figures to an ongoing ideological debate. In short, Blair and his supporters were identified with New Labour (vaguely 'progressive' but strongly supportive of free-market economics), while Brown was seen as the natural leader for the remaining advocates of 'old' Labour (suspicious of capitalism, committed to wealth redistribution in the interests of equality). In reality, although Blair and Brown did disagree over policy (notably, in relation to the desirability of adopting the euro), their feud was primarily personal. Certainly, those who hoped that Brown's (long-delayed) accession would produce a dramatic change in British foreign policy could only do so if they chose to overlook Brown's apparent determination to associate himself with Blair's various initiatives. After all, while Blair has been dubbed an 'Accidental American' (Naughtie, 2004), Brown's love affair with Britain's transatlantic ally was a matter of conscious choice. In any case, his brief spell as Prime Minister was bound to be coloured by the legacy of the interventions in Afghanistan and Iraq; the fact that these momentous issues were rivalled by the global financial crisis which began in 2007 served to prevent Brown from establishing a new foreign policy line, whatever his intentions.

Timeline of domestic political developments

August–September 2007 First symptoms of effect of global 'credit crunch'
May 2010 Inconclusive general election: formation of Conservative–Liberal Democrat coalition government under David Cameron
January 2013 Cameron's Bloomberg Speech signals capitulation to right-wing press and Conservative Eurosceptics and acceptance of referendum on EU membership before 2017
August 2013 Government loses House of Commons vote on military action in Syria by 285 to 272
June 2015 General election: Conservatives win a majority of 12
September 2015 Labour leadership election won by Jeremy Corbyn, vociferous critic of War on Terror and opponent of nuclear 'deterrent'
June 2016 'Leave' narrowly wins referendum on UK membership of EU
June 2016 Cameron resigns as Prime Minister; succeeded by Theresa May on 11 July
June 2017 May's Conservatives lose overall majority in snap general election

---

No Prime Minister is an exact replica of his or her predecessor, and this chapter will explore differences between the foreign policy outlooks of Blair and Brown. However, it would not be fanciful to characterise Brown as the 'heir to Blair' in this field, due to a continuity of constraints. In 2010 Brown's party was defeated at the polls and was succeeded by a coalition between the Conservatives and the Liberal Democrats. The coalition Prime Minister, David Cameron, had actually claimed the mantle of 'heir to Blair' in an unguarded conversation with journalists before winning the Conservative leadership in 2005. It has been reported that, long after public support for Blair's foreign policy had dissipated, Cameron continued to seek his advice (Oborne, 2015). Again, the contention that Cameron's foreign policy showed considerable continuity with that of Blair will be explored in this chapter.

One point of similarity can, however, be established at the outset. Blair and Cameron both became Prime Minister without serving a ministerial apprenticeship of any kind; and before rising to the leadership of their respective parties neither had served as Shadow Foreign Secretary. By contrast, as Chancellor of the Exchequer between 1997 and 2007, Gordon Brown obviously exerted considerable influence over the *implementation* of foreign policy decisions – all too often, his critics alleged, by denying adequate resources to Britain's armed forces. However, influencing policy from the outside is very different from taking direct responsibility for the policy itself. The classic illustration is the case of Harold Macmillan, whose view of the Foreign Office and its decisions underwent a sudden transformation when he left it for the Treasury in December 1955.

It would be wrong, however, to conclude on this basis that aspirant Prime Ministers were no longer interested in foreign policy. Rather, if anything it suggested that the post of Foreign Secretary had slipped from its presumed status as one of the great offices of state, whose tenure made the incumbent an obvious candidate for the biggest job of all should it fall vacant. Long before the advent of Blair, the 'Presidentialisation' of the British system gave the Prime Minister considerable potential to take the leading role in foreign policy – indeed, if a Prime Minister was reluctant to do so, pressures from the media and other sources would force her or him to push the Foreign Secretary into the background. Learning, as Foreign Secretary, to play second fiddle in one's area of policy responsibility could not be considered to be sound training for a subsequent leadership role. Margaret Thatcher had sensed the institutional weakness of the Foreign Secretary and made life almost impossible for the occupants of the office after the resignation of Lord Carrington in 1982. John Major, who knew something about the FCO, tried his best to delegate decision-making to Douglas Hurd (with whom, in any case, he tended to agree). Blair and his heirs reverted to the Thatcher model, with results which will be explored in this chapter.

The Brown interlude

The chances of New Labour maintaining its winning electoral streak would have been enhanced if Gordon Brown had used his belated accession as an opportunity to make a quick and clean break from his predecessor's foreign-policy commitments. Of the two major conflicts in Afghanistan and Iraq, the latter was the more deeply unpopular in Britain; and Blair had already announced plans for a phased withdrawal. However, Brown knew that he would face pressure from key allies to maintain Britain's presence in the Basra province, where existing instability was likely to increase. Given the state of domestic opinion, the only viable option was to act in a way which, while satisfying no one, was likely to cause the minimum damage. Accordingly, Brown expressed a willingness to learn from the mistakes of 2002–3, and in 2009 he established an inquiry, under the distinguished former civil servant Sir John Chilcot, with broader terms of reference than the previous Hutton and Butler reports. British combat operations in Iraq ended in April 2009. Brown's assertion that 'we leave Iraq a better place' was highly questionable, but it was difficult to see what else he could say (Watt, 2008).

Afghanistan was even more problematic for Brown. Initial British involvement had been far less controversial; and, although no one could claim that the intervention had been an unqualified success, it was easier to identify some positive results. However, Brown became Prime Minister at a time when Iraq and Afghanistan were beginning to merge in the mind of the average voter, producing a general feeling of war fatigue even among those who had once been enthusiastic about both ventures. This mood was accentuated in 2009, when more than a hundred British service personnel were killed in Afghanistan – only slightly fewer than the total British death toll during the whole of the country's involvement in Iraq. The following year was almost equally bad, and, aside from fatalities, more than 2,000 service personnel were wounded, often being maimed for life by improvised explosive devices (IEDs) which, rather than Saddam's WMDs, were a constant source of danger. Brown was heavily criticised for the government's failure to protect soldiers adequately against these weapons – an allegation which stuck, since he had carried the ultimate responsibility for defence spending throughout the period since 9/11. In November 2009 Brown announced that British troops would stay in Afghanistan until the security situation in the country was sufficiently stable. At the end of 2010 there were still around 9,000 British soldiers in Afghanistan.

Brown's dilemmas concerning Iraq and Afghanistan added to a natural interest in the fate of the 'special relationship' in the wake of the feverish encounter between Blair and Bush. In November 2007 Brown assured an audience in the City of London that:

> We will not allow people to separate us from the United States of America in dealing with the common challenges that we face around the world. I think people have got to remember that the relationship between Britain and America and between a British prime minister and an American president is built on the things that we share, the same enduring values about the importance of liberty, opportunity, the dignity of the individual.
>
> (Reynolds, 2007)

The emphasis on moral values in this speech was characteristic of Brown, who presided over a period of increased tension within the UK and (not least because of his own distinctive British/Scottish identity) was anxious to establish a coherent sense of Britishness on the basis of a shared ethical outlook. However, in foreign policy terms – and especially in the context of the 'special relationship' – this preoccupation raised serious questions. Neither Britain nor the US could persuasively claim that its actions during the War on Terror had been based upon an unshakable adherence to 'liberty' or 'the dignity of the individual'. At Guantanamo Bay the Americans had showed a willingness to deviate from these supposedly 'enduring values'. Apart from instances of misconduct by individual soldiers, the British had collaborated in the practice of 'extraordinary rendition', whereby terrorist suspects were transported to locations where they could be interrogated without the protection accorded by countries which recognised 'enduring values'.

The other arresting feature of Brown's speech was his presentation of the 'special relationship' in personal terms, as if the interactions between Presidents and Prime Ministers were indeed the key element in an alliance which, in reality, was based on multi-layered cooperation. Brown's choice of words can only be explained by his anxiety to move away from the mood-music of Blair–Bush. Bush, indeed, had been warned about Brown's personal idiosyncrasies before the 2007 transition. Anyone in Washington who longed for a continuation of the good old days when Blair and Bush had burbled happily about their favourite toothpaste was quickly disabused when Brown eschewed Christian names at press conferences and referred to his fellow leader as 'Mr President'.

Just before stepping down as Prime Minister, Tony Blair had signalled his acceptance of Brown as his successor by referring to his 'clunking fist'. In his diplomacy, however, Brown's chief characteristic was his cack-handedness. His unsubtle exhibition of personal coolness towards George Bush was echoed in his attempts to appear semi-disapproving of China's human rights record (by failing to appear at the opening of the 2008 Beijing Olympics then materialising for the closing ceremony) and to avoid the public signature of the EU's Lisbon Treaty (he was the only one of 27 European heads of government to find an 'opt-out' from the ceremony, appending his name later, in very unsplendid isolation).

These maladroit genuflections towards public opinion apparently justified the misgivings of Labour strategists who, back in 1994, had identified Tony Blair rather than Brown as their party's best hope. Brown's supporters could continue to argue that his problems were chiefly presentational and thus superficial, at a time when the world was in desperate need of leaders who could provide real *substance*. Unfortunately, rather than treating political spin with the contempt it deserved, Brown seemed to rival Blair himself in his obsession with presentation; it was just that he was very bad at it. Like most British Prime Ministers of the post-war period, he did not bring all of his misfortunes on himself. If Hillary Clinton had succeeded George W Bush in the White House, for example, Brown might have been able to establish cordial relations. As it was, for various reasons Barack Obama (who beat Clinton to the Democratic nomination for the 2008 election) treated his country's continuing alliance with Britain as a regrettable historical hangover. After visiting Washington in 2009, among other gifts Brown presented Obama with a pen-holder carved from the timbers of a ship which had been used by the British in the nineteenth century to extirpate the slave trade. In return, Obama bestowed on Brown a collection of 25 DVDs, which the British Prime Minister could have acquired at any car boot sale in his homeland.

This deliberate snub was all the more piquant because by 2009 Brown could claim more constructive achievement than Obama was to manage in his eight-year Presidency. Within weeks of Brown's ascent to the top of Westminster's 'greasy pole', evidence emerged of pressure on Britain's banking system. The problem had originated in the US, whose financial institutions had offered housing loans with insufficient attention to the likelihood of repayment. In the ensuing financial crisis banks across the world were reluctant to extend credit either to each other or to their clients. This was the kind of problem which played to Gordon Brown's strengths; while other world leaders dithered, he argued forcefully for a programme of global reflation, and his intervention was applauded both at the time and in hindsight. In the *New York Times* the Nobel Prize-winning economist Paul Krugman wrote that Brown and his Chancellor Alistair Darling 'have defined the character of the worldwide rescue effort, with other wealthy nations playing catch-up' (Krugman, 2008). However, even those who claimed to understand the complexities of the world economy were divided in their assessments of Brown's performance during the crisis; and since this constituency was thinly represented among the British electorate, the Prime Minister was never likely to gain much tangible benefit. Among Britain's post-war Prime Ministers, only Gordon Brown could have turned the episode into a humiliating gaffe, when in a garbled response to a Parliamentary question in December 2008 he apparently claimed credit for 'saving the world'. In fact, while Brown had certainly proved his mettle in his response to the economic crisis, his policies had helped to ensure that the crisis was particularly damaging for the UK. Not only had he lightened the regulatory load on British banks while he was Chancellor, but he had openly boasted about this irresponsible approach.

Some admirers of New Labour might still wonder 'what might have been' if only Tony Blair and Gordon Brown had been able to control their personal animosity. However, if one accepts that in 1994 these two ambitious politicians had decided to carve up future government policy, so that Brown had ultimate control of the domestic front and Blair had a free hand elsewhere, the only conclusion is that they proved equally adept in throwing away their advantages. When Brown became Prime Minister he had to clear up the foreign policy mess left by Blair and then was forced to address the consequences of the mistakes he had made as Chancellor. In domestic terms the various problems bequeathed by Blair and Brown to each other meant that the 2010 general election was a good contest for Labour to lose. But, contrary to the usual swings of the British electoral pendulum, there was no outright winner this time. Instead, Brown's government was succeeded by a Conservative–Liberal Democrat coalition, headed by David Cameron.

The foreign policy of 'liberal Conservatism'

When senior Conservatives and Liberal Democrats began to negotiate a coalition agreement in the wake of the inconclusive 2010 general election, it was easy to suppose that foreign policy would provide a major stumbling block. After all, the two parties had been on opposite sides of the debate over intervention in Iraq, and, arguably, the critical stance of the Liberal Democrats had been the main reason why, after the 2005 general election, the party could begin serious preparations for taking part in a British government for the first time since 1945. Cameron, by contrast, had voted for war – albeit 'grudgingly, unhappily, unenthusiastically' (Cameron, 2003).

Since then, however, the Conservatives had accepted that their support for the war had been based on flawed intelligence. In any case, the withdrawal of British forces from Iraq in 2009 effectively neutralised the issue. The 2010 Conservative manifesto described the continuing mission in Afghanistan as 'vital to our national security'. For their part, although the Liberal Democrats expressed a desire to end the mission before 2015, this objective was dependent on the stabilisation of Afghanistan.

Afghanistan and Iraq inevitably raised the question of the 'special relationship', and here the two parties could be expected to diverge. Certainly, the rhetoric was different. Addressing the British–American Project on the fifth anniversary of the attack on the World Trade Center, David Cameron denounced anti-Americanism and expressed an attachment to the Atlantic alliance that was both 'instinctive' and 'passionate'. For their part, in their 2010 manifesto the Liberal Democrats referred to 'the dangers of a subservient relationship with the US that neglects Britain's core values and interests'. However, after affirming his belief in the 'special relationship' Cameron had cautioned that:

> we will serve neither our own, nor America's, nor the world's interests if we are seen as America's unconditional associate in every endeavour. Our duty is to our citizens, and to our own conception of what is right in the world.
> (Cameron, 2006)

Although the 2010 Conservative manifesto included the phrase 'special relationship', it did so in reference to India rather than the US.

In any case, by 2010 the relationship with America was far less controversial in Britain, and the occupant of the White House, Obama, was as anxious as

Cameron and the Liberal Democrat leader, Nick Clegg, to bring a satisfactory end to the adventurism of Bush and Blair. In the published Coalition Agreement – an unprecedented document, essentially a manifesto for an election which had already taken place – the two parties spoke of maintaining a 'strong, close and frank relationship with the US'. The agreement also covered the subject of nuclear weapons, which had always been highly controversial among Liberal Democrat activists. The coalition reached a compromise on Conservative terms; the 'deterrent' would remain, and Trident would be renewed with due attention to 'value for money'. Liberal Democrats would be free 'to make the case for alternatives' (HM Government, 2010, 20, 16). In practice, during the coalition period this 'freedom to differ' meant that Liberal Democrats accepted Trident but argued that the submarine fleet could be reduced from the existing four vessels.

The really awkward area for the negotiating teams was always going to be 'Europe'. Unlike their two main rivals, the Liberal Democrats had always been positive about European integration, to the extent that many Conservatives regarded them as 'Eurofanatics'. This was in keeping with a general trend in Conservative politics, traceable to Mrs Thatcher's 1988 Bruges Speech, to regard anyone who was prepared to acknowledge positive features in the EU as 'unBritish'. Cameron himself was a genuine Eurosceptic, i.e. consistent with his pragmatic approach to most questions, he was prepared to base his decisions on the likely practical consequences of a proposal, whether or not it emanated from Brussels. However, in order to win the Conservative leadership in 2005, and to secure his position afterwards, he had made promises which were calculated to mollify members of his party who saw the EU as a conspiracy to diminish Britain's influence in the world, if not to destroy its identity. Thus Cameron had promised not to accept the Lisbon Treaty unless authorised to do so by a referendum. This 'cast-iron' pledge had to abandoned when the 27 EU member states ratified the treaty (after Ireland, which had rejected Lisbon in a 2008 referendum, reversed this decision in 2009). Cameron had to content himself with the fulfilment of another promise, this time to pull Conservative MEPs out of the main centre-right EU grouping, the European People's Party (EPP), on the grounds that it was insufficiently 'sceptical'.

On taking the leadership in 2005, Cameron had burnished his anti-European credentials by bringing the former Conservative leader William Hague into his team as Shadow Foreign Secretary. Hague had won the party leadership in 1997 thanks at least in part to strong support from Lady Thatcher, and in the 2001 general election campaign he had made antipathy towards the EU, rather than the domestic issues which mattered most to voters, a central theme of his speeches. However, by 2005 Hague – now, at just 44 years of age, considered an elder statesman – was far less pugilistic and could be considered, along with Cameron, as an unusual example of Conservative Euro-pragmatism. Insider accounts of the coalition talks suggest that the European issue was easily dealt with, but this should not obscure its importance to the overall deal. The Liberal Democrats were well aware that their adherence to the coalition would help Cameron stand up to the irreconcilable elements within his own party, and to that extent they were indispensable to him. On the other hand, if the Liberal Democrats refused to join a coalition and the eventual outcome was a minority Conservative government, Cameron might be forced into populist measures regarding the EU, causing lasting damage to Britain's (already uncertain) status within it. Thus, on European matters, the Liberal Democrats needed Cameron as much as he needed them; and the painless negotiations on the subject seemed to reflect the mutual recognition of these facts.

This amity on key foreign policy issues was underpinned by a considerable element of ideological convergence. Indeed, in his 2006 speech to the British–American Project Cameron had seemed to anticipate the possibility of a coalition with the Liberal Democrats by outlining a 'liberal Conservative' approach to international affairs, explaining that:

> I am a liberal conservative, rather than a neo-conservative. Liberal – because I support the aim of spreading freedom and democracy, and support humanitarian intervention. Conservative – because I recognise the complexities of human nature, and am sceptical of grand schemes to remake the world.
> (Cameron, 2006)

The pragmatic (or 'conservative') part of this formula might have been regarded with distaste by idealistic Liberal Democrats. However, the unusual circumstances of the Iraq War had turned many idealists into Realists, i.e. those who would have rejoiced if Iraqi citizens had truly been liberated from tyranny opposed the war because they deemed that Western-led action was unlikely to have that effect. In reality, Cameron's declaration of scepticism was designed to distance himself from the neo-conservatives who had imagined that the removal of Saddam would have triggered a series of benign, democratic revolutions throughout the Middle East.

Cameron's 'liberal Conservatism' suffused the relevant section of the 2010 Conservative manifesto – although, true to form, this appeared at the end of the document, under the impeccably Realist heading of 'Promote our national interest'. However, the manifesto referred to '*enlightened* national interest', which would provide justification for Cameron's promise to fulfil the long-standing UN target of spending at least 0.7 per cent of GDP on overseas aid. More generally, in the manifesto the Conservatives claimed that '[o]ur approach to foreign affairs is based on a belief in freedom, human rights and democracy'. This was considerably more laconic than the Liberal Democrat statement that '[w]e believe in freedom, justice, prosperity and human rights for all and will do all we can to work towards a world where these hopes become reality'; but it seemed to amount to pretty much the same sentiment. Above all, the wording of the manifestos implied that Cameron was trying to persuade his party to take a more 'liberal' view of the world, while Clegg, hoped to induce a realisation among his own party's supporters that power would necessitate compromise as well as providing an opportunity to promote radical change at home and abroad. Thus from very different points of departure the Conservatives and the Liberal Democrats had arrived at something like a philosophical consensus on foreign policy. This was probably just as well, since Clegg could be pretty sure that, under the coalition, effective control of key foreign policy decisions would lie with Cameron and Hague; as Deputy Prime Minister, his own sphere of influence would be in constitutional matters.

A 'networked world'

The emphasis on values, particularly concerning human rights, was identified by commentators as a new feature in Conservative foreign policy, suggesting that Cameron and Hague had been influenced by New Labour's approach (Beech, 2011). This certainly seems to be the case in respect of humanitarian intervention, which the 2010 Conservative manifesto endorsed 'when it is practical and necessary'. This, of course, was a direct echo of Blair's 1999 Chicago speech (Chapter 9), which had laid down a series of requirements before intervention could take place. Over Iraq, Blair had deviated from his own advice. It remained to be seen whether Cameron would be more prudent.

If New Labour's foreign policy record had been dominated by the War on Terror, Robin Cook's reference to an ethical dimension to foreign policy was still remembered as an expression of the government's initial aspirations. Subsequent developments made it unlikely that a Conservative would use that form of words, but senior figures in the party seemed to endorse the underlying sentiment. For example, in a key speech within weeks of taking office as Foreign Secretary, William Hague noted that:

> It is not in our character as a nation to have a foreign policy without a conscience or to repudiate our obligation to help those less fortunate. Our foreign policy should always have consistent support for human rights and poverty reduction at its irreducible core and we should always strive to act with moral authority, recognising that once it is damaged it is hard to restore.
> (Hague, 2010)

Although apparently more nuanced and carefully crafted than Cook's ethical dimension, this formulation furnished even more hostages to fortune. Moral considerations were now the 'irreducible core' of British foreign policy. In reality, Hague, like Cook, had merely given more explicit articulation to a theme which had been present since 1945, i.e. that whatever its relative hard power at any given time, Britain had always pursued the path of righteousness. As we have seen throughout this book, that claim was difficult to substantiate – not necessarily because British policy makers were more wicked (or even hypocritical) than the norm, but because all too often the pursuit of the perceived national interest had prevented the ethical dimension from playing more than a secondary role.

Why, then, did William Hague choose to make his own version of Cook's promise? The answer was suggested by the title of his July 2010 speech. In a 'networked world', transformed by a multitude of developments which could be designated by the umbrella term 'globalisation', Britain's good name was more important than ever. But it was also more vulnerable. Countries like the US and China could still hope to get away with actions which defied the moral conscience of the international community; but even they could not conduct their affairs without attracting notice in a world where, thanks to new technology, millions of people had become potential television journalists. In terms of international opinion, Britain (unlike its banking sector) was no longer deemed 'too big to fail'. Even if the 'moral' post-war narrative had once been an option – to console the British public for their country's relative loss of hard power – it was now a compulsory feature of ministerial rhetoric.

In fact, the majority of Hague's speech reflected the latest blow to Britain's traditional sources of power – the economic crisis which began in 2007 and which, according to Conservative propaganda, had been caused by the Brown government rather than developments in the 'networked world'. Apart from its general impact on Britain's diplomatic position, the crisis had a direct effect on the FCO, which was one of the main targets for government savings, being asked to absorb a 24 per cent budget cut over four years. Unabashed, Hague devoted most of his speech to the various ways in which Britain could use its privileged position in the 'networked world' to recover from its latest setback, so long as its diplomatic endeavours were sufficiently 'agile and energetic'. Multilateral institutions like the G20 and the UN were still important to Britain, which would play its full part. But New Labour had neglected the chance of strengthening bilateral relations with emerging superpowers like Brazil, India and China, not to mention Turkey and Indonesia.

Hague's mouth-watering menu marked the point at which the Conservatives finally abandoned the Churchillian perspective, in which the world was bounded by the three concentric circles of the US, the Commonwealth and Europe. According to Hague, New Labour had failed to capitalise on its relationship with the last two of these; and the Commonwealth, in particular, should be cultivated. But in a networked world Britain should develop a truly global gaze to further its national interest. The main target in Hague's sights was, of course, China. He could argue that this was no sudden infatuation – Britain, after all, had recognised the People's Republic (despite considerable American displeasure) in 1950. Sixty years later, Britain would still have to tread carefully in case friendship with China jeopardised the 'special relationship' with the US. There was also the question of human rights in China, which had improved markedly since the days of Chairman Mao but which still presented obstacles to a country which placed such considerations at the 'irreducible core' of its foreign policy. Accordingly, while the 2010 Conservative manifesto included a promise 'to seek a closer relationship with China', this course would be pursued while 'standing firm on human rights'.

Even without the advantage of hindsight, it was possible to detect features of the Conservative manifesto which could prove problematic. It was as if the party had studied New Labour's mistakes and committed itself to repeating them in a way which was a little less damaging to Britain's international reputation. On the one hand, the position on humanitarian intervention was insufficiently circumscribed: despite all the qualifying language, a party which favoured 'supporting human rights and championing the cause of democracy and the rule of law at every opportunity' would come under pressure to intervene in civil conflicts overseas whenever the arguments were finely balanced. On the other, there was ample evidence in the manifesto, and in Hague's subsequent speech, to suggest that economic self-interest would be a key driver of foreign policy decisions after 2010 – that whenever morality and materialism came into collision the latter consideration would prevail. These dilemmas, of course, were not unprecedented for British policy makers since 1945; but the Conservatives had spelled them out even more starkly than New Labour had done, and the cost of miscalculation was arguably greater after 2010 than it had ever been before. The hazards were given a cruel (if not crude) illustration in 2012, when Cameron's agreement to meet the Tibetan spiritual leader, the Dalai Lama, triggered a lengthy diplomatic *froideur* in which China displayed a level of arrogance worthy of Britain itself in its nineteenth-century heyday.

If Cameron's foreign policy approach contained novel features, he was also prepared to innovate in institutional terms. The 2010 manifesto proposed the establishment of a National Security Council (NSC) 'to coordinate responses to the dangers we face'. Beginning its work immediately after the election, the NSC included several Cabinet ministers, including both the Chancellor of the Exchequer and the Home Secretary. As well as reflecting the new and greatly enhanced security dimension of foreign policy, this new body promised to remedy the ad hoc decision-making which had preceded the Iraq War. On the face of it, William Hague's unruffled response to this reform was a surprise; the Foreign Secretary would obviously attend the weekly meetings, but there was a risk that he or she would be there to receive instructions rather than to offer advice, especially since senior figures from the military and intelligence communities would be present when relevant, bringing specific expertise and insights which not even the best informed Foreign Secretary could match (Chapter 2).

The Arab Spring

In his 'networked world' speech, Hague had asserted that '[t]he country that is purely reactive in foreign affairs is in decline' (Hague, 2010). Before the end of the coalition's first year it had been forced into a 'reactive' position by events in North Africa and the Middle East; but, then again, the 'Arab Spring', which began in Tunisia in December 2010, caught most governments by surprise. The unrest spread to Egypt, where President Hosni Mubarak was forced to step aside in February 2011, after three decades in which he had been regarded as a dependable ally by the West. As if to demonstrate the thin line between 'enlightened' and 'selfish' national interest, David Cameron became the first Western leader to visit Egypt just a few days after Mubarak had been toppled; but this was a hastily arranged detour from a long-planned Middle Eastern trip during which the Prime Minister had hoped to promote the sale of arms to equally unsavoury regional regimes. In this context it was interesting to note that while the 2010 manifesto had promised that human rights would not be overlooked when Britain dealt with China, no such pledge was made when the party expressed its intention to 'elevate our relations with many friendly nations, including in the Middle East'. Whatever one might say about Britain's relations with Gulf states like Bahrain, they certainly could not be considered to be 'elevated' from the moral perspective (Controversy 11.1). And yet the Gulf featured in the manifesto immediately below the reference to human rights in China.

Cameron arrived in Cairo as civil strife was erupting in Libya, and he denounced the Gaddafi regime's repressive response. However, if Britain's previous relations with Mubarak's regime would look awkward to anyone who cared to look closely, the Gaddafi problem was even less edifying. In March 2004 Tony Blair had met the Libyan dictator and hailed him as a reclaimed sinner, whose return within the fold of civilisation should be chalked up as a major success for the West's strategy in the War on Terror. Knowledge of this uncharacteristic example of Blairite realpolitik seemed to make Cameron all the more anxious to obliterate Gaddafi from the wallchart of world leaders. Along with France and the Lebanon, Britain took a leading role in the promotion and passage of UN Resolution 1973, which called for an immediate ceasefire in Libya and imposed both an arms embargo and a no-fly zone. Gaddafi's regime was accused of human rights abuses, possibly amounting to 'crimes against humanity' (Vickers, 2015, 232). In March 2011 a coalition of countries (Belgium, Canada, Denmark, Italy, Norway, Qatar and Spain, as well as France, the US and the UK) embarked on military action to enforce the UN resolution, as Gaddafi's forces attacked the city of Benghazi. In July Britain recognised the opposition National Transitional

Controversy 11.1 Bahrain, human rights and the return to 'east of Suez'

Bahrain, an oil-rich archipelago located just off the east coast of Saudi Arabia, had been a long-standing focus of British interest for several decades before it became a Protectorate in 1892. Just before the First World War Britain obtained exclusive rights to oil reserves, which began to be exploited in the early 1930s. In 1971 the state was granted independence, and (consistent with the commitment to withdraw from its bases east of Suez (Chapter 6)) the British Navy, which had made Bahrain its main Middle Eastern station in 1935, pulled out.

The government of Bahrain – which became a kingdom in 2002 – continued to value its close relationship with Britain, and commercial ties remained very strong. The War on Terror produced a step change in relations, and a series of agreements was reached in areas such as intelligence sharing and military training. However, Bahrain exemplified the politico-religious tensions which were helping to fuel general unrest in the Middle East, with a government dominated by Sunni Muslims denying full political rights to a population with a Shi-ite majority. During the Arab Spring of 2011 protestors demanding greater political freedom were attacked by troops, including a contingent from Saudi Arabia. Thousands were arrested, and allegations of systematic torture used by the Bahraini authorities were subsequently confirmed by independent investigators.

Far from persuading British ministers to distance themselves from Bahrain, this episode seems to have cemented the relationship. In 2015 work began on a new British naval base in Bahrain – the old one having been taken over by the Americans. Most of the cost, of around £15 million, was being met by Bahrain's royal family. Critics alleged that this was a gift to the British as a reward for their indulgent approach towards the regime's human-rights record. The stated purpose was to help defend Britain's allies in the region, rather than marking a resurgence of imperialism. Nevertheless, the Foreign Secretary, Philip Hammond, was clearly delighted by this development, which had symbolic significance as well as being a practical projection of British power at a time of economic austerity at home. In addition to the promised naval facility, a squadron of British Tornado fighter planes was stationed at the al Minhad airbase in neighbouring Dubai from 2013.

Council as the legitimate Libyan government. By the end of October Gaddafi had been captured and killed. Enthusiastic crowds in Tripoli hailed Cameron, along with France's President Sarkozy, as Libyan liberators. Sarkozy had been the first Western leader to call for Gaddafi's deposition, while Britain's initial response had been uncertain; in the light of subsequent events, the British premier would have been well advised to let Sarkozy take the plaudits on his own.

Britain's role in the fall of Gaddafi was the first item in the list of achievements paraded by the coalition government in the foreign policy section of its mid-term review and presumably was seen as the main justification for the headline boast that the country was once again 'standing tall in the world'. By that time, however (August 2013), it had become much more difficult to regard the Libyan intervention as an unqualified success. In hindsight, the obvious criticism against Cameron is that he engaged British forces against the Gaddafi regime without developing a workable strategy for the aftermath of an intervention which was clearly designed to effect regime change in Libya. As such, it seemed that Cameron had repeated Blair's misjudgements in advance of the 2003 Iraq War. However, Cameron can be regarded as more culpable than his predecessor, since (unlike Blair) he knew in advance that a miscalculation could have disastrous effects in Britain itself, as well as the area in which British forces were deployed. The most egregious mistake would be for Britain's Prime Minister to have authorised military action on the basis of over-optimistic assumptions concerning the true nature of the uprising in Libya and the Arab Spring as a whole. Yet this is precisely what David Cameron had done, according to a highly critical report published by the House of Commons Select Committee on Foreign Affairs in September 2016 (House of Commons Foreign Affairs Committee, 2016).

In September 2011 Cameron used his first speech to the UN Assembly to reflect on the Arab Spring. Presumably, his intention was to inspire national leaders to provide economic assistance to the countries which had undergone recent revolutions; hence his characterisation of the Arab Spring as 'a massive opportunity . . . only if we really seize it'. By 'seize it', Cameron could not have meant armed intervention in other states in order to spread Western values; he disclaimed any mission to impose such values by force, although he signalled his support for interventions when they were 'necessary, legal and right'. However, Cameron interpreted the Arab Spring as a sign that the people of the Middle East could 'do it for themselves'. After all, they had made their aspirations clear:

> They want transparency and accountability of government. An end to corruption. The fair and consistent rule of law. The chance to get a job and to have a stake in how their country is run. The freedom to communicate and the chance to participate in shaping society as citizens with rights and responsibilities.
>
> (Cameron, 2011)

If Cameron had referred back to the 2010 Conservative manifesto before delivering this speech, he would have been reminded that liberal Conservatism meant that '[w]e are sceptical about grand utopian schemes to remake the world. We will work patiently with the grain of other societies'. Instead of working 'with the grain' of Egyptian, or Libyan, society, Cameron had emulated American neo-conservatives who imagined that the Middle East and North Africa were swarming with individuals who were desperate for the chance to implement liberal democratic institutions. Among other things, the logic of this position constituted a heavy indictment of outside forces which had helped to prop up undemocratic states throughout the freedom-thirsty Middle East. These states included Bahrain, whose repressive regime was conducting business with British firms at the time that Cameron was delivering his moral message to the UN. In ideological terms, the left hand of the British government was acting (and speaking) as if its right hand was immobile. In reality, and in conformity with the programme sketched out in the 2010 Conservative manifesto, the right hand was energetically at work. The dissonance in British policy was sufficiently marked to endanger any gain in soft power which might have accrued from London's successful staging of the 2012 summer Olympic Games (one of the few positive legacies which Cameron had inherited from his New Labour predecessors).

A year later, when Cameron addressed the General Assembly once again, his remarks were more chastened. He acknowledged that some people now took the view that the Arab Spring was 'in danger of becoming an Arab Winter'. However, the establishment of liberal democracies was bound to be halting and gradual, and there were signs of progress in many places. There had been elections in Libya, for example, and in Egypt 'the democratically elected President has asserted civilian control over the military'. Maybe the verdicts of the ballot box were less than optimal from the viewpoint of Western governments – in Egypt, for example, the new President, Morsi, had been a key figure in the radical Muslim Brotherhood – but Cameron declared that 'nothing in the last year has changed my fundamental conviction [that] the Arab Spring represents a precious opportunity for people to realise their aspirations for a job, a voice and a stake in their own future' (Cameron, 2012).

Cameron also referred to the view that while some countries were beginning to benefit from the Arab Spring, its impact on Syria had 'unleashed a vortex of sectarian violence and hatred' which could plunge the region into turmoil. A 'political transition' in Syria was obviously needed, based on 'mutual consent'. However, he referred to atrocities which were 'a terrible stain on this United Nations' – particularly on those members (e.g. Russia) which 'aided and abetted Assad's regime of terror'. If the UN Charter was to have any meaning, its members should cooperate to provide the Syrian people with 'a future without Assad' (Cameron, 2012).

However, the 'rapid transition' which Cameron sought did not materialise, and a year after his emotional appeal Assad was still in place, using chemical weapons and barrel bombs against his own people. President Obama had declared that the use of such weapons would mean that the Syrian dictator had crossed a 'red line', entailing 'enormous consequences'. By stepping across the red line Assad had given Cameron the green light to step up his personal pressure on Obama. For understandable reasons, neither partner in the 'special relationship' was prepared to take military action without guaranteed support from the other. Cameron took the initiative, recalling Parliament from its summer recess on 27 August 2013 in the hope that it would provide the necessary authority. However, whatever his personal views, Labour's leader Ed Miliband knew that his MPs would not vote to provide Cameron with a blank cheque. Since the coalition parties themselves included potential dissenters, the Parliamentary motion was watered down to an invitation to endorse the possibility of military action, which could not proceed without a further vote. Ministers were evidently calculating that if Parliament could be made to agree on the principle of action, any subsequent vote was likely to be a formality. The opponents of British intervention were well aware of this, with the result that many of them persisted in their obstructive attitude despite frantic lobbying by Cameron himself (Ashcroft and Oakeshott, 2015, 443–4). The coalition duly went down to defeat, by 285 votes to 272. The majority of Labour MPs were joined by 30 Conservatives and 9 Liberal Democrats in the 'No' lobby.

In itself, this would have been a notable event in British political history – the first time that the executive's foreign policy had been negated by a Parliamentary vote since the eighteenth century. Among its penitent responses to the Iraq War, the Brown government had opened the possibility that British forces should not be committed to action in future without explicit Parliamentary approval. The Syria vote had no specific constitutional force in itself, but it seemed like a good way to establish a conventional practice and was by any standards a nasty blow to the power of the executive, which had interrupted everyone's summer holidays only to be humiliated. Labour's position could also be regarded (and denounced, predictably, in some quarters of the media) as a rare breach of the political consensus which is supposed to apply to significant decisions in foreign policy. The vote certainly took US officials by surprise; but things had changed since 2002, when the Bush administration felt strong enough to hint that it would go ahead with its Iraq adventure even if Blair was unable to enlist British support. Far from spiking Obama's guns, the Syria vote gave the President a plausible pretext for laying down his unloaded weapons. The Syrian crisis had proved that the 'special relationship' could still be useful but not in a way which was particularly flattering to the junior partner; it suggested that the US only liked the guarantee of a supportive partner in circumstances where it felt strong enough to act alone.

Immediately after the rejection of the government's motion, Ed Miliband challenged Cameron to pledge that he would not use the royal prerogative in order to evade Parliament's decision. In response, Cameron acknowledged that

MPs had reflected the views of the British people: 'I get that, and the Government will act accordingly' (*Hansard, House of Commons Debates*, 29 August 2013, Vol. 566, col. 1555). Yet it was clear that nothing he had heard during the debate was going to change his own view of the need for regime change in Syria.

Attitudes began to change when the Islamic State of Iraq and the Levant (ISIL, also known as the Islamic State of Iraq and Syria (ISIS) or Da'ish) organisation began to add territorial gains in Western Iraq, notably the country's second city of Mosul, to the areas of Syria already under its control. Since Da'ish was fighting Assad, British action against the Syrian regime would have helped its brutal campaign. The argument that Da'ish and other fanatical factions in the area were ultimately the products of Assad's own tyranny was hardly relevant in this context; apart from raising the possibility that the 2003 Iraq intervention was actually the main source of the trouble, the question now was not where Da'ish came from but how it should be dealt with. A humanitarian catastrophe was unfolding in Syria, as millions fled in terror at the prospect of further Da'ish advances. In September 2014 Cameron recalled Parliament again, in response to a request for military assistance from the government of Iraq. This time MPs gave overwhelming approval for air strikes, although more than a hundred withheld support (including the future Labour leader Jeremy Corbyn, along with six Conservatives and a Liberal Democrat).

By this time British foreign policy concerns were divided between the rise of Da'ish and the resurgence of Russia, which had seized the Crimea from Ukraine in February 2014. The coalition responded with vigorous rhetoric and support for economic sanctions, specifically aimed at the Russian leader, Vladimir Putin, and his closest associates. Tony Blair had tried to cultivate Putin, on his usual assumption that once he had established a rapport with world leaders they would continue to prioritise the maintenance of this personal friendship over the perceived interests of their nation states. Unsurprisingly, the divisions between Britain and Russia over Iraq had proved more powerful than the relationship between Blair and Putin, which in any case was strained by the fact that Britain had given refuge to a number of exiled Russian dissidents (repeating the favour which it had extended to Lenin and others before the 1917 Bolshevik Revolution). Putin's agents seemed to have a longer reach than their tsarist forebears. In 2006 one prominent dissident, Alexander Litvinenko, paid an ill-advised visit to a sushi cafe and subsequently succumbed to poisoning by the radioactive compound polonium-210.

It was obvious to all except pro-Russian conspiracy theorists that an unfriendly foreign power had been involved in an incident which – among its numerous astonishing features – could be considered a gross infringement of British sovereignty. Yet this was never going to be a subject on which Parliament would be asked to support military reprisals. If Britain looked impotent in the face of Russian aggression against Ukraine, at least it was not alone. The crisis had been generated by the prospect of an 'association agreement' between Ukraine and the EU, which Putin regarded as unacceptable. France and Germany were equally wrong-footed by the Kremlin's encouragement of Crimean separatists. Yet at least those countries took the lead in the search for a peaceful solution, in which the British government was conspicuously absent. Rather than being a country that punched above its weight, Britain now looked as if it was happy to act as a playground bully until a really big kid turned up, at which point it discovered that this was someone else's quarrel. Cameron, the 'Libyan liberator,' had suffered an abrupt transformation into a Crimean capitulator.

A month before the 2015 general election the *Economist* magazine characterised Britain as 'a shrinking actor on the global stage'. Harsh words were being uttered about Cameron and his coalition by retired British soldiers as well as US officials. Britain looked set to spend less than 2 per cent of GDP on defence, despite Cameron's emphasis on this minimum figure at the 2014 NATO summit. Britain had been a guarantor of Ukraine's territorial integrity in 1994, when that country agreed to relinquish its nuclear weapons. Yet Cameron, the *Economist* felt, had 'been not so much cautious as apathetic, ineffective and fickle' in his response to Putin's aggression (*Economist*, 2015).

While the *Economist* concentrated its fire on the Prime Minister, its article was intended as an indictment of the coalition as a whole. In defence of their record, ministers could reply that their main task when assuming office in 2010 had been the restoration of their country's finances, without which no future British Prime Minister would have enjoyed the option of looking 'apathetic', 'ineffective' or 'fickle'. However, at the outset the coalition had talked as if Britain's global standing could be improved *despite* the context of austerity, and the government's programme of spending cuts had turned out to be less drastic than initially expected. The *Economist*'s critique attributed the coalition's failure not to the need to save money but to its inability to make the most of its position within the EU.

The coalition and 'Europe'

The coalition government was unlikely to repeat all of New Labour's offences with regard to the EU, but its dominant Conservative members had already shown a clear propensity to offend. David Cameron might have abandoned his 'cast-iron' promise to hold a referendum on the Lisbon Treaty, but he had concealed his tactical retreat under a covering fire of rhetoric which implied that he would seize any plausible opportunity to obstruct European business.

In a concession to 'openness', the coalition had promised that if petitions published on the government's website (www.gov.uk/petition-government) won the support of 10,000 signatories, they would receive an official response of some kind; if they reached 100,000, their subjects would be considered for Parliamentary debate. A petition calling for a referendum on EU membership was duly started and quickly attracted the requisite support. The debate was held on 25 October 2011, on a motion which envisaged a referendum offering three options: that Britain should stay in an unreformed EU, remain a member subject to renegotiated terms or withdraw. Cameron imposed a three-line whip, which was never likely to deter the dissidents on his own side. In total (including the two tellers), 81 Conservative MPs voted in favour of the motion, and there were around 20 abstentions (Cowley and Stuart, 2012). This rebellion topped the Maastricht record by some 40 votes, although the survival of the government was not even remotely in question this time, since a cross-party combination ensured the motion's defeat by 483 to 111 votes. Even on the most imaginative construction of the voting, this implied that MPs were out of line with the majority of their constituents, since polling now suggested a clear majority for withdrawal from the EU (Ipsos MORI, 2016).

Fortunately for Cameron, an opportunity to appease the public mood – and his own troublesome backbenchers – was at hand. At a meeting of the European Council in December 2011 he refused to endorse a treaty amendment which would introduce new rules relating to the eurozone. The fact that Cameron had made use of Britain's veto gave the Eurosceptic press a rare opportunity to use language it expected its readers to understand. In gratitude, the *Daily Mail* applauded 'defiant Cameron' for resisting 'Euro bullies'; to complete the Prime Minister's new Churchillian image, the paper exulted that he had ordered 'a full English breakfast' the next morning (Chapman, 2011).

For anyone with memories of the 1992 Maastricht negotiations, the reaction to the 'historic' veto was unsettling. On that occasion the press had been briefed to say that it was 'game, set and match' for Britain – a phrase which aroused considerable irritation in European capitals. This time the London Mayor Boris Johnson helpfully suggested that the Prime Minister had 'played a blinder'. What Cameron had really done was to stipulate that Britain's financial institutions should not be affected by the eurozone rules. This had proved unacceptable to other EU leaders – particularly Cameron's former friend President Sarkozy, whose wrath, apparently, came close to provoking a physical confrontation. Having failed to protect crucial British interests through persuasion, Cameron really had no choice but to apply the veto. Subsequently, a French official summed up the controversy in a simile which would resonate with many tabloid readers, in Britain and beyond, claiming that Cameron had behaved 'like a man at a wife-swapping party who refuses to bring his own wife' (Chapman, 2011).

Conservative Eurosceptics were too well informed to fall for simplistic headlines which titillated the rank and file, but they could draw plenty of comfort from the details. The incident was a crushing blow to the coalition's plan for a constructive EU role; as the *Guardian* newspaper correctly predicted, it would increase Britain's isolation and thus enhance the case for complete withdrawal (in the end, only the Czechs followed Cameron's example by withholding support from the Eurozone reforms: Traynor *et al.*, 2011). The veto was likely to be unpalatable to many Liberal Democrats, bringing closer the prospect of an end to another dubious union – the coalition itself. Initially, Nick Clegg endorsed the use of the veto, albeit with reluctance. However, the furious response of his Parliamentary colleagues induced a rapid rethink. In a television interview Clegg revealed that he was 'bitterly disappointed' by the veto. His feelings were expressed in a physical form, though not the pugilistic variety which Sarkozy had allegedly attempted. When Cameron reported on the summit in the Commons, Clegg refused to sit next to him (Goes, 2013, 9–10).

Whatever the effect of his conduct on the audiences that really mattered – the British tabloid press, the Conservative Party and other EU leaders – Cameron really had 'played a blinder' *vis-à-vis* his coalition partners. In the initial stage of his game plan he would propitiate the real enemy – his own backbenchers – at the expense of his Lib Dem friends. However, once the hubbub had subsided, he could make concessions to Clegg which would create barely a ripple outside the 'hardest' of Eurosceptic households. Thus, just a month after his heroic stand, he agreed to empty much of its significance by conceding that the European Court of Justice (ECJ) could enforce the revised fiscal rules. As Cameron presumably calculated, this quiet climbdown could not be translated into screaming headlines unless the tabloid press was prepared to explain the complex procedures of the EU to its readers – a task which it was notoriously reluctant to undertake. As a result, Cameron got away with his tactical ploy – for the time being.

Almost exactly a year after the Conservative rebellion on an EU referendum Cameron's internal critics struck again, and on this occasion they had Labour's support. Indeed, it was Labour, rather than a Conservative backbencher, which provided this opportunity for revolt. The Opposition forced a vote on a real-terms cut in the EU's budget for 2014–20 in place of the planned 5 per cent increase; the coalition had been arguing for a real-terms freeze. This cynical ploy attracted the support of 53 Conservative MPs, leading to a government defeat by 307 to 294. Presumably, Labour's strategists calculated that although its proposal would cause annoyance within the EU, European leaders would still prefer to do business with Ed Miliband than David Cameron after the next election. If so, their tactics were too clever by half. Cameron might have alienated many of his partners by casting his veto over fiscal reform, but some of them (including Germany's Angela Merkel) recognised the publicity value of an EU budget cut at a time of austerity. In February 2013 Cameron was able to hail an agreement to reduce the 2014–20 budget; and although the British contribution would rise, he was able to blame that on concessions which New Labour had agreed back in 2005.

Before then, however, Cameron had decided to face up to the logic of his circumstances, both domestically and within the EU. The balance of opinion within his own party had forced him into a self-defeating scenario where every concession won through hard bargaining would merely serve as the prelude to more unrealistic demands from Conservative backbenchers, until every last objectionable power had been 'repatriated' to Britain. This process could only end in a row and a rebuff which would be taken as proof by members of the party and their media supporters that the EU was not susceptible to reform and that British withdrawal was the only sensible option.

On 23 January 2013 Cameron delivered a speech at the London headquarters of the US-based financial institution Bloomberg, in which he accepted the case for a referendum on EU membership. However, this was not a belated acceptance of the Liberal Democrat policy of 2010, in which an in–out referendum could only be triggered by a significant EU treaty change. Cameron was arguing that a referendum should be held whether or not a new treaty was being proposed. However, the vote would not take place immediately, since this would deny Britain the chance to explore possible reforms which would make it more likely that voters would opt for Cameron's own preferred option of continued EU membership. Indeed, the full text of the speech must be rated as one of the best expositions by a British leader of the 'case for the defence', when so many of Cameron's predecessors had chosen to pay lip-service to the prosecution argument. In view of Britain's role in Iraq, as well as Libya's ongoing descent into anarchy, it was perhaps unfortunate that Cameron should tell his audience that 'in any emergency you should plan for the aftermath as well as dealing with the present crisis'. However, Cameron outlined five principles which should guide the EU in the twenty-first century; and although some of the suggestions (particularly those relating to economic competitiveness) would have reminded his listeners that the Prime Minister had once anointed himself 'the heir to Blair', no one could doubt his constructive purpose (Cameron, 2013).

Nevertheless, the inevitable headline arising from the Bloomberg speech was that Cameron had finally caved in to his Eurosceptic critics and accepted that long-suffering Britons should finally get the chance to throw off the EU yoke. Tactically, his timing was excellent as usual; the pledge would keep his Eurosceptic critics (fairly) quiet until the next general election, and an announcement which would have wrong-footed any Labour leader, however gifted and far-sighted, was not calculated to make life any easier for Labour's Ed Miliband, who was struggling to win a reputation for statesmanship. Last, but not least on this occasion, whatever their private feelings, Cameron's Liberal Democrat partners were unlikely to lodge a vehement protest, since the logic of their previous policy suggested that 'the people' had every right to pronounce on 'Europe', so that the calling of a referendum on the subject was now a matter of timing rather than of principle.

However, even if the Bloomberg speech made a favourable impression in European capitals, Cameron managed to dissipate its effect through his attempts in 2014 to thwart the nomination of the former long-serving Prime Minister of Luxembourg Jean-Claude Juncker as European Commission President. As if to compensate for his previous run of luck, Cameron's persistent and high-profile campaign to contest Juncker's appointment was an almost incomprehensible blunder. Juncker, after all, was virtually guaranteed the Presidency as the nominee of the EPP, which commanded a majority in the European Parliament; and any influence Cameron could have hoped to exercise over this grouping had been jettisoned back in 2009, when he ordered Conservative MPs to abandon the EPP in favour of more exotic company. Cameron was not entirely devoid of support. Sweden and the Netherlands were sympathetic, and Germany's Angela Merkel was also reported to have private reservations about a 'federalist' candidate. Ominously, though, some of Cameron's own backbenchers were hoping that Juncker would prevail, since 'this would have a positive effect in accelerating a British exit'. 'You can find a lot of people [in the Tory party] who think he will be very helpful', commented Charles Walker, who, as Vice-Chairman of the 1922 Committee, was in a good position to gauge Parliamentary opinion (Helm, 2014). Perhaps it was Cameron's awareness of this Machiavellian line of thinking that prompted him to use up remaining political capital in Brussels by urging the case against Juncker long after it seemed certain to prove unavailing. A more immediate consideration was the perceived threat from the United Kingdom Independence Party (UKIP), which topped the poll in the 2014 European Parliamentary elections and was now emulating the destructive effect on the Conservative Party that the Militant Tendency had wreaked on Labour for much of the 1980s.

Conforming to the party's usual practice, the section on 'Europe' appeared towards the end of the 2015 Conservative manifesto. It reiterated the referendum pledge and promised that before the poll was held (no later than 2017) '[w]e will negotiate a new settlement for Britain'. The negotiations would result in an EU 'that helps Britain move ahead, not one that holds us back'. Readers were reminded that 'David Cameron vetoed a new EU treaty that would have damaged British interests' – 'the first time in history that a British Prime Minister has done so'. Whatever the result of the referendum, a Conservative government would honour it – even if the voters were silly enough to opt for withdrawal from an association which kept on producing treaties which 'damage British interests'. The implicit message of the manifesto was that only the Conservatives could be trusted to give the British people the chance to make the wrong choice.

Bring on the 'Brexiteers'

Before the 2015 general election David Cameron revealed that, whatever the outcome of that contest, he would not fight another one as Conservative leader. Following the creation of the US-style NSC, and New Labour's introduction of a Supreme Court, this was another sign that the UK's political system was morphing into an imitation of its former colony. Since Cameron was still relatively young and vigorous (certainly when judged on his performances at Prime Minister's Questions), his decision to step down suggested that Britain, like the US, should restrict its heads of government to just two terms in office.

In reality, Cameron's main motivation was to assure the sharks circling in Conservative Party waters that he would be dead meat before 2020, thus giving them every incentive to give the appearance of loyalty through the 2015 election campaign and a suitable ensuing period, after which they could begin to deliver codedly critical speeches. At the same time, Cameron's 'inadvertent' announcement conveyed a degree of confidence that his departure would be voluntary, rather than being enforced by the impending decisions of British voters. He managed to overcome the first obstacle – the general election of 2015. Despite opinion polls which suggested another 'hung' Parliament, the Conservatives secured an overall majority of 16 seats. Cameron had some reason to feel that his leadership of the party had finally been vindicated, since he had led it to victory and was clearly an electoral asset rather than a liability. His post-election euphoria was probably enhanced by the media's near-universal presentation of the result as a personal triumph for Cameron against impossible odds. In reality, the media were taken aback because they had been misled by the opinion polls; if none of those imperfect surveys had been conducted, hardly anyone would have been very surprised by the Conservative victory, since the main opposition parties (which now included the Liberal Democrats) had done little to invigorate even their most devoted supporters.

For Cameron, the real message of the 2015 general election was that his party's overall majority was too slender to cushion him from the Parliamentary rebellions he could expect from MPs who, judged by their rhetoric, had only sought election in order to liberate Britain from the EU. Once this harsh reality had registered with Cameron, he decided that the referendum should be called sooner rather than later, to make the most of any enhanced prestige the election result might have brought him in Brussels, along with a 'second honeymoon' with British voters. The problem for Cameron was that the rationale for this accelerated timetable was likely to convince other European leaders that the case for continued British membership of the EU would prevail even if they refused to make significant concessions on key issues, such as the principle of free movement of people between member states. This showed the folly of Cameron's decision to agree that a referendum should be held *without* significant EU treaty changes; in that instance, the task would have been the familiar one of reassuring British voters that the reforms were not very important after all, whereas in 2016 he had the far more onerous problem of proving that he had persuaded his EU partners to make changes which really were significant. This would probably have overtaxed the powers of any British Prime Minister since the 1986 Single European Act revived the process of deeper integration. Cameron, however, gambled that he could present his inevitable failure as a kind of success.

After all, he had presided over two referendums (on a change to the voting system for general elections (May 2011) and Scottish independence (September 2014) which had resulted in victories for the status quo. In February 2016 he announced that a referendum on EU membership would be held in June.

Any observers who were hoping that this crucial decision would be informed by a debate which included a thoroughgoing assessment of Britain's role in the world since 1945 were predictably disappointed. The case for leaving the EU was dominated by the issue of immigration. On this subject the most eloquent contribution was made not by any speech but by statistics released in late May which showed that net migration to Britain over the previous year had been 330,000 – the second highest figure on record. The magnetic attraction of the UK for migrants (from the EU and elsewhere) was due, in large part, to the popularity of English as a second language – the very factor which provided the country with a reliable source of soft power, whatever its economic or military prowess. However, the anti-European press had played on the idea that migrants from countries like Poland and Romania hoped to exploit the country's welfare system – which had not been particularly generous by European standards even before the advent of austerity. In parts of the UK migrants were indeed straining some aspects of the welfare state, particularly in education, since so many were couples with young families. However, the press focused on the effects on the National Health Service (NHS), which in reality was facing a funding crisis because retired people were staying alive for much longer despite chronic (and very expensive) health impairments. Unprepared (and perhaps unwilling) to spell out the realities behind the stark immigration statistics, the 'Remain' campaign was unable to make significant headway through its urgent warnings about the likely economic impact of withdrawal. Indeed, these (well-funded) interventions became increasingly shrill and counterproductive, giving the impression that the political 'elite' was having to resort to scare stories because it lacked any positive arguments.

As in the previous referendum campaign of 1975, the governing party was divided and the Prime Minister suspended the convention of collective Cabinet responsibility to allow a majority of ministers to campaign on either side. In another repetition of 1975, the majority of ministers favoured continued membership; and the 'Leave' campaign was dominated by controversial characters. In 1975, however, the main opposition party had, if anything, been even more active on the side of membership than the Labour government, whose leader, Wilson, had been lukewarm. In 2016 the Labour leader Jeremy Corbyn made Wilson look like a Eurofanatic; and his party's campaigning effort seemed half-hearted even after the assassination, during the campaign, of pro-Remain Labour MP Jo Cox. Meanwhile the Liberal Democrats, whose Liberal forebears of 1975 had been popular with voters even if their Parliamentary contingent was small, had been discredited by their participation in the coalition government. The most powerful pro-European voice was provided by the leader of the

Scottish National Party (SNP), Nicola Sturgeon; but it was doubtful whether her advocacy made a positive impression in England, where the newspapers which bellowed for British independence from Brussels were equally vociferous in opposing Scottish separation from London.

Overall, then, the political impetus behind the 'Remain' campaign was much weaker than it had been in 1975. In numerical terms, its representation among the 'elite' was not much reduced; but it carried far less *weight*, reflecting the diminution of respect for politicians in general since 1975. Against this background, it was more difficult to undermine the 'Brexiteers' by referring to the obvious ambition and personal indiscretions of the leading 'Leave' campaigner, Boris Johnson, since the public seemed satisfied that all politicians were seriously flawed. Johnson – unlike Tony Benn, who had played a similar role in 1975 and had been subjected to vicious abuse for his pains – enjoyed considerable support from the media, especially sections of the 'popular' press. This, it seems, was the decisive difference between 1975 and 2016. On the former occasion almost all of Britain's national newspapers had supported continued membership; in 2016 most supported 'Leave'. Apart from their coverage of the campaign itself, newspapers like the *Sun*, the *Daily Mail* and (especially) the *Daily Express* had attacked the EU for years, occasionally straying from strict verisimilitude in reports designed to please their anti-European proprietors. Even 'heavyweight' publications, like the *Daily Telegraph*, extended the sort of unsympathetic treatment to the EU which they had reserved for the Soviet Union in the 1980s.

The vote itself, conducted on 23 June 2016, produced a narrow victory (by 51.9 to 48.1 per cent) for 'Leave'. David Cameron immediately announced his intention to resign as Conservative Party leader and Prime Minister, presenting the result as a decisive rejection of the advice that he had given to the electorate. Evidently, Cameron was hoping to minimise any soul-searching or post-mortems, on the old Churchillian grounds that in any vote a majority of one is sufficient. Nevertheless, his attempt (echoed by almost every other senior politician) to portray the outcome as a reflection of unequivocal purpose on the part of the British people was so obviously misleading as to undermine his intention. For example, the four capital cities of the UK – Belfast, Cardiff, Edinburgh and London – had all bucked the overall trend by endorsing continued EU membership; and while they might seem unrepresentative of the UK as a whole for various reasons, it was at least arguable that they were 'different' because their populations were more dynamic (or, in common parlance, 'forward-looking') than the areas which voted for 'Brexit'.

Since the vote would affect young people more than pensioners, the narrow verdict was rendered even less satisfactory by the fact that the latter had provided 'Leave' with its key constituency, whereas a clear majority of 18–24-year-olds who bothered to vote had plumped for 'Remain'. The differential turnout between generations – around 90 per cent of those aged over 65 voted, compared to fewer than two thirds of 18–24-year-olds – could, of course, be a testimony to the superior arguments of the 'Leave' campaign; more likely, though, it was just another manifestation of a demographic doomsday scenario, in which across a range of key government policies 'grey' voters enjoyed disproportionate influence merely because they had been brought up at a time when more people considered voting to be a duty. Subsequently it emerged that many people who voted 'Leave' did so either because they thought this was a costless protest, since 'Remain' was sure to win, or because they supposed (in accordance with the message of the tabloid press) that a vote to leave would be followed instantly by a painless liberation from the infernal EU. While 'Remain' campaigners had exaggerated the likely economic cost of withdrawal, their opponents had distorted the net cost of Britain's membership.

Since British referendums have no formal constitutional status and can be treated as 'consultative' exercises unless otherwise specified, taking all of the accompanying context into account the 2016 poll could have been interpreted as a dishonourable draw, leaving the country's Parliamentary representatives to decide Britain's future. After all, other EU countries with more clearly defined constitutions had held referendums which produced the 'wrong' result, and without undue embarrassment they had asked their voters to think again until they came up with a more satisfactory answer.

Why did Britain's elite capitulate in the face of such a dubious verdict? David Cameron's instant overreaction presumably reflected a sense of personal shock and humiliation. But others could have taken a different line, asserting that although the case for membership of the EU had suffered a serious setback, the war was not over. The fact that they spurned this course of action is partly explained by the weakness of the British political elite, which had been badly shaken by a 2009 scandal over Parliamentary expenses. The main reason, however, was that the 2016 referendum reflected the continued popularity of a narrative which the politicians had themselves promulgated, i.e. that despite the setback of the Second World War, Britain remained a great power. From that perspective, the notion that politicians or bureaucrats from other European countries – the states which Britain had rescued during the Second World War – could deprive the UK of control over its own borders was not just intolerable: it was unfathomable. Something underhand must have happened since 1945 to produce this state of affairs, and whether the chief culprits were based at Westminster, in Whitehall or in Brussels, a vote for 'Leave' would be a sufficient slap in the face to all of the above to make it worthwhile.

A mainstream politician like David Cameron could hardly say in the wake of the 2016 vote that it had all been based on a misunderstanding of Britain's global status. After all, he and earlier exemplars had brought the disaster on themselves. At regular intervals since 1945 opportunities had presented themselves for truly 'responsible' politicians to dissipate the post-war myths. In 1961, for example,

Harold Macmillan (so soon after Suez) could have told the British public that he was committing his country to EEC membership because its global role was 'played out'. Instead, he chose to emphasise the economic case for membership. After this missed opportunity, the main political parties tended to acknowledge in their election manifestos that Britain had declined; indeed, opposition parties were usually eager to exaggerate the evidence, so long as the deplorable trend could be blamed on the inadequate stewardship of their rivals. Even Edward Heath, who came the closest to giving the British public a cold dose of reality, was not immune from this electoral ploy. Some governments had the temerity to claim that their achievements had reversed Britain's decline, implying that the dominant post-war narrative had been inapplicable for a while but was now wholly revalidated. Such propagandists and their media allies regarded those who tried to base their assessments on careful evaluations of relevant evidence as tedious at the best of times and almost treacherous during more intense periods like the Falklands War and the 'Brexit' referendum.

On this view, it would be unfair to regard David Cameron as an inept performer who brought a promising act to a premature end. Rather, he seems like an inexperienced impresario who, at an awkward moment, was forced to ask the audience for its opinion of a long succession of conjuring tricks which had only ever seemed adequate because the audience had been willing the performers to succeed. The act had seemed transparent to well-informed observers within the UK, and it baffled external actors like US Presidents, who found themselves having to learn about something called the 'special relationship' every time they visited London or played host to a British Prime Minister.

An optimist could discern among the wreckage of the 2016 referendum the chance of a new beginning for Britain without any need to resort to smoke and mirrors. The possibility of a positive outcome was apparently augmented when Theresa May emerged as the new Conservative leader and Prime Minister ahead of some implausible rivals. May, who seemed to have arrived at a more stable and sustainable understanding of 'liberal Conservatism' than her predecessor, was a second-rate conjuror's nightmare; no British politician seemed better equipped to dispel the illusions associated with the great-power narrative, and on that basis she had decided to support 'Remain' while making no secret of her reservations in some of the EU's key policy areas. However, this entirely rational decision left her exposed to the view that a country which had just voted for 'Brexit' should not be led by a 'Remain' campaigner, however lukewarm. As a result, she felt compelled to genuflect towards the over-familiar post-war narrative on the day she took office, stating that although the referendum had created difficulties for her country, 'I know because we're *Great* Britain, that we will rise to the challenge. As we leave the European Union, we will forge a bold new positive role for ourselves in the world' (May, 2016). In later speeches she gave the impression of having warmed to oft rehearsed post-war themes.

Boris Johnson, May's new Foreign Secretary, had already proved his ability to merge the (over)familiar post-war narratives by declaiming that 'Britain is a great nation, a global force for good'. Ironically, this purple passage adorned an article which Johnson drafted before he had decided to campaign for 'Leave', and was meant to support the case for Remain'! (Shipman, 2017, 175–6.) Serious divisions were exposed by the 2016 referendum, but it would be a mistake to assume that delusions about Britain's recent history were confined to one side.

Unsurprisingly, then, during the campaign before the 'snap' general election in June 2017 Mrs May gave no indication that she was contemplating a re-examination of Britain's foreign policy in the aftermath of 'Brexit'. When Labour's Jeremy Corbyn argued that the terrorism which overshadowed the campaign had been inspired at least in part by foreign policy decisions, May and her colleagues were quick to seize on this plausible suggestion as evidence that Corbyn was unfit to hold high office. May had already demonstrated an iron determination to uphold the 'special relationship' despite the fact that the new US President, Donald Trump was a stranger to sentiment in the diplomatic sphere and showed a propensity to treat Britain like an insolvent business partner.

The ghost of Dean Acheson would have been astonished to see so much continuity between Britain's position in 2017 and the dilemmas he had identified back in 1962. Britain and the world had changed out of recognition since then, but while 'realities' were different, the old illusions apparently had retained their hold over the British imagination. There was even a chance that the voters had made the right decision in the 2016 referendum, although this would depend, crucially, on a judicious deployment of the country's overstretched diplomatic resources. But, even for an ardent Brexiteer in possession of factual information, at best it could only be regarded as an astute decision taken for inappropriate reasons; and, insofar as Britain's voters had decided to use the 2016 referendum as an opportunity to reaffirm their attachment to a story about the country's recent past which rarely trespassed on reality, the prospects were dispiritingly dubious.

Summary, guide to further reading and topics for discussion

12

Introduction

Further reading

Robert Self, *British Foreign and Defence Policy since 1945: Challenges and Dilemmas in a Changing World* (Palgrave Macmillan, 2010) and Jamie Gaskarth, *British Foreign Policy: Crises, Conflicts and Future Challenges* (Polity Press, 2013) are excellent introductory texts which take a thematic approach to developments in post-war British foreign policy. David Reynolds, *Britannia Overruled: British Policy & World Power in the 20th Century* (2nd edition, Routledge, 2000); John Young, *Britain and the World in the Twentieth Century* (Bloomsbury, 1997); and David Sanders, *Losing an Empire, Finding a Role: British Foreign Policy since 1945* (Palgrave Macmillan, 1990) are chronological studies which are still well worth reading. Paul Kennedy, *The Rise and Fall of the Great Powers: Economic Change and Military Conflict from 1500–2000* (Fontana, 1989); Niall Ferguson, *Empire: How Britain Made the Modern World* (Penguin, 2004); Corelli Barnett, *The Audit of War: The Illusion and Reality of Britain as a Great Nation* (Papermac, 1987); and Mark Curtis, *Web of Deceit: Britain's Real Role in the World* (Vintage, 2003) are all highly recommended: but since they advance very distinctive interpretations of Britain's changing role they should be consulted *after* readers have gained an overview from one or more of the introductory texts.

Chapter 1: foreign policy and International Relations theory

Summary

This chapter provides a brief introduction to the main theoretical perspectives used by scholars of international relations. These are:

- **Realism** – the idea that international relations takes place in a condition of 'anarchy', where states act on the basis of calculations of national interest;
- **Liberalism** – the view that states (and non-state institutions) can cooperate, especially through peaceful trade, in a manner which promotes global peace;
- **Marxism** – theories which focus on economic relations, particularly those which involve exploitation, as the main feature of international politics;
- **Social Constructivism** – an approach to international relations which emphasises the importance of ideas and perceptions rather than material factors;
- **Feminism** – an approach which identifies and attempts to address a perceived lack of attention to the role of women in international relations;
- **Postmodernism/poststructuralism** – theoretical perspectives which try to build a critical understanding of power, language and social relations.

The argument of the chapter is that, although students might find some theories more persuasive than others, all of these perspectives can enhance our understanding of the foreign policy of a state like Britain, as seen in a case study of the Iraq War (2003).

Further reading

Excellent introductory books include Oliver Daddow, International Relations Theory: The Essentials (Sage, 2013); Cynthia Weber, *International Relations Theory: A Critical Introduction* (4th edition, Routledge, 2013); Scott Burchill et al., *Theories of International Relations* (5th edition, Palgrave Macmillan, 2013); Tim Dunne et al., *International Relations Theories: Discipline and Diversity* (3rd edition, Oxford University Press, 2013); and Chris Brown and Kirsten Ainley, *Understanding International Relations* (4th edition, Palgrave Macmillan, 2009). All of these books contain copious references to books and articles which exemplify the key perspectives on international relations. The 'interpretive' approach to British foreign policy, highlighting the importance of ideological considerations, has been explored in a special issue of *British Journal of Politics and International Relations*, Vol. 15, 2013.

Chapter 2: the shaping and making of British foreign policy

Summary

This chapter sketches the development of the foreign policy-making process in the UK, starting with the formation of the Foreign Office in 1782. It argues that the fortunes of this government department (now the FCO) in some respects mirror those of Britain itself over the twentieth century. This is not to say, however, that Britain is no longer serious engaged in foreign policy making. Rather, the FCO has been overshadowed in its specialist field by the power of the Prime Minister and rivalled by other Whitehall departments. The chapter also discusses the influence of Parliament, public opinion and other bodies such as think tanks.

Further reading

The classic work on this subject remains William Wallace's *The Foreign Policy Process in Britain* (Royal Institute of International Affairs, 1975), which is still well worth reading even if much of the detail has been superseded by subsequent developments. The same applies to James Barber's concise study, *Who Makes British Foreign Policy?* (Open University Press, 1976). John Dickie's *Inside the Foreign Office* (Chapmans, 1992) and his *The New Mandarins: How British Foreign Policy Works* (IB Tauris, 2004) can be read consecutively to get some sense of recent changes in the status and procedure of the FCO. See also Ian Hall, '"Building the Global Network?" The Reform of the Foreign and Commonwealth Office under New Labour', *British Journal of Politics and International Relations*, Vol. 15, 2013; the relevant chapters of Robert Self, *British Foreign & Defence Policy since 1945* (Palgrave Macmillan, 2010); and Jamie Gaskarth, *British Foreign Policy: Crises, Conflicts and Future Challenges* (Polity, 2013).

Chapter 3: the road to 1945

Summary

This chapter provides the essential background for the main text, charting Britain's relative decline from the 1890s, when it was an imperial power of unparalleled global reach, to the late 1930s, when, sensing that it had overstretched its resources, it was desperate to avoid war. Underlying this different approach to international relations was an economic position which had been virtually unchallenged in the mid nineteenth century, but which was beginning to fall behind rivals like the US and Germany by 1900. Evidence of Britain's decline – particularly apparent in the Boer War (1899–1902) – forced Britain to abandon its previous 'isolationism' and to seek allies, in Europe and beyond. The First World War accentuated Britain's relative weakness, particularly compared to the US. The nightmare prospect of war on two far-flung fronts – involving a fight for national survival within Europe and an attempt to defend the Empire – inspired a policy of 'appeasement' designed to satisfy Germany and its ally Italy with territorial gains which did not infringe on key British interests. Unfortunately for Britain and the leading champion of appeasement, Neville Chamberlain, Adolf Hitler interpreted appeasement as a token of British weakness, and even Chamberlain accepted the need for war when Germany invaded Poland in September 1939.

Further reading

This crucial period has been covered by some books which are worth reading for their own sakes, as well as their relevance. In particular, AJP Taylor's *The Struggle for Mastery in Europe: 1848–1918* (Oxford University Press, 1989) is an endless source of stimulation. Zara Steiner's *The Lights That Failed: European International History 1919–1933* (Oxford University Press, 2005) and *The Triumph of the Dark: European International History 1933–1939* (Oxford University Press, 2011) are vivid and thought-provoking portraits of a continent in crisis.

Taylor and Steiner have also provided studies which are more directly concerned with British foreign policy in these years. Taylor's *The Origins of the Second World War* (Hamish Hamilton, 1961) is typically provocative. A revised edition of Steiner's classic book *Britain and the Origins of the First World War* (written with Keith Neilson) was published by Palgrave Macmillan in 2003. Margaret Macmillan's *Peacemakers: The Paris Peace Conference of 1919 and Its Attempt to End War* (John Murray, 2001) and her *The War that Ended Peace: How Europe Abandoned Peace for the First World War* (Profile Books, 2013) belong in the same exalted company, along with Paul Kennedy's *The Realities Behind Diplomacy: Background Influences on British External Policy 1865–1980* (Fontana, 1989), which examines much of the period covered by the present volume but which is particularly good on the earlier decades. Ronald Hyam's *Britain's Declining Empire: The Road to Decolonisation 1918–1968* (Cambridge University Press, 2006) is indispensable for the whole of the period it covers.

On the inter-war years, FS Northedge's *The Troubled Giant: Britain among the Great Powers, 1916–1929* (Bell, 1966) still rewards close inspection, along with Philip Reynolds' *British Foreign Policy in the Inter-War Years* (Longmans, 1954). A notable and more recent study is Anne Orde, *The Eclipse of Great Britain: The United States and British Imperial Decline, 1895–1956* (Longman, 1996). Paul Doerr's *British Foreign Policy 1919–39* (Manchester University Press, 1998) is an invaluable summary of inter-war developments.

Readers who want to expose themselves to the continuing controversy over 'appeasement' are advised to begin with John Charmley's *Chamberlain and the Lost Peace* (Hodder & Stoughton, 1989), following up with Robert Self's magnificent *Neville Chamberlain: A Biography* (Ashgate, 2006). After this preparation, readers should be able to take a measured view of Robert Rhodes James (ed.), *'Chips': The Diaries of Sir Henry Channon* (Phoenix, 1996), which offers valuable insights into the psychology of appeasement, and Martin Gilbert and Richard Gott, *The Appeasers* (Weidenfeld & Nicolson, 1963), which is rather less sympathetic to Chamberlain and his supporters.

Chapter 4: the limping lion, 1945–55

Summary

The immediate post-war years, which are covered in this chapter, established several enduring themes in British foreign policy. On the one hand, Britain had experienced its 'finest hour' during its resistance to Nazi Germany and was recognised as one of the three great powers (along with the US and the Soviet Union) which presided over the post-war settlement. However, Britain was clearly the weakest of the three – indeed, compared to the superpowers it was puny. Its greatest potential asset, the Empire, was obviously impossible to defend either from outside attack or nationalistic unrest; and even if Britain had commanded sufficient resources to maintain its overseas possessions, the moral disapproval of the country's key ally, the US, made this unsustainable.

The chapter outlines the response of British politicians (from both main parties) to this dilemma. It argues that two 'narratives' were developed: the first simply denying that Britain had ceased to be a great power, and the second asserting that, even if its military might had diminished in relative terms, it *deserved* to retain its global significance because of its record of standing up for justice against tyrannical regimes like Nazi Germany. These narratives could be used interchangeably. Thus, for example, the Attlee governments of 1945–51 tried to prolong the wartime alliance with the US, partly to ensure the defence of Europe against a perceived Soviet threat, in what came to be known as the Cold War, and partly in the hope of retaining Britain's diplomatic weight. Attlee and senior colleagues also decided to develop nuclear weapons. Simultaneously, they began the process of disengagement from the Empire, using the 'moral' narrative as political cover for what otherwise might have been regarded as an admission of reduced global power. In reality, during these years Britain was selective in its approach to decolonisation, using force to maintain its position in some territories which provided it with much needed raw materials. One by-product of these narratives was Britain's (at best) ambivalent attitude to the early signs of European cooperation; officially, Britain decided to welcome this development, while reaffirming its belief in a global mission.

Further reading

Wide-ranging studies which are particularly useful for these years include FS Northedge, *Descent from Power: British Foreign Policy, 1945–1973* (Allen & Unwin,

1974); CM Woodhouse, *British Foreign Policy since the Second World War* (Hutchinson, 1971); and Anne Orde, *The Eclipse of Great Britain: The United States and British Imperial Decline, 1895–1956* (Macmillan, 1996). A highly relevant study of the economic background is Alan Milward, *The Economic Effects of the World Wars on Britain* (Macmillan, 1970).

On relations with the US and the origins of the Cold War, see John Charmley, *Churchill's Grand Alliance: The Anglo-American Special Relationship, 1940–57* (Hodder & Stoughton, 1995); D Cameron Watt, *Succeeding John Bull: America in Britain's Place 1900–1975* (Cambridge University Press, 1984); Anne Deighton, *The Impossible Peace: Britain, the Division of Germany and the Origins of the Cold War* (Oxford University Press, 1990) and her edited volume *Britain and the First Cold War* (Macmillan, 1990); and Nicholas Henderson, *The Birth of NATO* (Weidenfeld & Nicolson, 1982).

The retreat from Empire has been analysed by several scholars who have the ability to combine searching analysis with a very accessible style of writing. See, in particular, John Darwin, *Britain and Decolonisation: The Retreat from Empire in the Post-War World* (Macmillan, 1988); Piers Brendon, *The Decline and Fall of the British Empire* (Jonathan Cape, 2007); and Ronald Hyam, *Britain's Declining Empire: The Road to Decolonisation 1918–1968* (Cambridge University Press, 1988). On India, see Stanley Wolpert, *Shameful Flight: The Last Years of the British Empire in India* (Oxford, 2006).

Britain's role in the Middle East during these years has been the subject of some searching analysis. Wm Roger Louis and RW Stookey's edited volume *The End of the Palestine Mandate* (Tauris, 1968) is particularly useful, along with FS Northedge, 'Britain and the Middle East', in R Ovendale (ed.), *The Foreign Policy of the British Labour Governments 1945–51* (Leicester University Press, 1984). On the Iranian coup, see Steven Kinzer, *All the Shah's Men: An American Coup and the Roots of Middle East Terror* (John Wiley, 2003).

On Britain's (non-) engagement with Europe, see Hugo Young, *This Blessed Plot: Britain and Europe from Churchill to Blair* (Macmillan, 1998).

Chapter 5: Suez and 'Supermac', 1955–63

Summary

This chapter is dominated by the Suez crisis of 1956, which dispelled any illusion that Britain's relationship with the US was based on equal concern for each other's perceived interests. This policy disaster could have impelled Britain towards constructive engagement with its European allies, but, if anything, it made senior ministers more anxious to reassert the great-power narrative. In pursuit of this goal the Conservative government of Harold Macmillan sought to deepen nuclear cooperation with the US, culminating in the Nassau Agreement of 1962, which made Britain dependent on US ballistic-missile technology. By that time, however, the economic success of the European Economic Community (EEC) had persuaded Macmillan that Britain would have to apply for membership after all. France's President de Gaulle vetoed the application, partly for personal and nationalistic reasons but also on the more defensible grounds that Britain was far more attuned to the US than to the European mainland. This humiliating rebuff, coming so soon after the Suez fiasco, verified the earlier comment of the US statesman Dean Acheson that Britain had lost an Empire and had yet to find a role for itself.

Further reading

Although many excellent books have been written about the key event of this period, the classic study is Keith Kyle, *Suez: Britain's End of Empire in the Middle East* (2nd edition, IB Tauris, 2003). A special issue of the journal *Contemporary British History* (1999) was devoted to 'Whitehall and the Suez Crisis'. See also Wm Roger Louis and Roger Owen (eds), *Suez 1956: The Crisis and Its Consequences* (Oxford University Press, 1989).

For developments in the Empire/Commonwealth, most of the books listed in the further reading for Chapter 2 also provide coverage for this period. Along with the subject of 'Europe', they are also discussed in the excellent edited collection by Wolfram Kaiser and Gillian Staerck, *British Foreign Policy, 1955–64: Contracting Options* (Macmillan, 2000). Some piercing insights are offered from the US perspective by Kenneth Waltz in the relevant chapters of his *Foreign Policy and Democratic Politics: The American and British Experience* (Longman, 1967). CM Woodhouse's *British Foreign Policy since the Second World War* (Hutchinson, 1961) is particularly interesting on Europe, since the author (later Baron Terrington) was a Conservative MP who wrote this book when the British government was reluctantly accepting the need to apply for EEC membership (he had previously been a diplomat and a secret agent who was involved in the Iranian coup of 1953, before becoming Director of the respected think tank the Royal Institute of International Affairs).

Harold Macmillan's published diaries (edited by Peter Catterall and published by Macmillan in two volumes (2003 and 2011) are indispensable sources. See also Richard Aldous and Simon Lee (eds), *Harold Macmillan and Britain's World Role* (Macmillan, 1996) and Ritchie Ovendale, 'Macmillan and the Wind of Change in Africa, 1957–60', *Historical Journal*, Vol. 38, 1995.

Finally, for analysis of the most pertinent (or pestilential) comment on this period, see Douglas Brinkley, 'Dean Acheson and the "Special Relationship": The West Point speech of December 1962', *Historical Journal*, Vol. 33, 1990.

Chapter 6: symbols and substance, 1963–70

Summary

Blackballed by 'Europe' and wary of too close a commitment to a US which was becoming embroiled in the Vietnam War, Labour's Harold Wilson took office in 1964 determined to address Britain's relative decline at its source, i.e. its post-war economic stagnation. This initiative failed, largely for reasons outside his government's control. Britain reapplied for EEC membership, prompting another de Gaulle veto, and tried to act as an 'honest broker' in Vietnam with limited success. The decade was blighted by Britain's obvious impotence in the face of an illegal declaration of independence by its colony of Southern Rhodesia (later Zimbabwe). If Britain could no longer read the Riot Act even to small states run by racists, its moral stature was also endangered by its policy towards Nigeria, which was clearly dictated by its thirst for reserves of crude oil. Labour also jeopardised its ethical image by moving to restrict immigration to Britain on racial grounds, bowing to a public mood which was stirred in 1968 by Enoch Powell's 'rivers of blood' speech.

Further reading

On Britain's continuing withdrawal from Empire, the relevant chapters of books by Hyam, Darwin and Brendon listed in the further reading for previous chapters are highly recommended. On the final decision to withdraw from 'east of Suez', see Gill Bennett, *Six Moments of Crisis: Inside British Foreign Policy* (Oxford University Press, 2013), chapter 4. On Diego Garcia, see the blistering critique in Mark Curtis, *Web of Deceit: Britain's Real Role in the World* (Vintage, 2003), chapter 22.

On Europe, see Oliver Daddow (ed.), *Harold Wilson and European Integration: Britain's Second Application to Join the EEC* (Frank Cass, 2003) and Helen Parr, *Britain's Policy towards the EC: Harold Wilson and Britain's World Role 1964–67* (Routledge, 2006).

On Vietnam, see Peter Busch, *All the Way with JFK: Britain, the US and the Vietnam War* (Oxford University Press, 2003); Jonathan Hollowell (ed.), *Twentieth-Century Anglo-American Relations* (Palgrave, 2001), chapter 10; and John Dumbrell, *A Special Relationship: Anglo-American Relations in the Twentieth Century* (Macmillan, 2001).

Rhodesia is discussed in John Young, *The Wilson Governments 1964–70: International Policy* (Manchester University Press, 2003); Richard Coggins, 'Wilson and Rhodesia: UDI and British policy towards Africa', *Contemporary British History*, Vol. 20, 2006; and Rhiannon Vickers, 'Foreign and Defence Policy', in Andrew S. Crines and Kevin Hickson (eds), *Harold Wilson: The Unprincipled Prime Minister?* (Biteback, 2016).

Chapter 7: awkward partners and special relationships, 1970–83

Summary

In 1973 Britain finally achieved membership of the EEC, under a Prime Minister (Edward Heath) who wanted to break from the post-war narratives and forge a new role for Britain as a significant European power whose relations with the US were friendly but not subservient. Heath, however, had limited rapport with the British electorate and never came close to developing a convincing narrative of his own. Restored to office between 1974 and 1979, Labour continued to flounder, bedevilled by the economic and industrial problems which had floored Heath. It did, however, participate in constructive dialogue with the Soviet Union and acted decisively when the British Overseas Territory of the Falkland Islands came under potential threat from Argentina.

After Heath's downfall, the Conservative Party had chosen as its leader Margaret Thatcher, who was an unquestioning expositor of the great-power narrative. When her party regained office in 1979 her timing could hardly have been better; the Cold War was about to re-enter the deep freeze, and in 1980 America elected a President (Ronald Reagan) who genuinely liked Thatcher and apparently shared many of her views. In her first term Thatcher was broadly successful in branding those who disputed the great-power narrative as either defeatists or crypto-Communists. Since her instinctive support for America was accompanied by a suspicion of Europeans, she reactivated the fears of EC partners who doubted that Britain could ever be more than an 'awkward partner'. Despite her bellicose rhetoric, her government's resolve to cut public spending encompassed the armed forces, particularly the Navy. Among its effects, this policy consciously left the Falkland Islands without an effective defence, and attempts at a negotiated settlement were thwarted by Conservative backbench MPs who shared Thatcher's own view that Britain was still a great power. In the ensuing conflict over the islands, Thatcher proved a very effective war leader, not least because she was able to draw on support from the US. Her attempts to depict the victory as testimony to Britain's enduring great-power status proved effective among parts of the electorate which were influenced by elements of the tabloid press.

Further reading

For aspects of the Heath government's foreign policy, see two chapters in Stuart Ball and Anthony Seldon (eds), *The Heath Government 1970–1974: A Reappraisal* (Longman, 1996); John Young's 'The Heath Government and British Entry into the European Community' and 'The Foreign Policy of the Heath Government' by Christopher Hill and Christopher Lord. Heath's own Godkin Lecture of 1967, published as *Old Worlds, New Horizons: Britain, the Common Market and the Atlantic Alliance* (Oxford University Press, 1970) offers invaluable insights into his foreign policy thinking.

On Mrs Thatcher's first term, Charles Moore's *Not for Turning*, the first volume of his authorised biography (Allen Lane, 2013) provides a wealth of useful information. *Signals of War: The Falklands Conflict of 1982* (Faber and Faber, 1991) by Lawrence Freedman and Virginia Gamba-Stonehouse is an authoritative study. Freedman's 'Britain and the World', in Dennis Kavanagh and Anthony Seldon (eds), *The Thatcher Effect: A Decade of Change* (Oxford University Press, 1989) is a convenient summary written before the end of the Thatcher period. For sources dealing with the 'special relationship' under Thatcher, see the further reading for Chapter 8.

Chapter 8: from Falklands fanfare to Maastricht misery, 1983–92

Summary

The Conservatives were re-elected in 1983 – partly thanks to the 'Falklands factor' but mainly due to the fact that anti-Conservative sentiment was divided. In particular, Mrs Thatcher benefited from Labour's policy, which in the 1983 general election was opposed both to the 'special relationship' with the US *and* to the supposed alternative role of positive engagement with 'Europe'. However, between 1983 and her resignation in 1990 Thatcher gradually ran out of luck, in a manner which exposed the unreality of her argument that the Falklands Conflict had confirmed the great-power narrative. By the end of the decade her anti-Communism seemed obsolete, since the Soviet Union had collapsed; before its demise her supposed 'soulmate', President Reagan, had come close to a deal with the Soviet leader, Mikhail Gorbachev, which would have removed the protection of America's 'nuclear umbrella' from Europe. Although Thatcher liked Gorbachev personally, she had good reason to resent his rise to power since one of its effects was the prospect of a reunified Germany. For someone whose mindset had been constructed by the Second World War, this was an unpalatable prospect, which increased an existing hostility towards the EC. Thatcher's attempt (in her 1988 Bruges speech) to construct the EC into a threat to British identity was thought-provoking, to say the least, since in other contexts she had hailed a sense of Britishness which was capable of surmounting any challenge; and in the same speech she seemed to concede that citizens of other European nations could accept 'ever closer union' without suffering an existential crisis.

Mrs Thatcher could have hoped for succour from across the Atlantic; but Reagan's replacement, George Bush, was unswayed by sentiment and regarded German reunification as a positive development. The 'special relationship' with the US was revived to some extent by cooperation during the Gulf War of 1991; but the British beneficiary was Thatcher's successor as Prime Minister, John Major.

Further reading

On the 'special relationship' in the 1980s, see the contrasting studies by Geoffrey Smith (*Reagan and Thatcher*, Bodley Head, 1990) and Richard Aldous (*Reagan & Thatcher: The Difficult Relationship*, Hutchinson, 2012). Again, the relevant volume of Charles Moore's authorised biography (*Anything She Wants*, Allen Lane, 2015) is very useful, particularly for the relationship with Gorbachev and Thatcher's attitude to the FCO. The same is true of Percy Craddock's discreet insider account, *In Pursuit of British Interests: Reflections on Foreign Policy under Margaret Thatcher and John Major* (John Murray, 1997). Paul Sharp, *Thatcher's Diplomacy: The Revival of British Foreign Policy* (Macmillan, 1999) should be consulted, even though some might consider its title to be an oxymoron and harbour some doubts about its subtitle.

The Thatcher period is crucial to an understanding of Britain's relationship with 'Europe', and all good books on that subject will provide useful coverage of the Bruges speech and its aftermath. However, readers are advised to consult the whole text (available at www.margaretthatcher.org/document/107332). Stephen Wall's *A Stranger in Europe: Britain and the EU from Thatcher to Blair* (Oxford University Press, 2008) is particularly recommended.

John Major: The Autobiography (HarperCollins, 1999) contains excellent material on the Gulf War and Maastricht. Douglas Hurd's *Memoirs* (Little, Brown, 2003) are also well worth consulting in conjunction with other sources (in particular, William Wallace's 'Foreign Policy', in Dennis Kavanagh and Anthony Seldon (eds), *The Major Effect* (Macmillan, 1994)).

Chapter 9: ethics and interventions, 1992–2001

Summary

After making a conscious effort to step out of Thatcher's considerable shadow John Major found it impossible to plot a new course for British foreign policy. His biggest handicap was Britain's first-past-the-post electoral system, which ensured that although the Conservatives won the largest-ever tally of votes in the 1992 contest, they were left with an overall majority which handed effective power over key decisions to a relatively small clique of MPs, who were dubbed 'Eurosceptics', but who in reality were not sceptical at all. After Britain's enforced ejection from the Exchange Rate Mechanism (ERM) of the European Monetary System (EMS) in September 1992, these individuals made it impossible for Major to fulfil his self-declared intention to act positively in what was (after the 1992 Maastricht Treaty) the EU. Other forces at work within the Conservative Party confirmed Major's own reluctance (shared with his Foreign Secretary, Douglas Hurd) to commit British troops to any war-fighting role. This outlook was particularly damaging in the former Yugoslavia, where Britain tried to obstruct effective military action against Serbia, which sought to expand its territory through 'ethnic cleansing'. Since it had made no attempt to refute Thatcher's great-power narrative, the government was forced to adopt its own version of Neville Chamberlain's position that the inhabitants of countries outside Western Europe were 'far away' and that Britons were scantily informed about them.

The overwhelming Conservative defeat in the 1997 general election provided the incoming Prime Minister, New Labour's Tony Blair, with an opportunity to reassess Britain's place in the world without fear of disruption from troublesome backbenchers or, at least during his 'honeymoon' period, from the wrecking tactics of the tabloid press. However, Blair decided not to press the case for British involvement in the proposed European single currency. His main foreign policy focus was the promotion of 'humanitarian intervention', as expressed in his 1999 Chicago speech. This approach, apparently, was vindicated in the former Yugoslav province of Kosovo, despite US reservations which created tensions between Blair and his supposed ideological ally President Bill Clinton.

Further reading

The academic literature on Major's second government is not voluminous. There is relevant material in the memoirs of Major and Douglas Hurd (see previous chapter) and in *Major: A Political Life* (Weidenfeld & Nicolson, 1997) by Anthony Seldon and Lewis Baston. John Coles' *Making Foreign Policy: A Certain Idea of Britain* (John Murray, 2000) is the thought-provoking account of a very senior diplomat of the Major years. On the Scott Report into 'arms to Iraq', see Stephen Cook and Mark Lloyd, *Knee Deep in Dishonour: The Scott Report and Its Aftermath* (Victor Gollancz, 1996). On the ERM crisis, see Philip Stephens, *Politics and the Pound: The Conservatives' Struggle with Sterling* (Picador, 1996).

On the first Blair government, see John Kampfner, *Blair's Wars* (Free Press, 2003). The text of Blair's Chicago speech is available at www.pbs.org/newshour/bb/international-jan-june99-blair_doctrine4-23/. Robin Cook's 'ethical foreign policy' statement also deserves to be read in full, at www.theguardian.com/world/1997/may/12/indonesia.ethicalforeignpolicy. See also Richard Little and Mark Wickham-Jones (eds), *New Labour's Foreign Policy: A New Moral Crusade?* (Manchester University Press, 2000); Paul Williams, *British Foreign Policy under New Labour* (Palgrave Macmillan, 2005); and Brendan Sims, *Unfinest Hour: Britain and the Destruction of Bosnia* (Allen Lane, 2001).

Chapter 10: 'not in my name', 2001–7

Summary

Having forfeited the chance of a leading role within the EU by deciding not to campaign on behalf of Britain's adoption of the euro, Tony Blair needed to establish a good relationship with the new US President, George W Bush, if he was to cement his continuing popularity at home by creating the impression that Britain mattered on the world stage. Even if the terrorist attack of 11 September 2001 had been averted, he might have established a good relationship with Bush, since despite their ostensible party allegiances they had a similar view of a world divided between good and evil.

If 9/11 had happened on the watch of an articulate US President – like Bill Clinton – the British response might have been more nuanced. As it was, Blair expressed Britain's support for the US in more eloquent words than Bush could hope to find. Although America's grateful response could hardly change military realities, in which Britain could only hope for a subsidiary role, Blair enjoyed his moment of global recognition and decided to act as if he was Bush's Foreign Secretary. If he had considered the way in which he treated Britain's own Foreign Secretary, who was effectively excluded from decision-making long before 9/11, he might have thought twice about this self-adopted role on behalf of a President whose closest advisers held impracticable views on foreign policy in general and about the Middle East in particular.

While British public opinion was generally in favour of military action in Afghanistan in retaliation for 9/11, it was more divided about the long-planned attempt to remove the brutal dictator Saddam Hussein from Iraq. However, early in 2002 Blair assured Bush of British support for a war against Saddam's regime whenever America chose to act; and subsequent attempts to gain public 'consent' for this decision were almost laughably cynical. However, it was still possible to argue that regime change in Iraq was compatible with Britain's national interests. Subsequent events suggested that even this rationale for military action – a Realist argument which represented a departure from the 'moral' narrative underpinning British foreign policy after 1945 – could not be sustained.

Further reading

For this chapter, the problem is an overabundance of material, much of it available online. For example, the Hutton Inquiry can still be perused in full (www.webarchive.org.uk/ukwa/target/102325), along with the 2004 Butler Report (https://fas.org/irp/world/uk/butler071404.pdf) and the 2016 Chilcot Report (www.iraqinquiry.org.uk/), which contain plenty of relevant material for those who are interested in the policy-making process as well as the events leading up to the Iraq War.

In the secondary literature, contemporaneous reflections are always particularly interesting. William Shawcross' *Allies: The United States, Britain, Europe and the War in Iraq* (Atlantic Books, 2003) presents the argument for intervention without recourse to the second thoughts that might have arisen in hindsight. Peter Riddell's *Hug Them Close: Blair, Clinton, Bush and the Special Relationship* (Politicos, 2003) left far fewer hostages to fortune. Alastair Campbell's diary for the period, published as *The Burden of Power: Countdown to Iraq* (Hutchinson, 2013), is especially valuable, since it chronicles the daily reactions of protagonists and provides insights into their thinking. Blair's own memoir, *A Journey* (Hutchinson, 2010), is unrepentant – or, more accurately, defiant – in a way which makes his own reflections more revealing than the accounts of most Prime Ministers and therefore worth reading even by those who reject his reasoning. For such readers, William Wallace's article 'The Collapse of British Foreign Policy', *International Affairs*, Vol. 81, 2005, will provide an effective antidote. See also Mark Curtis, *Web of Deceit: Britain's Real Role in the World* (Vintage, 2003), chapters 1–2.

Chapter 11: heirs to Blair and 'Brexiteers', 2007–17

Summary

Whatever the problems it brought upon itself, Tony Blair's New Labour enjoyed a relatively trouble-free run in economic terms. The era of apparently painless prosperity came to an end almost as soon as Blair's successor, Gordon Brown, realised his long-nurtured ambition by becoming Prime Minister. Saddled with the consequences of Blair's wars in Afghanistan and Iraq, Brown tried his best to extricate British troops, but his attention was distracted by the global financial crisis. Since he had prided himself on his economic expertise even before becoming Chancellor of the Exchequer in 1997, he had good reason to regard this challenge as the testing ground for his premiership. Whether or not the crisis would have been more damaging without his personal interventions, qualified observers applauded his performance.

However, whether or not Brown 'saved the world', British voters were not in the mood to show gratitude, and New Labour lost office in 2010 amid predictions that the country faced a period of economic austerity. The incoming government – a coalition between the Conservatives and the Liberal Democrats – promised a foreign policy which combined the familiar post-war narratives. It would work in the national interest while paying due attention to 'moral' considerations.

Unfortunately for the coalition, its first serious test – the outbreak of the Arab Spring, which began in Tunisia early in 2011 – presented a challenge which its 'moral' side could not resist. The Prime Minister, David Cameron, seemed to regard the rebellious forces across the Arab world as if they faced the same challenges which confronted young people in the West, rather than being contestants of a highly complex political environment which included an explosive mixture of religious sects and tribal divisions.

If Cameron's Arab Spring quickly turned to winter, there was never any chance of a warmer prospect from 'Europe'. Whipped up by unrelenting media stories about EU misdeeds, public pressure for a referendum on membership resulted in rising support for the United Kingdom Independence Party (UKIP), and in January 2013 Cameron capitulated, promising a poll before 2017, whether or not the EU moved to even deeper integration. When he made this pledge, Cameron was Prime Minister of a government which included the pro-EU Liberal Democrats. After the 2015 general election Cameron became the head of a government comprised only of Conservatives; but by that time the small faction of Europhobes had grown to the extent that it could exert effective control over the whole party.

After announcing that the referendum would be held in June 2016 Cameron tried to extract meaningful concessions from his EU partners but without success. As a result, rather than presenting a European role as a ticket to the kind of glittering future promised by the post-war narratives, the 'Remain' campaign tried to convince voters that Britain would be doomed if its citizens voted to leave the EU. Understandably, many voters who had never relinquished the great-power narrative reacted strongly against this kind of campaign; and they were joined by people who felt that the EU's inflexible policy on the free movement of labour was undermining British living standards as well as presenting a potent threat to national security, despite the fact that most British terrorists had been 'home grown'.

The result of the 2016 referendum – which, if it had been an opinion poll, would have been regarded as interesting but inconclusive, even as a snapshot of British opinion at that particular time – suggested that the challenge implied in Dean Acheson's speech of 1962 was as pertinent as ever. Acheson had argued that Britain could not find a viable role if it was subordinate to the US or unwilling to join other European states in a union which was political as well as economic. More than 50 years later Britain still seems to be faced with that challenge.

Further reading

The 'Brexit' referendum is likely to dominate academic discussion relating to the Conservative government elected in 2015. On the previous coalition government, see Michael Clarke, 'The Coalition and Foreign Affairs', in Anthony Seldon and Mike Finn (eds), *The Coalition Effect, 2010–2015* (Cambridge University Press, 2015). On the continuity between Blair and Cameron, see Oliver Daddow and Pauline Schnapper, 'Liberal Intervention in the Foreign Policy Thinking of Tony Blair and David Cameron', *Cambridge Review of International Affairs*, Vol. 26, 2013. See also Michael Harvey, *Perspectives on the UK's Place in the World* (Chatham House, 2011). On the EU, see Cameron's Bloomberg speech, at www.gov.uk/government/speeches/eu-speech-at-bloomberg, and Eunice Goes, 'The Coalition and Europe: A tale of reckless drivers, steady navigators and imperfect roadmaps', *Parliamentary Affairs*, Vol. 66, 2013.

Bibliography

Adler, E (2005), *Communitarian International Relations: The Epistemic Foundations of International Relations*, Routledge.
Angell, N (1910), *The Great Illusion*, Putnams.
Ashcroft, M, and Oakeshott, I (2015), *Call Me Dave: The Unauthorised Biography of David Cameron*, Biteback.
Ashdown, P (2001), *The Ashdown Diaries*, Vol. II, Allen Lane.
Baldwin, S (1937), *The Service of Our Lives: Last Speeches as Prime Minister*, Hodder & Stoughton.
Barnett, C (1986), *The Audit of War: The Illusion and Reality of Britain as a Great Nation*, Macmillan.
Baylis, J (1997), *Anglo-American Relations since 1939: The Enduring Alliance*, Manchester University Press.
BBC (2007), 'Iraq War Survey', March, http://news.bbc.co.uk/1/shared/bsp/hi/pdfs/20_03_07_iraq_poll.pdf.
Beckett, A (2010), *When the Lights Went Out: A History of Britain in the Seventies*, Faber and Faber.
Beech, M (2011), 'British Conservatism and Foreign Policy: Traditions and ideas shaping Cameron's global view', *British Journal of Politics and International Relations*, Vol. 13, issue 3.
Beetham, R (2006), written contribution to witness seminar in M Kandiah and G Staerck (eds), *The Helsinki Negotiations: The Accords and Their Impact*, Institute of Contemporary British History.
Beisner, R (2006), *Dean Acheson: A Life in the Cold War*, Oxford University Press.
Beloff, Lord (1986), 'The End of the British Empire and the Assumption of Worldwide Commitments by the United States', in WR Louis and Hedley Bull (eds), *The 'Special Relationship': Anglo-American Relations since 1945*, Oxford University Press.
Benn, T (1988), *Office without Power: Diaries, 1968–72*, Hutchinson.
Benn, T (1994), *Years of Hope: Diaries, Letters and Papers 1940–62*, Hutchinson.
Bennett, G (2013), *Six Moments of Crisis: Inside British Foreign Policy*, Oxford University Press.

Blair, T (1999), 'Doctrine of the International Community', Economic Club of Chicago, 24 April, www.britishpoliticalspeech.org/speech-archive.htm?speech=279.

Blair, T (2001), statement on 11 September 2001, http://news.bbc.co.uk/1/hi/uk_politics/1538551.stm.

Blair, T (2002), 'Foreword', *Iraq's Weapons of Mass Destruction: The Assessment of the British Government*.

Blair, T (2003), Address to British ambassadors in London, 7 January, www.theguardian.com/politics/2003/jan/07/foreignpolicy.speeches.

Blair, T (2010), *A Journey*, Hutchinson.

Brendon, P (2008), *The Decline and Fall of the British Empire*, Penguin.

Brown, C (with K Ainley) (1997), *Understanding International Relations*, Palgrave Macmillan.

Bush, GW (2002), State of the Union Address, 29 January, http://whitehouse.georgewbush.org/news/2002/012902-SOTU.asp.

Butler, D, and Pinto-Duschinsky, M (1971), *The British General Election of 1970*, Macmillan.

Buzan, B (2004), *From International to World Society? English School Theory and the Social Structure of Globalisation*, Cambridge University Press.

Cameron, D (2003), 'Time to Be Counted', *Guardian*, 17 March.

Cameron, D (2006), Speech to the British–American Project, *Guardian*, 11 September.

Cameron, D (2011), Speech to the UN General Assembly, 22 September, www.gov.uk/government/speeches/prime-ministers-first-speech-to-the-un-general-assembly.

Cameron, D (2012), Speech to the UN General Assembly, 26 September, www.gov.uk/government/news/the-arab-spring-represents-a-precious-opportunity-for-people-to-realise-their-aspirations-for-a-job-a-voice-and-a-stake-in-their-own-future.

Cameron, D (2013), EU speech at Bloomberg, 23 January, www.gov.uk/government/speeches/eu-speech-at-bloomberg.

Campbell, A (2011), *Diaries, Vol. II, Power and the People*, Hutchinson.

Campbell, A (2012), *Diaries, Vol. III, Power and Responsibility*, Hutchinson.

Carr, E (1937), *International Relations since the Peace Treaties*, Macmillan.

Carr, E (1939), *The Twenty Years' Crisis*, Macmillan.

Castle, S, and Routledge, P (1997), 'Blair is Mr 93%', *Independent*, 28 September.

Catterall, P (ed.) (2011), *The Macmillan Diaries, Vol. II, Prime Minister and After, 1957–1966*, Macmillan.

Chapman, J (2011), 'Day the PM Put Britain First', *Daily Mail*, 10 December.

Charmley, J (1989), *Chamberlain and the Lost Peace*, Hodder & Stoughton.

Churchill, W (1930), article in *Saturday Evening Post*, 15 February.

Churchill, W (1950), *Europe Unite: Speeches 1947 and 1948*, Cassell.

Clark, C (2013), *The Sleepwalkers: How Europe Went to War in 1914*, Allen Lane.

Coe, S (2012), *Running My Life: The Autobiography*, Hodder & Stoughton.

Cook, R (1997), Mission statement for the Foreign and Commonwealth Office, www.theguardian.com/world/1997/may/12/indonesia.ethicalforeignpolicy.

Cook, R (2003), *Point of Departure*, Simon & Schuster.

Cowley, P, and Stuart, M (2012), 'The Cambusters: The Conservative European Union Referendum rebellion of October 2011', *Political Quarterly*, Vol. 83, issue 2.

Cox, R (1981), 'Social Forces, States, and World Orders: Beyond International Relations Theory', *Millennium: Journal of International Studies*, Vol. 10, issue 2.

Cradock, P (1997), *In Pursuit of British Interests: Reflections on Foreign Policy under Margaret Thatcher and John Major*, John Murray.
Crowley, D (1963), *The Background to Current Affairs*, Macmillan.
Curtis, M (2003), *Web of Deceit: Britain's Real Role in the World*, Vintage.
Dell, E (1996), *The Chancellors: A History of the Chancellors of the Exchequer, 1945–1990*, HarperCollins.
Denver, D, and Garnett, M (2014), *British General Elections since 1964: Diversity, Dealignment, and Disillusion*, Oxford University Press.
Dibelius, W (1930), *England*, Jonathan Cape.
Dickie, J (2004), *The New Mandarins: How British Foreign Policy Works*, IB Tauris.
Dillon, M (1989), *The Falklands, Politics and War*, Palgrave Macmillan.
Doerr, P (1998), *British Foreign Policy 1919–39*, Manchester University Press.
Donaldson, F (1984), *The British Council: The First Fifty Years*, Jonathan Cape.
Dumbrell, J (2001), *A Special Relationship: Anglo-American Relations in the Twentieth Century*, Macmillan.
Dundabin, J (1994), *The Post-Imperial Age: The Great Powers and the Wider World*, Pearson.
Dutton, D (1985), *Austen Chamberlain: Gentleman in Politics*, Ross Anderson.
Economist (1997), 'Cook's Tour', 15 May.
Economist (1999), 'Addicted to the Arms Trade', 16 September.
Economist (2015), 'Punch and Duty', 4 April.
Ehrman, J (1996), *The Younger Pitt, Vol. III, The Consuming Struggle*, Constable.
Finnemore, M (1996), *National Interests in International Society*, Cornell University Press.
Frankel, J (1975), *British Foreign Policy, 1945–1973*, Royal Institute for International Affairs.
Franks, OS (1983), *Falkland Islands Review*, HMSO.
Freedman, L, and Gamba-Stonehouse, V (1990), *Signals of War: The Falklands Conflict of 1982*, Faber and Faber.
Fukuyama, F (1989), 'The End of History', *The National Interest*, Summer.
Fukuyama, F (1992), *The End of History and the Last Man*, Free Press.
Garnett, M (2007), *From Anger to Apathy: The British Experience, 1975–2005*, Jonathan Cape.
Garnett, M (2015), 'Iain Macleod', in R Hayton and A Crines (eds), *Conservative Orators from Baldwin to Cameron*, Manchester University Press.
Garnett, M, and Mabon, S (2016), 'Think Tanks and Foreign Policy in the United Kingdom', in D Abelson, S Brooks and X Hua (eds), *Think Tanks, Foreign Policy and Geo-Politics: Pathways to Influence*, Routledge.
Gaskarth, J (2013), *British Foreign Policy: Crises, Conflicts and Future Challenges*, Polity.
Geddes, A (2004), *The European Union and British Politics*, Palgrave Macmillan.
Gilbert, M (1986), *Road to Victory: Winston S. Churchill, 1941–1945*, Heinemann.
Gilbert, M (1988), *Never Despair: Winston S Churchill 1945–1965*, Heinemann.
Gilbert, M (1990), *Prophet of Truth: Winston S Churchill 1922–39*, Minerva.
Goes, E (2013), 'The Coalition and Europe: A tale of reckless drivers, steady navigators and imperfect roadmaps', *Parliamentary Affairs*, Vol. 67, issue 1.
Green, EH (2010), *Thatcher*, Hodder Arnold.
Greenwood, S (2000), *Britain and the Cold War, 1945–91*, Palgrave Macmillan.
Hague, W (2010), 'Britain's Foreign Policy in a Networked World', www.gov.uk/government/speeches/britain-s-foreign-policy-in-a-networked-world-2.

Hague, W (2011), Evidence to House of Commons Foreign Affairs Select Committee, HC 438.
Hamilton, K (2006), 'Britain and the Conference on Security and Cooperation in Europe, 1972–77', in M Kandiah and G Staerck (eds), *The Helsinki Negotiations: The Accords and Their Impact*, Institute of Contemporary British History.
Helm, T (2014), 'David Cameron in New Bid to Stop Jean-Claude Juncker', *Guardian*, 7 June.
Henderson, N (1979), valedictory despatch, www.margaretthatcher.org/archive/1979_Henderson_despatch.asp.
Hennessy, P (1992), *Never Again: Britain, 1945–51*, Jonathan Cape.
Hennessy, P (2006), *Having It So Good: Britain in the Fifties*, Allen Lane.
Herz, J (1950), 'Idealist Internationalism and the Security Dilemma', *World Politics*, Vol. 2, issue 2.
HM Government (2010), *The Coalition: Our Programme for Government*, www.gov.uk/government/uploads/system/uploads/attachment_data/file/78977/coalition_programme_for_government.pdf.
Home, A (1976), *The Way the Wind Blows: An Autobiography*, Collins.
Hopf, T (1998), 'The Promise of Constructivism in International Relations Theory', *International Security*, Vol. 23, issue 1.
House of Commons (2006), *Report of the Official Account of the Bombings in London on 7 July 2005*, HC 1087.
House of Commons Foreign Affairs Committee (2002), Seventh Report from the Foreign Affairs Committee Session 2001–02, *Foreign Policy Aspects of the War against Terrorism*, HC 384.
House of Commons Foreign Affairs Committee (2003), Ninth Report of Session 2002–3, *The Decision to Go to War in Iraq*, HC 813.
House of Commons Foreign Affairs Committee (2011), Seventh Report of Session 2010–12, *The Role of the FCO in UK Government*, HC 665.
House of Commons Foreign Affairs Committee (2016), Third Report of Session 2016–17, *Libya: Examination of Intervention and Collapse and the UK's Future Policy Options*, HC 119.
Howard, A, and West, R (1965), *The Making of the Prime Minister*, Jonathan Cape.
Hurd, D (1997), *The Search for Peace: A Century of Peace Diplomacy*, Little, Brown.
Hurd, D (2003), *Memoirs*, Little, Brown.
Hurd, D (2010), *Choose Your Weapons: The British Foreign Secretary – 200 Years of Argument, Success and Failure*, Weidenfeld & Nicolson.
Hyam, R (2006), *Britain's Declining Empire: The Road to Decolonisation 1918–1968*, Cambridge University Press.
Ipsos MORI (1983), 'Cruise Missiles – Trend: British opinions in the 1980s', November, https://ipsos-mori.com/researchpublications/researcharchive/3243/Cruise-missiles-trend.aspx?view=wide.
Ipsos MORI (2001a), 'British Reaction to Attacks on America', September, www.ipsos-mori.com/researchpublications/researcharchive/1343/British-Reaction-To-Attacks-On-America.aspx.
Ipsos MORI (2001b), 'War of Afghanistan', October, www.ipsos-mori.com/researchpublications/researcharchive/1276/War-of-Afghanistan-Poll.aspx.
Ipsos MORI (2003a), 'Blair Losing Support on Iraq', January, www.ipsos-mori.com/researchpublications/researcharchive/829/Blair-Losing-Public-Support-On-Iraq.aspx.

Ipsos MORI (2003b), 'Iraq: The last pre-war polls', March, www.ipsos-mori.com/newsevents/ca/287/Iraq-The-Last-PreWar-Polls.aspx.

Ipsos MORI (2016), 'European Union Memberships – Trends', June, www.ipsos-mori.com/researchpublications/researcharchive/2435/European-Union-membership-trends.aspx.

James, L (1994), *The Rise and Fall of the British Empire*, St Martin's Press.

Kampfner, J (2003), *Blair's Wars*, Free Press.

Karsh, E, and Rautsi, I (1991), *Saddam Hussein: A Political Biography*, Free Press.

Kennan, G (1946), 'The Long Telegram', at http://nsarchive.gwu.edu/coldwar/documents/episode-1/kennan.htm.

Kennedy, P (1981), *The Realities behind Diplomacy: Background Influences on British External Policy, 1865–1980*, Allen & Unwin.

Krugman, P (2008), 'Gordon Does Good', *New York Times*, 12 October.

Kyle, K (2003), *Suez: Britain's End of Empire in the Middle East*, IB Tauris.

Lamb, R (1995), *The Macmillan Years, 1957–63: The Emerging Truth*, John Murray.

Lane, A (2004) 'Foreign and Defence Policy', in A Seldon and K Hickson (eds), *New Labour, Old Labour: The Wilson and Callaghan Governments, 1974–79*, Routledge.

Lawson, D (1990), 'Saying the Unsayable about the Germans', *Spectator*, 14 July.

Lawson, N (1992), *The View from No. 11: Memoirs of a Tory Radical*, Bantam Press.

Louis, W (1977), *Imperialism at Bay, 1941–1945*, Oxford University Press.

Lynn, J, and Jay, A (1986), *Yes, Prime Minister: The Diaries of the Right Hon. James Hacker*, Vol. 1, BBC.

McCullough, D (1992), *Truman*, Simon & Schuster.

Macmillan, H (1973), *At the End of the Day*, Macmillan.

Major, J (1999), *The Autobiography*, HarperCollins.

Mason, E, and Asher, R (1979), *The World Bank since Bretton Woods*, Brookings Institution.

May, A (1998), *Britain and Europe*, Routledge.

May, T (2016), Statement from new Prime Minister, www.gov.uk/government/speeches/statement-from-the-new-prime-minister-theresa-may.

Meyer, C (2005), *DC Confidential*, Weidenfeld & Nicolson.

Montague Browne, A (1995), *Long Sunset: The Memoirs of Winston Churchill's Last Private Secretary*, Cassell.

Moore, C (2015), *Margaret Thatcher, The Authorised Biography, Vol. II, Everything She Wants*, Allen Lane.

Morgan, K (1984), *Labour in Power 1945–51*, Oxford University Press.

Morgan, K (1997), *Callaghan: A Life*, Oxford University Press.

Morgenthau, H (1948), *Politics among Nations: The Struggle for Power and Peace*, Alfred A Knopf.

Mullin, C (2010), *A View from the Foothills: The Diaries of Chris Mullin*, Profile.

Naughtie, J (2004), *The Accidental American*, Macmillan.

Nicolson, H (1937), 'British Foreign Policy and Public Opinion', *Public Opinion Quarterly*, Vol. 1, issue 1.

Nicolson, H (1946), *The Congress of Vienna – A Study in Allied Unity, 1814–22*, Constable.

Northedge, F (1962), *British Foreign Policy: The Process of Readjustment, 1945–1961*, Allen & Unwin.

Northedge, F (1966), *The Troubled Giant: Britain among the Great Powers, 1916–1929*, Bell.
Northedge, F (1974), *Descent from Power: British Foreign Policy, 1945–73*, Allen & Unwin.
Nye, J (2002), *The Paradox of American Power*, Oxford University Press.
Oborne, P (2015), 'David Cameron Truly Is the Heir to Tony Blair', *Daily Mail*, 21 November.
O'Keeffe, L (2006), '… And the Walls Came Tumbling Down', in M Kandiah and G Staerck (eds), *The Helsinki Negotiations: The Accords and their Impact*, Institute of Contemporary British History.
Orde, A (1996), *The Eclipse of Great Britain: The United States and British Imperial Decline, 1895–1956*, Longman.
Pimlott, B (1992), *Harold Wilson*, HarperCollins.
Ponting, C (1989), *Breach of Promise: Labour in Power, 1964–70*, Hamish Hamilton.
Porter, B (2008), *Critics of Empire: British Radicals and the Imperial Challenge*, IB Tauris.
Price, L (2010), *Where Power Lies: Prime Ministers v The Media*, Simon & Schuster.
Pulzer, P (1967), *Political Representation and Elections in Britain*, Allen & Unwin.
Reynolds, D (2000), *Britannia Overruled: British Policy and World Power in the Twentieth Century*, Routledge.
Reynolds, P (1954), *British Foreign Policy in the Inter-War Years*, Longman.
Reynolds, P (2007), 'The Subtle Shift in British Foreign Policy', http://news.bbc.co.uk/1/hi/uk_politics/6897313.stm.
Rhodes James, R (1986), *Anthony Eden*, Macmillan.
Richards, P (1967), *Parliament and Foreign Affairs*, Allen & Unwin.
Riddell, P (1996), 'Labour Reaps Poll Rewards of Scott', *The Times*, 29 February.
Riddell, P (2003), *Hug Them Close: Blair, Clinton, Bush and the 'Special Relationship'*, Politicos.
Riddell, P (2005), 'Europe', in A Seldon and D Kavanagh (eds), *The Blair Effect, 2001–5*, Cambridge University Press.
Ruggie, J (1998), *Constructing the World Polity: Essays on International Institutionalisation*, Routledge.
Roberts, I (2006), valedictory despatch, www.gov.uk/government/uploads/system/uploads/attachment_data/file/513213/0520-15_Valedictory_Note.pdf.
Sampson, A (1962), *Anatomy of Britain*, Hodder & Stoughton.
Sampson, A (1965), *Anatomy of Britain Today*, Hodder & Stoughton.
Sampson, A (1971), *The New Anatomy of Britain*, Hodder & Stoughton.
Sampson, A (1983), *The Changing Anatomy of Britain*, Random House.
Sampson, A (2004), *Who Runs This Place? The Anatomy of Britain in the 21st Century*, John Murray.
Seeley, J (1883), *The Expansion of England*, Macmillan.
Seldon, A (2004), *Blair*, Free Press.
Seldon, A (2007), *Blair Unbound*, Simon & Schuster.
Seldon, A, and Baston, L (1997), *John Major: A Political Life*, Weidenfeld & Nicolson.
Self, R (2006), *Neville Chamberlain: A Biography*, Ashgate.
Self, R (2010), *British Foreign & Defence Policy since 1945*, Palgrave Macmillan.
Sellar, W, and Yeatman, R (1930), *1066 and All That*, Methuen.
Sharp, P (1997), *Thatcher's Diplomacy: The Revival of British Foreign Policy*, Palgrave Macmillan.

Shipman, T (2017), *All Out War: The Full Story of Brexit*, Collins.
Shlaim, A, Jones, P, and Sainsbury, K (1997), *British Foreign Secretaries since 1945*, David and Charles.
Snyder, W (1964), *The Politics of British Defence Policy, 1945–1962*, Ernest Benn.
Steiner, Z (2005), *The Lights That Failed: European International History 1919–1933*, Oxford University Press.
Straw, J (2012), *Last Man Standing: Memoirs of a Political Survivor*, Macmillan.
Taylor, AJP (1954), *The Struggle for Mastery in Europe 1848–1918*, Oxford University Press.
Taylor, AJP (1964), *The Origins of the Second World War*, Penguin edition.
Taylor, AJP (1965), *English History 1914–1945*, Oxford University Press.
Thatcher, M (1988), Speech to the College of Europe ('The Bruges Speech'), 20 September, www.margaretthatcher.org/document/107332.
Thatcher, M (1993), *The Downing Street Years*, HarperCollins.
Thatcher, M (2002), *Statecraft*, HarperCollins.
Thorpe, DR (2010), *Supermac: The Life of Harold Macmillan*, Chatto & Windus.
Traynor, I, Watt, N, Gow, D, and Wintour, P (2011), 'David Cameron Blocks EU Treaty with Veto, Casting Britain Adrift in Europe', *Guardian*, 9 December.
Truman, H (1965), *Memoirs, Vol II: Years of Trial and Hope, 1946–1952*, Signet.
Tunzelmann, A von (2016), *Blood and Sand: Hungary and the Crisis that Shook the World*, Simon & Schuster.
Turner, J (2000), *The Tories and Europe*, Manchester University Press.
Urban, G (1996), *Diplomacy and Disillusion at the Court of Margaret Thatcher: An Insider's View*, IB Tauris.
Vickers, R (2015), 'Foreign Policy and International Development', in M Beech and S Lee (eds), *The Conservative–Liberal Coalition: Examining the Cameron–Clegg Government*, Palgrave Macmillan.
Wallace, W (1975), *The Foreign Policy Process in Britain*, Royal Institute of International Affairs.
Wallace, W (1994), 'Foreign Policy', in D Kavanagh and A Seldon (eds), *The Major Effect*, Macmillan.
Wallace, W (2005), 'The Collapse of British Foreign Policy', *International Affairs*, Vol. 81, issue 1.
Waltz, K (1967), *Foreign Policy and Democratic Politics: The American and British Experience*, Little, Brown.
Waltz, K (1979), *Theory of International Politics*, Addison-Wesley.
Watt, DC (1984), *Succeeding John Bull: America in Britain's Place, 1900–1975*, Cambridge University Press.
Watt, N (2002a), 'Blair's Midnight Dash to the Kabul War Zone', *Guardian*, 8 January.
Watt, N (2002b), 'The Lost Straw', *Guardian*, 4 January.
Watt, N (2008), 'Brown: British military to withdraw from Iraq', *Guardian*, 17 December.
Weaver, P (2010), 'English Rebels Who Ignored Apartheid Cause Still Show a Lack of Shame', *Guardian*, 11 January.
Wendt, A (1992), 'Anarchy Is What States Make of It: The social construction of power politics', *International Organization*, Vol. 46, issue 2.
Wendt, A (1994), 'Collective Identity Formation and the International State', *The American Political Science Review*, Vol. 88, issue 2.

Wheatcroft, G (2013), 'Not-so-special Relationship', *Spectator*, 5 January.

Wheeler, N (2002), *Saving Strangers: Humanitarian Intervention in International Society*, Oxford University Press.

Williams, P (2004), 'Who's Making UK Foreign Policy?', *International Affairs*, Vol. 80, issue 5.

YouGov (2014), 'Afghanistan: The public verdict', https://yougov.co.uk/news/2014/04/04/afghanistan-final-verdict/.

YouGov (2015), 'Memories of Iraq: Did we ever support the war?', https://yougov.co.uk/news/2015/06/03/remembering-iraq/.

Young, H (1991), *One of Us: A Biography of Margaret Thatcher*, Macmillan.

Young, H (1998), *This Blessed Plot: Britain and Europe from Churchill to Blair*, Macmillan.

Young, J (1996), 'The Heath Government and British Entry into the European Community', in A Seldon and S Ball (eds), *The Heath Government 1970–74: A Reappraisal*, Longman.

Young, J (2004), 'Europe', in A Seldon and K Hickson (eds), *New Labour, Old Labour: The Blair, Wilson and Callaghan Governments*, Routledge.

Youngs, T, and Dodd, T (1998), *Kosovo*, House of Commons Library Research Paper 98–73.

Youngs, T, and Oakes, M (1999), *Iraq: 'Desert Fox' and Policy Developments*, House of Commons Library Research Paper 99–13.

Index

Acheson, Dean 119, 122, 154–6, 159, 167, 217, 325
Aden 162, 166–7, 170
Adenauer, Konrad 142
Adler, Emanuel 18
Afghanistan: Soviet invasion 195, 198, 215, 218; US-led intervention 269, 273–6, 277, 286, 298, 299, 300, 303
Al-Assad, Basher 46, 274, 313–14
Al-Qa'ida 24, 271, 273
Amin, Idi 183
Amritsar massacre (1919) 77
Andropov, Yuri 214
Angell, Norman, 62
Annan, Kofi 203
Anschluss (1938) 88
appeasement 74, 87–96, 125, 159
Arab League 103, 148
Arab Spring (2010–11) 309–12
Argentina 171–2, 200–3, 205, 256
arms industry 173, 255, 309
'arms to Iraq' scandal (1988) 251
Ashdown, Paddy 278, 279
Asquith, Herbert 71
As-Said, Nuri 127
Atlantic Charter (1941) 117
Attlee, Clement 4, 107, 108, 109, 118, 119, 120, 121–2, 130, 172
Australia 63, 75, 138, 184
Australia, New Zealand, United States Security Treaty (ANZUS Pact, 1951) 120

Baghdad Pact (1951) 126–7, 134, 148
Bahrain 44, 309, 312
Baldwin, Stanley 69, 84, 86–7, 92, 96, 104, 254
Balfour, Arthur 70, 76–7, 80, 81, 92, 103, 186, 240
Barnett, Correlli 100
Bay of Pigs Invasion (1961) 153
Beckett, Margaret 291
Benn, Tony 180, 182, 322
Benson, Arthur Christopher 60–1, 67
Bentham, Jeremy 8
Berlin blockade 111–13
Bevan, Nye 116, 118, 150–1, 153
Bevin, Ernest 31, 38, 99, 107, 108, 109, 113, 121, 123, 125, 130, 131, 183
Biafran War 56, 173–4
Birch, Nigel 160
Blair, Tony 4, 24, 35–6, 49, 51, 57–8, 116, 153, 252, 253, 254, 255, 257, 297–8, 299, 301, 302, 304, 314; Chicago speech (1999) 25, 37, 44, 266, 267–8, 273, 278, 280, 285, 293, 294, 306; downfall 288–92; and Europe 257–60, 286–8; Kosovo 262–8; and 'special relationship' 260–3, 265–86, 293, 294, 295–6, 301; and 'War on Terror' 269–87, 289, 293–4, 311
Boer War 60, 63, 64–5, 66, 79
Bosnia 238, 246–50, 263, 265
Brazil 307
Bretherton, Russell 143
'Brexit' 1, 5, 29, 31, 43, 46, 48, 52; effect on Foreign Office, 54; *see also* EU referendum (2016)
Brezhnev, Leonid 187, 214

Briand, Aristide 84
Bright, John 62, 81
Britain, economic decline of 62, 77–8, 100–1, 103, 116, 164–6, 167, 169–70, 174, 176–8, 181, 187, 192, 224, 302, 307
British Broadcasting Corporation (BBC) 1, 4, 174, 283–4; World Service 4, 174
British Council 4, 174
British Guiana (Guyana) 160
British Nationality Act (1948) 172, 184
Brown, Chris 21
Brown, Gordon 37, 259, 260, 282, 287, 291, 296, 297–8, 299–303; and 'special relationship' 301–2
Brussels, Treaty of (1948) 111–12
Burma (Myanmar) 105
Bush, George HW 221–2, 230, 231, 233, 234, 235, 244, 245, 254, 273, 293
Bush, George W 4, 24, 51, 268, 271, 274, 275, 276, 277, 279, 281, 293, 294, 295–6, 300, 301, 304, 313
Butler, 'Rab' 161, 166
Butler Report 282, 283, 300
Buzan, Barry 22

Callaghan, James 31, 183–4, 187, 188, 189–90, 191–2, 194, 200, 201, 209, 210
Cameron, David 5, 45–6, 52, 286, 298, 299; and 2016 referendum 318–24; and Arab Spring 309–15; and 'Europe' 304, 315–24; 'liberal conservatism' 305–6; and 'special relationship' 303–4
Campaign for Nuclear Disarmament (CND) 49, 56, 150, 198
Campbell, Alastair 272, 274
Canada 82, 100, 102, 114, 141, 274, 309
Carr, EH 9–10, 85–6
Carrington, Lord 36–7, 196, 201, 206, 299
Carter, Jimmy 188–9, 195, 215
Castle, Barbara 30, 174, 180
Castlereagh, Lord 53
Castro, Fidel 153
Central African Federation 106–7, 168–9
Central Intelligence Agency (CIA) 126
Ceylon (Sri Lanka) 105
Chamberlain, Austen 84–5
Chamberlain, Joseph 62, 65, 80
Chamberlain, Neville 5, 34, 48, 80, 84, 87–90, 91, 92, 94–6, 119, 125, 128, 140, 141, 159, 250, 269
Charmley, John 94
Chernenko, Constantine 214

Chilcot Inquiry 277, 282, 284, 285, 300
China 51–2, 115, 117, 118–19, 127, 170, 256–7, 301, 307–8
Chirac, Jacques 273, 287
Christmas broadcasts 55–6
Churchill, Winston 1, 48, 63, 78, 80, 82, 84, 86, 91, 93, 97–8, 101, 102, 105, 107, 109, 113–14, 117, 121, 124, 125, 128, 135, 141, 142, 154, 155, 156, 180, 186, 197, 203, 225, 233, 246, 291, 294, 307; 'concentric circles' concept 102, 140, 307; Fulton speech (1946) 117–18, 109, 120; and 'special relationship' 113–14, 140–1; Zurich speech (1946) 120–1
Clark, General Wesley 265–6
Clarke, Kenneth 244
Classical Realism 12
Clegg, Nick 304, 306, 317
Clemenceau, Georges 13, 75
climate change 41, 289
Clinton, Bill 245, 253, 255, 260–1, 266, 267, 268, 271, 278, 280, 293
Clinton, Hillary 301
Coe, Sebastian 215, 289
Cold War 14, 15, 17, 107–13, 152–3, 155, 189, 194–9, 203, 205, 211–19, 224, 230, 253, 256, 260, 287, 293, 294; end of 218–19; onset of 108–11
Colonial Office 29, 146
Commonwealth 4, 34, 55–6, 82, 93, 102, 104, 105, 107, 118, 123, 144, 145, 151, 159, 162, 167, 168, 169, 172, 177, 178, 179, 183, 184, 188, 196, 216–17, 219–21
Commonwealth Relations Office (CRO) 29
Constructivism 6, 9, 17–20, 25, 26
Cook, Robin 37, 38, 251, 254–5, 259, 272, 280–2, 284, 306–7
Corbyn, Jeremy 282, 314, 325
Council of Europe 121–2
Cox, Robert 20
Cradock, Percy 35, 222
Crimean crisis (2014) 314–15
Crimean War 64, 65, 115
Cripps, Stafford 166
Critical Theory 8–9, 15, 16, 20–2, 23
Croatia 247, 263
Crowe, Eyre 66
Crowley, Desmond 2
Cuba 196
Cuban Missile Crisis (1962) 153, 160, 293
Cyprus 162–4, 184–5, 199

Da'ish (or Islamic State) 46, 314
Darling, Alistair 302
Darroch, Kim 78
defence budget cuts 170, 200, 206, 253, 299
de Gaulle, Charles 154–6, 158, 170, 179, 185
Delors, Jacques 225–6, 227–8, 229, 236, 254, 258
Denman, Roy 193
Department for International Development (DfID) 30, 44, 53, 174, 250, 284, 305
Dependency Theory 16–17
Derrida, Jacques 20
Devlin Report (1959) 146
Dickinson, Goldsworthy Lowes 74
Diego Garcia 171
differentiated polity model of governance 42–3, 53
Dimbleby, Richard 101
Disraeli, Benjamin 64
Dominions Office 29
Dulles, John Foster 125

Eden, Anthony 5, 30, 32, 34, 87, 88, 94, 124, 125–8, 130, 133–44, 147, 148, 155, 156, 158, 163, 170, 291
Egypt 65, 105, 126–7, 133–42, 185, 186, 309, 312
Eisenhower, Dwight 125, 128, 138–9, 147, 149, 150, 151, 152
Elizabeth II 55–6, 101, 199, 271
English School of International Relations 22–3
Entente Cordiale 65
European Coal and Steel Community 120–2, 142–3
European Court of Human Rights (ECHR) 163
European Defence Community (EDC) 124
European Economic Community (EEC) 131, 143–4, 151, 158, 159, 170, 173, 175, 177–81, 182, 183, 185, 186–7, 191–4, 203, 204, 207, 208, 209, 210–11, 220, 224–7, 240, 252, 254, 258; and 1975 referendum 182–3, 237, 322
European Free Trade Association (EFTA) 143–4
European Monetary System (EMS: also European Exchange Rate Mechanism (ERM)) 209–10, 211, 227–8, 229, 236, 238, 241, 253; British ejection from, 242–3
European single currency (euro) 244, 258–9, 287, 292, 316
European Union (EU) 1, 3, 5, 29, 41–2, 45, 47, 49, 50, 54, 236, 241–4, 252, 253, 255, 257–60, 261, 265, 269, 273, 281, 286–8, 292, 293, 295, 304, 315–24; and 2016 referendum 318–25
'extraordinary rendition' 301

Falkland Islands 171–2, 191; 1982 War 36–7, 48, 54, 56, 199–204, 205, 207, 230, 238, 256, 276, 293, 310
feminist theory 21
Festival of Britain (1951) 101
Finnemore, Martha 18
First World War 12–13, 62, 66–7, 100; consequences of 68–77, 102; *see also* Versailles, Treaty of
Fontainebleau Summit (1984) 210
Foot, Michael 201
Foreign and Commonwealth Office (FCO) 5–6, 28–58, 87, 96, 109, 115, 135, 171, 174, 200–1, 232, 246, 267, 272, 278, 285, 291, 293, 296, 299, 307, 324; decline of 38–9, 52, 272, 307, 308; history of 5–6, 29–30; structure 30–4
Foucault, Michel 8, 20
France 65, 66, 67, 72, 73, 74, 79, 82, 83, 84, 85, 88, 89, 92, 110, 111, 117, 122, 124, 125, 127, 137–8, 141, 148, 234, 241, 262, 273, 274, 287, 288, 289, 309
Frankfurt School 20
Franks, Oliver 116, 199, 200
Freedman, Lawrence 44
Freeman, John 175
Fukuyama, Francis 15, 275

Gaddafi, Muammar 231, 285, 309–11
Gagarin, Yuri 153
Gaitskell, Hugh 116, 118, 150–1, 158, 159
Galloway, George 290
Gandhi, Mahatma 82, 106
Geneva Accords (1954) 127
Germany 61–2, 65–7, 79, 83, 84, 85, 87, 88, 89, 90, 91, 92, 93, 96, 97, 103, 234, 274, 287, 293; and First World War 68–77; partition of 110, 111; reunification 221–4, 234, 242; *see also* West Germany
Gladstone, William 70, 81
Glubb, John 135

Gold Coast (Ghana) 106
Goldsmith, Peter 282
Gorbachev, Mikhail 208, 213, 214, 216, 217, 218, 223, 232, 234–5, 256
Gordon-Walker, Patrick 166, 172
Government Communications Headquarters (GCHQ) 33
Gramsci, Antonio 21
Grant, Mark 38
great-power narrative 2, 17–18, 58, 59, 68, 97–9, 113, 140, 142, 150, 164, 165, 169, 179, 185, 203–4, 224, 227, 238, 239, 246, 323–5
Greece 79, 89, 103
Greene, Graham 129–30
Greenwood, Anthony 167
Grenada 196, 199, 208, 230
Grenville, Lord 47
Grey, Lord 44
Grey, Sir Edward 66, 70
G8 50, 288–9, 295
Guantanamo Bay 301
Gulf War (1990–1) 230–5, 238, 245, 247, 251, 253, 261, 263, 279

Habermas, Jurgen 20
Hague, William 5, 28, 38, 47, 304, 306–9
Haig, Alexander 202, 212
Hammond, Philip 210
Healey, Denis 166, 208
Heath, Edward 145, 164, 177–9, 181, 183, 184, 185, 186, 190, 191, 193, 194, 210, 227, 243, 245–6, 324
Helsinki Conference (1975) 187–9, 190
Henderson, Nicholas 37, 38, 40, 202
Hennessy, Peter 114
Herz, John 11
Heseltine, Michael 198, 215, 244
Hezbollah 291–2
Hills, Denis 183
Hitler, Adolf 73, 78, 79, 80, 84, 85, 87, 88–9, 90, 91, 94, 95, 117, 159
Hobbes, Thomas 8, 10–11, 15, 19
Hogg, Quintin 161
Hola Camp massacre (1959) 146–7, 172
Home, Alec 31, 159, 161–2, 164, 292
Hong Kong 115, 256
Hopf, Ted 18
House of Commons (and role in policy making) 45–7, 49, 114, 144, 171, 180–1, 190, 201, 241, 242, 251, 257, 262, 280, 281–2, 313–14; Foreign Affairs Select Committee 46–7, 278, 283, 311
House of Lords 47, 81
Howard, Michael 286
Howe, Geoffrey 35, 210, 214, 222, 227, 228, 236, 245, 281
human rights 32, 187–9, 190, 235, 305, 306, 308, 309
Hungary 111, 139, 214, 218
Hurd, Douglas 35, 127–8, 215, 245–6, 247, 248, 249, 250–1, 254, 299
Hussein, Saddam 24–5, 38, 44, 45, 55, 153, 232, 234, 251, 261–2, 271, 276, 277, 278–9, 280, 281, 294, 295, 300, 305
Hutton Inquiry 282, 283–4, 300

immigration 56, 172–3, 184, 222
imperialism 62–3, 71–2, 75, 91, 105, 160, 310
India 29, 63–4, 77, 81–2, 92, 100, 103–4, 107, 133
Indonesia 255, 307
International Institute for Strategic Studies (IISS) 43
International Relations theories 7–27; and Iraq War 23–6
Iran 24, 75, 81, 109, 125–6, 127, 135, 195, 196, 271, 276, 281
Iraq 75, 81, 127, 135, 148, 251, 261–2, 313; and War on Terror 4–5, 23–6, 38, 45–6, 48, 51, 57, 137, 138, 238, 276–86, 290, 294, 295, 298, 299, 300, 303
Ireland 77, 80–1, 92, 231
Ismay, Lord 221
Israel 103, 127, 134, 137–8, 169, 174, 185, 186, 273, 291–2
Italy 75, 84, 88, 89, 92, 93, 110, 112, 153, 241, 309

Japan 64, 65, 74, 79, 82–3, 89, 105, 127; 1902 alliance with Britain 64, 65, 82–3
Jenkins, Roy 183, 189, 192, 193, 194
Johnson, Boris 6, 32, 52, 314, 322, 325
Johnson, Lyndon 167
Joint Intelligence Committee (JIC) 278
Jordan 75, 135, 148
Juncker, Jean-Claude 318–19

Kant, Immanuel 8, 14, 19
Karzai, Hamid 275
Keating, Frank 217
Kelly, David 282, 283

Kennan, George 109
Kennedy, Charles 290
Kennedy, John 151–2, 153, 155, 160, 162, 245
Kenya 106, 145–6, 172
Keohane, Robert 14
Keynes, John Maynard 93
Kinnock, Neil 208, 252–3
Kipling, Rudyard 71
Kirkpatrick, Jeane 202
Kissinger, Henry 26, 185
Kohl, Helmut 207, 221, 223, 224, 236, 242
Korean War 10, 115–18, 127, 167
Kosovo 238, 249, 273, 280, 294
Krugman, Paul 302
Krushchev, Nikita 138–9, 150
Kuwait 25, 148, 230–4, 251, 261

Lawson, Nigel 210, 227, 228, 229, 281
Leach, Henry 206
League of Nations 13, 16, 74–5, 79, 83, 84, 86, 89, 92, 96, 102
Lebanon 148, 291
lend-lease 114
Lennon, John 175
liberalism 6, 8, 9, 12–17, 20, 62–3, 80–1, 91–2, 304; and Iraq War 24–5, 26, 294–5
Libya 47, 51, 105, 231–2, 285, 309–11, 318
Lisbon, Treaty of (2007) 288, 292, 301, 304, 315
Litvinenko, Alexander 314
Livingstone, Ken 289
Lloyd, Selwyn 34, 135, 136, 137, 147, 158–9
Lloyd George, David 34, 71, 72, 73, 77
Locarno, Treaties of (1925) 84, 88, 92, 95
Locke, John 19
Lockerbie bombing (1988) 285
London terror attacks (July 2005) 290

Maastricht, Treaty of (1992) 236, 241–4, 245, 257, 260, 316
MacArthur, Douglas 115, 119
Machiavelli, Niccolo 8, 10, 285
Macleod, Iain 146
McMahon Act (1946) 114, 149
Macmillan, Harold 30–1, 34, 51, 120, 132, 135, 141, 144, 146–56, 157, 158–9, 160–1, 163, 165, 168, 197, 217, 245, 292, 299, 324; 'Wind of Change' speech (1960) 146–7

McNamara, Robert 152
Mahathir, Mohamad 250
Major, John 31, 35, 57, 240, 251–2, 254, 258, 260, 283, 293, 299; and Balkans 246–50; 'Europe' 235–8, 241–4; and Gulf War 232–5; outlook of 233, 235; and US 244–5
Makarios, Archbishop 163–4
Malaya (Malaysia) 105, 145, 250
Mandela, Nelson 217, 220–1
Manning, David 272, 284
Mao Tse-Tung 115, 127, 308
Marshall, George (and Marshall Aid) 110–11, 113, 121, 123
Marxism 6, 8, 9, 16–17, 20, 25, 91
Maudling, Reginald 161
Mauritius 171
May, Theresa 5–6, 52, 324–5
Mearsheimer, John 12
Melrose, Dianna 44
Merkel, Angela 292, 317, 319
Meyer, Christopher 271, 285
Miliband, Ed 313, 317, 318
Milosevic, Slobodan 264, 267, 279
Mitterand, Francois 211, 225
Mollet, Guy 142
Molotov–Ribbentrop Pact (1939) 90–1
Morgan, Kenneth 119
Morganthau, Hans 9
Mossadegh, Mohammed 125–6
Mountbatten, Louis 103–4
Mubarak, Hosni 309
Mullin, Chris 282
multi-level governance 41, 50
Munich conference (1938) 88, 89, 94, 111, 119, 269
Murdoch, Rupert 258, 284
Musharraf, Pervez 273
Mussolini, Benito 89, 90, 95

Nassau conference (1962) 3, 152, 153, 154, 155, 159, 166
Nasser, Gamal 126–7, 134–6, 137, 139, 140, 148, 153, 162, 169
National Security Council (NSC) 38, 40, 308–9, 319
Neo-Realism 12
New Zealand 63, 179, 184
Nicolson, Harold 47
Nigeria 106, 173–4
Nixon, Richard 175, 245

North Atlantic Treaty Organisation (NATO) 3, 49, 51, 112, 115, 117, 123, 124, 139, 145, 152, 163, 185, 200, 218, 223, 246, 247, 260, 264–6, 267, 274–5, 281
Northedge, Frederick Samuel 2
North Korea 24, 115, 271, 276; see also Korean War
Nott, John 200–1, 206
nuclear weapons 3, 10, 11, 14, 128, 130, 148–53, 159, 166, 170–1, 185, 189, 194, 195–6, 208–9, 211–12, 213, 217–18, 254, 304
Nyasaland (Malawi) 106, 146, 168
Nye, Joseph 23

Obama, Barrack 301–2, 312–13
oil crisis (1973–4) 181
Olympic Games 4, 56, 87, 195, 214–16, 288–90, 301
Oman 147–8
Onuf, Nicholas 17–18, 19–20
Operation Desert Fox (1998) 263, 265, 267, 280
Organisation for European Economic Co-operation and Development (OEECD) 121
Orientalism 25–6
Osborne, George 28
Ottawa conference (1932) 80
overseas aid; see Department for International Development
Oxfam 44

Pakistan 104, 127, 273
Palestine 75, 76–7, 81, 92, 103, 105, 186, 224
Parsons, Anthony 202
Patten, Christopher 257
Peace Ballot (1934–5) 86
Pinochet, Augusto 256
Pleven Plan 123–4
Poland 73, 89, 90, 111, 114, 125, 212, 218
Pompidou, Georges 179, 185
Portugal 187
positivism 8–9
poststructuralism 21
post-war foreign policy 'consensus' 98–9, 107–8, 118, 130, 180
Powell, Charles 35, 223
Powell, Colin 272

Powell, Enoch 56, 146, 172–3, 179
Prime Minister: role in foreign policy making 34–9, 53, 57, 268, 272, 274, 284–5, 299, 311
Profumo scandal (1963) 160
public opinion 70, 71–2, 74, 79, 85–7, 89, 90, 92, 118, 139, 141–2, 144, 157, 160, 164, 169, 180–1, 182, 194, 198, 240, 249, 276, 281, 282, 285–6, 291, 294, 299, 316, 322–3; role in foreign policy matters 47–9; and War on Terror 24, 276, 285–6
Putin, Vladimir 273, 314–15
Pym, Francis 37, 206

Reagan, Ronald 37, 195–6, 199, 202, 208, 212, 213–14, 217, 219, 220, 221, 224, 231–2, 244, 252, 254, 261
Realism 6, 8, 9–12, 17, 20, 23, 24–5, 68, 91–3, 102, 108, 109, 154, 229–30, 247–9, 281, 295, 305
Redwood, John 244
Rhineland, remilitarisation of 84–5, 87
Rhodes James, Robert 125
Rice, Condoleezza 26
Ricketts, Peter 38
Ridley, Nicholas 36–7, 223
Roberts, Ivor 38, 40
Robertson, George 264
Rome, Treaty of (1957) 143, 178, 211
Roosevelt, Franklin Delano 88, 95, 114–15, 117, 142
Rothschild, Walter 76
Royal Institute of International Affairs (Chatham House) 43
Royal United Services Institute (RUSI) 43
Ruggie, John 17–18
Russia: post-Soviet era 262, 264, 267, 314–15; pre-Soviet era 64–5, 67, 73, 76, 77, 82, 88, 109
Rwandan genocide (1994) 248–50

Saint-Malo Declaration (1998) 259–60
Salisbury, Lord 70
Sampson, Anthony 5, 38
Santer, Jacques 243
Sarkozy, Nicholas 292, 310–11, 316–17
Saudi Arabia 147, 230, 271, 274, 310
Schröder, Gerhard 263, 273
Schultz, George 213
Schuman Plan 120–1, 122–3, 142
Scott Report (1996) 251–2

Second World War 9, 97, 100, 107–8, 121, 130, 154, 184, 207, 227, 293, 323
Seeley, John 59–61
Self, Robert 94
Serbia 246–50, 264–7, 281
Sevres, Treaty of (1920) 75
Sharon, Ariel 273
Short, Clare 284
Sierra Leone 238, 267–8, 273, 294
Singapore 83, 105, 120, 289
Single European Act (1986) 211, 225, 226, 236, 237, 238
Smith, Ian 168–9, 173, 197
Smith, John 253
Smuts, Jan 79
Soames, Christopher 197
soft power 4, 11, 23, 54, 55–6, 101–2, 153, 174–5, 176, 290
Somoza, Anastasio 15
South Africa 63, 75, 100, 106, 146–7, 168, 173, 197, 216–17, 219–21
South East Asia Treaty Organisation (SEATO) 125
sovereignty 8, 10, 112–13, 117, 123, 144–5, 191, 237; and 'Europe' 144–5, 151, 191, 237; and NATO 112–13
Soviet Union 89–90, 91, 96, 103, 113, 115, 116, 117, 119, 127, 128, 134, 135, 139, 143, 148–9, 153, 159, 167, 170–1, 174, 178, 186–7, 188, 194, 209, 212, 214, 215, 218, 223, 238, 252, 253, 254, 294; and Cold War 108–10, 111–12; collapse of 234–5, 238
Spain 111, 227; Spanish Civil War 87–8, 89, 93
Sputnik 148–9
Srebrenica massacre (1995) 246, 263
Stalin 90, 91, 96, 103, 108–9, 110, 114–15, 128, 142
Steiner, Zara 68
Stettinius, Edward 114
Strategic Arms Limitation Talks (SALT) 189
Strategic Defence Initiative (SDI) 212–13, 217
Straw, Jack 37–8, 126, 272, 291
Stresemann, Gustav 84
Sturgeon, Nicola 322
Sudan 65
Suez Crisis (1956) and repercussions 2, 5, 34, 48, 54, 55, 57, 105, 126–7, 133–42, 143, 144, 147, 148, 150, 151, 155, 156, 157, 158, 163, 167, 169, 170, 174, 217, 269, 324
Syria 45, 148, 185, 186, 274, 312–14

Taiwan 115
Tanzania (Tanganyika) 75, 107
Taylor, AJP 66, 81, 85, 87, 89
Templar, Gerald 105
Templewood, Lord 104
Test Ban Treaty (1963) 159
Thatcher, Margaret 35–7, 48, 57, 169, 183, 186, 188, 190, 235–6, 238, 242, 244, 245, 246, 250, 252, 256–7, 261, 268, 281, 292, 293, 294, 296, 299; Bruges speech (1988) 226–7, 304; and Commonwealth 219–21; downfall 224–30; and 'Europe' 191–4, 207–11, 224–30, 237, 243; and Falklands War 199–205; and Germany 221–4; outlook 206–7, 227, 293, 295; and Soviet Union 194, 211–19; and 'special relationship' 194–5, 211–19; and sporting boycotts 215–17; and Zimbabwe 197–8
think tanks 43–4
Thorpe, DR 139
Thucydides 10
Tiananmen Square massacre (1989) 256
Treasury, role in foreign policy making 40–2, 53, 299
Truman, Harry 15, 108, 110, 112, 115–16, 119, 125, 154
Trump, Donald 325
Turkey 103, 109, 127, 153, 164, 184–5, 234, 307

Uganda 76, 183–4
Ukraine 51, 314–15
United Kingdom Independence Party (UKIP) 319
United Nations (UN) 37, 50, 51, 103, 117, 118, 136, 138, 148, 174, 188, 200, 202, 230, 233, 234, 247, 250, 261–3, 264, 266–7, 271, 274, 277, 279, 280, 281, 305, 307, 309, 311–12
United States 3, 13, 24–6, 51–2, 57–8, 61–2, 65, 68, 71, 74, 75, 77, 78, 79, 82, 83, 88, 93, 95, 101, 103, 109, 110, 11–12, 113, 117, 118, 121–2, 123, 125–6, 128, 136, 138, 167, 171, 178–9, 186, 189, 195, 202–4, 206, 207, 211–19, 244, 249, 255, 260–3, 266–7, 268, 293, 294, 295–6, 300–1, 303–4, 307; anti-imperialism

113–15, 148–9, 160; and Iraq War 269–84; and 'special relationship' 3–4, 113–14, 119–20, 129–30, 140–1, 144, 147–56, 158, 172, 175, 185, 199, 219, 221–2, 224, 230, 231–2, 293, 301, 303–4, 308, 313; and UK membership of 'Europe' 3, 130–1, 261
Urban, George 206, 222

Van Rompuy, Herman 292
Vansittart, Robert 87, 126
Vietnam 127–8, 129–30, 167–8, 175, 188, 293
Versailles, Treaty of 13, 71–5, 77, 80, 83, 84, 85, 90, 92, 94, 95

Walesa, Lech 218
Wallace, William 42–3, 252
Wallerstein, Immanuel 17
Waltz, Kenneth 10, 12, 154
Washington Naval Conference (1921) 78–9
Weimar Republic 72, 84
Weinberger, Caspar 202
Weizmann, Chaim 76
Wells, HG 77
Wendt, Alexander 17–19

Western Europe Union (WEA) 124–5
West Germany 101, 124–5, 142, 144, 152–3, 165, 189, 207, 218–19, 222–4
'Westminster model' of governance 41, 53
Westminster, Statute of (1931) 80
Westphalia, Treaty of (1648) 8
Williams, Paul 57
Wilson, Harold 116, 161, 162, 164–75, 182–3, 185, 187, 191–2, 194, 199
Wilson, Woodrow 13–14, 71–2, 74, 75, 88, 117, 177
World Systems Analysis 16–17
World Trade Center, attack on (9/11) 38, 39, 51, 269, 270–1, 290, 293, 294, 303
World Trade Organisation (WTO) 50

Yalta conference (1945) 114–15, 142
Yeltsin, Boris 264
Yom Kippur War (1973) 185–7
Younger, Kenneth 120

Zambia (Northern Rhodesia) 106, 146, 168
Zimbabwe (Southern Rhodesia) 106, 146, 168–9, 196, 197–8